W9-BXP-911

A RAHNER READER

A
RAHNER
READER

edited by Gerald A. McCool

CROSSROAD · NEW YORK

1981
The Crossroad Publishing Company
575 Lexington Avenue, New York, NY 10022

Grateful acknowledgment is extended to the following
publishers for permission to reprint material originally
published by Benziger Verlag, Zurich, for selections from
Schriften zur Theologie, Volumes I-VIII; Kösel-Verlag
Munich, for selections from *Hörer des Wortes;* Verlag
Herder, Freiburg, for selections from *Das Dynamische in
der Kirche* and *Episcopal und Primat;* Search Press,
London, for selections from *The Church and the
Sacraments;* and Sheed and Ward, London, for selections
from *Nature and Grace* and *Christian Commitment.*

Copyright © 1975 by
The Crossroad Publishing Company

The English editions of the materials in this volume are
identified at the bottom of the page on which they first
appear, which pages constitute an extension of this
copyright page.

All rights reserved. No part of this book may be used or
reproduced in any manner whatsoever without the
permission of the publisher, except for brief quotations in
critical reviews and articles.

Library of Congress Cataloging in Publication Data

Rahner, Karl, 1904–
   A Rahner reader.

   Reprint. Originally published: New York:
Seabury Press, 1975.
   Bibliography: p. 363
   1. Theology—Collected works—20th century.
2. Catholic Church—Collected works.
I. McCool, Gerald A.   II. Title.
BX891.R253   1981   230'.2   81-17394
ISBN 0-8245-0370-8   AACR2

Josepho Donceel, S. J.
Bene Merenti de Universitate
Fordhamensi

Acknowledgments

A special word of thanks is due to Father Joseph Donceel, S.J., for permission to print his translation of the first edition of *Hörer des Wortes (Hearers of the Word)* in *A Rahner Reader*. This service to Transcendental Thomism is one more contribution added to the many which have already been made by this distinguished scholar. During his brilliant teaching career at Fordham University, stretching over more than two decades, Father Donceel, through his translating and editing of important texts and through his own books and articles, had done more than any other American scholar to acquaint his countrymen with the European tradition of Transcendental Thomism.

A very sincere word of thanks is also due to Father Alfons Deeken, S.J., of Sophia University, Tokyo. Father Deeken first suggested the publication of a "Rahner reader." Without his encouragement and occasional friendly prodding the work would never have been completed.

I would also like at this time to express my gratitude to Father Vincent Potter, S.J., Chairman of the Philosophy Department at Fordham, for his understanding cooperation with my work in preparing the manuscript.

Finally I would like to thank the graduate students of my own Department and of the Theology Department at Fordham. Their response to Rahner's transcendental anthropology during the past few years has done a good deal to strengthen my own conviction that Rahner's intellectual appeal is not confined to his own country or even to his own continent.

G.A.McC.

CONTENTS

Chapter XI   Moral Theology

Chapter XII   The Church and the Sacraments

Chapter XIII   Spirituality

Chapter XIV   Ideology, Eschatology, and the Theology of Death

Introduction: Rahner's Philosophical Theology

Karl Rahner was born in Freiburg im Breisgau on March 4, 1904, and entered the North German Province of the Society of Jesus on April 20, 1922. After his noviceship and one year of philosophical studies at Feldkirch, Austria, he was sent to the Berchmanskolleg at Pullach, near Munich, for two more years of philosophical study. In 1929 he went to Valkenburg, Holland, for four years of theology. After his third year of theology he was ordained by Cardinal Faulhaber in St. Michael's Church in Munich and, upon the completion of the full course of priestly formation in the Society of Jesus, was sent by his superiors to take an advanced degree in philosophy at the University of Freiburg.

MARÉCHAL'S TRANSCENDENTAL THOMISM

During his years at the Jesuit scholasticate in Pullach Rahner made an extremely thorough study of Kant and Maréchal. Joseph Maréchal, S.J., for many years a professor at the Jesuit Faculty of Philosophy at Louvain, is generally considered to be the father of Transcendental Thomism. Maréchal's *Le Point de départ de la métaphysique*, especially its famous fifth volume, *Le Thomisme devant la philosophie critique*, exercised a profound influence on his fellow Jesuits in Belgium, France, and Germany between the First and Second World Wars. Maréchal's principal thesis was that if Kant's transcendental reflection on human knowledge is applied consistently, it leads to metaphysical realism and not to critical idealism, as Kant had mistakenly supposed.

Kant himself was unable to extricate himself from critical idealism because he failed to observe that the dynamism of the human mind is one of the a priori conditions of possibility for the *speculative intellect's* objective knowledge. In *The Critique of Pure Reason* objectivization is considered to be a *static* union of empirical data, the forms of space and time, and the categories of the understanding. Consequently the innate ideas of the world, the soul, and God cannot be a priori conditions of possibility for the objective categorical judgments of man's *speculative reason*. They are purely regulative ideals, whose function is to make possible speculative reason's organization of its *already constituted* objective judgments into a coherent, intelligible whole. Thus, since the regulative ideals do not enter into the constitution of the categorical judgments themselves, they cannot be valid sources of objective knowledge. Although it is true that the human mind has a natural tendency to mistake the three regulative ideals for innate ideas which can give it genuine objective knowledge of the world, the soul, and God as noumenal realities, this tendency must be resolutely resisted as a metaphysical illusion. Genuine objective knowledge can only be obtained through the categorical judgments of the speculative reason. And, since these judgments are constituted by the application of the forms and categories to the raw data of sensation, their valid cognitional content is necessarily confined to the subjective realm of human experience. God and human freedom are indeed *postulates of practical reason,* but speculative reason can have no objective knowledge of them. The agnosticism of speculative reason makes way for the faith of practical reason.

Kant's successors endeavored to bridge the gulf which Kant had opened between noumena and phenomena, sense and intellect, speculative and practical reason. Fichte proposed the dynamism of the human spirit as the philosophical basis on which a reconciliation between Kant's speculative and practical reason could be effected. According to Fichte, the human subject has an intellectual intuition of his own spiritual activity of knowing and willing. Because of this intuition he becomes aware that his activity of knowing and willing is fundamentally a striving toward the Infinite Absolute. Towards the end of the nineteenth century Maurice Blondel transformed Fichte's spiritual dynamism into a dialectic between the innate dynamic orientation of the human will to God and the finite objects of man's concrete choices. Blondel's *Action* and Bergson's dynamic spiritualism had a deep and widespread influence on Catholic philosophers and theologians in France and Belgium during the early years of the twentieth century. Pierre Rousselot's *L'Intellectualisme de saint Thomas* remains an impressive monument to their combined influence on the historical studies of the Thomists who were trying at that time to free the genuine philosophy of St. Thomas from the Cartesian distortions of the nineteenth century manuals.

Maréchal was familiar with the work of Blondel and Rousselot when he began the fifth volume of his *Le Point de départ de la métaphysique*. Like Blondel, he had been impressed by Fichte's reconciliation of Kant's speculative and practical intellect through the dynamism of the human spirit. If, as Fichte claimed, the dynamism of the mind is a constitutive element of both speculative and practical reason, Kant's critical idealism can be overcome. A real dynamism demands that its goal or term also be real. It follows therefore that, if the mind's real striving toward the Infinite Absolute is one of the a priori conditions of the speculative reason's objective judgments, God's real existence is an a priori condition of possibility for every categorical judgment of the speculative reason. From this discovery two others immediately follow. Firstly, far from showing that the idea of God is merely a regulative ideal for speculative reason, a transcendental reflection on human knowledge manifests that God's real existence is an a priori condition of possibility for any speculative judgment whatsoever. Thus a judgment which doubts or denies his existence is a contradiction and destroys itself in its very utterance. Secondly, since God's real existence as First Cause is a necessary condition of possibility for any speculative judgment whatsoever, the judgments of speculative reason are *metaphysical affirmations*. Critical idealism is a contradiction and the judgment which affirms it destroys itself in its very utterance.

The dynamism of the intellect not only bridges the gulf between noumena and phenomena by its grounding of metaphysical affirmations, it unites speculative and practical reason by showing that the Infinite Final Cause of the metaphysical order is the condition of possibility for both. Furthermore, it bridges the gulf between sense and intellect. The dynamism of the intellect explains how, through the causality of the active intellect, man's passive intellect can abstract an intellectual form from the phantasm and reunite it to its sensible subject in a metaphysical affirmation. We should not be surprised therefore that, once Kantianism is made coherent with its basic principles, its philosophy of knowledge is quite similar to the philosophy of St. Thomas. St. Thomas, of course, proceeded as a metaphysician of knowledge and not as a critical philosopher. Nevertheless, his understanding of sensation is quite like Kant's; his explanation of abstraction and conversion to the phantasm reminds the modern reader of Kant's schematism of the categories; and the drive of St. Thomas' active intellect to the Infinite God grounds the analogous knowledge of God, derived from the content of sense knowedge, which Kant denied only because he overlooked the implications of the intellectual dynamism which the coherence of his own system demands.

One of the basic contentions of Maréchal's *Le Point de départ de la métaphysique* is that the metaphysics of knowledge is an integral part of a more general metaphysics of finite and infinite reality. The basic structure of one is dependent upon the basic structure of the other. Therefore a consistent application of the transcendental method to human knowledge should lead to a remarkably similar dynamic structure of human knowledge in both Kant and in St. Thomas and to the metaphysical affirmation of the Pure Act of Being. Consequently it is reasonable to anticipate, Maréchal believed, that the transcendental method could be extended beyond epistemology and be used to ground a general metaphysics whose form and structure would resemble the metaphysics of St. Thomas. Kant and Thomas both agree that man is a receptive knower. Human knowledge must begin with sensation and man's conceptual knowledge depends upon the senses for its objective content. Consequently the unity of sense and intellect in the single act of the receptive knower's existential affirmation demands as the condition of its possibility that both the receptive knower and the sensible objects of his knowledge be composed of matter, form, and existence. How else would the synthesis of intelligible form, sensible subject, and existential affirmation in the judgment be possible? Maréchal was content, however, to indicate the possibility of such a transcendental metaphysics in *Le Point de départ de la métaphysique*. He left the task of working it out to his successors in the movement which has since become known as Transcendental Thomism.

RAHNER'S EARLY PHILOSOPHICAL WORKS

Rahner continued the study of Kant and St. Thomas which he had begun at Pullach at the University of Freiburg. It was his good fortune to be admitted to the famous seminar conducted by Martin Heidegger. Like another distinguished Transcendental Thomist, Johannes B. Lotz, S. J., a fellow student in Heidegger's seminar, Rahner carried his dialogue with German philosophy beyond Kant's critical idealism to the absolute idealism of Hegel and the phenomenological ontology of his professor, Martin Heidegger. Hegel and Heidegger have since replaced Kant as the principal dialogue partners of the German Transcendental Thomists (Rahner, Lotz, Coreth).

Rahner's desire to engage in a Maréchalian dialogue with Heidegger became evident in his doctoral dissertation, subsequently published as *Spirit in the World*. Rahner's dissertation was basically an historical and systematic study of *Summa Theologiae* I, q. 84, a.7, the text in which St. Thomas affirms the necessity of the intellect's conversion to the phantasm in human knowledge. Rahner's dissertation, however, went beyond the bounds of a purely historical study of St. Thomas's metaphysics of the judgment. It contrasted St. Thomas's philosophy of knowledge with the philosophy of Kant and, even more, with the philosophy of Heidegger. Thomas's dynamism of the human mind is compared with Heidegger's fundamental question about Being. Rahner's human subject, like Heidegger's *Dasein*, is a being-in-the-world who reaches self-awareness by raising the question of Being in a world of sensible objects. For man can become aware of his own existence as a free knower only by setting the world over against himself in a judgmental affirmation. Thus the dynamism of man's fundamental question about Being must carry human knowledge through the process of abstraction and conversion to the phantasm without which no judgment about a sensible object can be made. But abstraction of a concept is possible only if the intellect recognizes that the universal conceptual form is *more* than the limited sensible singular in which the human knower first encounters it. And the metaphysical affirmation of the judgment is possible only if the intellect recognizes that the Absolute of Being is *more* than any finite conceptual form or any complexus of finite conceptual forms. Thus the human intellect, in order to come to know itself through the process of the judgment, must have an implicit, pre-conceptual pre-grasp *(Vorgriff)* of Infinite Being. Heidegger was right when he said that *Dasein* was the questioner whose fundamental question about Being "runs through" the beings of the world in its pre-grasp of the world's Horizon. Heidegger was wrong, however, when he affirmed the essential finitude and historicity of Being because he thought that man's question about Being runs through the beings of the world only to terminate in Nothing. For man's question about Being, Rahner claims, is identical with man's conscious awareness of the fundamental dynamism of the human mind, and the term of that dynamism is not Nothing. On the contrary, it is Infinite Existence. Thus the finite historicity of *Dasein* and *Dasein's* world is anchored in God's Infinite Eternity. For without the human mind's pre-grasp of its Infinite Horizon the historicty of the human world could not be known.

Man is a spirit because he is aware of himself as the self-presence of knowing and loving. As spirit he is aware of himself as being-present-to-itself because his conscious drive to the Absolute is a real pre-grasp of Infinite Existence. Yet man is spirit in the world because he is a receptive knower who can come to know himself only through his prior affirmation of sensible realities. His discursive knowledge bears the marks of space and time whose root is matter.

Both *Spirit in the World* and Rahner's later work on the philosophy of religion, *Hearers of the Word* (cf. summary before Chapter I), endeavor to provide a systematic grounding of the Thomistic metaphysics of essence and existence, matter and form, action and finality through a transcendental reflection of the human knower's fundamental question about Being. Their stress on metaphysics rather than epistemology is characteristic of German Transcendental Thomism. However, Rahner's Transcendental Thomism differs from the Transcendental Thomism of Maréchal by more than its stress on a self-grounding metaphysics. It also gives much greater emphasis to the human subject's conscious, although implicit, awareness of God as the Horizon of his spiritual dynamism. Rahner's preoccupation with Heidegger's phenomenological ontology, which is evident in this concern with man's *conscious* pre-grasp of his spirit's Horizon, also appears in the importance which Rahner places on the role of freedom in man's authentic grasp of himself, his world, and the world's Horizon. The same preoccupation manifests itself in the emphasis which Rahner gives to the historicity of the human subject. In short, both the way in which Rahner develops his argument in his second philosophical work and the Heideggerian flavor of its terminology make it very evident that his *Hearers of the Word* is intended to be a Thomistic dialogue with his former professor.

Hegel's influence on Rahner is also apparent in these two early philosophical works. Rahner describes the human spirit as being-present-to-itself *(bei-sich-sein)*. The union of knower and known in the spirit's act of knowledge demands their prior identity in Absolute Being as the condition of its possibility. Sensation is required as a necessary moment in the unified act of human knowledge because sensation is the only way in which the human spirit can "go out of itself" in order to "return to itself" through its "identity with its other" in a judgment about a sensible object in its world. The reader who is acquainted with *The Phenomenology of the Mind* will find many familiar echoes in the metaphysics of knowledge of *Spirit in the World* and *Hearers of the Word*. Rahner revealed in these early works his conviction that Hegelian dialectic is quite compatible with a dynamic interpretation of Thomas's metaphysics of being and knowledge. This conviction would have very important consequences in Rahner's systematic theology of the Trinity, the Incarnation, and grace.

RAHNER THE THEOLOGIAN

However, Rahner was not destined to become a professional philosopher like his classmate, Johannes B. Lotz, S.J. Transcendental Thomism has never enjoyed unanimous approval among Thomists. One of the most distinguished Thomists of this century, for example, Étienne Gilson, has never been willing to admit that Transcendental Thomism is either good Thomism or good philosophy. In Gilson's opinion Transcendental Thomism makes fatal and unnecessary concessions to Kant and the philosopher who uses this method can never work his way out of Kant's idealism. Martin Honecker, the mentor of Rahner's dissertation, took an equally negative view of Transcendental Thomism. He refused his approval to Rahner's dissertation on St. Thomas's metaphysics of the judgment, forcing Rahner to leave Freiburg without his degree. Rahner then transferred to Innsbruck where he received his doctorate in theology in 1936. The dissertation which Honecker had rejected was published at Innsbruck in 1939 under the title *Geist in Welt (Spirit in the World),* and the fifteen lectures which Rahner delivered at the Salzburg summer school in 1937 on the foundations of a philosophy of religion appeared in book form under the title *Hörer des Wortes (Hearers of the Word)* in 1941.

Rahner began his career as a professor of theology at the Jesuit theological faculty in Innsbruck in 1938. His innovative and systematic spirit manifested itself almost at once in his new scheme for a dogmatic theology *(Theological Investigations,* vol. I, pp. 20–37) and in his projected series of monographs on theological themes which evolved many years later into Herder's famous series, *Quaestiones Disputatae,* in which some of Rahner's own significant monographs have appeared. In 1939 the Nazis, after having suppressed the faculty of theology, closed the Jesuit college in Innsbruck and ordered Rahner himself to leave the city.

From 1939 to 1944 Rahner devoted himself to pastoral work and theological lecturing in Vienna. During this period he was a theological consultant to the Archdiocese of Vienna and was closely connected with its pastoral institute. He also lectured in Leipzig, Dresden, Frankfurt, and Cologne. After a year of pastoral work in rural Bavaria, he resumed his post as professor of theology in 1945, first at Pullach and then at Innsbruck after the reopening of its theological faculty in 1948. He remained at Innsbruck until 1964 when he returned to his native Germany to teach, first at the University of Munich and finally at the University of Münster.

Rahner's combination of pastoral work and theological lecturing during the war years gave him a keen appreciation of theology's pastoral implications. His personal experience of a big city diocese torn by war and persecution and his pastoral contact with large numbers of priests, religious, and laity during an agonizing and turbulent period in the history of Central Europe provoked the theological reflections on the diaspora Church, the parochial principle, the charismatic and hierarchical elements in the Church, the apostolic spirituality of the laity, the formation of priests, and the religious life which attracted popular attention to Rahner in the years before Vatican II and contributed greatly to his influence on the bishops who took part in it.

The principal characteristics of Rahner's theology had already begun to take shape during these turbulent years of pastoral and theological activity. From the beginning the theoretical base of his theology was the transcendental reflection on man's conscious activity as spirit in the world which he would later call his philosophical anthropology. With Heidegger in mind, Rahner pictured man as an historical, spatio-temporal being whose spiritual dynamism was consciously, although implicitly, directed toward Infinite Being. Again with Heidegger in mind, he insisted that man is the free subject whose authenticity or inauthenticity springs from his fundamental choice of himself. The intentionality of this fundamental choice contains, albeit implicitly, a choice of man's fundamental attitude

toward his world and the Infinite Being who is its Horizon. In Rahner's
Heideggerian Thomism, however, the intentionality of man's inescapable
choice of himself in his choice of attitude toward the world is declared to
be either an implicit loving acceptance or an implicit egoistic rejection of
God, the world's Absolute Horizon. Furthermore, as Heidegger has
also seen, man is a social being whose destiny is entwined with the destiny of his fellow men in an historical world. He is a member of a race in
the course of whose history a free personal God can speak a word of
revelation.

Rahner has always been insistent on the fact that Christian revelation
contains strict mysteries. God's historical revealing Word is not to be
reduced to purely philosphical knowledge or to merely natural mysticism.
Nevertheless his systematic turn of mind and his schooling in German
idealism made him receptive to the idea that historical revelation should
be looked upon as God's self-revelation and not simply as an arbitrary
collection of facts. As God's self-revelation, the Christian mysteries
should be linked intrinsically to each other and form a coherent system.
As God's self-revelation to man, the Christian mysteries should have
some intrinsic connection with man's personal experience of himself and
of his world.

As early as 1933 and 1934 Rahner had published two articles on St.
Bonaventure. Bonaventure's remarkable synthesis of philosophy, theology, and spirituality is structured around the Trinity and its relation to
redeemed creation. The human mind is the image of the Trinity and
corporeal reality is its vestige. Since the Word of God is the consubstantial expression of the Father within the Trinity, the Word is the home of
the divine ideas. Thus the Word is the Medium through whom the Holy
Spirit, who proceeds from both the Father and the Son, communicates
their dynamic intelligibility to spiritual and corporeal creation. The Word
Incarnate is the Medium of the supernatural grace, without which the
human soul, the created image and expression of the Trinity, cannot
return to its Triune Source. Thus for Bonaventure the Word of God is the
source of both the natural illumination without which the human mind can
acquire no genuinely metaphysical knowledge and of the supernatural
illumination without which the redeemed soul cannot travel the road to
God which leads it from a contemplation of sensible reality to a contemplation of its own spiritual reality and ultimately to a contemplation of the
Truth and Goodness of the Trinity.

Both Bonaventure and Hegel regard the Trinity as the indispensable
key to man's understanding of himself, the world, and God. Hegel considered Chrisianity the Absolute Religion precisely because Christianity is
the religion of the Trinity. For, in his opinion, the theology of the Trinity
is the finest expression of the dialectic of the Spirit which can be found on

the level of religion. According to the dialectical law of its being Spirit must go over into its "other" in order to return to itself in its self-knowledge. The Father must "pass over" into the Son, who is his other within the Trinity, in order to become aware of himself as Father. The Son in his turn continues the dynamic emanation of his procession from the Father by passing over into his "finite other" through the divine creation of the world which Hegel identifies with the Incarnation of the Son.

We can see the effect of Rahner's reading of Hegel and Bonaventure in his later systematic theology. From Bonaventure and Hegel Rahner learned that the Trinity is the key to a religious understanding of the universe. Both of them focused their attention on the pre-Augustinian Patristic theology which affirms that there is an intrinsic metaphysical connection between the procession of the Word from the Father within the Trinity and the relation of the Word to the world through creation and the Incarnation. Both of them bolstered Rahner's own confidence in the possibilities of a metaphysics of the human spirit as a means of linking man's natural knowledge of himself and his world to the supernatural knowledge of the Trinity which comes to him through revelation and mystical experience.

Thus the intellectual and pastoral experience acquired in the troubled early years of his theological career provided Rahner with the main outlines of the synthesis which he would later call his theological anthropology. Its philosophical basis was man's reflection on his own spiritual activity. A knower, the content of whose judgments must be derived from sense experience, is a spatio-temporal knower, composed, like the beings of his world, of matter, form, and act of existence. The dynamism of his knowledge and free choice are inexplicable unless they are directed toward the Infinite Free Existent. Thus both God's freedom and man's historicity ground the possibility of revelation.

The historical Word of revelation which God has actually spoken, however, is his revelation of himself to man in Christ. Christ is God's free communication of his personal depths to man through his Word and his grace. Thus the aim of the Word's Incarnation is the indwelling of the Trinity in the human soul through Uncreated Grace. Moreover, grace, by its intrinsic nature, must be the grace of Christ because, if God is to communicate himself to the created world through a Hypostatic Union, only the Word can become man. Only the Word can do so because the Word alone is the Father's consubstantial self-expression within the Trinity. Consequently the Word alone, as the Father's self-expression, can be the Divine Person through whom God can express himself in his creation through a Hypostatic Union. Since man, composed of matter and form, is a social and historical being, once the Word becomes man, he enters history as a member of the human race. Therefore his abiding self-revelation in word and grace should take social and historical form in the indefectible society which is his Church.

Thus Rahner's theological anthropology unfolds into a coherent theological synthesis structured around the Trinity, the Incarnation, and grace. It resembles Bonaventure's Trinitarian synthesis in the dynamic role which it assigns to the Word of God in God's self-expression in the world through creation and the Incarnation. Both creation and salvation history are understandable only in terms of their relation to the Word of God. That relation, in its turn, is understandable only in terms of the place of the Word within the dynamic processions of the Trinity. The metaphysics of the uncreated and created spirit which undergirds Rahner's Trinitarian synthesis is the Thomistic metaphysics of matter, form, and act of existence which he has justified by his transcendental reflection on man's intellectual and volitional activity. Nevertheless, in addition to the Heideggerian stress on man's conscious pre-grasp of God, which distinguishes Rahner's anthropology from non-Transcendental Thomism, Rahner's metaphysics contains Hegelian elements. The metaphysics of the Son's relationship to the Father within the Trinity and the metaphysics of the Son's relation to the world in creation and the Incarnation, which are essential to the coherence of Rahner's system, have an unmistakably Hegelian origin. They all follow the Hegelian metaphysics of the spirit which, abiding changelessly "in itself," changes "in the other," into which it "goes over" in order to return to itself.

Theologians have questioned the coherence of the "Hegelian Thomism" without which Rahner's theological synthesis would not hold together. Whatever may be the merits of the arguments advanced against it, however, Rahner's metaphysics cannot be dismissed as mere eclecticism. There is an historical and systematic relationship between the Augustinian and Dionysian mysticism which undergirds Bonaventure's *The Mind's Road to God* and the German philosophical tradition to which both Hegel and Heidegger belong. Rahner is well aware of this relationship and of the possibility which it offers of incorporating the best elements of the German philosophical tradition into a Thomistic system which, like Bonaventure's medieval Augustinianism, would link the theology of the Trinity, the Incarnation, and grace to philosophy, mysticism, and personal experience in a synthetic understanding of man, his world, and God.

RAHNER'S THEOLOGICAL WRITINGS

Rahner has been a prodigiously productive writer. Although he has written systematic works of considerable length such as his much discussed work on the Trinity or his recently published fundamental course in theology, Rahner's favorite forms of expression have been the theological monograph and the short article. The range of topics covered in these publications is extremely wide. Rahner has produced profound and original studies on the Trinity, Christology, grace, ecclesiology, scripture, tradition, and eschatology. His important contributions to moral theology have had a significant influence on its development both in Europe and America. His devotional and ascetical writings, among them two priests' retreats, have reached a large audience on both sides of the Atlantic, and his articles on celibacy, the evangelical counsels, religious and lay spirituality have had considerable effect on the Church's interior life during the past two decades. Rahner's influence on pastoral theology has been equally great. His distinction between the charismatic and hierarchical element in the Church, his defense of free speech and public opinion in the Church, and his advocacy of a pastoral practice aimed at fostering personal decision rather than social conformity attracted much attention immediately before and after Vatican II.

Rahner's pastoral preoccupation has not only led to the great diversity of his theological writings, it has brought about a definite evolution in their content and approach. It would not be too hard to trace the course of European theology during the past twenty years by following Rahner's reaction to its development in his multifarious articles. From his early concern with nature and grace, situation ethics, and the pastoral practice of the diaspora Church, Rahner moved on to engage in the debate over Scripture and tradition, the development of doctrine, and religious authority which engaged the Church's attention during and after Vatican II. Later, following the changing focus of theological attention, he took part in the debate over ecumenism, the theology of hope, ideology, eschatology, and political theology. More recently the intellectual problems connected with theological pluralism and the disturbing moral problems of war and peace, scientific development, and technological manipulation of man and nature have become the object of his theological reflection. Despite the profoundly metaphysical character of his systematic theology Rahner has shown himself consistently to be an extremely pastoral theologian both in the style and content of his writings. He has never abandoned his early conviction that a genuine theology must be able to bring light to ordinary Christians as they endeavor to confront the moral and spiritual problems of their age.

The sheer volume of Rahner's writings, however, can present problems to his readers. Very few readers have been able to make their way through the vast number of monographs and articles which he has produced. Fortunately, *Theological Investigations,* the collection of his more important articles, of which twelve volumes have been translated into English, enable the interested reader to acquaint himself with

Rahner's views on most of the major topics which he has treated. Still, Rahner's practice of expressing himself in short articles does not make it easy for the ordinary reader to appreciate fully the force of what he is saying. Rahner is a systematic theologian and his treatment of individual topics is shaped by the basic presuppositions of his theological anthropology with which the reader of an individual article may not be acquainted. Furthermore, Rahner's articles in one area of theology are closely linked to the articles which he has written in other areas. Thus the reader who confines his attention to a single topic will fail to appreciate the remarkable synthetic power of Rahner's theology. He will fail to understand just why Rahner is a great *pastoral* theologian *precisely because* he is one of greatest *systematic* theologians of this century. Again Rahner is difficult to read because he often fails to indicate the contemporary sources which have influenced his own theological anthropology. Thus the unwary reader can fail to grasp the *originality* of Rahner's understanding of Thomistic metaphysics and the daring nature of his Trinitarian and Christological theology. Finally Rahner can confuse an unwary reader when he fails to indicate that his ongoing dialogue with contemporary thought has caused him to modify philosophical or theological positions which he formerly held.

PHILOSOPHISING WITHIN THEOLOGY

To enable the reader to acquire some insight into the synthetic unity of Rahner's world-view the texts devoted to individual theological topics in *A Rahner Reader* are preceeded by texts in which Rahner establishes the basic principles of his philosophical and theological anthropology. In addition, the texts on individual topics are grouped together and prefaced by a brief introduction indicating both their own internal unity and their relation to the basic principles which structure Rahner's system. It is hoped that the reader will be helped thereby to acquire a better understanding of Rahner's unusual ability as a systematic theologian. On the basis of his metaphysics, grounded on man's inner experience, Rahner structures the data of Scripture and tradition into the synthesis of his theological anthropology whose main lines have been sketched above. He is then in a position to address the individual moral, social, and religious problems of contemporary life as a philosophical theologian. For Rahner insists that the theologian today cannot simply "take over" a "ready-made" philosophy. He must establish his own philosophy on the basis of his personal experience, his confrontation with God's revealing Word, and his dialogue with the science, culture, and technology of the modern world. Rahner's moral, pastoral, and spiritual theology *is precisely* this "philosophising within theology" in dialogue with his contemporaries.

For Rahner, like Bonaventure and the great medievals, pastoral and spiritual theology are not something *added on to* a systematic theology with which they have little or no connection. Spiritual and pastoral theology are moments of the same *unified theological activity* from which systematic theology arises. They are a *sharing of experience* by the theologian and his dialogue partner. Both the theologian and his dialogue partner are spirits in the world, sharing a common experience of God's natural and supernatural presence within them. On the basis of a shared contemporary experience both are trying to discern the meaning of the revealing Word which God speaks to them as free individuals within the Church. Therefore the theologian, in Rahner's understanding of the term, should be a sure pastoral guide and spiritual director. The theologian's experience has the breadth which comes from a wide ranging, coherently unified grasp of the data of Scripture and tradition. It has the personal depth which has come from prolonged philosophical and religious reflection. And it has also the relevance which comes from its ability to distinguish between the changeless structures of the human mind and the mutable, culturally determined categories of contemporary science. Rahner's own publications testify to his remarkable success in achieving this ideal of systematic theology. The reader who follows the dialectical spiral of Rahner's thought from experience to system and back to experience again by going carefully through the collected texts on the Trinity, Christology, grace, the theological virtues, ecclesiology, spirituality, and eschatology will get some idea of the breadth and unity of thought required of a great theologian. Students of theology may also gain some understanding of the habit of mind which enables a great pastoral theologian to *think like a theologian* in his retreats, conferences, and talks to the laity.

THEOLOGICAL ANTHROPOLOGY: THE STRENGTH AND WEAKNESS OF RAHNER'S SYSTEM

The transcendental anthropology which is the heart of Rahner's theological synthesis is obviously the place at which it is most vulnerable. This is true, of course, of any metaphysical system. Metaphysics, after all, is not revelation, and Christians today, perhaps more than ever, are divided in their philosophical allegiances. Rahner's system, however, may be more vulnerable than some other philosophical theologies because of the extent to which its conclusions depend on his own transcendental metaphysics of knowledge and love. The dialectic between the mind's categorical knowledge of sensible reality and its conscious, though unobjective, grasp of God as the term of its dynamism, is crucial for

Rahner's dogmatic theology. His theology of mystery, of Christ's human knowledge, of the development of dogma is based on this dialectic. So is his theology of hope, his eschatology and his theological justification of the evangelical counsels. The same dialectic is essential to Rahner's theology of the supernatural existential. For, even if one grants Rahner's contention that the divine decree which raises man to the supernatural order must of its nature produce an ontological effect in man, man's *conscious drive* to God is required as the subject in which the ontological "existential" which raises man to the supernatural order is received. Again, the same dialectic between man's categorical objective knowledge and his conscious, unobjective drive to God, elevated now by the "supernatural existential," supplies the indispensable grounding for Rahner's theology of the anonymous Christian and of the salvific character of the non-Christian religions.

Furthermore, this dialectic between man's objective and unobjective knowledge is equally necessary for Rahner's moral and pastoral theology. Without it Rahner could justify neither his defense of the changeless principles of the natural law nor the individual divine commands which he claims can come to the charismatic Christian. The same dialectic is required for Rahner's pastoral theology of the free individual within the Church and for his theology of the discernment of spirits and of the experience of grace.

The dialectic between man's objective knowledge and his pre-grasp of God is also needed to justify the role which Rahner assigns to freedom in man's fundamental response to God through his response to his world. For, it is only the conscious dynamism of man's spirit to God which makes it necessary for the human agent to accept or reject *God* in the self-choice entailed in taking up his fundamental attitude toward the world. Yet some of Rahner's most significant contributions to theology—his theology of the unity of love of man and love of God, his theology of the fundamental option (through which he has greatly influenced contemporary moral theology), his theology of concupiscence, and his theology of death—depend completely on Rahner's metaphysics of the choice of God entailed in man's choice of a fundamental attitude toward the world.

It is regrettable therefore that Rahner has not provided a more careful and detailed account of the metaphysics of the supernatural existential which is such a vital element in his whole system. Rahner's commentators have had difficulty understanding its precise metaphysical status. In Heideggerian philosophy an existential means one of *Dasein*'s stable conscious structures. Yet Rahner is a Transcendental Thomist. Is his supernatural existential then to be considered an accident inhering in the soul? Clearly it is not justifying grace. But if it is a supernatural accident, what is its precise relation to the order of grace?

The major difficulty of Rahner's critics, however, is not with the supernatural existential but what they consider the excessive dependence of his whole system upon Transcendental Thomism. Gilsonian Thomists do not accept Rahner's Maréchalian contention that the dynamism of the mind can ground his metaphysics. They also reject Rahner's metaphysical account of abstraction through the mind's conscious pre-grasp of God. In their opinion such an understanding of abstraction is both un-Thomistic and philosophically unwarranted. Phenomenologists can hardly be expected to accept either Rahner's metaphysics of being or his account of the origin of conceptual knowledge through abstraction. They also deny Rahner's claim that the intentionality of human consciousness is directed to an Infinite God. As a philosophical theologian, however, Rahner would simply refer these critics to the texts in which he has tried to justify his basic metaphysics of knowledge and being. There is little more that a philosophical theologian can do.

Even Transcendental Thomists, however, have their problems with Rahner's Hegelian metaphysics. Rahner's theology of the Trinity and his Christology, as we have seen, depend on his contention that a being can express itself in its other. This metaphysics, which Rahner calls the metaphysics of the real symbol, is essential to his Christology. Without it Rahner's proof that all grace is the grace of Christ, a vital element in his theology of the anonymous Christian, will not hold up. Neither will Rahner's theology of Christ's real identity with the history of the world on which he builds his theology of the identity of world and salvation history and of Christ as the world's Absolute Future.

Nevertheless, Rahner's Hegelian metaphysics of the real symbol leads to a philosophy of God which is quite startling to traditional Thomists. God is the Pure Act of Being. Therefore he is immutable. Still, while remaining immutable "in himself," the Incarnate Word *really changes in his divine nature*. The Word, however, changes in his other, his human nature. Thus, because of the Son's Incarnation, God is *really involved* in world history. Some Thomists have criticized Rahner's metaphysics of the Incarnation as an incoherent and un-Thomistic blend of classical and process theology. Others have hailed it as a breakthrough to an authentically Thomistic panentheism. Once more Rahner can only direct his critics to the texts in *Spirit in the World* in which he has endeavored to establish the validity and the Thomistic character of his controverted metaphysics of the real symbol.

Rahner's readers can only regret, however, that his pastoral preoccupations have prevented him from writing at greater length on the philosophical foundations of his theology. This is particularly true, since his later theological writings reveal his keen awareness of the complexity and pluralism of contemporary philosophy. Nevertheless, although Rahner has shown that he understands thoroughly the variety and the historical character of our conceptual frameworks, he has never explained how this awareness is to be reconciled with the comparatively straightforward Thomism of his account of conceptualization in his early philosophical works. Again, Rahner has given great importance in his recent theological works to the Church's acceptance of contemporary theological pluralism. He insists that, given the unbridgeable philosophical pluralism which exists today, the Church must learn to live with an unbridgeable theological pluralism. Her theologians can hope to reach agreement only about a very small number of fundamental Christian mysteries. Yet Rahner's own theological anthropology is built on the changeless a priori structure of the human mind, which, as Lonergan has shown, is the unrevisable revisor of all conceptual frameworks. And Rahner's theological anthropology has proposed answers to a broad range of theological questions. How much of Rahner's actual theology represents *the changeless and unrevisable theology*? How much of it should be taken as just *one more theology* among the unbridgeable multitude of theological systems? How coherent are Rahner's recent statements about theological pluralism with his lifetime commitment to transcendental method?

There is no doubt that Rahner could give cogent answers to these questions. On the basis of what Rahner has already written, an attentive reader would even have a shrewd idea of how he would go about answering them, if he thought it worth while to do so. Rahner, however, is pastoral theologian rather than methodologist. He is more interested in responding to vital questions as they arise than in justifying the systematic coherence of what he has already written. We should not expect Rahner to duplicate the work which Lonergan has done in *Insight* and in *Method in Theology*. Rahner knew years ago that, when he chose the short article as his chief means of expression for pastoral reasons, the price of this choice would be loose ends in his theology. Rahner can only be judged on the basis of what he set out to do. Judged on that basis, he is without question one of the greatest systematic and pastoral theologians of this century.

Gerald A. McCool

Note: Throughout this collection the italicized matter introducing the individual chapters and sections are the editor's.

A RAHNER READER

I

The Openness of Being and of Man

In Hearers of the Word *Karl Rahner inaugurates a transcendental reflection on conscious human activity which opens out into a general metaphysics and a philosophy of religion. His own self-awareness manifests to the human knower that he is a conscious subject who cannot fail to raise the question of Being. His primordial, even though implicit, question about Being, which is the condition of possibility for every other act of human knowledge, reveals, in the dynamic process of the question itself, the original unity of Being and knowing. The human subject must possess at least an implicit knowledge of Being since he inquires about it. In the activity of human questioning Being reveals its fundamental characteristic. It is luminous self-presence: the union of Being and knowing.*

Man's awareness of himself and Being comes about in the intellectual activity of making judgments. Yet, since man is a discursive knower, his knowledge must begin with sense experience and move through the abstraction of the concept to its culmination in the objective affirmation of the judgment. Through that objective affirmation, which sets the concrete objects of sense experience over against him in the realm of being, man grasps his own independent reality. He is spirit, the union of being and knowing. But, since he is a discursive knower, whose knowledge must begin with sensation, he is not pure spirit. A discursive knower, who must progressively increase his knowledge of himself and Being through the step-by-step process of ongoing inquiry, cannot be by identity the pure luminosity of Infinite Being. He is not Being by identity. He has being by participation in his own finite measure. Furthermore, since part of his reality eludes his intellectual grasp, there is in the human subject, besides the intelligibility of being, the unintelligible non-being which Aristotle and St. Thomas called matter.

The objective judgment, which is the necessary condition for self-

*awareness, requires both the abstraction of the concept by the active intel-
lect and the conversion to the phantasm without which the concept cannot be affirmed of a sensible singular object. Abstraction of the concept
by the active intellect is therefore an a priori condition of possibility for
human self-awareness. But abstraction is possible only if the human intellect has a conscious, even though implicit and unobjective, pre-grasp of
Infinite Being. For only this conscious pre-grasp of Infinite Being, the
goal of its inborn natural dynamism, enables the human intellect to understand that the universal form represented in the concept is more than
the sensible singular which embodies it and that the fullness of Being is
more than any intelligible form or any finite system of intelligible forms.*

*Thus the process of the judgment brings to light two irreducibly distinct
forms of intellectual knowledge. The first is the objective, categorical
knowledge expressed through the universal concepts of the judgment.
The second is the human knower's unobjective grasp of himself and of
Infinite Being which is the inseparable concomitant of every act of affirmation.*

1. The Luminosity of Being*

We may then tackle our next and proper task: to draw the great lines of
a metaphysical analysis of man with regard to his ability to perceive the
Word of God that may come to him, within the purview of history, as the
revelation of the unknown God.

Now, to ask a question metaphysically means to ask it as a question
about being. This implies that every metaphysical question must somehow encompass the whole of metaphysics. If such is the case, it is obvious that we undertake our task only with the proviso that it will be enough
to draw the major lines of such an ontology of man as the possible recipient of a divine revelation. It is quite impossible to do more.

Moreover we must keep in mind that such a procedure continually
contradicts the inner nature of a metaphysical investigation. For we have
metaphysics as science only where slowly and painstakingly that which is
always already known is developed in a systematic and strictly conceptual way, where man tries to put into concepts that which he has always
already anticipated in his being and in his activity. If we make bold,
nevertheless, to call the abbreviated procedure which we are forced to

* From *Hearers of the Word*, chapter 3. The new translation of the original edition of *Hörer des Wortes* used throughout chapters I-III of *A Rahner Reader* is by Joseph Donceel. An edition of *Hearers of the Word*, revised by J. B. Metz and translated by Michael Richards, was published by Herder and Herder in 1969.

adopt, a metaphysical investigation, we feel ourself entitled to do so only because, in our considerations, we shall, as often as possible, appeal to the metaphysics of Thomas Aquinas. That which we cannot do here may be presupposed, because it has been done by him and it may be done with him by anybody who cares to study his works. Yet our task consists not merely in telling what Thomas has thought, because the point of view from which we consider the great lines of his metaphysics, namely the analysis of the human person as a being who can listen to a revelation of God, has not been expressly considered by Thomas.

Our aim is a metaphysical analysis of the being of man. But, as we mentioned above, such a problem includes the whole of metaphysics. Metaphysics is the question about the being of beings as such, it inquires about the meaning of "being." Such is the way in which metaphysics has always been understood and is still, under various disguises, understood today. Man can never stop, in his thought or in his activity, at this or that reality taken in isolation. He wants to know what reality is all about in its unity within which he gets to know whatever he knows. He inquires about the ultimate foundations, about the one ground of all reality. Insofar as he knows every reality as being, he inquires about the being of beings, he practices metaphysics.

Even when he does not bother to ask such a question or explicitly refuses to do so, he still answers the question. He calls the question irrelevant or meaningless and he has *ipso facto* already given an answer: being is that something which stares at us out of every being as irrelevant, dark, and meaningless. Or man implicitly makes of some particular existent being as such. It may be matter, or business, the vital urge, or death and nothingness. Every time man makes of some reality his be-all and his end-all, he makes of it the center of that which is around him and of all that he is. All the rest is but a means for or an expression of this unique reality. This is the way in which he says what he means and wishes to mean by being. He is practicing metaphysics. Therefore we must practice metaphysics, since we are always already practicing it. We must ask the question: what is the being of beings?

But every question has a "whence," a principle from which may derive an answer. A question which does not want any answer at all does away with itself. If it wants an answer, it necessarily implies already a certain basis, a well-defined ground, upon which it may and must be asked, whence the answer will have to come. Otherwise any answer would be right, even the most arbitrary one. A question to which any answer at all may be given is no longer a question. When the answer does not matter, the question too no longer matters, and no answer is expected.

But whence should the universal question of metaphysics about being as such derive its answer? The "whence" of the answer cannot be questioned itself, since it is supposed to constitute the ground on which the answer can stand. But where shall we find the principle of an answer to the question of being in general, since this question questions absolutely everything by questioning that which always comes first, being as such? It looks very much as if the starting point for the answer can only be the question itself. Hence the starting point of metaphysics is the question: what is the being of beings? It is this question itself, inasmuch as man necessarily asks it. If we had no right to presuppose that this question is really and necessarily asked by all human beings, then he who refuses to ask it or to admit that he does would have done away with every "whence" of an answer and made the answer itself impossible.

Thus we have shown that the question about being itself is the solid positive starting point of metaphysics, the premise for every metaphysical answer and statement. Of course, we do not consider only the content of the question; as important at least is the fact that man, the questioner, actually and necessarily brings it up. Man cannot abstain from answering the question about being; an answer is always forthcoming, because the question belongs always and necessarily to man's existence. Always and of necessity man posits in his existence the "whence" for an answer, hence implicitly the answer to the question of being itself.

This point is important enough to deserve a few more comments. The question about being belongs necessarily to man's existence, because it is implicitly contained in everything man thinks or says. And without thinking and speaking man is not human. Every statement is a statement about some being. Hence it occurs against the background of a previous, although unthematic knowledge of being in general. Every true statement, every judgment, every intentional activity (the activity of a man with "sound judgment," and in every human activity, even when it is "unwise," there still subsists a bit of judgment) contains two components: (1) a synthesis of two concepts, with the claim that this synthesis is correct; (2) the referring of this mental synthesis to "reality in itself," to the objective synthesis of which the mental synthesis is a reproduction. But how can man have access to this reality in itself, to which he refers the synthesis of subject and predicate of his every statement? Precisely through his previous knowledge of being as such.

St. Thomas held similar views. For him too our knowledge of being as such does not derive from but is previous to (not chronologically, of course) our knowledge of single beings. We are speaking, of course, of our immediate and implicit, not of our explicit, knowledge of being as such. We advert explicitly to this knowledge only in the reflective knowledge of metaphysics.

In short, whenever man knows anything, he also possesses an unexpressed co-knowledge of being as the condition of every knowledge of single beings. This always implies the question what being is, whose co-awareness accompanies all our knowing of and dealings with the single objects of our knowledge and of our activity. The question about being emerges necessarily in the existence of man.

Thus the inquiry about the being of beings is a necessary constitutent of man's being and the starting point of every metaphysical question and answer. Since this starting point of every metaphysical investigation is characteristic of the being of man, it follows that every metaphysical inquiry about being as such will also be an inquiry about the being of that being which necessarily asks this question, an inquiry about man. Hence human metaphysics is also always and necessarily an analytic study of man. We may be assured, therefore, that we are not looking away from man when, at first, we seem to be concerned only with the most general principles of metaphysics.

The metaphysical question about the being of beings as such is the only possible starting point of every metaphysics. The analysis of this question must tell us about the nature of beings in general and, in particular, about the nature of the being which, in its existence, necessarily asks this question about being. That which follows from this analysis must be accepted by man as necessarily as, in all his judgments and actions, he asks, at least implicitly, the question about being and he fundamentally always also already answers it. On account of the mutual implication and of the unity of the question about being and about questioning man himself, as they follow from the nature of every metaphysical question, the analysis will always have to be at the same time a general ontology and a metaphysical anthropology.

What is the being of beings as such and in general? This question which we cannot elude in our existence is our starting point and our only starting point. The whole of metaphysics is contained in its analysis. This question has three aspects:

> 1) It inquires about *all* being as such. Not in the sense of the sum total of all beings in all their multiplicity and diversity. But in the sense that it inquires about being that, as one and as (at least analogically) always itself, belongs to every being.
> 2) It has to *inquire* about it.
> 3) It has to inquire about being as such in such a way that the question aims at the being of a being as such, making a distinction between *Sein* (the act of being) and *Seiendes* (that which is, the many beings to all of which belongs the same "act of being").

There is no need of a long explanation to show that these three aspects belong to the question about being. We inquire about being *as such*; it is precisely in this way that metaphysics differs from all other sciences. They inquire about some domain of beings and from a restricted point of view. Metaphysics inquires about all beings, insofar as they are. It inquires about the being of beings as such. Next, this question is really an authentic *question*. This means: what being is, is not always obvious. We know of it *(bekannt)* but we do not really know it *(erkannt)*. Although we know of being, our question is not a rhetorical one. We ask it, because we do not yet really know what we are inquiring about. Finally, our question always makes a distinction between being and beings. It is precisely this which enables us to inquire about being. We know of beings, we know beings, we have continually to do with them, our knowledge refers to them. But we do not know what the being of these beings is. That is why we inquire. This need of inquiring shows in its turn that we necessarily distinguish between being and beings.

We have now to submit these three aspects of the one question about being to a metaphysical analysis, in order to find out what this question itself tells us about the meaning of being and about the nature of the one who inquires about it.

In the metaphysical question about being we inquire first about *all* being as such. This implies that the nature of being is to know and to be known in an original unity. We shall call this the self-presence or the luminosity of being. This is the first statement of a general ontology, as it concerns us here. On the other hand, man's nature is absolute openness for all being or, to put it in one word, man is spirit. This is the first statement of a metaphysical anthropology, insofar as we study it here. In the following chapters we have to establish and to explain these two statements, as they derive from the first aspect of the general question about being.

The nature of being is to know and to be known in a primordial unity; in other words, it is self-presence, luminosity. First, when we inquire about the being of all beings, we admit that we have already a provisional knowledge about being in general. It is impossible to inquire about that which is in every respect and absolutely unknown. Thus some kind of knowledge is asserted and expressed when we inquire about the meaning of being. And since the question about being as such inquires about everything, the knowledge contained in it cannot know what it knows as something distinct from that which we inquire about. Mysterious though it may be, the being we inquire about is also always already a being we know about. For metaphysics being is all at once the whence and the whither, the beginning and the end of all questions.

Since to the extent and under the aspect that it is inquired about in metaphysics being is always already known, we thereby implicitly affirm that all being is basically knowable or intelligible. A being whose being would of its nature be unknowable is a contradiction. We would be inquiring about it, since the possibility or impossibility of our knowing it is in question. But whence would this inquiry come? We cannot inquire about something absolutely unknown, since every inquiry starts by positing as known to some extent that about which it inquires, and since something absolutely unknowable cannot be known to any extent. The first metaphysical question, the most universal question about being, is already the affirmation of the fundamental intelligibility of all beings. *Omne ens est verum.* (Every being is true.) Beings and possible objects of knowledge are identical.

This implies further that every being, as possible object of knowledge, has of itself and on account of its being, hence *essentially,* an inner ordination to possible knowledge and so to a possible knower. For we have seen that intelligibility is asserted as a determination of the being itself. This inner ordination of every being to possible knowledge is an a priori and necessary statement. This is possible only if being and knowledge constitute an original *unity.* Otherwise this relation of every being by itself to some knowledge might at the most be a factual one, and not a feature of every being, belonging to the very nature of its act of being. An essential relation of correlativity between two states of affairs must, in final analysis, be founded in an original unity of both of them. For if they should originally be unconnected, i.e., if they were not by their very origin related to one another, their relation would never be necessary, but, at the most, factual and fortuitous. *Non enim plura secundum se uniuntur.* (Many things do not constitute a unity by themselves.)

Therefore being and knowledge are related to each other because originally, in their ground, they are the same reality. This does not imply anything less than that being as such, to the extent that it is being, is knowledge; it is knowledge in original unity with being, hence it is a knowledge of the act of being which the knower himself is. Being and knowing constitute an original unity, that is, to the nature of being belongs a relation of knowledge with regard to itself. And the other way round, the knowledge which belongs to the essential constitution of being is the self-presence of being. The original meaning of knowing is self-possession, and being possesses itself to the extent that it is being. Such is the first statement of our general ontology which derives from the first aspect of our general question about being: the essence of being is to know and to be known in an original unity which we call the (knowing) self-presence of being. Or, if we wish to say the same thing with a term which is used in contemporary philosophy: being is self-luminous. Being is of itself luminosity.

This short deduction may become clearer, first, if we compare it with the principles of Thomistic metaphysics; next, if we take care of a possible misunderstanding, which may affect this statement and which has in fact affected it in the metaphysics of German Idealism. This will provide us with a first idea of the analogy of the concept of being.

First we explain our first statement of a general ontology by means of the axioms of Thomistic ontology (cf. *Spirit in the World,* p. 67ff.). We have already mentioned the principle *Omne ens est verum.* Intelligibility is a transcendental property of every being. "Transcendental" is used here first in the Scholastic sense of "surpassing the categories." More specifically it means here that intelligibility does not accrue to being from without, or that it does not consist only in a relation, extrinsic to the being itself, to some knowledge which happens to grasp the being in question. Rather it means that the intelligibility belongs intrinsically, from the start, by its very nature, to its essential make-up, that it only expresses explicitly what we affirm already when we affirm being itself. Hence, according to this Thomistic axiom, intelligibility belongs to the basic make-up of every being. Thus Thomistic metaphysics excludes at once all metaphysical irrationalism, i.e., an irrationalism that not only claims that some knowers have no access to all beings (thus denying them the possession of *logos*), but that some domains of being (whether they be called values, life, or anything else) are in principle inaccessible to any logical knowing. *Quidquid enim esse potest, intelligi potest* (For whatever can exist, can be known) (*S.c.G.*, II, 98).

But even for a Thomistic ontology this principle is but the way of access to the more essential insight of the original identity of being and knowing in a self-presence, in the luminosity of being for itself, to the extent that and insofar as it is being.

For Thomas the original and fundamental concept of being, hence of knowable object from which all other objects of knowledge and all other "beings" are but derivations, is actual being, *esse*, or, even less likely to be misunderstood, *esse actu* (the act of being). We must keep this in mind if we are to understand the following statements of Thomas in their real meaning and especially in their universal and fundamental significance and validity.

Thus Thomas emphasizes the original unity of knowable and knowing, which implies more than that one refers to the other. *Intellectum et intelligibile oportet proportionata esse*: The intellect and its object must be proportionate (not merely proportionally related to each other but) *et unius generis*: they must have the same origin. And Thomas indicates the logical ground for this requirement: *cum intellectus et intelligible in actu sint unum* (since the intellect and that which is intelligible in act are one). Otherwise we cannot understand the possibility of the factual unity in the act of knowing of the knowing and of that which is known (*In Metaph. Prooem.*).

Hence for St. Thomas being and knowing are also *unius generis*, coming from the selfsame, unique root in an original unity. Being is in itself knowing, and knowing is the self-presence of being that is inseparable from the make-up of being. It is the reflection of being upon itself.

It is in the light of this basic metaphysical conception of being and of knowledge that St. Thomas also interprets every instance of knowing, the single act of knowledge. He rejects the popular conception of the act of knowledge as a bumping into something, as an intentional reaching "outwards." Knowing does not occur *per contactum intellectus ad rem* (through some contact between the intellect and the thing). *(S. c. G.* II, 98) If knowing and intelligibility are inner features of being, a single actual act of knowing cannot be understood in its metaphysical nature if one interprets it as a referring of some knower to an object distinct from him, as "intentionality." This can, at least, not be the right starting point for a metaphysical understanding of the nature of the act of knowledge. We must rather start from this: that being is of and by itself knowing and being known, that being is self-presence. *Intellectus in actu perfectio est intellectum in actu (S.c.G.,* II, 99). The complete ontic reality of the intellect is that which is actually known. Since this statement refers to the essence, it is also reversible: in order to be actually known, that which is knowable must basically be the ontic reality of the intellect itself. We would totally misunderstand St. Thomas—our interpretation would be cheap and shallow and reduce his profound metaphysics to something quite pedestrian—if we were to interpret the identity of the knowing and the knowable, which is asserted in this and similar formulas, as if it simply meant that the known as such must be known by some "knower," that the knower as such must know "something," and that in this sense both must be "one." In the statement we have quoted "perfection" means an ontic reality of the intellect as a being. *Idem est intellectus et quod intelligitur* (the intellect and that which it knows are the same thing—I, 87, 1, ad 3). *Intellectum est perfectio intelligentis* (that which is known is the perfection of the one who knows) *(S.c.G.,* II, 98).

Hence the *species* is not for St. Thomas something like an "intentional image." It is an ontic perfection of the spirit insofar as it is a being. The problem of how I can know something which is distinct from me is not solved by appealing to the species as an intentional image. Rather for St. Thomas this word brings up the following problem: how can an ontic determination of a knowing subject, by reaching consciousness, bring about the knowledge of an object distinct from the species and from the knowing subject? However, we do not yet have to consider this problem. We have referred here to the correct meaning of species in St. Thomas so as to avoid the danger of a too hasty interpretation. This might make us unable to understand the real starting point of the whole Thomistic metaphysics of being and of knowledge: that knowledge, in its first and original sense, is the self-presence of being, that something is known to the extent that it becomes in its being identical with the knowing subject.

We attempted to summarize our interpretation in the statement: knowledge, in its original nature, is the self-presence of being. St. Thomas says practically the same thing. What we called the self-presence is called by him *reditio subjecti in seipsum* (the return of the subject into himself). For St. Thomas to know is an activity by which the knower returns into himself; it results therefore in a self-presence. This shows how he basically rejects the popular interpretation of knowledge as what he calls a *spargi ad multa,* a being spread out over many things. Knowledge essentially takes place through the return of the knowing subject into himself, it is coming-to-oneself, a self-presence. Of course this presents the Thomistic metaphysics of knowledge with the following problem: if knowing is ultimately a coming-to-oneself, how can a knowing subject ever know anything distinct from himself? It will have to solve this problem (to which we shall return later) without giving up its basic insight into the nature of knowledge. That St. Thomas considers this coming-to-oneself, this power of self-presence, as the basic constituent of being is evident also from the fact that, in a remarkable chapter of his *Summa contra Gentes* (IV,11) he claims that the degrees of being (we might say the degrees of possession of being, of intensity of being) correspond to the degrees of the power of coming-to-oneself, of returning into oneself. A being possesses being to the extent that it possesses the possibility of such a *reditio in seipsum.*

We feel that in this way we have sufficiently shown, within the framework of what is possible here, that in a Thomistic ontology there is really room for our first statement of a general ontology: the essence of being is to know and to be known, in an original unity which we have called the self-presence of being, the luminosity of being for itself.

Of itself being is luminosity. That which is, to the extent that it is, is not something which may be experienced and known only in obscure urges, in the chaotic turmoil of dark powers. Of itself at least it is luminous, it has always been light. Sure, being is more than knowledge, it is life and action, decision and execution; but it is all this in such a way that all life and action, every decision and execution, insofar as they are (and insofar as they are not, they are nothing), are luminous for themselves, are self-present in knowledge, because, although they differ conceptually from knowledge, they are moments that belong intrinsically to being itself, to being that is self-present in its luminosity in all the dimensions in which it unfolds its nature.

2. The Analogy of Being*

Before we continue our investigation we have to consider an obvious difficulty against our conception of being. If being implies the original

*From *Hearers of the Word,* chapter 4.

unity of knowing and of its object, if it belongs to the basic nature of being to be self-present, then it seems impossible that there may exist any being that is not at once knowing and known in identity. But then we have strayed into the basic assertion of the philosophy of German Idealism, as it finds its peak in Hegel: being and knowing are identical. It cannot be our task here to undertake the arduous attempt of explaining what this statement implies in German Idealism, to what extent it means a deep insight and to what extent a fateful error. Such formulas must always be understood as results of former thinking and must be interpreted in the framework of their historical and philosophical development. Hence it is by no means certain that we have understood this assertion of German Idealism simply by stating it. And if it can be understood only together with that which German Idealism has deduced from it, it is clear that we cannot go into more details about its exact meaning. Otherwise we would have to explain the whole philosophy of Hegel. It will be enough here, with respect to this pantheistic thesis of German Idealism, to explain *our* statement of the original unity of knowledge and being in such a way as to show clearly that it has nothing in common with any kind of pantheism or of idealism (or that which is usually known under this name).

We reached our statement because it is presupposed by the possibility that every being can, in principle, be known. We have shown that this possibility was implicitly affirmed in the first metaphysical question about the meaning of beings as such and in general. Hence in order to explain our first statement about the luminosity of beings we must return to its origin, to the fact that man *asks the question* about being. But a question is meaningful only if it is possible and necessary. Possible: that which we inquire about must, in principle, be knowable. Necessary: that about which we inquire is not so obvious that it allows of no further questions.

In other words, we can inquire about being only if the question is not, from the start and from every point of view, made superfluous by an an answer, by a complete knowledge of the object, only if a question and also an answer (which always presupposes an authentic question) is not rendered impossible by some knowledge which no longer allows of any questions. The fact that the question is possible implies that being is self-presence, an original unity of being and knowledge. The fact that the question is necessary seems to contradict what we have just said about it. Why should we inquire about being if it is self-presence, a reflecting upon itself?

If the questioner inquires about being, he must be being, since his inquiry shows that he knows already about being and since (according to the first principle of our general ontology) he can know about it only insofar as he himself is what he knows. Yet the inquirer cannot be being, about which he inquires, since otherwise, according to the same principle, he should be in unquestioning possession of the being he inquires about.

Hence the being that inquires is both being and non-being; its basic inner being is weak; it is not that act of being to which the first principle of our general ontology strictly applies. The act of being of the inquirer is not simply and from every point of view the act of being to which our first principle applies.

On the other hand, the inquirer must possess an act of being, to which this first principle applies in some way, since we have deduced the principle from the first metaphysical question about beings as such and in general, that is from a question which comprises the inquirer himself and his act of being. But this makes of the concept of being, to which our first principle applies, a fluctuating concept. We cannot clearly grasp and delimit it. We cannot derive from it any precise statements about its content, that is, about being as self-presence, as luminosity, by simply predicating being of a being.

The material insight which we had first reached that being is self-presence, self-luminosity, turns into a formal insight: the *degree* of self-presence, of luminosity for oneself, corresponds to the intensity of being, to the *degree* in which being belongs to some existent, to the *degree* in which, notwithstanding its non-being, a being shares in being. And the other way round: the degree of intensity of being shows in the degree in which the being in question is able to return into itself, in which it is capable, by reflecting upon itself, to be luminous for itself.

Hence our first metaphysical principle about the luminosity of being applies only with the restriction that a being is self-present and constitutes a unity of knowing and being only to the extent that being belongs to it. This extent is intrinsically variable. The same starting point from which we derived our first statement shows us also that we must, in principle, consider this being not as something unchangeable, always and everywhere the same, not, so to speak, as a constant quantity, but rather as a variable function. We have seen that "being" in itself and in the most formal sense cannot be intrinsically fixated. Being is an analogous concept. And this analogy shows in the purely analogical way in which each single being returns to itself, can be present to itself. We shall have to apply this finding in detail to man and to the first and original object of his specific human knowledge. In this way it will become even clearer when we shall have to treat of the second and third aspects of our question about being.

At this stage of our investigation we wish to refer once more to Thomistic ontology (cf. *Spirit in the World*, p. 71 ff.). St. Thomas was undoubtedly convinced of the fact that being is the self-presence of being. However, as a rule, he prefers to express this basic idea of his metaphysics of knowledge and of being in the more formal way we have just established. This way emphasizes the fact that the concept of being cannot be fixated; it expresses at once its analogical character.

St. Thomas affirms two things. First that the concept of the being of a being is itself a fluctuating concept, which cannot in its universality, be pinned down to a determined, univocal meaning (hence to a determined manner of self-presence). Next, that the inner luminosity, the degree in which being knows itself and is known, corresponds perfectly to and varies with the variability of being. The concept of being is analogous, as follows from the very starting point from which we were able to get an idea of how for Aquinas too being, self-presence and luminosity are analogous concepts, which cannot be pinned down, which go through continual inner transformations, and which show themselves as such there where being manifested its nature as presence to itself.

This enables us, in a way which will do for the time being, to reject an interpretation of our first metaphysical principle in the sense of German Idealism, as it is generally and rightly interpreted in a pantheistic sense. True, being is knowledge. But only to the extent that a being is or has being. Now this being is an analogous concept, analogous for the same reason from which we derived this first principle. Hence not every being is "knowledge" or "true" in the same sense and measure. A being is conceivable, nay, it is already asserted as actually existing, although as such, it is not an inner moment of a knowledge of the "absolute consciousness." Only the pure act of being is the absolute identity of being and knowing, and perfectly realizes what is meant by the concept of being. In this case of an absolute identity of being and knowing in the pure act of being, in the absolute Being, there remain no more questions to be asked. The being that is absolute Being itself possesses at once in absolute identity, hence in pure luminosity, the object of all questioning: being as such. Hence the question is always already overtaken by an unquestioning knowledge. It is the *noesis noeseos* (the thought of the thought).

It belongs to man's basic make-up not only that he *can* inquire about being, but also that he *must* do so. It follows that he is not absolute consciousness but, precisely in his metaphysics, hence *as* transcendental consciousness, a *finite* spirit. His metaphysical inquiry does not imply absolute consciousness. This absolute consciousness does not come to itself in man, not even in his transcendental consciousness. When man feels that he has to inquire about being, he shows the finiteness of his spirit in such a way, however, that the question itself reveals that being is, of itself, self-presence, luminosity, the original unity of knowing and of being known.

We are in the midst of the most authentic philosophy of religion, insofar as it should be for us a vindication of the possibility of a divine revelation. If revelation is to be the manifestation of the Absolute by himself to the finite spirit, this presupposes two things: first, that, in principle, every being may be expressed in a "true" discourse, in a communication addressed to the spirit. This is required if we are to speak of the possibility of the communication of a state of affairs hidden in the absolute Being. And this (at least this, although there is more to it) is what we mean by revelation. That is precisely what we have been discussing. The ultimate unity of being and knowledge is the ultimate presupposition of the communication of the ultimate being, of pure being in its "divinity," to man through discourse, through the word. Only if being is from the start "logos" can the embodied Logos say in the word that which is hidden in the depths of the Godhead. Only if these depths are not a dark urge, an abysmal night, a blind will, but eternal light (even though inaccessible to man left to his own devices) can the word be the bearer of all grace and of all reality.

3. Man as Spirit*

Every judgment affirms a being as such in one of its peculiarities: this is such or such. That is in a sense the most general form of a judgment; it is present also in every action, since here too man has always to do with something that is such or such, of this or that kind. But grasping a single object *as* such or such, of this or that kind, is nothing but grasping the single object of our thought or action under a universal concept. The single object, as given originally in and through the senses, is subsumed under a concept. And this grasping of the single object under the concept (the knowledge of the object as possessing the universal quiddity mentioned by the statement's predicate) is but the other side of what we have called the self-subsistence in knowledge of the knowing human subject. For it is precisely because through his concept the knowing subject knows something of something, because he can refer his universal concept to a *this* to which it applies, that he opposes this *this* to himself as his object and thus reaches his knowing self-subsistence. Inquiring about the ultimate ground of the possibility of this self-subsistence is identically asking the following question: what makes it basically possible for man to subsume the single sense object under a concept, to grasp the universal in the singular?

In Thomistic metaphysics of knowledge the technical term for this problem is *abstraction*. Abstraction enables us to grasp the universal in the singular, in the particular. It is the condition of the possibility of judging, hence of knowing self-subsistence. We are looking for that which makes this self-subsistence possible; we must therefore investigate what makes abstraction possible.

* From *Hearers of the Word*, chapter 5.

"Abstracting" means "detaching." When we abstract, we find out that the quiddity given in sense knowledge may be detached from the individual thing in which it presents itself to us. It is not of the essence of this "what" to be realized in this and only in this individual object. To abstract means therefore to discover that the quiddity given in the individual object is illimited, in this sense that we grasp it as a possible determination of other individual objects. The whatness (the *forma* or *quidditas* in scholastic terminology) is grasped as a determination which, in principle, applies to more than this individual object in which it happens to appear and to affect our senses.

This leads us to the question: what is the transcendental condition which enables the knowing subject to discover that the quiddity is illimited, although it is experienced as the quiddity of one single individual. We are inquiring about the *transcendental* condition of this possibility. That means we are looking for a condition which must exist in the knowing subject prior to any knowledge or abstraction, as the previous condition of their possibility. In scholastic terms: we are inquiring into the inner nature of the "power" of abstracting. Since in Thomistic terminology this power is also called *agent intellect,* we may express our question as follows: what is the nature of the agent intellect?

The power of abstraction is the power of knowing that the quidditative determination presented by the senses in its singularity is, of itself, illimited. The quidditative determination is first presented to us as restricted to a single sense object. If then we know at once that this determination as such is illimited, we must somehow grasp that its limitation comes from the single sense object as such. If we are aware of this limitation as such, and as brought about by the "thisness" of the single object, we are also aware of the illimitation of the quiddity as such.

Now a limit is experienced as such (we do not simply say: we are aware that there is in fact a limit!) when it is experienced as an obstacle to something which wants to get beyond it. Let us apply this to our present case. We are aware that the quiddity given in sense knowledge is limited in and through the single sense object. The fact that we are aware of this limitation reveals to us the illimitation which belongs to the quiddity as such. This is possible only if the activity which grasps this individual sense object reaches out, prior to this grasping, beyond this individual object, for more than the latter is.

Now this "more" can obviously not be a single object of the same kind as the one whose abstracting knowledge it is supposed to make possible. Otherwise the same question would come up again. This "more" can only be the absolute range of all knowable objects as such. We shall call this "reaching for more" the *Vorgriff* (anticipation, pre-apprehension). Human consciousness grasps its single object in a *Vorgriff* which reaches for the absolute range of all its possible objects. That is why in every single act of knowledge it always already reaches beyond the individual object. Thus it does not grasp the latter merely in its unrelated dull thisness, but in its limitation and its relation to the totality of all possible objects. While it knows the individual object and in order to know it, consciousness must always already be beyond it. The *Vorgriff* is the condition of the possibility of the universal concept, of abstraction. The latter in its turn makes possible the objectivation of the sense datum and so man's knowing self-subsistence.

We must explain more clearly what is meant by the *Vorgriff*. It is an a priori "power" given with human nature. It is the dynamism of the spirit as it strives towards the absolute range of all possible objects. In this movement of the mind the single objects are grasped as single stages of this finality; thus they are known as profiled against this absolute range of all the knowable. On account of the *Vorgriff* the single object is always already known under the horizon of the absolute Ideal of knowledge and posited within the conscious domain of all that which may be known. That is why it is also always known as not filling this domain completely, hence as limited. And insofar as it is *thus* known *as* limited, the quidditative determination is grasped as wider in itself, as relatively illimited. In other words, it is abstracted.

This is possible only if this *Vorgriff* and the range of the knowable revealed by it is conscious (in a way which we shall have to explain more precisely). Of course, this consciousness emerges only in and with the knowledge of the single object, as a previous condition of the possibility of our knowledge of it. The *Vorgriff* makes man conscious by opening up the horizon within which the single object of human knowledge is known.

We can determine in more detail the nature of this *Vorgriff* only by determining more precisely the range of the horizon which it opens up and in which it posits the single object of knowledge. As briefly mentioned above, it is obvious that this "whither" of the *Vorgriff* cannot be an object of the same kind as the one whose abstractive and objective knowledge it makes possible. For such an object would require a similar *Vorgriff* to be known. Likewise the *Vorgriff* is conscious (otherwise it would have no meaning for our problem). Yet it is not, by itself alone, an act of knowledge. It is a moment of such an act, which, as such, intends a single object.

Nevertheless, although the *Vorgriff* is only the condition of the possibility of knowledge, we cannot help conceiving it (we do not say: affirming it) as some kind of knowledge in itself, because this is the only way we can form an idea of this reaching out of our knowledge to ever further objects. Now, if we must think of the *Vorgriff* as some kind of knowledge, we must be ready to state what the "object" of this "knowledge" is. In this sense we ask then what the object of the *Vorgriff* is.

We have already said above that this object is the totality of the possible objects of human knowledge, since it cannot be a single object. Such a single object would, as such, also have to be known in conceptual abstraction. How shall we more precisely determine this totality? What is the absolute totality of all possible objects of knowledge, in whose horizon the single object is grasped? It might even be more prudent not to speak of the "totality" of all objects of knowledge, and to ask simply: whither does man's anticipating knowledge transcend the single object which it grasps?

There are in the history of Western philosophy three typical directions in which an answer to this question has been attempted: the direction of the perennial philosophy which, in this case, goes from Plato to Hegel; the direction of Kant; and that of Heidegger. The first one answers: the range of the *Vorgriff* extends towards being as such, that possesses no inner limit in itself and that therefore includes also the absolute being of God. Kant answers: the horizon, within which our objects are conceptually given to us, is the horizon of sense intuition, which does not reach beyond space and time. Heidegger says: the transcendence which serves as the basis for man's existence heads for nothingness.

It is of course—and unfortunately—not possible, within the scope of these considerations, to investigate this problem and the suggested solutions in a way which befits its importance. We shall have to content ourselves with outlining very briefly at least the answer of perennial philosophy, as given by Scholastic philosophy. The least we can say is that human knowledge intends that which exists, means a Yes. Our problem is to explain how man knows about the finiteness of the immediately given object. As long as we can explain this by means of some positive knowledge, of some anticipation which says Yes, which aims at being and not at nothingness, we cannot and may not interpret transcendence as a transcendence aiming at nothingness.

The only reason why this transcendence towards nothingness might be required is that it renders possible our experience of the inner finiteness of the things and persons that are immediately given to us in knowledge. But the *Vorgriff* toward more than what the single object is constitutes a sufficient and plausible explanation for this negation, for the knowledge of the finiteness of the immediate object of our experience. Nothingness does not come before negation, but the *Vorgriff* towards the illimited is already in itself the denial of the finite, because and insofar as, as condition of the possibility of its being known, it reveals its finiteness by reaching beyond all the finite. Hence the Yes to that which is illimited in itself makes the negation possible, and not the other way round. So we need not admit a transcendence towards nothingness which, previous to and as the foundation of all negation, would alone reveal the finiteness of a being. The positive illimitation of the transcendental horizon of human knowledge shows by itself the limitation of all that which does not fill this horizon. Hence it is not "nought that noughtens," but it is the infinity of being, at which the *Vorgriff* aims, which unveils the finiteness of all that which is immediately given.

Hence our problem can only be this: whether this *more* of the *Vorgriff* implies only a relative illimitation, as Kant believes, or the absolute illimitation of being as such, so that the *Vorgriff* opens up a domain beyond the field of spatio-temporal knowledge. But the former hypothesis contains a contradiction—not a contradiction between the content of the concepts, as if there were a conceptual and immediate contradiction between the concept "finite" and the concept "totality of the objects of human knowledge"—but there exists a contradiction between the act by which the statement is asserted and the content of the statement.

We can know that the totality of the objects of human knowledge is finite only if we reach beyond this finiteness. Otherwise the latter might actually exist, but it would not be known as such. This *Vorgriff* beyond the inner finiteness of the field of human objects, of the domain of sense knowledge, which alone can make manifest this finiteness *as* such, would have to aim at nothingness, since, *ex hypothesi*, it cannot reach for the being that is illimited in itself. Thus Heidegger is the logical outcome of the Kant who opposed German Idealism. But we have just shown that this *Vorgriff* towards nothingness is an inadmissible hypothesis. Thus the presupposition of perennial philosophy is the only possible and admissible one.

The *Vorgriff* which is the transcendental condition of the possibility of an object known as object, hence of man's self-subsistence, is a *Vorgriff* towards being as illimited in itself.

Our first and most general question about being is only a formalized way of expressing every judgment, as it underlies all our actions and thoughts. Therefore we may say of every judgment that it contains the *Vorgriff* towards being as such in its illimitation. Insofar as this question (like judgment and free activity) is of man's very essence, the *Vorgriff* towards being as such in its essential infinity belongs to the basic make-up of human existence.

The same necessity which drives man to anticipate being as such makes him co-affirm the infinite being of God. It is true that the *Vorgriff* does not immediately put God as an object before the mind, since, as the condition of the possibility of all knowledge of objects, the *Vorgriff* itself never represents an object in itself. But in this *Vorgriff*, as the necessary and always already fulfilled condition of every human knowledge and action, the existence of an absolute being, hence of God, is always already co-affirmed, even though not represented. The *Vorgriff* co-affirms as objectively possible that which, as a possible object, may come to stand in its range; otherwise it would once more aim at nothingness. An absolute being would wholly fill the range of the *Vorgriff*. Hence it is co-affirmed as real, since it cannot be grasped as objectively merely possible, and since the *Vorgriff* intends primarily not merely possible, but real being. In this sense we may and must say: the *Vorgriff* aims at God. Not as if it intended God so immediately that it should immediately represent the absolute Being in its own self, as an object, and make this being immediately known in itself. The *Vorgriff* intends God's absolute being in this sense that the absolute being is always and basically co-affirmed by the basically illimited range of the *Vorgriff*.

This is by no means an a priori demonstration of God, like that of Augustine, derived from the "eternal truths," or like that of Anselm or of Leibniz. The *Vorgriff* and its range, as the always present and necessary condition of all knowledge, can be known and affirmed only in the a posteriori knowledge of a real being and as the necessary condition of this knowledge. Thus the way we understand our knowledge of God is but a translation in terms of the metaphysics of knowledge of the traditional proofs of God, as formulated in terms of the metaphysics of being. Instead of saying: this finite being, which I affirm as actually given, demands, as its condition, the existence of an infinite being; we only say (and we mean the same thing): the affirmation of the real finiteness of a being demands as condition of its possibility that we affirm the existence of an absolute being. We do this implicitly in the *Vorgriff* towards being as such, since only through it do we know the limitation of the finite being as such a limitation.

Once more we must say that it is unfortunately not possible to show in detail how the ideas which we have exposed have been traditionally formulated in Thomism (cf. *Spirit in the World*, pp. 117–236). We would have to speak of the connection between the "complete return of the subject upon himself" as performed by the human spirit in all its thinking and the abstraction, hence between what we have called the self-subsistence of man and the grasping of the individual sense datum as an object under its concept. Starting thence we would have to show what the power of abstraction, what the agent intellect is. It would turn out to be the power of the *Vorgriff* towards being.

The agent intellect is the light that permeates the sense object, i.e., puts it within the domain of being as such, thus revealing how it participates in being as such. On the other hand, the actually intelligible object which comes about this way makes that light, i.e., knowing about being as such, in its illimited extension, emerge into man's consciousness. This allows us to understand the correct and profound meaning of the simple sounding statement that the formal object of the spirit is *ens commune* (being in general) and not *ens principium numeri* (spatio-temporal being) and that the spirit is spirit because it grasps everything *sub ratione entis* (from the point of view of being). This grasping of all objects in the horizon of being as such is often misunderstood. It does not mean that, after he knows the single objects, man combines them under a general point of view. It means rather that man is a spirit because, from the start, in his dynamism towards being as such, he grasps his single objects as moments of this unending movement of his, he sees them right away under this horizon of being as such, on account of which man is always already open for the absolute being of God. That is why St. Thomas can truly say: "All knowing beings [he means, of course, those that possess spiritual knowledge] implicitly know God in everything they know" (de Ver., 22, 1 ad 1). For St. Thomas the concept of God is that which comes last in all our knowledge. But the Vorgriff towards the infinite being is the previous condition of our very first conceptual knowledge, so that in every such knowledge God is already implicitly known. These simple allusions to the way in which our ideas have been formulated by St. Thomas will have to do.

Once more, as we did already in the last chapter, we must ask: have we not strayed too far away from our theme? And once more we must answer: we are in the midst of a philosophy of religion which, as metaphysical anthropology, has to establish the possibility of a revelation addressed to man.

We started with the question what our first metaphysical question about being had to tell us, in its first aspect, about the nature of man as the possible subject of a revelation. The answer has been that it belongs to man's fundamental make-up to be the absolute openness for being as such. Through the Vorgriff, which is the condition of the possibility of objective knowledge and of man's self-subsistence, man continually transcends everything towards pure being. Man is the first of these finite knowing subjects that stand open for the absolute fullness of being in such a way that this openness is the condition of the possibility for every single knowledge. Hence there is no domain of being which might lie absolutely outside the horizon in which man knows his objects; and, through this knowledge, he is self-subsistent and capable of freely acting and deciding his own destiny. We call this basic make-up of man, affirmed by him in every act of knowledge and of freedom, his spiritual nature.

Man is spirit, i.e., he lives his life while reaching unceasingly for the absolute, in openness towards God. And this openness towards God is not something which may happen or not happen to him once in awhile, as he pleases. It is the condition of the possibility of that which man is and has to be and always also is in his most humdrum daily life. Only that makes him into a man: that he is always already on the way to God, whether or not he knows it expressly, whether or not he wills it. He is forever the infinite openness of the finite for God.

A divine revelation is possible only if the subject, to whom it is to be addressed, offers to it by himself an a priori horizon within which something like a revelation may occur. And it is only if this horizon is absolutely illimited that no law or restriction is imposed from the start on a possible revelation concerning that which might and should possibly be revealed. A revelation which is to unveil the depths of Divinity and which is basically the first moment of the invitation addressed to man to share in the life of Almighty God himself, is conceivable and possible only if man is understood as spirit, i.e., as transcendence towards being pure and simple. A more restricted horizon of human knowledge would at once and a priori drive possible contents of a revelation outside this horizon and render them incapable of being revealed.

Hence when we state that the transcendence of his knowledge towards being pure and simple is the basic make-up of man as a spirit, we have made the first statement of a metaphysical anthropology aiming at a philosophy of religion that may establish the possibility of a verbal revelation.

The knowledge of this transcendence, a knowledge that does not affirm this transcendence as if it were one property of man among many others, but as the condition of the possibility of his thought and action within the world, is the first chapter of an ontology of the obediential potency for a possible revelation. It is also the essential part of a Christian philosophy of religion. Being is luminous, it is *Logos*; it may be revealed in the word. Man, on the other hand, is a spirit and this fact permeates his whole humanity. Hence he has an open ear for every word that may proceed from the mouth of the eternal. This is the statement which understands man's nature in its very origin and whose meaning and truth we have tried to understand in the present chapter.

At this stage it is already clear that every philosophy of religion is basically wrong which declares that the object of religion corresponds to any finite aspect of man. No objectivated projection of racial peculiarities, of blood or nation, of world or of anything else, not even the absolute idea of man, can possibly be considered as the divine. As a spirit man has always already transcended all these finite realities towards something that differs from all this not only in degree, but basically and in kind. Man is spirit and, as such, he always already stands before the infinite God, who, as infinite, is always more than only the ideal unity of the essentially finite powers of human existence and of the world. He does not only acknowledge God in fact, but in the daily drift of his existence he is man, self-subsistent, capable of judgment and of free activity, only because he continually reaches out into a domain that only the fullness of God's absolute being can fill.

II

The Hiddenness of Being

If the human knower must be aware of God's Infinite Reality, at least implicitly, what place is there for an historical revelation which would communicate to man further knowledge of God, knowledge which, in principle, lies beyond the limits of man's natural powers? In other words, if every man already knows God implicitly, how can man be called in any meaningful sense an obediential potency *for a supernatural revelation?*

Man discovers that he is an obediential potency for a further word of historical revelation when he examines the deeper implications of his own self-awareness. For the very act through which man affirms his own existence has as its a priori condition of possibility the existence of a free personal God who can speak a word of historical revelation. The human knower must affirm his own existence. In doing so, he must also affirm that he exists as a contingent being in an intelligible world whose ground is the Infinite Intelligibility of Being. As a contingent being man has proceeded causally from the world's Luminously Self-Present Ground. God's luminous self-presence excludes the possibility that man has proceeded from him either through chance or through unintelligible necessity. Man's ineluctable contingence excludes the possibility that he has proceeded from God through the intelligible necessity of impersonal Idealist thought. Man therefore has proceeded from God through an act of creative freedom. For freedom is the only ontological ground whose defining characteristic is intelligible contingency. *Thus when man affirms his own contingency he implicitly affirms that his ontological ground is a person whose creative relation to the world has its source in an act of freedom. Since God is the infinite free creator of a contingent world, He is capable of disclosing the hidden riches of his personal depths in a further historical revealing word.*

Being therefore is not only luminous self-possession, in its highest expression it is also freedom. As St. Thomas clearly saw, a human spirit whose goal is Infinite Being is capable of free choice. Thus the human

*knower, the goal of whose spiritual dynamism is Infinite Freedom, is also
a free knower. God and the human knower therefore are linked in an
ontological relation which is fundamentally interpersonal.*

*Yet, if the ground of man's existence, as indeed of any finite existence,
lies in an act of freedom, how can that ground become intelligible to
man? Granted that a free act is intelligible to the agent who elicits it,
since it is a modification of his own spiritual reality, how can it become
intelligible to another agent who is a distinct spiritual subject? As Scheler
has shown, it can become known by empathy. Empathy, whose condition
of possibility is a fundamental attitude of loving self-surrender, enables
the lover to penetrate the spiritual reality of his beloved. Because of their
personal interpenetration through the empathetic identity made possible
by self-surrender, the lover can acquire an interior knowledge and understanding of his beloved's free act of love toward him. An act of interpersonal knowledge therefore is, by identity, an act of love. Consequently
the human subject can acquire a true knowledge of his Infinite Ground
only by eliciting, at least implicitly, an act of free loving surrender to
God. Love is the lamp of knowledge. Authentic knowledge of God and
the world will be reached only through the dynamism of a fundamental
act of human freedom by which man determines his basic attitude toward
the world and its Infinite Horizon.*

1. The Problem and How to Solve It*

Our purpose is to explain the nature of the philosophy of religion by
outlining it on the basis of Thomistic metaphysics in such a way that it
may be seen as an ontology of man as the being who, in his history, listens
for an eventual revelation. From the first aspect of our general question
about being, as it inquired about *all* being as such and in general, derived
two basic statements. On the one hand, our first statement of a general
ontology: the nature of being is to know and to be known in an original
unity. We have called this the self-presence or the luminosity of being. On
the other hand, the first statement of a metaphysical anthropology: to
man's fundamental make-up belongs the a priori absolute transcendence
towards being pure and simple. That is why man is called a spirit. From
the first statement followed the insight into the basic possibility of a bar-
ing of all being in the word. From the second statement the insight that,
a priori at least, man is open for every kind of knowledge and does not
restrict the scope of a possible revelation.

*From *Hearers of the Word,* chapter 6.

The previous considerations may have provided us with a first insight into the possibility of a revelation. But they also bring up a difficulty which seems to militate against such a possibility. We have seen that man is the infinity of absolute spiritual openness for being. He has to be this since he is spirit only on account of this transcendence towards being as such. Thus man does not a priori put any limits to the possibilities and extent of a revelation through the narrowness of his receptivity, and revelation is not from the start excluded because there is no room within which it may unfold. Now precisely this first statement of our philosophy of religion and of our anthropology seems once more to show that revelation is impossible because of man's basic spiritual make-up. Man is the infinity of the absolute spiritual openness for being. In scholastic terminology he is, through the formal object of his spirit, "as it were everything." Does it not look then as if the whole of intelligible being falls within the reach of his transcendental openness, in such a way that the opening up of a divine domain, to which he has no access by his own power, is from the start excluded? Moreover, "theology" speaks of a *new subjective* "openness," through the *inner* light of grace and of faith. This too seems to have become impossible on account of the absolute range of man's natural transcendence.

Since every possible datum lies a priori within the reach of man's transcendence, the revelation of some data might at the most mean an actual and merely provisional help. In scholastic terminology, revelation would be possible only with God's help, but this help would be due to man's nature, that is, to man's essential make-up, as he himself can know it. Revelation would come from the God of the philosophers, not from the God of Abraham, Isaac, and Jacob. And it should be possible, at least in theory, to transpose every content of revelation into some knowledge which may be deduced from the a priori structure of man or which is at least due to it. Revelation would only be a propaedeutic to philosophy. In Hegelian terms, it would be the knowledge of the absolute spirit that breaks through in man on the level of representation and that develops necessarily into absolute knowledge, in which the finite spirit becomes aware of its unity with the infinite spirit in the form of the concept.

Upon closer examination the same difficulty might have arisen earlier already, from our first statement of ontology, not just from the first statement of a metaphysical anthropology. Speaking very generally, the difficulty consists in this: what we have said hitherto might produce the impression that a revelation, in the sense of the free unveiling of something which of itself is essentially hidden, is impossible, because in principle every being is always already manifest, and does not need to be revealed. In this event revelation would be nothing else than the immanent and necessary unfolding of this openness of being which is from the start always present in the spirit as such.

We have met this difficulty first when treating of the absolute transcendence of man as a spirit. It looks as if, for man as a spirit, every knowledge of being is always and in every case but the actualization of his infinite potentiality, hence the necessary unfolding of his own infinity. The statement of metaphysical anthropology which we have established in order to make place for a possible revelation seems to imply too much. It seems to imply the basic idea of the philosophy of religion of German Idealism, which—having in mind the semirationalism of Günther, Hermes and Froschammer—the Vatican Council has formulated as follows: "man can and must by himself through constant progress reach the possession of all truth and goodness" (Dz. 1808). As mentioned above, the same difficulty seems to arise already from the first statement of our general ontology, at least when taken in connection with the first statement of our philosophical anthropology. If being by itself and necessarily means self-presence, inner lucidity, and reflection-upon-oneself; if being is luminous to the extent that it is being; if it is not being, but only non-being which is dark, then it looks as if being should already be manifest by itself, at least for that being which is endowed with an absolute openness for every self-luminous reality, that is for the spirit.

The highest being, pure being, must always already be manifest for man, at least to the extent that man is spirit and becomes ever more spirit. Thus revelation would be nothing else than man's spiritualization, as it slowly progresses according to the inner law of man himself. God himself would by himself always be the one who is manifest and revealed. Revelation could not possibly be the free activity of God, since his light always already necessarily shines and illuminates every man. "Inaccessible light" seems to be a contradiction, because of itself light necessarily radiates in all directions wherever there is room for it to shine.

This brings up a problem for a Christian anthropology and metaphysics. How can they explain the nature of man in such a way that, without giving up his transcendence towards being as such and the inner luminosity of being, man's transcendence does not anticipate the content of a free revelation? The solution of the problem will have to show how a free self-manifestation of the free personal God remains possible despite the fact that this free revelation can be addressed to a being who is capable of perceiving it. We shall find the elements of such a solution when we treat of the second and the third aspects of our initial question.

Since this difficulty derives already from the first statement of our general ontology about the luminosity of being, it is our first duty to look for its solution within this ontology. We must inquire why, despite and in its luminosity, pure being is that which is utterly concealed, why being, to the extent that it is being, is not only present-to-itself, but also hidden, present-only-to-itself. We must once more go through the transcendental deduction of the luminosity of being in such a way that it may turn into the transcendental deduction of the presence-only-to-itself, of the inaccessibility which belongs properly to the eternal light. We shall further have to take up the same problem in its connection with the first statement of our anthropology.

Our remaining task will materially coincide with the analysis of the second aspect of our initial metaphysical question. This second aspect emphasizes the fact that, in the problem of being, we do really *ask a question*. Not only *can* we inquire about being (first aspect), we *must* inquire about it (second aspect). This is the problem which we must briefly consider now.

At first sight it might seem as if the infinity of God's being, as co-affirmed in the *Vorgriff*, suffices to explain why God is essentially the Unknown One for the finite spirit. And since the finiteness of the human spirit became evident, as shown above, by the fact that he had to inquire about being, the analysis of the second aspect would be over. It would be enough to say that, even as a spirit, man is finite. The fact that man must inquire about being, that he feels this need of asking questions, is sufficient proof of the finiteness of the questioner as such. The absolute transcendence of man as a spirit would reveal the infinite. But this infinity of being stands revealed only in the illimited range of *Vorgriff*. Now this *Vorgriff* does not represent the infinite in himself, it only co-affirms him as the ultimate whereunto of the illimited dynamism of the spirit that we call *Vorgriff*. On the other hand the *Vorgriff* occurs and we know about it only as the condition of the possibility of conceptual knowledge of finite objects. It seems to follow that we know of God's infinity only in connection with *finite* beings.

Thus this infinity would in itself remain unknown to man, since it is grasped explicitly as such only when man denies and rejects the finite, the knowledge of which makes the *excessus* (a Thomistic term for the *Vorgriff*) emerge in consciousness. If then man knows the infinity of God only when, through negation, he moves beyond the finite, this infinity seems to be sufficiently unknown, to stand sufficiently unrevealed and shrouded in mystery, so that a new self-manifestation of the infinite remains meaningful and has still something that may be revealed. The fact that we must inquire about being seems not only to exclude any kind of absolute idealism, insofar as it manifests the analogy of being and the finiteness of the human spirit (as explained above), it seems also to manifest sufficiently the essential hiddenness of all positive aspects of the infinite being. This follows from the fact that the reason why we know the infinite, pure spirit, namely, the absolute range of the *Vorgriff*, hence also the infinity of being itself, becomes explicitly conscious only when we negate the finite being whose knowledge is made possible by the *Vorgriff*.

All this is true, it may serve as a first provisional answer to our difficulty. Let us once more go over this first stage of our answer. From the fact that we must inquire about being as such it follows that we know about being as such and about its infinite ground only because we deal with single, finite beings. Hence we may explicitly know the infinite being (about which we always already know on account of the absolute range of the *Vorgriff*) only by turning towards this finite object and by making explicit the negation which is necessarily implied in the fact that our intellect always moves beyond it by negating the finiteness of the finite object. This, however, does not provide us with a positive knowledge of that which is beyond this finiteness. The positive aspect of this infinity, which only the concept, not the *Vorgriff* alone, might make known, remains hidden, despite the basic openness of this domain of infinity, which results from the spirit's transcendence. Once more: this first provisional answer is correct. And it is also the only answer which is given to this problem by the textbooks of fundamental theology.

Yet it does not seem to be sufficient for the following reasons. What we have said hitherto shows us only that, in the present state of his knowledge, man cannot reach by himself a positive knowledge of that which is "beyond" the domain of the finite world, although the anticipation of this beyond is the condition of his knowledge of things in the world. But this seems to establish only a de facto hiddenness of the infinite being. For we have not yet excluded two possibilities.

The first one is this: man might (or even may) by himself reach a stage at which he would, as it were, to stay within our present terminology, become aware of the absolute range of his *Vorgriff* without requiring a finite object as the "matter" in which alone the *Vorgriff* comes to be known as its "informing light." Let us suppose, moreover, that this is the only and highest way in which a finite spirit may get to know the absolute as such immediately, that God can only be grasped in the *excessus* of the finite spirit (without the intermediary of a finite object, of a finite "image" which represents the object to the spirit). Nevertheless, in such a hypothesis a positive revelation would no longer be possible. Man might, by his own powers, be able to reach the highest knowledge of the Absolute. On the one hand, this knowledge would not be merely the usual "negative" theology of rational metaphysics because the absence of the finite image of a finite object which must be transcended and denied would, from the start, radically do away with the negative aspect of such a theology. On the other hand, it would not be a "beatific vision" in the sense of Christian theology, because this way of knowing God's infinity would occur only in the immediate grasping of the transcendence of the spirit without the intermediary of any object. If this were the highest knowledge of the Absolute of which man were capable, and capable by his own forces, a revelation of God by God in the word would no longer be required.

This is not a purely arbitrary hypothesis, an intellectual exercise by which we think of things which are not absolutely impossible. We believe that this represents essentially, as stated in our own terminology, the basic conception of every non-Christian mysticism, expressed metaphysically in the Plotinian mysticism, as it continues to exert an undeniable influence upon the Christian mysticism say of Gregory of Nyssa or of the Pseudo-Areopagite. The philosophical interpretation of the mysticism of the "dark night" of John of the Cross, as worked out by Baruzi, moves in the same direction.

As a rule, wherever one opposes or seems to oppose "mystical piety" to the "prophetic piety" of a revealed religion, our hypothesis is at work: a mystical experience (usually involving "night" and "ecstasy") in which man reaches out beyond his finiteness and experiences the infinite, is considered as one which surpasses and supersedes a revelation through the word. To him who has ecstatically experienced God's infinity, a human word, the kind in which God's revelation must speak to us, can no longer convey anything. If our thesis of the absolute transcendence of the finite spirit should end up in a natural mysticism, a revelation through the free word of God would from the start be superseded by a more profound knowledge which man can acquire by himself. Absolute transcendence might not lead to the absolute philosophy of German Idealism (which is to some extent the sober daylight-mysticism of reason), but it would lead to a philosophical mysticism of a "night ecstasy." Both would have the same destructive consequences for the possibility of a free revelation of God. Mystical piety, even in its simple form of an obscure experience of God in the illimited infinity of the spirit itself, would have rendered superfluous the prophetic piety of the revealed word with its historical restrictions.

We must further mention a second hypothesis which, if we admit our statement of the absolute transcendence of the spirit, would make a revelation impossible. What we said above about God, that he remains hidden even to man's transcendence, would not quite take care of such a hypothesis. Somebody might reason as follows: the absolute openness of man's spirit, its dynamism which strives towards the infinite being, demands the possibility of an immediate intuition of God as the only definitive fulfillment of the absolute range of the spirit. Such an intuition might suppose some divine initiative, but this initiative would simply consist in making possible man's natural fulfillment. The natural end of man as a spirit would be the beatific vision. The summit of his spiritual life in its immanent natural development would not merely be a "nightlike" ecstatic experience of God's infinity contained, as was the case in our first hypothesis, in the experience of the soaring, absolutely transcendent infinity of one's own spirit. It would rather be the immediate intuition of the essence of God's infinite being itself, as given to man in itself. This would lead us very near the heretical position of the mysticism of the

Begards: "that every intellectual nature is naturally blessed in itself, and that the soul does not need the light of glory to raise it to the vision and the happy fruition of God" (Dz. 475).

We cannot reply to this hypothesis that the question of whether or not the beatific vision is due to man or only bestowed upon him as a grace has nothing to do with the question of the possibility of a revelation, since these two questions treat of quite different things. This is precisely not the case. If man's natural end is the beatific vision, which unveils God's essence more than can be done by any possible revelation in mere words and in finite signs, we can no longer conceive of a revelation as a supremely free act of a God who manifests himself freely and gratuitously. At most it might still be conceivable as a verbal anticipating disclosure of a God who is, at least in principle, always already the final term of man's knowledge.

To this objection we may give the following answer, which is undoubtedly important and fundamental: we have admitted the absolute range and illimitation of the human spirit's transcendence as a condition of the possibility of an objective knowledge of finite beings and of the self-subsistence of man. The purpose of this transcendence is to make possible the peculiar mode of being which turns a finite being into a spiritual being. This purpose has been reached even when the capacity of this transcendence is never immediately filled by the manifestation of the infinite being itself. We have posited and we were able to establish this transcendence *only* as the condition of *this* possibility. We have not presented it as a function which had its own *telos* (end) for itself alone. Hence we have no right to demand that this transcendence should, in itself, independently of the make-up of man's spirit, receive a fulfilment other than the one on account of which we affirmed its existence.

In a philosophical anthropology we know only of a human knowledge which demands, as a condition of its possibility, besides the dynamism towards being as such, also the representation of a finite object, to render the dynamism conscious. It follows that philosophically we cannot say whether the spirit's transcendental capacity may ever be filled without the help of a finite sense object. We cannot say whether the beatific vision is intrinsically possible, much less whether it is due to man.

Once more: all this is true and must be taken into consideration. But our conclusion that the beatific vision cannot clearly be assigned as man's natural end does not yet prove that it is essentially supernatural and utterly undue to man; it does not prove that, despite man's absolute transcendence, God continues to stand before him as the one who is still Unknown, and that in this way there remains an object for an eventual revelation. And we might even wonder whether man as such, that is "naturally," has received his finality towards the infinite for no other purpose (even if this is the only purpose for which we can show that it has been given to him) than to roam forever, a perpetual wanderer, through the domain of the finite, in order to greet the Infinite always only from afar, without every discovering the direct road that would lead him before the face of God.

St. Thomas himself speaks of a natural desire for the immediate intuition of God. It is not quite certain what Thomas meant exactly by this expression. Every theologian who has written about it seems to have his own interpretation. At any rate, it shows that Thomas admitted between man's spiritual nature with its immanent dynamism (its *desiderium*) and the beatific vision relations that do not merely derive from the fact that man has been called by grace to the immediate intuition of God, but that are previous to this invitation and rooted in man's "nature."

What we have just said about the difficulty deriving from the natural possibility of a beatific vision applies also, *mutatis mutandis,* to the difficulty arising from the hypothesis of natural mysticism. It is not possible to demonstrate positively the possibility of such a mysticism, as interpreted above, at least not in a deductive metaphysical anthropology, whose only starting point is the nature and the function of transcendence. Such a transcendence has a purpose and a meaning even if such a mysticism does not or cannot exist. On the other hand, what we have said hitherto does not allow us positively to exclude such a hypothesis.

Thus we have not yet discovered a final answer to our question: why does the absolute transcendence of the spirit as the a priori opening up of a room for revelation, combined with the pure luminosity of pure being, not render superfluous from the start any possible revelation?

We have merely reached the following conclusion: man stands before God as before one who is, at least for a time, unknown. For he is the Infinite, whom man can know in his infinity only by denying the finite and referring to that which lies beyond any finiteness. This referring is the condition of the objective knowledge of finite realities.

If God is known in this way, he remains hidden in the positive content of his infinity. But is it not possible that God remains hidden simply because man does not yet know him, because man, as a finite spirit, has not yet reached the end of his spiritual dynamism? This has not yet become clear. Hitherto we have explained the fact that God remains hidden only by studying man, more specifically the merely factual structure of his spiritual being. Thus we have explained it more through man's blindness than through God's inaccessibility in himself. We shall understand the possibility of a divine revelation as a free act of God only if we can establish that God remains hidden in himself before every finite spirit as such, and not only before man in the actual structure of his knowledge. It is not enough for us to know that God is more that what we have hitherto grasped of him in our human knowledge, as we get to know it in anthropology. We must also know that he may speak and that he may refrain from speaking. Only then can a real speaking of God, if it really happens, be understood for what it is: the unpredictable act of his personal love, before which man falls upon his knees in worship.

2. *God Free and Unknown**

How can we then explain more precisely the necessity of affirming the luminosity of being as such? We cannot see it in the absolute Being. Neither can we, by simply examining the content of both concepts (being, intelligibility) discover that they are essentially connected when applied to being itself. In fact, when we deduced the first statement of our general ontology, we have already mentioned the reason of this necessity.

That we know enough about being to inquire about it, must be explicitly affirmed, since we affirm it implicitly in the question about being, as it arises unavoidably in human existence. Should anybody be able to abstain from inquiring about being, he would not have to affirm the statement that being is intelligible in itself. But in every judgment and activity of man there is some knowledge about being as such. Thus the question is always implicitly raised: what is being which man always already knows by anticipation, whenever he deals with individual beings in his thinking and activity?

Thus the evidence of metaphysics is based upon the necessity revealed in human existence. The last metaphysical evidence available to man is not a material, but a formal evidence. It is not the material evidence of an insight into being as such, which would be an insight into absolute being. It is the formal evidence rooted in the necessity for man of being what he is: one who inquires about being in his every thought and action, one who, while he inquires about being, and despite its basic hiddenness, has always already affirmed that he knows it enough to inquire about it, that it is luminosity. He can affirm this only insofar as he affirms his existence and because he has to affirm it with its own human characteristics. Being as such essentially opens up for man when, as it cannot refrain from doing, human existence takes possession of itself.

The existence of man, which permeates in this way the insight into an ultimate necessity, is a purely factual existence. It is contingence, "thrownness," to use Heidegger's term. To deny this fact would be a denial of man's finiteness. It would amount to an endeavor to put man in the very midst of being, as it extends into infinity before human transcendence. It would do away with man's need of inquiring about being. Thus

*From *Hearers of the Word,* chapter 7.

man must assume his existence in its mere thrownness, if he is to be human existence, i.e., if he is to stand before being's luminosity which he necessarily affirms. Hence the first metaphysical affirmation of an absolute necessity is at the same time the affirmation of human contingency and thrownness. Only the man who resolutely assumes his own finiteness and thrownness finds access to being's true infinity.

What follows from this? We have discovered the starting point for a new basic insight in our general ontology (which always includes also a statement about God) as well as for our metaphysical anthropology. Our next task is to develop this new insight as regards general ontology.

Once more we start from the peculiar structure of human existence as we have come to know it from all our previous considerations. In his self-subsistence and in the objective nature of his thought and activity man develops necessarily an attitude towards himself. He must necessarily be present to himself, affirm himself, posit himself absolutely. On account of this necessity he inquires about being as such, and insofar as he inquires within this necessary acceptance of his being, he knows about being as such. He affirms the luminosity of being and his own transcendence towards being as such and in this way he stands before God.

Insofar as he must *inquire*, he affirms his own finite thrownness; insofar as he *must* inquire, he affirms it necessarily. And as he affirms it necessarily, he affirms his existence, in and despite its thrownness, as unconditioned, as absolute. In other words: because the affirmation of the *contingent* fact is unavoidably *necessary*, the contingence itself reveals something absolute: the unavoidable way in which the contingent fact demands to be affirmed. Despite its contingency it excludes the possibility of being denied. This implies that man necessarily assumes a relation of absolute affirmation with regard to his finite and contingent existence. It is only in this necessity of a conscious relation to the non-necessary that man is the transcendence towards being that is luminous and affirmed as such.

Now to posit something contingent absolutely is to will. Such a positing must intrinsically be more than a mere static insight, it must be volition. Mere understanding as such can derive the reason of its affirmation only from the object itself. Now something contingent as such does not have in its *quidditative* essence any ground to be absolutely affirmed. If its present existence itself is considered as the reason for affirming it, for positing its quiddity absolutely, this existence would be posited as necessary, since only such an existence can be the ground of an absolute affirmation. Hence this existence would be the necessary existence of something contingent, which would be a contradiction.

Hence the affirmation of the contingent does not simply find its ground in the object as such. The ground is thus first the ground of the act of affirmation, and only afterwards the ground of the object as affirmed. But such a ground is called will. Therefore in the ground of human existence we discover within the primordial transcendence towards being the (necessary) act of the will. The fact that being opens up for human existence is brought about by the will as an inner moment of knowledge itself. We must now first examine this knowledge in the direction in which it includes a statement about being itself, hence in the direction of general ontology. The next chapter will consider what it can tell us for metaphysical anthropology.

We have seen how the fact that man wills himself is a condition of the possibility and of the necessity of the question about being and so a condition of our knowledge of being as such. What follows thence for the nature of being, especially of pure being, and for its relation to finite beings, especially to finite human existence? At the basis of human existence we always discover a necessary and absolute affirmation of the contingent reality that man himself is, that is, we discover the will. It goes always together with an affirmation of the luminosity of being as such. It follows that the necessary volitional affirmation can only be conceived as the *Nachvollzug* (the ratification) of a free absolute positing of something which is not necessary. For should this absolute positing of contingent human existence not originate from a free will, the basic luminosity of being as such would be eliminated. In that case, the necessary positing of something contingent, which is known to be contingent, hence not to be posited absolutely, can only derive from a ground which is dark, not luminous for itself, not aware of itself. For let us suppose that man, the contingent reality which is being posited, should derive from a ground which cannot not posit him. Then we have the choice between these two hypotheses: man, the reality which is posited, is as necessary as the act by which he is posited. Or the positing cause is of such a nature that any attempt to clarify it, by means of a "logical" connection between it, the act of positing, and that which is posited, would be frustrated by the peculiar nature of the cause. But both hypotheses are unacceptable. The former, because that which is posited is contingent. The latter, because being, the positing cause, must in final analysis be luminous and because the connection between a necessary act of positing and a contingent, not necessary, object of this act can never be made luminous.

It follows that the volitional necessary positing of something contingent, as it occurs in man's affirmation of his own existence, can only be understood if we affirm it as posited by a *free* voluntary act. Man is necessarily posited because he is posited by a free will. We necessarily posit a contingent reality absolutely while in the same breath affirming the luminosity of being. This makes sense only if, by doing so, we ratify and endorse the act by which this contingent being has been freely and voluntarily posited as absolute. This free, voluntary, original positing of the being that man is (for we are thinking of him in all our considerations) can only be the work of the absolute being of God. We have already mentioned above that God must be affirmed as the universal ground of all that which is. Here our purpose was only to show that this positing of the finite being by God must be an act of the will.

This implies that in his necessary and absolute relation to his thrownness as it affirms the luminosity of being, man affirms himself as a freely willed effect of God. He knows that his being is carried by the free power of pure Being. It follows that he does not stand before pure Being, the final horizon of his *Vorgriff*, as if it were a lifeless ideal which, always at rest, must always be available to his grasp; he stands before it as before a being who freely disposes of himself. God is the whereunto of the *Vorgriff* of the human spirit, but he is such because he looms before the finite as free power. Thus, when finite knowledge knows God, this knowledge is carried by God's own free positing of this finite reality, which we call creation. Thus it is always already a reply to a free word, spoken by the Absolute himself, which is implicitly affirmed as such a free action when, on account of his transcendence, the finite spirit perceives the distant radiance of the infinite light.

Central in this whole discussion are the following points: man as a spirit who knows the absolute Being stands before the latter as before a person who freely disposes of himself. When God thus looks like a person, it is not because, having discovered him, we have afterwards provided him with human features. Rather God appears as a person when absolute being becomes manifest for human transcendence, because this being assumes the form of the totality of being about which man not only can but must inquire.

When the object of our knowledge is a free, autonomous person, our knowledge turns into lack of knowledge. Because of his freedom a person manifests of himself only that which he wishes to manifest. In the case of the free positing of something which is not necessary, there is no previous a priori whence it might be known. We may receive this knowledge only from itself. Insofar as the free positing of God makes him look to us as a person, the knowledge of this personal God depends always on his own free decision.

Thus man always stands already before a God of revelation, before a God who operates in history. For if, from the start, God appears to man's transcendence as the free power, it takes only two more conditions to make him known as the God of a possible revelation: (1) the possibility for his freedom to bring something about must not be exhausted by the creation of a finite being who is capable of knowing him. In other words, his creative possibilities must not have come to an end when he created man. God must still have further possibilities of free activity with regard to this creature of his. (2) That which has been created must still have a capacity for the knowledge of such an additional free operation of God with regard to itself. In one word, there must still be room for the object of a further free activity to be known by a knowledge that has not yet reached its limit.

Now both these conditions are fulfilled. The free creation of the finite and the contingent by God implies already as such that God's further activity with regard to his creature cannot be simply and altogether the logical consequence of his first creative action. The contingency of this finite creature implies as such that it is changeable, hence that by itself it may be the object of further possible free interventions of the Absolute. Since the creature depends wholly on God's free will, it cannot unfailingly tell us about the direction of God's free activity. The second condition too is fulfilled. The horizon of possible beings opened in the spirit's transcendence extends in principle beyond everything which is not the immediate vision of God's Absolute Being. We have already said that this vision cannot be shown to be the connatural end of the spirit's absolute transcendence. Hence as long as this vision is not granted to man there remains room for accepting further communications of God which he may in his freedom deem fit to bestow.

Therefore insofar as, in his absolute and not wholly fulfilled transcendence, man stands before the free God, his first question about being (a question which characterizes him as man) puts him before the possibility of a free activity of God with regard to him; hence it puts him before the God of a possible revelation. Now a free activity is always unpredictable, hence final and unique. Therefore such a revelation is not simply the continuation of the manifestation of being which would already, although only inchoatively, have started for man in its definitive and final direction with his natural knowledge of God.

In order correctly to evaluate the scope of these considerations we must keep in mind what follows. They do *not* intend to demonstrate that there exist in the depths of God mysteries that belong to God's necessary essence (for instance, the Trinity) and are, nonetheless, essentially mysteries, that is, accessible to man only if God in his grace freely reveals them to him. They intend to show only that, through transcendence, as it occurs in him in its human form, man does not merely stand before the Absolute Being as *semper quiescens* (always at rest), but before the God for whose free activity with regard to man there still remains actual possibilities and in man the power of knowing them. Will this God enter in contact with man and how will he do it? Can he thus make known mysteries of his own necessary essence, mysteries in the strictest theological sense? We shall not try to answer these questions but leave this task to the a posteriori knowledge which derives from the actual revelation of this God.

3. The Free Listener*

We must now answer a further question: what does the analysis of our general question about being under its second aspect tell us about the nature of *man*? It is quite natural to expect that the problem of general ontology discussed in the preceding chapter has something to tell us about this nature.

Man is that being which, as a finite spirit who inquires and must inquire about being, stands before the free God, affirms his freedom in the way he raises the question of being, and must therefore take this divine freedom into account. Because of this freedom God can manifest his personal countenance and reveal his nature in a way which we cannot discover a priori in some other manner. These findings of the last chapter gave us several data for an analysis of human nature.

In connection with them we have also discovered that there occurs, at the core of our finite knowledge of being, especially of the absolute Being, a necessary volitional affirmation of our own contingent existence. Being opens up for the human spirit through and in a voluntary attitude towards itself. Not in the sense that our knowledge of being should be preceded by a blind impulse and volition, resulting in a dull unintelligibility and only afterwards giving rise to some knowledge or to a "spirit" that would remain imprisoned in its dull origin without ever being able to make it translucid. This would be a shallow and wholly false interpretation of the important insight which has been brought up as a presupposition of our former findings.

This insight has nothing to do with a metaphysical irrationalism, except for the kernel of truth that is necessarily contained in such a false conception. When we established that, in knowledge itself, there is an element of volition, we have only said what is evident for a Thomistic ontology: that being is always spirit and will, true and good, that knowledge is being and that it is knowledge only as being, so that it cannot be adequately grasped in its own essence, unless it be also grasped as will. It follows that willing is not merely an inner aspect of knowledge, it is also at the same time a transcendental determination of being, that proceeds in a certain sense *beyond* knowledge. But this is another problem, which we shall not examine here, although this idea was already germinally present in the last chapter.

This insight in the volitional moment of knowledge as such is the starting point for our further investigations. For this and for other reasons it is important to see this point clearly. Therefore we shall once more come back to it.

*From *Hearers of the Word*, chapter 8.

Our considerations ran as follows: man necessarily affirms the luminosity of being because he necessarily assumes an affirmative stance towards himself, as he necessarily is present to himself in objective knowledge and' in action. Man necessarily assumes an affirmative stance towards himself, because, even when in thought or in action he says No to himself, he still affirms himself as being, because in the very act of such a denial he still presupposes himself as the possible object of such an act, hence as being. But in such a necessary attitude towards himself man affirms himself as finite, as contingent, as fortuitous. Insofar as he affirms himself necessarily, his existence is for man, despite and in its contingency, something unavoidable, which he has to take up, in that sense something absolute. Despite its contingency it is not submitted to the decision of the finite being, to his choice between Yes and No; it raises an absolute claim to acceptance, it demands to be accepted and despite its contingency it has always already imposed this acceptance.

In this irresistible acceptance of something contingent, of a double possibility which has already been decided in favor of one side, which presents man with a free choice, and thus does not justify or "make luminous" the choice as it favors one side, man affirms in the transcendence at work in this choice the luminosity of being as such. How is this possible? Something is luminous when it is intelligible. But the contingent seems to be basically unintelligible. We say that something is intelligible only when it is grasped in connection with its ground, when it is, as it were, replaced into its ground and viewed as emerging from it as its necessary consequence. Our statement about the intelligibility of being in itself derived from the fact that, always and also in the first question about being, every possible object of knowledge is already viewed by anticipation under the general aspect of being as such. Hence there can be no being which does not, by itself, positively range itself in the context of being as such.

This is precisely the reason why it is intelligible. Something contingent that would, in its mere contingency, stand loose and unconnected, in absolute isolation, would not possibly, on account of its being, range itself within being's totality. And it is precisely this connection with being's totality that makes the particular beings intelligible. Therefore such an entity would be basically unintelligible. But this contradicts the first general statement of our ontology. Hence the term intelligible must be reserved for either absolute being itself, because, as the whereunto of human dynamism, it causes the spirit's openness for the totality of its possible objects, or for the single finite being that is object of knowledge when and insofar as it is grasped as grounded in this pure absolute being. Otherwise this single being would have no ground of its intelligibility, since the latter means that something stands within the absolute horizon of the possible objects of knowledge. This is the case only if either this being itself constitutes the absolute horizon of knowledge (as a finite being it is unable to do this, it does not fill this horizon) or it must be grasped as connected with the objective horizon of knowledge. It must have its ground (the ground of its being, of its intelligibility, of its being ranged within the horizon of being as such) in the absolute being. We have made clear enough in the last chapter that this standing of the finite reality, its being grounded in absolute being, must be conceived as voluntary and free.

We must now take up again more thoroughly our previous considerations. Is it possible, after that which we have said above, to reconcile the contingency of human existence, which man must necessarily affirm, with the luminosity of being as such? At first it looks very much as if the unintelligibility, i.e., the fact that the single contingent being could not be ranged in the context of being as the totality of the possible objects of knowledge, had simply been displaced from the contingency of that being itself to the contingency of the act which posited it, from contingency to the contingent fact of God's freedom.

First we must admit that, even when we are given such a ground of its being posited and of its intelligibility, the posited reality remains unintelligible for us in its contingency. For we see the act of creation only in that which has been created. Hence for us, who do not see directly the free act of creating, this act remains as dark as that which has been created. However, we are not trying to reconcile the contingency of the finite being with *our* finite knowledge of being, but with its luminosity, which belongs to it in itself.

The question is now whether, in its free creation by God, the contingent itself is luminous? Is the free act of creation itself (as distinct from that which is created) not once more something unintelligible, since a free act as such has no reasons which determine it and thus explain it and make it luminous? In other words, does the free God himself understand his free action? Or does it, in its "contingency" and its "groundlessness," stand before him as something unintelligible?

It is clear at once that this question cannot and must not be answered in such a way that the expected luminosity of the free act would jibe with a concept of intelligibility that would arbitrarily have been set up before our question had been answered.

Since we are still busy with our first explanation of the general question of being, we are still trying to find first of all the right concept of the luminosity of being which is supposed to be that essence of being into which we are inquiring. We must try to reach this right concept of being's luminosity by starting also from the freedom of the act. Thus we are entitled to reverse the question and to inquire: how should the luminosity of being be understood so that God's free activity may be understood as luminous in itself?

Basically knowledge is self-presence of a being in its act of being. Hence where the self-presence is complete, knowledge too is complete. When a being has totally taken possession of itself, knowledge too has reached its fullness. Now, a free act is originally not so much the positing of something else, of something external, of some effect which is distinct from and opposed to the free act itself. It is rather the fulfilment of one's own nature, a taking possession of oneself, of the reality of one's own creative power over oneself. Thus it is a coming to oneself, a self-presence in oneself.

The action is free and cannot be deduced, but it is not something which faces the one who knows it *in the very act of performing it* as something other in its contingency. It is, at bottom, the agent himself. That is why it is luminous for *himself*, even though it may be dark for *another* who is present only to that which is performed and not to the performing itself. The fact that the free act belongs to the innermost meaning of self-subsisting being shows at the same time that it is most intimately luminous for the free self and dark for all others.

It is most perfectly self-present, hence it is something which is most luminous in and for itself, something also which is least accessible to others: light for itself and darkness for another. It can become luminous and understandable for another only when he co-posits *(mitvollzieht)* it himself as free act, when he himself loves it.

Hence the free action is luminous in itself. And if it seems to be dark and unintelligible, it is so only for a knowledge which tries to understand it while standing outside of it. But this does not detract from its intelligibility. It is only an invitation extended to knowledge to work itself, as it were, into the free activity in order to understand it and its effects. This happens when one tries to understand the free action of the other not after it has already been carried out, but when one takes part in the performing itself, or by ratifying it *(Nachvollzug)* lets it, as it were, emerge also from oneself. In this emerging itself the free activity may be present to itself, i.e., it may be understood.

We may note in passing that the concept of luminosity (which we have already mentioned before this last chapter, where we explained it in function of freedom) shows that freedom and intelligibility may be reconciled. Above we explained intelligibility as the possibility of ranging a reality within the totality of possible objects, either because it is pure being itself, the last whereunto of all efforts at understanding, or because it is ontically connected with this pure Being. This way of explaining what is intelligible shows that a free act of pure being itself is at once intelligible in itself. We have, however, avoided this shorter road in behalf of the opposite procedure, from freedom to luminosity, because it provides us with new insights that are important for us.

To start again where we left off, the finite has its ground in the free, luminous act of God. Now, a free self-present act is love. For love is the luminous will aiming at the person in its irreducible unicity. It is precisely such a will that God sets in action when he creates a finite being. It is his way of loving himself in his free creative power. Thus the contingent is understood in God's love and only in it. The finite contingent being becomes luminous in God's free love to himself and to what he freely creates. Thus love is seen to be the light of knowledge. A knowledge of the finite that is not willing to understand itself in its ultimate essence as reaching its own fulfilment only in love turns into darkness. It must erroneously consider the contingent as necessary, or leave it in its absolute unintelligibility (an unintelligibility which does not exist and which knowledge steadily denies), or it must explain being as a dark urge, in whose depths there shines no light. For the finite may be grasped only when it is understood as produced by the divine freedom. Now this free action of God is luminous for us only when we do not merely take it as a fact. We must also ratify it in our love for it, thus re-experiencing it, as it were, in its origin and its production. Thus love is the light of the knowledge of the finite, and, since we know the infinite only through the finite, it is also the light of the whole of our knowledge. In final analysis, knowledge is but the luminous radiance of love.

Hence insofar as God, in his love of himself, freely loves as the creator of the finite, he understands the finite itself in this love. In this light the contingent too is raised to the light of being. Because and insofar as God loves the finite, it shares in the luminosity of pure being. There is for it no other way of sharing this light. Only in the logic of love does logic reach the understanding of free being.

However, our purpose was not simply to shed light upon some obscure points of our previous considerations. We wished to inquire into the being of man, as it looks to us from the second aspect of our question about being. We are making progress in this direction.

We have already said that the necessary welcoming of our own existence could, on account of its contingency, be understood only as the continuation and the ratification of its original free production by the absolute being. It has thus become clearer why, in this transformation of pure knowledge into knowing love, the absolute affirmation of the contingent becomes so luminous that the affirmation of something contingent in God's knowing love does in no way contradict the luminosity of being. This provides us also with some insight into the ratification of this affirmation by man. It is a ratification of the self-luminous power of God's supremely free love, which is basically his love for himself.

This means that at the heart of the finite spirit's transcendence there lives a love for God. Man's openness towards absolute being is carried by his affirmation of his own existence. This affirmation is a voluntary attitude of man with regard to himself and, in final analysis, a reaching out of finite love for God, because, as love of the spirit, it can affirm the finite only as carried by God's affirmation of his own being. This implies that man's standing before God through knowledge (which constitutes man's nature as a spirit) possesses as an inner moment of this knowledge a love for God in himself. Man's love for God is not something which may happen or not happen once man has come to know God. As an inner moment of knowledge it is both its condition and its ground.

In the previous chapter our analysis of the fundamental nature of man has shown that he is the being who stands before the free God of a possible revelation. He stands there through a voluntary (even a necessary) attitude towards himself. We see now that this attitude is based on an attitude to God in himself. So if we wish to think our anthropological analysis through to its end, we must inquire what follows for it from the mutual relation between willing and knowing as the two inseparable moments of the one basic structure of man, as he stands before God.

The opening up of the transcendental horizon of being as such, which makes man stand before God, takes place in a voluntary attitude of man towards himself. This is the ratification and the outcome of the free positing of this finite knower by God. In the heart of knowledge stands love from which knowledge itself lives. We do not mean that knowledge is *preceded* by a blind urge. Rather knowledge and love constitute originally the one basic stance of the one human being, so that neither can ever be understood except as turning into the other, as grasped in function of the other.

To come back very briefly to a scholastic formula, we might say that we have only developed the meaning of the scholastic axiom: "being-truth-goodness are convertible." We might, of course, also say: "being-intellect-will are convertible." This amounts ultimately to saying: even while maintaining the conceptual distinction between them, we must conceive of knowledge and of will as essentially inner moments of being and of each being insofar as it is being. Thus something is knowledge only to the extent that it is being. Being is something only to the extent that it is also understood as will, so that knowledge too may be understood in its fullness and in its origin only when it turns into will, so as to reach the fulfilment of its own nature in the total makeup of a being (that is also will). Will and knowledge can only be understood in a *reciprocal* priority with regard to each other; their relation is not a one way affair.

We have hitherto always spoken of this voluntary attitude, entailed by the spirit's openness, as being necessary. Man necessarily has an attitude towards himself. In this dynamism of self-assertion he affirms himself. We must now have a closer look at this necessity.

This voluntary self-affirmation, which occurs in the transcendence towards being as such, is necessary in this sense that it cannot be avoided. It should not be confused with a blind, dull fate or with some kind of metaphysical inertia. It is a form of understanding. Man affirms *himself as* something because his affirmation, although implicit, happens consciously. Thus this self-affirmation may be necessary in its occurrence without having to be necessary in the concrete manner of this occurrence. Because this self-understanding is a *conscious* one, its necessity is not of such a kind that its concrete manner is fixed once and for all. Man necessarily understands himself in some way. But the *way in which* he concretely assumes an attitude towards himself may nevertheless depend on his original freedom. Again this does not mean that man might understand himself in the full autonomy of his decision about himself, as if the way he understands himself were wholly left to his choice. The necessity of his self-affirmation implies already a directive which tells him how he must understand himself. All that which we have hitherto said of man was but the explanation of this directive. But even so this self-understanding is, in the manner that it happens, an act of man's freedom. We must show why this is so.

Insofar as the things which are given in human knowledge are grasped by the *Vorgriff* in the horizon of being as such, they are known as objects of a self-subsisting subject. Insofar as this transcendence contains a volitional moment, these objects are grasped as possible goals of a voluntary attitude, of an emotional decision, i.e., as values. This means that being itself is grasped as a value. Thus man is the absolute transcendence towards the absolute value which is God's pure being. At first this absolute value is not given as object, but only as the "whereunto" of the *Vorgriff* that is always also volition. To put it in Scholastic terms, we know it only as "beatitude in general," not as an object; it is given only as the condition of the possibility of our grasping finite values.

We have seen that, in the line of knowledge, the spirit, through its transcendence towards absolute being, objectivates the finite reality whose finiteness it knows and grasps itself as self-subsisting. Likewise in the awareness of values, the spirit, in its transcendence towards the absolute value, knows of the finiteness of the single values which it encounters and knows itself as actively self-subsisting with respect to such values, i.e., as endowed with freedom. In the affirmation of a value it is subject to necessity and in this sense not free only to the extent that the affirmation belongs to the conditions of the spirit's necessary openness to value as such. Only this a priori condition is necessarily affirmed, together with what is implied by it (and only insofar as it is immediately such a condition).

Before single values, insofar as they are given in his representation, man is free because they are always represented as finite (although not necessarily affirmed as finite). In this way man is also free with regard to the conditions of the possibility of his openness to value as such, if and insofar as they become, in his reflection, objects of knowledge. This makes it possible to understand suicide or the hatred for God, although implicitly man continues to affirm himself and the Absolute Value, as the conditions of the possibility of his negative attitude with respect to his own existence and to the Absolute Value. As objects they are not conditions of possibility and that is why man can be free with respect to them.

What is the relation between this possibility of man's freedom with regard to values and his necessary affirmation of the right order of values, as implicitly contained in the transcendence towards being and value and thus belonging to the basic makeup of man?

We may first reply that there exists more than some kind of logical agreement or opposition between this necessarily affirmed correct order of values and the order of values implied in the free choice between values. Of course, some such agreement exists and it is the first point we have to mention here. The love for God, which is necessarily present deep down in man's existence, may be explicitly welcomed by him in his free activities, or the latter may contradict it, exactly as a single judgment may agree with the first laws of being and of thinking or may stand in contradiction to them.

But this is not all, nor is it what matters most. Rather it is a fact that the free decision about single values (among which belongs also the decision about the Absolute Value as objectivated by man's reflection in his a priori openness to the values) has a repercussion upon man's fundamental openness for the right order of values. This does not mean that this openness may be altogether destroyed. But a free decision about a single value is ultimately always a decision about and a molding of the person himself. In every decision man decides about himself, not about an action or a thing. Thus in his free decision man works back upon himself, he affects the very criteria of his love, which determine his own being. To the extent of his power and of what is possible, man sets up, in his free decision about single values, in what he accepts and in what he rejects, the criteria of his possible further decisions. He not only *assumes* the basic laws that govern his love and his hatred, but he himself freely *ratifies* anew the right laws, which he always already welcomes unconsciously, or he sets up his own laws in opposition to the right order of love. Thus he does not merely string out without any connection single actions one after the other. But in every action he sets down a law of his whole activity and life. He does not simply perform good or bad actions, he himself becomes good or bad.

In this way man constructs, above the true order of love, which he always implicitly affirms (the ancient philosophers called this *synderesis*) his own order of love. Man knows and acts according to his self-chosen order, according to what he himself has freely decided. He can behave according to the right order of love only after having rendered it explicit before his mind. That is why he knows this order, as established by God, only in combination with the freely constructed order of his love, which he has rightly or wrongly set up through his free reaction to the single values.

At this point we must remind the reader that, within man's transcendence towards God, there stands a voluntary attitude of man towards himself. Thus some love is the condition of man's knowledge of God. Of course, we have first said this about man's necessary love for God, that is always already given with human existence. Now, however, we see that in man's free activity this necessary love is never present by itself alone, as "pure" love; it is always combined with the order of love freely set up by man, which may agree or disagree with it.

This implies that concrete man's concrete transcendence towards God always contains, as one of its inner moments, a free decision. The free decision does not merely follow from knowledge, it also influences the latter. It follows that the deepest truth is also the freest truth. The way man knows and understands God is always also carried by the order or disorder of his love. Man does not first know God in a "neutral" way and afterwards decide whether he will love or hate him. Such a neutral knowledge, such objectivity, is an abstraction of the philosophers. It is real only if we suppose that man's concrete order of love is correct, that it agrees with the necessary order of love which comes from God and rules in man's innermost being. The concrete way in which man knows God is from the start determined by the way man loves and values the things that come his way.

Metaphysical knowledge never meets its object in itself, but comes to know it only in function of the subject's own transcendence, of man's dynamism towards this object. Thus such metaphysical knowledge can never be evaluated in function of the object itself; moreover, it depends on all the concrete peculiarities of this transcendence. This by no means detracts from its strictly objective and logical character. But such knowledge always is a commitment of the whole person in a free decision. A change in this knowledge is, in this domain, always also at the same time a "conversion," not merely a modification of one's opinion or the result of some investigation. Thus every man has the god who corresponds to his commitment and the nature of this commitment. He who loves matter more than the spirit, will adore it as the absolute, as his god. He who centers the understanding of his nature around the vital urge will—to speak metaphysically with St. Paul—make his belly into his god. And so forth.

The truths which all people admit, those of mathematics for instance, are not demonstrated more certainly or more strictly than those of a metaphysics of God. But they are admitted by all only because they belong to man's surface (that of numbers and space) and thus can never contradict the basic option contained in man's understanding of being as determined by the way he freely loves. Metaphysical knowledge may be demonstrated in a stricter and more consequent way, because man's innermost being always necessarily co-affirms it. But that which is thus co-affirmed can become the object of explicit knowledge only to the extent that this knowledge fits in the structure of the love for which man has opted in his concrete conduct. The fact that it is possible clearly to establish for a scoundrel a mathematical truth, but not a proof of God's existence, demonstrates neither the strength of the former nor the weakness of the latter. It only goes to show the extent to which a demonstration needs a commitment of man himself.

Ascetics may be understood in the sense of a readiness to criticize one's own order of love and to evaluate it in the light of the remainder of this order as it subsists in everybody and to organize it ever anew and more correctly in the growing light of true insight. In that sense it constitutes an inner moment of the philosophy of the real person. This truth has practically been totally overlooked in the philosophical activity of the later centuries, with the results which we know only too well. Only he who, in spirit, lives in temples and cloisters, can be a philosopher.

What follows from this for our philosophy of religion? We have already said that man is the being who stands before a free God and before the still unfulfilled possibilities of his freedom, hence before the God of a possible revelation in the sense which has been more precisely explained above. We have now advanced one step further and shown that the openness of man's knowledge for this God of an eventual revelation, which belongs to man's basic makeup, is always at the same time and essentially an openness which, in its inner concrete structure, is determined by man's free attitude.

We have seen that the openness towards God is a question of the moral self-determination of man. When we consider the knowledge of God as a real event in a real person, we see that it is intrinsically a moral or rather (since it refers to a decision with respect to God) a religious problem. Thus we may formulate the second statement of our metaphysical anthropology as follows: man is the being who stands in free love before the God of a possible revelation. Man listens to God's word or God's silence to the extent that he opens up in free love for this message of the word or of the silence of God. He hears this possible message of the free God when he has not, on account of a wrongly directed love, narrowed the absolute horizon of his openness for being as such, when he has not, in this way, made it impossible for the word of God to say what it might please him to say, to tell us under what guise he wishes to encounter us.

III

The Place of the Free Message

A human knower who is both free and spatio-temporal is an historical knower. Man is a discursive knower whose judgments affirm universal ideas of a multiplicity of mutable objects, distinct from each other in space and time. Like the sensible objects affirmed through his judgments, man himself is a form received in matter. As such he is a member of a species, inseparably associated with the history of his race. Since God is capable of giving man true, though imperfect knowledge of his Infinite Reality through the word of conceptual expression, the place where this word would be spoken would be human history. Thus man, who is by nature historical and social, is a potential hearer of an historical word of revelation. Indeed, even the silence of a God who can speak in human history has a revealing character. It is the free silence of the God who has chosen not to speak. Man therefore must examine this history of his race and endeavor to discover whether God has chosen to utter the revealing word of speech or the revealing word of silence.

1. Explaining the Question*

The manifestation of something unknown may occur in two ways: either it is presented in its own self or some knowledge of it is mediated in a word, where "word" is taken at first in the sense of a vicarious sign of that which is not given in itself. Insofar as man is the absolute openness of the spirit for being as such, hence also for pure, absolute being, the possibilities of a revelation through the self-presentation of its object are wholly exhausted only if man were to see the absolute God immediately in his own self.

*From *Hearers of the Word*, chapter 9.

Therefore, as long as God does not immediately manifest himself to man in his own self, man must always take into account the possibility of a revelation of this God in the word (*word* meant in the above sense). Hence as long as man is not given the immediate vision of God, he is always and essentially, on account of his basic makeup, one who listens for God's word, one who has to reckon with a possible revelation of God that consists not in the immediate presentation in his own self of the one who is revealed, but in a communication through a vicarious sign, whereby another reality points to the one that is to be revealed.

There is a second remark which we may make here about this place of a possible revelation. This place cannot, from the start, be determined in such a way that it points to a specific part of man's basic makeup which would be the only chosen place for such a revelation. God can only reveal that which man can hear. This statement is immediately evident. It does not imply by itself any previous limitation of the possible objects of a revelation, because of the transcendence of the human spirit towards being as such. This entails also at once that the absolute openness for being as such must be an inner moment of this place of a possible revelation. Suppose now that we modify this statement in such a way as to say: God can only reveal that which man can perceive through this or that side of his nature, through this or that fundamental experience, through this or that religious feeling, through this or that religious experience. In this case we would do away as well with the illimited openness of the spirit as with the free and imprevisible nature of a possible revelation of God.

Yet the place of the possible revelation of God has not yet been clearly determined when we say that it is man's illimited possibility, resulting from the spirit's transcendence, to hear any word that comes from the mouth of God. For we have not yet adequately described this transcendence of man as a spirit. We have not yet grasped it in its specifically *human* peculiarity. We have said above that the only thing we can say about the place of a possible revelation is that man himself is to be this place.

Thus when, in the following pages, we try to determine this place more precisely, we are always thinking only of the peculiar nature of human transcendence, of an inner moment of it, not of something distinct from it. Thus we must determine the nature of man himself more completely than we have done hitherto through the abstract statement that man is a finite spirit. We must find out in what precise way man is spirit. To show the purpose of these considerations, so that their scope may become clearer, we may say that man is spirit as an *historical* being. The place of his transcendence is always also an historical place. Thus the place of a possible revelation is always and necessarily also the history of man.

General ontology has already shown us that a possible revelation must have a certain historicity. When God is known by man as the pure, absolutely luminous being, he also stands before man as one who acts freely, who has not yet exhausted the possibilities of his freedom with respect to man by the free creation of this finite being. But free activity is essentially historical activity. In a first, general, and metaphysical sense, there is history wherever there is free activity, because in such an activity things happen which cannot be deduced or computed from some general, previous ground.

Such a free, undeducible happening is also always a unique happening which cannot be repeated. It can only be understood in itself, it is not one application of some general law. Now such an event is totally unlike an object of the natural sciences, i.e., of a knowledge that aims at necessary and general laws which totally explain the single case. We call it an historical event, as opposed to an event in nature. Thus when we consider it from God's side, revelation is already seen as an historical event.

However, this brief outline of the concept of history is not yet an adequate description of what the historical is in a human history. Thus when we say: revelation is an historical event, because the place of a possible revelation for man is his history, we do not mean this in the general metaphysical sense of history as such, but in the sense of *human* history.

But what is human history? We must not merely set down a definition of it. The meaning of human history should become clear to us from an examination of the historicity of man in the midst of his transcendence. We must establish this historicity of man not merely through empirical observation, nor through the simple accumulation of concrete facts. We must understand historicity as belonging to man's basic nature. As long as this had not been done, we might always imagine that, because of his spiritual nature, man might believe that he can try to put himself as spirit above his history, to emancipate himself from it, and thus to exclude history from the start as the possible place of a revelation. As a spirit man possesses the absolute possibility of attempting this, not of succeeding in it. Thus we must show that turning towards his history is an inner moment of man's spiritual nature. If we succeed in this, we have also shown that the place of a possible revelation of God, namely, man's openness for all being as such, is also necessarily situated within human history.

2. Man as a Material Being*

We are standing before a new starting point for our insight into the essential make-up of man. Man is receptive knowledge in such a way that his

*From *Hearers of the Word*, chapter 10.

self-knowledge, his cognitive self-subsistence derives always and necessarily from a stepping out into the world, from the grasping of something other distinct from him, that constitutes the first object of human knowledge. Hence we concluded that man must be one of these beings whose act of being is that of an empty possibility of being distinct from him. We must now further explain this statement.

Insofar as we derive this insight from a consideration borrowed from the metaphysics of knowledge, it is obvious that it applies to man precisely insofar as his knowledge is receptive. In other words: man knows as receptive, and insofar as his knowledge is the reception of an object, not the a priori possession of some knowledge of himself, man is the act of being of matter. Now a knowledge which, as such, in its being, is the act of a possibility of being, that is distinct from it, real and wholly undetermined in itself, a knowledge that is the act of being of matter, the knowledge of a material being, is known as sense knowledge. This means that receptive knowledge in the above sense is essentially *sense* knowledge. Thus we have reached a *metaphysical* idea of human sense knowledge. We have established it not simply as the cognitive power which man happens to possess (which would not bring us beyond an a posteriori description of the concrete forms of this sensibility, beyond a description which would have to start from the different sense organs). But from the metaphysically deduced essence of receptive knowledge we have concluded that this knowledge is necessarily sense knowledge. In return we have also understood the metaphysical essence of sensibility. Sensibility is the knowledge possessed by a being that, in order to have the other as its first object, must itself be the act of being of matter.

We must here draw the attention upon a methodical insight that is important for the whole of our metaphysics. The present instance provides a very clear example for it. We have just established a concept of matter, of subsisting-in-another, as ontological correlates of corresponding concepts in the domain of knowledge. This shows that, in general, really metaphysical ontological concepts can be grasped only when combined with the corresponding concepts of the metaphysics of knowledge. The former are but the translation of the latter in the language of being, and the other way round. This insight is basically but the application of our first ontological principle about the luminosity of being. For this principle implies that a being possesses being to the extent that it is self-present in knowledge and the other way round. The intensity of being in its analogy, and thus also all concepts that are connected with it and explicitate it, can be known in their proper nature only when we consider the corresponding degree and peculiarity of self-presence in knowledge.

Receptive knowledge is sense knowledge, i.e., the self-presence of a being whose act of being is the reality of matter. Thus we must answer the question how this matter, in which subsists the act of being of one who knows receptively through the senses, can be further elucidated. For this would also shed light on the nature of man as one who possesses such receptive sense knowledge.

In order to answer this question, we start with a previous question: what must be the metaphysical structure of the being which is the first known *object* of a receptive knowledge? If knowledge is originally self-presence of being, we may also say: the ontological structure of the knower is the a priori law of his possible objects as such. The structure of a being that has a certain intensity of being may be translated into the structure of a self-presence, therefore in that of its *first* known object as such. For if being is self-presence and if knowledge is self-presence of being, then the first known object is always the knower's own being itself, so that the structure of a knowing subject as a being is the structure of that which is known and the other way round.

And when that which is first known is the other, and when this is so because the being that knows becomes being of the other, we reach again the same conclusion: the structure of the knowing subject as a being is the structure of that which is known. This implies that, if the act of being of the subject who knows through the senses is the act of being of matter, the object of knowledge itself must be material in this sense.

Thus we may say: the original object of receptive knowledge can only be the act of being that is rooted in matter as its reality. The object of sensibility, of human receptive knowledge, is the material being. Thus the insight into the nature of material things as the first, original objects of human receptive knowledge provides us, in its turn, with the possibility of explaining more precisely our notion of matter and thus of interpreting better the essence of man as material being.

We may now return explicitly to the third aspect of our general question about being. We grasp being always as being of a being. We always grasp an existing reality, a real whatness of this or that determined kind, as that of a "subject." As shown in the most general and formal way precisely in this manner of formulating our question about being, we distinguish in every object of our knowledge between a *what* in a *something* and this *something itself,* as determined by this *whatness,* between a form and a subject, between an essence and that which possesses it. An object is represented in our knowledge always only in the peculiar way of such a distinction.

The subject, to which the whatness is attributed as its substantial determination and to which the whatness which is known and expressed in the concept is referred, in other words, the "wherein" of a whatness and the "whereunto" of our attribution of it cannot itself in its turn be an act of being. For, as such, it would be an existing reality, that can be grasped, that is self-luminous. Hence it might be expressed itself as a whatness and it should itself in its turn be referred to another subject.

Therefore this wherein of an existing reality and whereunto to which in knowledge we refer a conceptually grasped whatness can only be the empty undetermined possibility of being. Thus we stand once more before matter, this time by considering the peculiar way in which man grasps a being, and we arrive at similar conclusions. However, the present approach may help us better explain what matter is. We saw it as the empty, undetermined wherein of an existing reality which we grasp conceptually and attribute through a judgment precisely to this matter. Now in the judgment, in which it is present as the content of the predicate, this whatness always comes up as general, whereas matter (as the whereunto to which the predicate is referred) is seen as the undetermined bearer, that can of itself be the indifferent subject of several possible whatnesses. Because the whatness is general, matter appears as the ground which, on account of its emptiness and its indifference for any determined whatness, makes it possible for this multipliable whatness to be this or that well determined whatness. As the whereunto of the statement and the underlying wherein of the whatness itself, matter is thus the cause of the thisness of a being, whose whatness may be reproduced. In this sense matter is the principle of individuation. Not, of course, in the sense of an individuality which, through its peculiar fullness, would be, in the unique nature of its determinations, the opposite of something which may be reproduced. But in the sense of an individuality which belongs to a being whose several quidditative determinations, even when combined in the possibly most complex way, may, in principle, still always be repeated.

Hence matter is the principle of individuation, not in the sense that it is the cause of the unicity of a certain quiddity, but in the sense that is the cause of the multiple individuation of the same quiddity. From this explanation of matter we may now derive further information both about man's nature and about the nature of the object which is to be received by his receptive knowledge. We shall speak of this in the following chapter.

At any rate, we have reached the following conclusion: man is spirit in such a way that, in order to become spirit, he enters and he has ontically always already entered into otherness, into matter, and so into the world. This is not simply another statement about man, which is to be added to the assertion of his spiritual nature. It is an inner determination of his spirituality itself. This should not be understood as if spirituality, as a *peculiar* power of man, were sensible. Such a statement would contain an inner contradiction. It is meant in the sense that man is a spirit in a peculiar way. His spirit is *receptive—anima tabula rasa—*and because of its receptivity this spirit needs, as its own, indispensable means, produced by itself, a sense power through which it may strive towards its own goal, the grasping of being as such. In this sense man is sense-endowed spirituality. The intellectual soul, i.e., the spirit, really and essentially informs the body, to use the words of the Council of Vienne. The soul is spirit; enters by itself, *per se,* into matter. We have also already discovered a starting point which helps us better understand matter. Matter is the principle of individuation. We shall now further have to inquire what it means for the spirit that man wends his way through the world precisely as spirit.

3. Man as an Historical Spirit*

The soul, form of matter. This was the statement which the last chapter started to establish. At the same time we had discovered a starting point which helped us understand prime matter. It is the empty, undetermined, although real possibility of being and, as such, the ground of the multiple individuation of the same quiddity. We have also already said that such an explanation of the nature of a material being told us something about man as endowed with receptive knowledge and about the first objects of this knowledge, which have to show themselves in order to be known. The empty potential indetermination of matter, as real and by itself pure possibility, allows us to state two more things about it. It is the ground of the *spatiality* and of the *temporality* of the being of which it is an essential component.

It is the ground of the spatiality of a being. The quiddity, the object of our knowledge, appeared to us as by itself universal, indifferent to be a particular this or that, hence as a determination which can come to stand as often as one pleases in the wherein of the matter that bears it. When such a form, such a quiddity, does in fact repeatedly subsist in matter, so that the same reality is several times repeated, it becomes possible to add up these several reproductions. Counting is possible only where that which is to be counted appears, previous to the counting, as the repetition of the same. And since matter is the principle of the possible repetition of the same, we must necessarily consider it the principle of number. But number implies quantity. Matter is the principle of quantity, since the latter is but the multiple repetition of the same.

Now matter is such a principle not only with respect to several things that are really distinct from each other; it must necessarily also carry out this, its essential function, within the single thing into which it enters as an essential principle. Hence it makes of the single thing something quantitative *in itself*. Now the repetition of the same within one and the same

*From *Hearers of the Word,* chapter 11.

thing is nothing but its spatiality, its being innerly affected by quantity, the real diversity of the same thing within its unity. Thus we may say: a being whose innermost make-up contains matter as an inner essential principle is spatial.

The further basic determination of a material object is its inner temporality. We saw that matter is the in itself undetermined possibility of real determinations. This implies that it is always wider than the determined reality whose substratum it is in this or that determined being. The determined quiddity, which subsists in matter, does not fill matter's whole potentiality. Thus, because of the ever wider range and incompleteness of its matter, a material being always points towards new determinations, it is always "in motion" towards new realities of being which always open up in the ground of its nature, because of the undetermined range of the possibilities of matter.

Hence the material being is one which always points towards the totality of the realization of its possibilities as the future of its inner movement and keeps striving towards it. Since these possible determinations, whose simultaneous realization would constitute the realization of matter's illimited potentialities, exclude each other at least partially as simultaneous determinations of the underlying matter, the totality of the possible realizations of the potentiality of matter is always delayed and is never given all at once.

The total realization of the possibilities of a material being is possible only in the succession of the latter's inner movement. In other words, the being is temporal. Temporality is meant here in the original sense, not as the extrinsic measure of the thing, but as the inner protracting of the thing itself in the realized totality of its possibilities. As realized these possibilities cannot at once determine this being. Because it is material, each one of them is perishable, and dynamically finalized towards another possibility which will overtake it. Thus we must say that a material being is intrinsically temporal. In this way we have established three determinations of matter: It explains how the same may be repeated over and over again; it provides the being of which it is an essential constituent with an inner spatiality and temporality.

We have seen that man is the knower, whose knowledge is essentially receptive, that he is being in matter. On account of the inner nature of his knowledge, his act of being is that of matter. In this sense, he is a material being. We must now use this deeper insight into the nature of matter to reach a metaphysical concept of man.

Man is one among many. He is essentially in space and in time. Insofar as his quiddity is, by itself, the quiddity of matter, it is a reality that may, in principle, be identically reproduced. Individual man is, in principle, one of a kind. Of course, no attempt is made here to deduce a priori in a metaphysical deduction, the fact of a biological bond through reproduction or the concrete manner of such a biological connection. This is the task of empirical observation of facts. But something may be known a priori and through metaphysical insight: that, because man is essentially a material being, he may be repeated in his quiddity, in his nature, that there may exist many men.

This implies also that, should there in fact exist only one human person, he would, by his very essence, have to carry in him an ordination to a possible multiplicity of other men. When we spoke of the temporality of a material thing, we have already stressed the fact that a single material being can never wholly and at once realize the ever greater range of its possibilities that always are already contained in its materiality. It follows that a single man can never exhaustively and at one time actualize that which belongs to him by way of possibilities as a material being. That is why referring to other beings of his kind, which every man does as this particular individual, is not something unimportant; it is a referring to a multitude of men, to a humanity which, only as a whole, can really make manifest that which is essentially given to each single man deep down in his possibilities, but only as possibilities. Man is real only in a humanity.

Everybody knows what we mean by saying that man, as a material being, is spatial and temporal. Man is not put into a spatio-temporal world after having first been made into man. He is not simply put on a spatio-temporal stage to act out his life. Spatio-temporality is his inner make-up which belongs properly to him as man. Because matter is one of his essential components, it is by himself that he constructs space and time as inner moments of his existence.

When we say man is essentially one among many of his kind with whom he is together in space and time on account of his inner essence, we say nothing but: he is historical in the concrete sense of a *human* history. Above we have already, in a true and necessary, although wider sense, attributed a historicity to man's activity. Man is historical insofar as he is the one who acts freely, even in his transcendence towards God, hence in determining his relation to the Absolute. Of course, this moment belongs essentially to man's historicity. There is authentic historicity only where there is the unicity and the imprevisibility of freedom. Although nature changes and undergoes movement, it has no real history, because all stages of its movement, although their direction may be irreversible, are but necessary moments and consequences of the initial setup and therefore instances of a general law. There is history only where unicity and originality triumph over being only an instance or an item in a series. There is history only where there is freedom.

But there is history in the *human* sense only where, in a togetherness of free persons in their multiplicity, the activity of freedom expands in a world, i.e., in space and time, where the intelligible acts of freedom must, in order to become manifest, extend in space and time, where they need space-time in order to be themselves.

And precisely such a historicity is found in man because he is essentially a free, self-subsisting personality, which must freely realize itself through a multiplicity of such personalities as the total realization of the very essence of such a personality in space and time.

Man is a historical being. This is now for us no longer a mere observation, resulting from the accumulation of disparate facts, which are then afterwards put together. It is an essential insight, whose elements we understand as they derive from their original starting point in their necessary and inner connection.

4. Spirit and Historicity: Being and Appearance*

If we wish to show the connection between the transcendence of the human spirit and man's historicity, we must once more explain how we arrived at this historicity of man. We have not simply established it as a fact, but we have transcendentally deduced it from a peculiarity of the spirit of man as such. For we started from the fact that, despite its transcendence towards being as such, man's spirit is receptive knowledge.

Man views the illimited domain of all being as such not in such a way that he anticipates this knowledge by starting from a certain fund of knowledge which would be available to him a priori together with its nature. Man's openness for being as such does not derive from a previous, albeit narrower openness, which would come to him with his very nature, making known to him some objects, such as his essence itself. Rather transcendence opens up for man when he receives an object given from without, showing itself by itself. This peculiarity of man's spiritual nature and transcendence was the starting point whence we arrived at man's historicity. This implies that historicity is not a property which belongs also to man, who happens besides also to be a spirit. Rather it is an essential element of the transcendental spirituality itself. Historicity derives from the specific spiritual nature of man. Hence it is the historicity of human spirit as such. We must now examine what this means.

We have said that man has his transcendence, his outlook on being as such, only because and inasmuch as he is receptive knowledge. Now we have also shown that receptive knowledge is intrinsically sense knowledge. Hence man knows of being as such only because and insofar as he knows through the senses.

We must not understand this statement as if man had some sense knowledge and, subsequently, as a spirit, would, as it were, try to find out what

*From *Hearers of the Word*, chapter 12.

he can do with it and the objects it offers to him. We have seen that sense knowledge, with its sensible and material characteristics, is a necessary condition of that transcendence towards being as such, which possesses its openness only because a single object manifests itself to it by itself. This implies that human sensibility is correctly interpreted only when we understand it as deriving from the spirit and its necessity. This spirit which, by itself and despite its transcendence, is *tabula rasa* can reach the fullness of its nature only if it produces a sensibility as its own power. A spirit of this kind penetrates into matter in order to become spirit. Man penetrates into the world in order to reach being as such, that extends beyond the world.

Such a conception of human sensibility corresponds fully to St. Thomas's metaphysics of knowledge (see *Spirit in the World,* pp. 246 ff.) which explicitly conceives sense knowledge as a power which emerges from the spirit as the latter reaches for and pre-apprehends the end which belongs to it as spirit: to be openness for being as such. Man's sensibility is not to be understood as a power which exists mainly for itself, but from the start as a power of the spirit for its own purpose. It follows that the spirit possesses its openness, its stance before being as such, hence also before pure Being, only because and insofar as, through its entrance into matter, it acquires an openness for, a stance before, the material things in space and time.

Hence for man as a finite and receptive spirit there exists a luminosity of being as such only in the luminosity of material realities; he turns towards being as such only when turning to material being, he goes up towards God only by going out into the world. And insofar as the access to God is given to man only in his a priori structure as a spirit, only in the transcendence which belongs properly to him, hence in his return into himself, we may also say: only by stepping out into the world can man so enter into himself that he encounters being and God.

When, in this connection, we speak of material things, this concept should not be restricted to the entities that, on account of their sense qualities, are immediate objects of our external senses. This concept comprises all that which can immediately be given to a receptive knowledge which grasps single objects. Thus we are not thinking only of outside sense objects, but also of man himself, insofar as he grasps himself in his concrete singularity while knowing such objects and dealing with them. We may designate all this in one word as the "world."

Insofar as all these things, which constitute the world, are objects of a receptive knowledge, they must show themselves by themselves. They must and can appear by themselves in their own nature. So we may designate all this as "appearance" (*Erscheinung*), without in the least implying that what is thus receptively known only "seems" to be real. The word only wishes to convey the idea that these objects "appear" in their own selves and are not simply known on the basis of a knowledge of something else which shows itself; further that, in these immediate objects of the receptive knowledge of a spirit, being as such is given by the *Vorgriff* in such a way that it appears in them and only in them. In receptive knowledge the world appears in its own self and it causes being, which is always more than the being of the world, to appear in the self of the world, so far as this is possible for the finite human spirit on account of its receptive nature.

Thus we may formulate the question which concerns us here as follows: we must investigate more thoroughly the relation which obtains in the spirit's transcendence between appearance and openness of being as such.

We must first remember what we have said above about transcendence itself. We said that man does not stand in an environment as a passive part of it, but that he stands as self-subsisting before a world of objects. Through his judgment and his activity he extraposes these objects as things in their own selves. This allows him to return into himself, to be self-subsistent in knowledge. In this self-subsistence he grasps the objects under concepts, under a universal point of view. This comes out in every statement, since such a statement always attributes to a subject a universal quiddity (the predicate).

We have shown about how the *Vorgriff* towards being as such is the transcendental condition of the possibility for this self-subsistence and this grasping of the things under universal concepts. By *Vorgriff* we meant the a priori power, given with the very nature of the spirit, to represent to oneself the single quiddities brought up by receptive sense knowledge in a dynamic a priori reaching out of the spirit for the absolute range of its possible objects. The single object is grasped as a stage in the reaching out of the spirit for the complete fulfilment of its capacity. Thus from the start it is always already seen under the horizon of the last end of the spirit as such.

The *Vorgriff* is the transcendence of the spirit, the "surpassing" of the spirit, in which the latter grasps the single object because, in a certain sense, it already looks beyond it into the absolute range of its possible objects as such. We have also shown that this transcendence is not simply a transcendence towards a finite circle of possible objects, that is, not originally a transcendence towards nothingness, but that it is a transcendence towards pure being that has no inner limits in itself.

It is evident that we should not understand this *Vorgriff* as an inborn idea of being as such, and even less as an objective intuition of some separate idea of being or of God's pure being itself. For all this would stand in contradiction with the statement that man's knowledge is originally receptive. Should we think of the *Vorgriff* in one of the above mentioned ways, man would be in possession of a knowledge that is absolutely independent of receptive sense knowledge of single objects in the world, hence absolutely independent of that which appears. Hence the *Vorgriff* as such is not an a priori knowledge of an object, but the manner, given with man's very nature and in that sense a priori, in which man takes up a sense object given a posteriori, the a priori way of knowing that which appears a posteriori. It is not a self-subsisting grasp of being as such, but the anticipating grasp of being which is possible only in the grasping of the appearance.

This enables us to determine more precisely the relation between transcendence and appearance. We may distinguish three moments in an appearance. (1) The appearance insofar as it is given to us only by receptive sense knowledge as such. Hence the sense object insofar as, through its own operation, it imprints itself by itself into our material sense receptivity and thus makes an appearance. (2) The outlook upon being as such opened up in the *Vorgriff*. Because sensibility is a power which the spirit begets in order to reach its own end, the single sense object is from the start grasped by human knowledge in the dynamic striving of the spirit towards being as such. Hence in the grasping of the sense object the *Vorgriff* itself enters into action. It becomes conscious and thus, through its own unlimited range, it opens up for the spirit the illimited range of being as such. In the grasping of the appearances being itself is by anticipation grasped in its wider range. (3) The appearance insofar as it is grasped itself under the *Vorgriff* towards being as such. We must not imagine the process as if the appearance were given to human consciousness in its mere sense givenness, and as if, besides it, there would open up an outlook upon the domain of being as such. We have established the *Vorgriff* in a transcendental deduction only as the condition of the possibility of grasping the appearance in the specifically human way, i.e., under universal concepts and in the self-subsistence of the knower.

In other words, the sense object is, as it were, informed by the *Vorgriff* and by the knowledge of being as such provided by it. A synthesis is made of the mere material appearance and the knowledge opened up in the *Vorgriff* of being as such. The appearance is grasped as being, *sub ratione entis,* and only because the appearance is grasped as a being does man acquire a knowledge of being as such. Hence we have three elements: the sense appearance as such, the knowledge of being (*Sein*), the being (*Seiende*) as the synthesis of sense appearance and knowledge of being as such. The two first elements, if we may call them that, appear first in immediate knowledge always only as synthesized in the being which is known. Were this not the case, sense knowledge and *Vorgriff* would represent two powers in man each of which would by itself alone and independently of the other grasp an object. But this is impossible for the *Vorgriff* because of the receptive character of human knowledge and for sense knowledge because we have seen that the spirit causes it to emanate from itself as its own power.

Thus, looking backward, we understand better why we said that the third aspect of our general question of being is that being is grasped as being of a being, whereby we both separate and connect being and a being, and we refer being to a subject distinct from it and whose being it is. This is but another way of saying that through the *Vorgriff* we grasp being only by grasping a certain single being given through the senses. Being and a being are not the same thing, for pure being is the ultimate whereunto of the spirit in its absolute transcendence. Here it can no longer be analyzed into being and a subject which only shares being. But what being is becomes clear to the finite receptive knowledge of man only in the reception of a sense object, that is grasped as a stage of the spirit on its way to being as such. That is why it is grasped as a participation of being as such, as in possession of being to the extent of its essence.

The *Vorgriff* and that which is manifested by it are known only insofar as the *Vorgriff* is the form of the appearance and constitutes the horizon under which the appearance is seen. Yet precisely as such it stands revealed as reaching beyond the circle of possible appearances. We have shown that its absolutely illimited range is that which allows it to make of the sense appearance as such an *object* opposed to man's self-subsistence.

5. The Human Historicity of a Possible Revelation*

As spirit man is destined for being as such. He possesses this transcendence only in connection with the spatio-temporal appearance in which he himself belongs, hence in connection with the historical appearance. But when he grasps it, he stands open for all being. Is this true only in the sense of a knowledge of the transcendental characteristics of being as such? Or can a specific supramundane being be made known through the appearance? And in what way is this conceivable? This is the question which we must now consider.

We reply with a statement, which is at the same time the third one among the statements in which we tried to formulate the relation between man's transcendence and innerworldliness. This third statement is: every being can be made manifest in the appearance *by means of the word*. This statement, the most important one for our further considerations on the philosophy of religion, needs a more thorough explanation.

*From *Hearers of the Word*, chapter 13.

First we must keep in mind two things which we know already. The *Vorgriff* opens up the horizon for absolutely all being. Hence we know already about positive determinations of absolutely every being. On the other hand, not every being can in itself be presented to receptive knowledge. How then can such a being be known nonetheless in its specific nature?

We answer first: through negation. In order really to understand this manner of knowing something that is not presented in itself, we must first come back to the analogy of being. A being may not be conceived as a sum of sundry properties, each of which, shut up as it were within itself, stands besides the others in mere juxtaposition. Rather that which we call the properties of a being is nothing but the expression of the degree of intensity of being which something possesses. Now this intensity of being may be negatively determined by negation. In this way we may also reach a certain being outside of the realm of appearance.

Through the *Vorgriff,* in the analogy of our concept of being, we reach from the start, although in an empty way, all possible degrees of the intensity of being, from the pure possibility of prime matter up to pure being. On the other hand, in the appearances specified degrees of the intensity of being are made immediately accessible to our intuition. By denying the limits of such a specified, immediately accessible intensity of being, by displacing these limits upwards in the direction of pure being, it is possible to determine, in some way, albeit only negatively, extramundane beings as such and not only in their most general determinations which they share with all beings. We are capable of doing this because we know the relation of these beings to the degrees of being that are immediately known to us (by such beings we do not mean, of course, only substantial entities, but also states of affairs pertaining to them).

The concept of being is not merely a static one, of the most empty and meaningless generality. For all its empty universality it possesses an inner dynamism towards the fullness of being (that is the meaning of the analogy of the concept of being). That is why it has, by itself, the possibility of growing innerly as it were and of taking on a richer content, from within and not through the adding of external properties derived from elsewhere. Thus it becomes possible to let the concept of being, together with its transcendental determinations, grow by and out of itself until, stopped as it were at a certain point in its dynamism by negation, it designates a certain extramundane intensity of being.

Since the positive fullness in such a concept always has its start in the appearance and remains dependent on it, it remains always necessary to turn towards the appearance when, by means of negation, we widen the concept up to the level of supramundane being. If we may express this whole state of affairs in a geometrical image, we would say: suppose a field given in its whole extension, further a certain segment of this whole field, in which certain points may be reached at will and determined immediately, independently of others. In that case it is possible, by starting from these points, to define and determine with certitude every other point of the whole field through its relation to the points which are immediately accessible and known in themselves.

This does not mean at all, of course, that man by himself can, by starting from these, his immediately accessible objects, know the actual existence or the inner possibility of each being in the extramundane domain of possibilities. This is excluded already by the simple fact that at least the actual existence of extramundane beings too depends on a free act of God and that therefore their existence cannot be established by man left to his own devices. The same thing may, at least in some cases, be true of the knowledge of the mere possibility of such facts outside of the world of appearance.

When several negations meet (or eventually necessarily meet) in the concept of such a being, if it is to be conceivable at all for human knowledge, it is quite possible that, on the basis of such a concept alone, the inner possibility of such a being can no longer be known, although this concept does in fact still really reach and define this being and provide a knowledge of it.

To return to our geometrical image: the field of being as such is illimited. This illimitation is experienced as the absence of a certain limit in the *Vorgriff*, not in its infinity in itself. Hence this field is not for man a clearly defined reality. When, on the basis of two or more points within the field of our experience, we try to define a real or possible point lying outside the intramundane field, it might be impossible to find out whether we are not intending a point that does no longer lie within the field, in other words, something impossible in itself. Nevertheless, if such a doubt is removed by revelation or in some other way, a real knowledge of such a being may be possible by means of such a negative determination.

Thus we have hitherto established what follows: in principle every being may be determined in function of that which appears. This determination can take place only through a negation. This does not mean that man can determine every reality in such a way that he can, by himself alone, come to know every being in its inner possibility or even in its actual existence. On the other hand, we have already established that an extramundane being cannot, in its own reality, be given to a receptive knowledge. If we take all this together we reach the conclusion that an extramundane being can be given to the finite spirit through the word.

Hence "word" is no longer here, as it was at an earlier stage of our investigation, meant as merely some kind of vicarious sign, but as a *conceptual* sign of the spirit, immediately intended for the latter. A negation as such can only take place in the word, which is, of course, not the same as a phonetic sound.

Hence every extramundane being may be grasped in the word. For, on the one hand, the word does not represent the being in itself; on the other hand, through the negation which it (and only it) can assume, it is capable of determining in function of what appears every being, even one which never appears. Therefore, insofar as it always refers to an appearance, the human word can be the way in which every being may be revealed. Insofar as the human word refers to a concept which, through negation, represents an extramundane being, it may, when spoken by the extramundane God, reveal to man the existence and the inner possibility of such a being.

Hence we may summarize our three statements as follows. Even in the appearance alone an extramundane being may be revealed to man by the human word, as the bearer of a concept of such a being derived through negation from the appearance. We have already seen that man is the being who must necessarily listen to a possible revelation of the free God. Since we have now shown that everything, including extramundane beings, may be made known by the human word, as it combines negated appearance and negating transcendence, we have also said that man is at least the one who must listen to a revelation of this free God *in a human word*.

We have shown that the human word does not mean an a priori restriction of that which may be revealed. The fact that man must wait upon such a word that may eventually be spoken is no limitation of God's freedom to reveal what he pleases. Hence there is no need for inquiring further whether God might also reveal himself without using such a word which reaches supramundane realities through a negation of the appearance. This would at any rate be possible only by giving up the structure of human knowledge, as we have discovered it, a structure that combines spiritual transcendence and sense appearance. Since man understands himself only as endowed with such kind of knowledge, he does not have to wait for a revelation which might take place only if this combination were given up. Whether and why such a revelation might be possible should therefore not further concern us here, especially since it may be shown that such an eventual different kind of revelation must finally be transformed into one whose inner possibility we have just established.

For as long as man is not raised above his basic makeup, as explained by us, such a different kind of revelation, should it ever determine and shape his normal being and activity, must be transposed by him into the kind whose structure we have tried to explain, i.e., into one that is grasped in the human word. This implies that man is the being who has at least to take into account the occurrence of a revelation of the free God through the human word. But in this way we have already anticipated the more thorough considerations that are still to follow.

Our first task here was to answer the question how transcendence and historicity are related to each other. What we have called appearance is nothing but what man meets in his history: everything which exists within the world, not only the objects that can immediately be known through the senses, but man himself too in his whole being and activity, as, through his knowledge of and his dealings with the things of the world, he arrives at grasping his own being.

We have now sufficiently answered this question so that we may say: every transcendent reality may in principle be represented to man not only in its most general determinations, but also according to its specific properties. It may be represented negatively through this historical appearance that we call word. This word itself is in its turn the synthesis of an inner-worldly, historical reality and of a negation. Thus we have established that the word is the place of a possible encounter with and revelation of the free God, before whom, because of his transcendence, man is always already standing.

But this does not yet clearly enough explain the relation of man as an historical being with a possible revelation. It is true that we have established that man must pay attention to a possible word of God that is spoken in his human language and that may nonetheless say everything that is to be revealed. But it has not yet become clear *where* man is to wait for this word. This points to the further question that must occupy us.

We have come to know man as spirit and therefore as one who stands open for the free revelation of God. Thus we have also, because of the peculiar way in which he is a spirit, understood that man is an historical being, who as *spirit* may come to know *every* being and as a spirit *endowed with senses and living in history* may come to know every being in the *word*, at least if this word is spoken to him in his human language by the free God. Thus there only remains to find out where he is to hear this word of God as a human word.

In order to find an answer to this question, two of the previously established points must work together: the insight into man's historicity and the insight into the historicity which necessarily belongs to a possible revelation of God.

We start with the historicity which belongs necessarily to God's revelation. We have understood God's revelation as his free activity with man. It remains a possibility, even when man's creation by God is already presupposed, because of man's finiteness and of his absolute transcendence. Therefore man must always reckon with it. Such a free action of God, which takes place within the empty, but already real space of the human being, is already historical by itself. It is not pre-historic, like the creation of the human being which, although free, had no partner, so that in it God acted only with himself. Moreover it is not universal and necessary. It is free, hence imprevisible. We can grasp and understand it only in itself. There is no point, no presupposition in the world, from which its actuality and its proper nature might be determined. Hence, although we must always reckon with it and wait for it, it is the unexpected. Such a free revelation is, of its very nature, historical, that is, the unique, gratuitous activity of a free agent. But how does such an activity of God stand in man's space? Can it, despite its divine historicity, be humanly *un*historical, i.e., not occupy a certain point in the space and the time of human history? Or is it also essentially historical for man, i.e., shall it, on account of its divine historicity, occupy a certain place also in human history, enter in contact with this history and its spatio-temporal extension at a certain point, so that man has to turn towards this specific point of his history if he is to perceive God's revealed word?

We hold that the latter possibility is the one which corresponds to the inner nature of a possible revelation of God. We have already given the reasons above. For we have already said that, in whatever way revelation may originally take place, it has to be transposed into the human word, if man is not to be taken by revelation out of his human way of existing.

It is inadmissible that man should be permanently and miraculously raised above his natural way of thinking and of acting by God's revelation. This would ultimately reduce God's free revelation again to be but an essential element of man himself, since we would no longer come to know it as the unexpected, as the act of God's freedom with regard to man as already constituted in his essence. Therefore, at least within the existence of the individual human being, the free revelation can occur only at a definite point. For all other times man can keep revelation only by way of a human word. He must forever refer back again to this certain exceptional point as to the unique point in human history at which God's revelation has originally emerged. Hence revelation takes place once in human history, at least in *this* sense that it cannot be permanently coexistent with all the single moments of a single human history. Thus, in order to meet revelation, man must refer back again, in historical knowledge, at least to certain exceptional moments of his own history. But once we have come that far, there can be no theoretical difficulty in admitting that man must reckon with the possibility that such a revelation does not occur at a certain point in *every* individual history of each person, but only in the history of *some* individual human beings. For the whole life of the single person, who can permanently possess a revelation only by turning back to a certain point of history that can never be repeated, who can possess it only in the words in which it has been expressed, it makes no essential difference whether he has to turn to one point of his *own* history or to one in the history of *another* person, as long as he can come to know that at this point of a human history a revelation has really taken place. There would exist an essential difference only if man were always able, in his own life, to repeat this revelation at will in its original form. In that case it would be true that the outer historical demonstration of an original revelation in another person would be no substitute for a revelation experienced from within in one's own existence. But this hypothesis stands in contradiction with the free divine historicity of revelation, at least if we presuppose that, in general at least, man would continue to exist with his usual human makeup even if a revelation occurs. Hence we must think of the historicity of a possible revelation in itself as historical also in the sense of a *human* history, i.e., we must look out for it as an event which has occurred at a certain point of space and time within the total history of man.

IV

Philosophy and Theology

1. Theology and Anthropology*

Transcendental anthropology is not only the method of philosophy; it is the method of theology as well. Far from opposing a theocentric or Christocentric focus in theology, theological anthropology enables the Christian to understand and correlate the Christian mysteries in a way which relates them to the fundamental a priori structures of his own experience. By doing so theological anthropology can make the central Christian mysteries of the Trinity, the Incarnation, and grace more credible and significant to the contemporary Christian than they appear to be in the more familiar presentation of the traditional Scholastic manuals. Modern philosophy's focus on the human subject and the great difficulty which modern men have in making sense of traditional Catholic theology make it imperative that Catholic theologians relate the Christian mysteries to the inner experience of modern man through a theology built upon transcendental anthropology.

This short paper is intended to show that dogmatic theology today must be theological anthropology and that such an 'anthropocentric' view is necessary and fruitful. The question of man and its answering may not be regarded, therefore, as an area of study separate from other theological areas as to its scope and subject-matter, but as the whole of dogmatic theology itself. This statement does not contradict the 'theocentricity' of all theology as expressed, for instance, in St Thomas' doctrine that God is as such the formal object of revelation theology. As soon as man is understood as the being who is absolutely transcendent in respect of God, 'anthropocentricity' and 'theocentricity' in theology are not opposites but strictly one and the same thing, seen from two sides. Neither of the two aspects can be comprehended at all without the other. Thus, although anthropocentricity in theology is not the opposite of the strictest theocentricity, it *is* opposed to the idea that in theology man is one particular

*From *Theological Investigations*, vol. IX, pp. 28-30, 33-42.
© 1972 by Darton, Longman & Todd Ltd.

theme among others, e.g. angels, the material world; or that it is possible to say something about God theologically without thereby automatically saying something about man and vice versa; or that these two kinds of statements are connected with one another in respect of their object, but not in the process of knowing itself.

Similarly, this anthropological focus in theology is not opposed to or in competition with a Christological focus. It is not possible to demonstrate this in more detail here; we merely observe that anthropology and Christology mutually determine each other within Christian dogmatics if they are both correctly understood. Christian anthropology is only able to fulfil its whole purpose if it understands man as the *potentia oboedientalis* for the 'Hypostatic Union'. And Christology can only be undertaken from the point of view of this kind of transcendental anthropology; for in order to say today what the 'Hypostatic Union' is without being suspected of merely reproducing no longer feasible 'mythologies', the idea of the God-man needs proof of a transcendental orientation in man's being and history under grace. A purely *a posteriori* Christology, unable to integrate Christology correctly into an evolutionary total view of the world, would not find it easy to dismiss the suspicion of propounding mythology.

This anthropology is naturally to be understood as a transcendental anthropology. A *transcendental investigation* examines an issue according to the necessary conditions given by the possibility of knowledge and action on the part of the subject himself. Such an investigation presupposes that the subject of the act of knowing is not simply a 'thing' among others which can be made at will the object of a statement including other objects, but which is not present at all—even implicitly—in statements purely about other objects. If I speak of Australia I have not said anything, not even implicitly, about Java. But in such a statement (from the point of view of its content and import) I have said something implicitly about man as its subject (in so far as the statement, in order to be possible at all, necessarily presupposes various things about man). I have expressed and affirmed this by means of subjective implication. Therefore, if one wishes to pursue dogmatics as transcendental anthropology, it means that whenever one is confronted with an object of dogma, one inquires as to the conditions necessary for it to be known by the theological subject, ascertaining that the *a priori* conditions for knowledge of the object are satisfied, and showing that they imply and express something about the object, the mode, method and limits of knowing it.

In general, transcendental investigation does not assume that the material content of the object in question can be adequately deduced from the transcendental conditions whereby it is known by the subject, nor that this content, known *a posteriori,* is unimportant for the subject's existence (his 'salvation') and for the truth of his knowledge. It does not regard this content as in itself merely indifferent material whereby the subject experiences his own *a priori* and necessary being. This applies fundamentally and decisively to a theological transcendental investigation and method as well. For instance, not only is it important for a true Christology to understand man as the being who is orientated towards an 'absolute Saviour' both *a priori* and in actuality (his essence having been elevated and set in this direction supernaturally by grace), but it is equally important for his salvation that he is confronted with Jesus of Nazareth as this Saviour—which cannot, of course, be transcendentally 'deduced'.

On the other hand, to interpret the whole of dogmatic theology as transcendental anthropology means that every dogmatic treatment must also be considered from its transcendental angle, and that one must therefore face the question, what measure of actual material content subsists in the theological subject's *a priori* 'structures' implicit in a particular theological statement? In other words it means that the transcendental side of knowledge must not be overlooked but taken seriously. The problem we mentioned of the relationship between transcendental, *a priori* theology and descriptive, historical and *a posteriori* theology is not solved, of course, by what we have just said. The problem only reveals its depth and acuteness when one is aware of the fact that in theology the final *a priori* precondition for the subject's theological knowledge, i.e. grace (ultimately the self-communicating God, acting freely in history) is the real content, or rather, the objective foundation of what is known and experienced *a posteriori* in history. One finds that in theology the *a priori* character of the subject and the *a posteriori* quality of the historical object enjoy an exclusive and unique relationship.

We must now ask *why* this anthropological change of direction in theology is *necessary*. There are fundamental reasons from the nature of the case, i.e. from theology and its object. Besides this there are reasons from the contemporary situation and reasons of basic theology and apologetics.

1. First of all the *reasons* or reason from the nature of the case. As a consequence of the nature of every occurrence of intellectual (and hence also theological) knowledge, the question of the object of such knowledge raises at the same time the question as to the nature of the knowing subject. This inextricable interrelation of the 'objective' and 'subjective' side of knowledge does not need, of course, to be discussed or to be equally explicit in every sphere of study. A concrete discipline in natural science does not have to investigate its philosophical foundation as well: the latter is concerned with the mode of being and structure of the subject who is concretely engaged in science. But where the study of a particular field becomes really 'philosophical' in a specific sense—and theology must do this of its very essence—every question concerning any object whatever also formally implies the question of the knowing subject.

A question is first stated philosophically by being put formally as the question concerning a particular object as such in the *totality* of reality and truth, for it is only in this way that the highest reasons, the philosophical ones, are sought out. If this is done, the subject is also investigated, not only because it is a 'material' part of the totality, but because the totality (as that to which man is transcendentally orientated) can only exist in the subject as such according to the latter's own subjective uniqueness. The philosophical question as to a particular object is necessarily the question as to the knowing subject, because *a priori* the subject must carry with it the limits of the possibility of such knowledge. Thus the 'transcendental' structures of the object are already determined *a priori*. A really *theological* question can only be put, however, if it is understood as being simultaneously a philosophical one in the sense we have shown. For it is only a theological question as long as it sees the individual object with its origin in and orientation towards God.

But God is not one object among others in the realm of man's *posteriori* knowledge but the fundamental ground and the absolute future of all reality.

As such he can only be understood as the absolute point of man's transcendental orientation. Thus every theology of this kind is necessarily transcendental anthropology; every *onto*logy is ont*ology*.

If one wishes to avoid falling into a heretical and positivistic fideism, what has been said must be applied also to revealed theology. Revealed theology has the human spirit's transcendental and limitless horizon as its inner motive and as the precondition of its existence. It is only because of this transcendental horizon that something like 'God' can be understood at all. 'Natural', 'philosophical' theology is first and last not one sphere of study side by side with revealed theology, as if both could be pursued quite independently of each other, but an internal factor of revealed theology itself; if philosophical theology, however, is transcendental anthropology, so is revealed theology too.

However, the thesis in question can be given a still more direct theological basis. Firstly, revelation is revelation of salvation and therefore theology is essentially salvation theology. What is revealed and then pondered upon in theology is not an arbitrary matter, but something which is intended for man's salvation. By this statement we do not imply the sort of principle (as in the case of a 'fundamentalism') according to which certain objects can be excluded at the outset from the sphere of possible revelation, for what salvation really is is determined materially for the first time in the event of revelation. But the statement must be taken seriously. Only those things can belong to man's salvation which, when lacking, injure his 'being' and wholeness. Otherwise he could eschew salvation without thereby being in danger of losing it. This does not entail a rationalistic and unhistorical reduction of man to the status of an abstract transcendental being in his merely formal structure as such, as if what is historical and not deducible and what is experienced concretely *a posteriori* had no significance for salvation. It means that everything of significance for salvation is to be illuminated by referring it back to this transcendental being (which is not the same as *deducing* the significance *from* the transcendental being). In this sense, 'reduction' does not mean diminution but the process of establishing by reflex investigation. A comparison may clarify what is meant: the concrete beloved person who is the object of my love and in whom it is realized (and without whom it does not exist) cannot be deduced *a priori* from human possibilities, but is rather a historical occurrence, an indissoluble fact which has to be accepted. But in spite of this, such love for this concrete person can only be understood when one comprehends man as the being who must of necessity fulfil himself in love in order to be true to his nature. Even the most unpredictable, concrete love, occurring in history, must therefore be understood transcendentally in this way, in order that it may be what it should be. And this applies above all in the case of salvation. For even if this is a historical event, what it concerns is precisely man's actual nature; it is his nature which is to be consummated in salvation or the loss of it. If revelation and theology are essentially concerned with salvation as such, theology's structure when confronted with any object whatsoever is bound to imply the question as to man's nature, in so far as this nature is susceptible to 'saving' influence from the object involved. In other words, a theological object's significance for salvation (which is a necessary factor in any theological object) can only be investigated by inquiring at the same time as to man's *saving receptivity for* this object. However, this receptivity must not be investigated only 'in the abstract' nor merely presupposed in its most general aspects. It must be reflected upon with reference to the concrete object concerned, which is only *theologically relevant* as a result of and for the purpose of this receptiveness for salvation. Thereby the object also to some extent lays down the conditions for such receptiveness.

In addition to these more formal considerations there is a decisive and clearly outlined issue. The Council's Decree on Ecumenism emphasises that not all articles of faith in the 'hierarchy' of truths are equally close to the 'fundamentals' of the Christian Faith. Thus according to the Council there is a foundation, an inner core in the reality of faith, to which all other realities (and articles of faith) are related. In the nature of the case this 'foundation' can only be God himself in so far as he is our salvation through his absolute self-communication, i.e. what we in theology usually call 'uncreated grace'. Salvation is mediated exclusively in and through this grace. Grace must therefore belong at least to the core of the salvation/revelation reality. If grace and the Trinity are understood, the reality of the triune God as such is given as well. For a full understanding of this grace another important condition must be presupposed: this grace is the grace of *Christ* (and he is not merely external to it as the reason for its being conferred), even in the case of prelapsarian grace. At the same time this means that, within the history of grace (as the self-communication of God acting freely in history), the history of humanity has come *in Christ* to its own historical and eschatological apogee, irreversibly manifested. If Trinity and Incarnation are implicit in the mystery of grace, it becomes intelligible that grace not only *belongs to* the core of the salvation/revelation reality, but *is* this core. (Of course the same could be said of the Trinity, especially *qua* 'economic' Trinity, and also of Christ as the apogee of God's self-communication to the world, precisely because these three realities mutually imply each other.)

Now it is only possible to speak of this grace in a meaningful way at all within a transcendental anthropological context. For, without destroying the fact that grace is God himself in self-communication, grace is not a 'thing' but—as communicated grace—a conditioning of the spiritual and intellectual subject as such to a direct relationship with God. The most objective reality of salvation is at the same time necessarily the most subjective: the direct relationship of the subject with God through God himself. If what 'grace' is must not merely be expressed in a mythological-sounding verbalism which communicates no experience, it can only be understood from the point of view of the subject, with his transcendental nature, experienced as being-in-reference-to the reality of absolute truth and free-ranging, infinite, absolutely valid love. It can only be understood in one's innermost regions as an immediacy before the absolute mystery of God, i.e. as the absolute realisation of man's transcendental nature itself, made possible by God in his self-communication.

Without an ontology of the transcendental subject a theology of grace (and hence all theology whatsoever) remains fixed in a pre-theological picture-language and cannot give evidence of a starting-point for transcendental experience. This transcendental experience is indispensable today if theology is to do justice to modern man's question as to whether all the talk of 'Divinization', 'Sonship', 'God's Indwelling' etc. is not merely poetic concepts and indemonstrable mythology. Let us emphasise once more that this transcendental direction in the theology of grace means a similar direction for the whole of theology. For today even ontic Christology itself (in spite of its abiding validity) urgently needs translating into an onto-logical Christology, i.e. one which at the outset understands the 'nature' to be assumed not as a thing but as a transcendental spiritual quality. Since nature and being not only 'has', but *is* actuality and transcendence, the substantial unity with the Logos must be basically expressible in the terms of actuality and transcendence. It must be translated into these terms in order that what is meant by the 'Hypostatic Union' is said really clearly enough and is sufficiently protected from being misunderstood as mythology. All theology stands in need of this transcendental and anthropological change of direction because all theology is dependent upon the mutually determining doctrines of the Trinity, Grace and Incarnation, and these three basic doctrines today fundamentally require a transcendental approach.

2. A considerable objection could be made against what has been said: if it really is so necessary for all theology, surely there must always have been this kind of transcendental anthropological programme and method of investigation?—for good theology has not emerged today for the first time. Since, however, there has clearly been no such investigation, the demand for it cannot be legitimate.

First of all we must draw attention to the very basic difference between proclamation and theology, although in practice proclamation always contains an element of theological reflection, and conversely theology can never adequately transmute the proclamation into theological reflection. Modern theological eschatology for instance has been left behind almost totally in a pre-theological stage of proclamation. By and large the ecclesiology of Vatican II has still not progressed beyond a certain systematization of biblical picture-language, apart from particular sections on Constitutional Law. Seen from this point of view it is by no means *a priori* impossible that there is as yet no really scientific, i.e. transcendentally reflected theology in many areas and topics. Why should it be impossible? The fact that there is a lot of thinking, talking, writing and 'systematizing' in some way or other in theology (and this is all good and laudable in itself) is no proof that theology has reached that stage of conceptualisation and reflection which must differentiate it from proclamation. This qualitative difference only really occurs, however, where and in so far as there is expressly transcendental thought, i.e. where the *a priori* presuppositions for knowledge and realisation of the particular realities of faith are explicitly included in one's reflections, determining the choice of terms for theological objects.

At the same time we by no means wish to imply that this transcendental anthropological method has been utterly absent from theology until now. There can be no question of that. We cannot give detailed examples here to show how this transcendental method has been at work everywhere in theology (even if in different intensities), at least since St Thomas, even if it had not yet become completely aware of itself nor comprehended itself explicitly in formal principles.

But in the end whatever the historical facts may have been, we must say that today's *contemporary situation* demands a transcendental anthropological programme and method. Plato, Aristotle and Thomas will remain immortal philosophers from whom we must learn. But this does not alter the fact (even if the kind of philosophy studied in the Church has only taken notice of it in the last forty years or so) that philosophy today and hence theology too *cannot* and must not return to the stage before modern philosophy's transcendental anthropological change of direction since Descartes, Kant, German Idealism (including its opponents), up to modern Phenomenology, Existentialism and Fundamental Ontology. With few exceptions, e.g. Blondel, it can be said that this whole philosophy is most profoundly un-Christian in so far as it pursues a transcendental philosophy of the autonomous subject, who stands aloof from the transcendental experience in which he experiences himself as continually dependent, with his origin in and orientation towards God. But this same philosophy is also most profoundly Christian (more than its traditional critics in modern scholastic professional theology have grasped), for according to a radically Christian understanding man is not ultimately one factor in a cosmos of things, subservient to a system of co-ordinate ontic concepts drawn from it, but the subject on whose freedom as subject hangs the fate of the whole cosmos: otherwise salvation-history and profane history could have no cosmological significance, and Christological cosmology would be infantile concept-poetry. This inner dividedness is, however, not only a symptom of modern philosophy but of all man's works, and hence a symptom of philosophy in all ages; we must not let it hinder us from seeing what is Christian in this significant epoch of modern culture. We must accept the situation in all its fundamental essence, as a factor henceforward indispensable in a modern Christian philosophy, and so too in modern Christian theology.

Modern man feels that thousands of statements in theology are just forms of mythology and that he is no longer able to believe them in all seriousness. Of course this is ultimately false, but there are real reasons behind the impression. It is due not merely to pride and stupidity on the subjective side, and objectively to the mysterious quality of the truth and reality of faith. Let us look dispassionately at today's real cultural situation: if a modern man who has not been brought up as a Christian hears the words 'Jesus is God made man' he will straight away reject this explanation as mythology which he cannot begin to take seriously nor to discuss, just as we do when we hear that the Dalai Lama regards himself as a reincarnation of Buddha. If this modern man hears of two people dying in similar state and condition, and one is said to go straight to heaven because he happens to be the recipient of a Papal Indulgence, whereas the other spends many years in Purgatory because the Pope, as Keeper of the Keys of Heaven, has not opened up straight away; he will regard Indulgences, represented in this way, as a clerical invention against which his own idea of God radically protests. It will not be easy to convince him that God desires the salvation of all men, including children dying while not responsible for themselves, even *after* the Fall, and yet is unable to allow children dying unbaptised to approach his face because he cannot dispense with his own rule of the necessity of Baptism.

One could multiply these examples at length. There ought not to be so many. Furthermore, it does not seem to me that theology has dealt with these countless difficulties in a sufficiently intellectual way; above all, not in a way which holds out much promise for the practice of religious education. Let us repeat that in apologetics it is little or no use appealing in a positivistic manner to the 'mystery' actually revealed by God. If the *fact* of a verbal revelation were psychologically so absolutely compelling that doubts were utterly impossible, one could impose acceptance of its content in this positivistic manner as a mystery beyond all discussion. But if modern man finds the *content* of revelation unworthy of belief through the fault of theology, he will think himself justified, not illogically, in further doubting the *fact* of revelation. Incidentally these remarks show that we need to strive for a much larger area of mobility for fundamental theology and dogmatics than is usually the case. All these difficulties of modern man can be traced to a common formal structure: theological statements are not formulated in such a way that man can see how what is meant by them is connected with his understanding of himself, as witnessed to in his own experience.

Of course one cannot demand (and it would be heretical Modernism to do so) that the attempt must be made simply to deduce strictly all theological statements *from* man's experience of himself as if they were the latter's objectifying conceptualisation and articulation. That is not what is meant, although this problem is more difficult than the traditional opponents of Modernism mostly think for there *is* also an *experience* of grace, and this is the real, fundamental reality of Christianity itself. If we leave this question here, it must be remembered that the connections between man's experience of himself and the content of the statements of dogma must be conceived otherwise than simply as logical connections of deduction or explication. There are correspondences, above all by virtue of the fact that 'nature'—understood as personal, intellectual and transcendental—is an inner and necessary constituent not abstractly of grace *per se*, but of the actuality and process by which grace can be conferred. If these connections were uncovered and thought about as the subject-matter required by dogma, rightly understood, dogmatic statements would not only appear more worthy of belief from the point of view of religious education and doctrine; rather, thorough reflection on these correspondences would enable one to penetrate deeper and more effectively to the significance of particular statements and would lead to the elimination of latent misunderstandings, unsuitable schemes of presentation and unjustified conclusions. The discovery of such connections between the content of dogma and man's experience of himself is, in actual fact however, nothing else but the required change to a transcendental anthropological method in theology. Thus today's demand for it is founded on reasons of fundamental theology and apologetics.

2. Philosophy and Theology*

Transcendental anthropology recognizes that philosophy must always be part of the dynamic structure of theology. Just as the order of grace and redemption requires the autonomy of the natural order as an intrinsic moment within itself, so too the order of revelation requires the autonomy of reason within itself. For the Christian thinker must confront God's revealing word with his understanding of his own existence and of the world. Since this must always be the case, we will always find philosophising going on inside theology. This philosophising, however, will not be "pure philosophy." For, since the mind of even the anonymous Christian is raised to the supernatural order by the grace of Christ, philosophy is not a purely "secular" activity. The best of modern philosophy should be considered the self-reflection of a mind to which God has revealed himself implicitly through his grace.

It can be said to begin with that just as the concrete reality of grace includes nature as an inner moment within itself, so also in our question . . . philosophy is an inner moment of theology. Grace is not a thing, but a particular condition of a spiritual person (really of this person *himself,* even though not owed to him). As the determination of a subject, it is—as such—formally distinct from this subject, in fact in no way owed to it. But it can also exist *as* this determination of this subject, as a particular manner-of-being of this spiritual person. It can exist and be understood in this way only in the sense that through it the *person,* i.e. 'nature', exists, viz. exists *in this way* and is understood as being in this way. Fulfilment in grace is necessarily also fulfilment of the natural person. In *this* sense, therefore, the latter is an inner moment of the concreteness of grace, just as potency is the potency of *act* and act is the act of the *potency,* and both therefore mutually embody one another in the concrete so as to exist and to exist as such themselves. Grace exists by affecting a spiritual, personal substantiality, by being the divinising condition *of the latter,* and hence presupposes and incorporates into itself the whole reality of this person as the condition of its own possibility and makes it part of the factors of its own concrete being.

This is also the way in which we must understand the relationship between revelation and theology, on the one hand, and philosophy, on the other. First of all, revelation understood as something heard and believed, is necessarily also already theology. It may be only the rudimentary beginnings of theology, but it really is already theology. After all, revelation—wherever and indeed because it is taken as historical and

*From *Theological Investigations,* vol. VI, pp. 72-75, 78-81.
© 1969 and 1974 by Darton, Longman & Todd Ltd.

propositional revelation—is heard by a human being who already knows other things besides this revelation, a revelation which does not occur always and everywhere but only here and now. But the hearing of a message by someone who already has other knowledge can only be possible—since it takes place in the unity of this one person—in confrontation with this other knowledge, however undefinitive this confrontation may be; it is hearing by means of categories already possessed from elsewhere, a reception within previously given horizons, however much these horizons themselves may be altered by this hearing; in other words, it is already an active effort of thought by man; in short, it is theology, however much this theology may in certain circumstances be thought of as being subject also to the direction and control of the original process of revelation. Such theology, however, being a necessary and unavoidable element of the hearing of revelation and hence of revelation itself, necessarily implies philosophy, i.e. a previous, transcendental as well as historical self-comprehension of the man who hears the historical revelation of God. Whether or not this self-understanding may already be called philosophy in the technical sense is quite immaterial in the final analysis, as long as one admits that even philosophy in the strictest sense cannot be anything other than the methodically exact, reflected and most expediently controlled representation and articulation of this original and never quite attained self-understanding. In other words, anyone who admits that in the unity of the one subject, every bit of knowledge is also the function of every other part of knowledge possessed by this subject, and who does not maintain by this that every knowledge has to do with revelation (a point to which we will have to return), must admit that revealed knowledge is also the function of philosophy, given that philosophy is understood as the basic formula of man's self-understanding in so far as the latter is not simply itself an effect of revelation.

If, however, this relationship of dependence is not to detract from the dignity and autonomy of revelation and theology, then it can be understood only in the sense that revelation is the highest entelechy and norm of this knowledge, unified in the unity of the one subject and thus presupposes this different 'philosophical' knowledge—precisely *as* a different kind of knowledge—as the condition of its own possibility. Only under this condition is it possible to avoid the dilemma of considering revelation either as being dependent on a knowledge different from it or as having to be quite independent of philosophy. This is especially true since the inner objective reconciliation and the original unity of what remains indifferent in knowledge cannot be brought about by the simple expedient of falling back on the one objective source of both kinds and powers of knowledge.

This brings us to a problem which we cannot really consider in its *formal* nature more exactly, viz. the general question as to whether and how a being can presuppose another being—precisely in so far as it is *another*—as the real condition of its own being, and thus presuppose itself, and whether and how the other—precisely as other—can be the inner condition of an existent (without reducing this to the category of the relationship of efficient causality) and how one can recognise this kind of thing. We intend to leave this problem to one side and will turn again to our own more limited question. That something like philosophy is an inner moment of theology (and therefore also of revelation), poses no difficulties in itself, since every being can be conceived as constructed of different constitutive elements and hence one moment of theology might very well be called—philosophy. The difficulty, however, is to understand the fact that, and the way in which, theology distinguishes this moment within its own being as something other than itself and at the same time introduces it into its own autonomous being; this being the only way in which it can make it a real condition of its own being. The difficulty in all this lies in the fact that the indispensable *ancilla theologiae* can be such only if it is at the same time *domina* in its own house without the role of *ancilla* being simply a part-time job alongside the principal job of being master, and that this mastery is possible only through the services to theology rendered as *ancilla*. What is the reason for this?

We can make this clear by a series of connected theological reflections. We must first of all fall back again on the relationship of nature and grace, and ask: why cannot the reality called 'nature' be conceived simply as an inner moment in the concrete relationship to God, which is known as the order of grace, in such a way that if it is not given grace, it must always be thought of as always and completely meaningless and hence simply sinful? The answer is: because grace, understood as the absolute self-communication of God himself, must always presuppose as a condition of its own possibility (in order to be itself) someone to whom it can address itself and someone to whom it is not owed; which therefore means also someone who can be thought of without contradiction even apart from this communication. Accordingly, it must be said that since revelation is a moment in this free self-opening-out by gratuitous grace, it presupposes as a condition of its own possibility the one to whom this revelation remains unowed; revelation taken as the gnosis of the child adopted gratuitously by *grace* presupposes the servant as the condition of its own possibility. God has created the servant only in order to make him his child; but he was able to create the child of grace, in distinction to his only-begotten Son, only by creating the addressee without claim to sonship, i.e. the servant. In the same way, God has willed the truth of philosophy only because he willed the truth of his own self-revelation, i.e. the absolute, beatifying truth which he is himself and which for us is the vision which is the nearness and not the distance of the absolutely Incomprehensible. He could, however, only will precisely this divine truth which is given out and away from himself, as the truth which is a gratuitous grace and expressed in and out of love. For this reason he had to create the one from whom he could keep this truth a secret, i.e. the philosopher who, because he himself experienced God as the one who conceals himself, could accept revelation from him *as a grace*.

The depth of the human abyss, which in a thousand ways is *the* theme of philosophy, is already the abyss which has been opened by God's grace and which stretches into the depths of God himself; and this precisely when and where the philosophising man cannot attain this fact of his spiritual existence by exact reflection, when and where he cannot distinguish nature and grace in the accomplishment of his spiritual existence.

It follows from this, however, that where the official, explicit Christian revelation presupposes philosophy as the condition of its own possibility, and brings it into its freedom, this in no way takes the form of a positing of the *pure* possibility but inevitably takes place in the form of a philosophy already actuated to some extent by Christianity. This is so not only when men engage in philosophy who are explicitly conscious of being Christians but also when those men philosophise whom we might call anonymous Christians (and this applies in principle to all men who do not explicitly call themselves Christians). The anonymous Christians—whether they know it or not, whether they distinguish it from the light of their natural reason or not—are enlightened by the light of God's grace which God denies to no man. From this point of view, it is correct to say that in every philosophy men already engage inevitably and unthematically in theology, since no one has any choice in the matter—even when he does not know it consciously—whether he wants to be pursued by God's revealing grace or not. Only we Christians are on the whole too blind or too lazy to recognise this latent 'Christianness' in the history of human existence, of religion in general and of philosophy. Unconsciously we are often guilty of living in the selfish narrow-mindedness of those who think their knowledge is more valuable and more blessed with grace if it is possessed only by a few; we rather foolishly think that God himself only makes an impression on men with His truth when *we* have already made an impression on them with our thematic and sociologico-official and explicit form of this truth.

Before thinking this out further, it must be remembered also that the philosophy of the West has been freed to live its own life in a thousand different explicit and historically tangible ways by Christian revelation and theology. This is well known and has been stated often. Yet it is perhaps well to acknowledge that this does not happen only in patristic and medieval philosophy but also in modern philosophy right up to the present day. The philosophers themselves may often have been only lukewarm Christians or no Christians at all; their philosophy in its propositional results (which are not indeed the be all and end all of philosophy) may often have to be rejected in the name of Christianity; yet the questions, the development of themes, the opening up of new horizons in all this dialogue contain many more Christian elements than we faint-hearted Christians—if we serve more the letter than the spirit of a Christian philosophy—would be prepared to admit. One could say quite rightly that the turning from a cosmocentric objective philosophy of the Greeks to the anthropocentric transcendental philosophy of the moderns is perfectly Christian in principle and basically already begins with St Thomas; it would be quite true to say, therefore, that the ecclesiastical 'philosophy of the schools' has still much to catch up on and to save with regard to what has been developed apart from it, though without being fully conscious of itself, as a partial realisation of what in fact is possible only in the *kairos* of Christianity and yet is still genuinely independent philosophy outside the orthodoxy of the magisterium.

After these reflections, we now go on to presuppose that the Church —and secondarily, by derivation from her, the Western world—still have the historically unfulfilled and still valid mission and commission to proclaim Christ's revelation to the whole world and to the future, globally unified history. What follows then—under this presupposition—from what has been said up to this point, with regard to the philosophy of the West?

1. First of all, the West need not abandon its own synthesis of theology and philosophy in favour of an attempt to hand on the, as it were, naked message of Christianity without the so-called 'overlay' of Western philosophy. This need not happen because there can be no proclamation of revelation without theology and no theology without philosophy. One can only spread abroad what one has heard . . . but whatever is to be spread abroad, is heard only in the measure of its acceptance within the whole of one's own spiritual existence. An unphilosophical theology would be a bad theology . . . and a theology which is bad, cannot render its necessary service to the proclamation of revelation.

2. This does not mean, however, that the Western world should be simply allowed to extend its traditional philosophy in a traditional way into a world-philosophy, perhaps even with the tacit view that a philosophical garb which has become unfashionable with us, will still be good and modern enough for the barbarians. This philosophy is necessary and useful for the proclamation of Christianity precisely if it is adequate enough for the really sufficient hearing of revelation by *ourselves*. This is so, however, only if we attain this philosophy anew in and out of our own actual spiritual situation, which really is ours here and now, and thus when it is not merely 'the handed-down' but a creatively and newly fashioned philosophy. After historism, and in the age of microphysics and cybernetics, of a history which is becoming planetary and in an age or a more deeply structured society, etc., *our* own existential situation that is

to be illumined by philosophy is different from what it was before; and hence our philosophy too must be different. This includes even the philosophy by which, in the evening of its existence, the Western world must deliver the gospel message.

3. Furthermore, this situation which is also the *kairos* of our philosophy today, embraces also encounter with the existence and hence with the explicit or implicit philosophy of those to whom we, in the evening of our history, may and must still bring the ever-young message of the Lord. The listeners change the situation of the speakers, and this even in favour of the *Christian character* of our own situation as philosophers. As we have said already, there can be no philosophy which could be simply a-Christian. The Western message of Christianity, even by means of the philosophy which precedes and accompanies it, has also undoubtedly the task of furthering the philosophical self-understanding of the non-Western world and of helping it to become more conscious of itself and free itself both from error and the abbreviation of its self-interpretation. Yet, since the Western world, during its wanderings into strange lands while carrying Christ's message, always encounters a world in which Christ's grace has long been at work even though not called by its own name, the reverse must necessarily also happen if everything runs its proper course: the anonymous Christianity (i.e. humanity and endowment with grace) of non-Western philosophy can bring to light and eradicate abbreviations of its Christian nature in the explicitly Christian philosophy of the West; it can liberate latent possibilities of its nature which even Christian philosophy, in spite of its name and of its inherent possibilities, and even as a specifically Christian philosophy, has not caught up with. In brief, the proclaiming West can itself become more Christian and more philosophical by having to listen in order to become comprehensible. Whether and to what extent there thereby arises anything like a common Christian world-philosophy—or whether and how national and historical individual and incommensurable traits may unfold themselves in multiple philosophies which need not necessarily contradict each other and yet may be multiple—all this depends on the question (which we cannot enter into here) as to whether and how the unity and interlacement of the until now separated historical spheres will produce a homogenous and yet still and indeed even more differentiated world-culture.

3. Philosophy and Philosophising in Theology*

Contrary to the assumptions of dogmatic positivism and biblicism, there must be philosophising inside theology. The philosophising, how-

*From *Theological Investigations*, vol. IX, pp. 47-49, 51-62.
© 1972 by Darton, Longman & Todd Ltd.

*ever, can no longer be equated with the theologian's uncritical accep-
tance of one or other ready-made system. The multitude of philosophical
systems which exist today, the variety of intellectual and cultural view-
points from which philosophers look at the world, to say nothing of the
vast range of data with which the physical and social sciences confront
the philosopher, eliminate the possibility that any one philosophical system could give an adequate representation of reality. Therefore the
theologian must undertake his own personal dialogue with the sciences,
work out his own philosophical positions to meet the problems which he
must solve in the course of his own theological reflection.*

*The unavoidable consequence of this new way of philosophising within
theology will be a pluralism of theologies. For pluralism cannot be
avoided once theological systems are structured by irreducibly distinct
philosophies. Nevertheless pluralism need not lead to relativism.
Theological anthropology can justify a limited core of epistemologico-
metaphysical positions which will be unrevisable because they are the a
priori conditions of human knowledge itself. Yet the historically and culturally conditioned nature of man's empirical knowledge makes it very
hazardous to extend the number of unrevisible concepts and principles
very far beyond the limited number which can be grounded on the a priori
conditions of knowledge. Neither theologians nor the Church's magisterium can any longer refuse to admit the pluralistic and historical
character of theology. Both must consciously accept the problems and
opportunities which the historical and pluralistic character of theology
entails.*

There must be 'philosophising' within theology if by 'philosophising' we
understand the activity of thinking about the revelation of God in Christ
in the Church's proclamation, implemented with the support of all the
means and methods of the intellect and by relating the act and content of
faith to everything which man experiences, questions and knows. In the
last analysis it is not so important whether this sort of activity should be
called 'philosophising' or not. On the one hand one might say for instance
that what is meant thereby is precisely what is meant by the business of
theology; on the other hand it can also be asked whether, even if one
considers the secular material in such theology, it can still be called
'philosophy' today or whether something else has assumed the position
previously held by philosophy as constituting the secular element and
function within theology. This something else would not have to be called
'philosophy' if the word were to retain its historically given meaning.

We shall need to speak of this later on. But if we exclude these questions, I think that the statement *'Within theology there must be
philosophising'* retains an intelligible and important sense which is not as
common an assumption as one might imagine, at least in the practice of
theology. According to the statement, this 'philosophising' must take

place *within* theology. This ought really to be discussed explicitly, since it can be questioned whether theology today can assume the existence of a ready-made and thought-out 'philosophy'—as maintained in the theory and practice of Neo-Scholasticism—which needs only to be kept in view and 'applied' in theology, or whether this is to a large extent no longer practicable today, even if one has no wish to proclaim the 'demise of metaphysics'. To this question we merely reply as follows: *in actual fact* and thus for the purposes of instruction *there no longer exists today any philosophy which can be assumed as ready-made and already adapted to the needs of theology. This applies equally to the Catholic Christian.* In this sense there is no longer a Neo-Scholastic philosophy as a (relatively) complete 'system', since Neo-Scholasticism has in actual fact dissolved into a wealth of philosophies which, while maintaining a more or less conscious and productive contact with the Scholastic philosophy of the Middle Ages and the Baroque, have taken up such a profusion of modern themes and complexes of problems (even though in very differing degrees) that it is scarcely possible today to speak any longer of a *single* circumscribable Neo-Scholasticism, able to function as *the* given instrument and *the* given partner-in-dialogue of theology. And the reverse is true as well: as a result of its own approaches, methods and needs, theology itself puts so many questions and demands before philosophy as far as concepts and the possibilities of systematisation go, that traditional Neo-Scholasticism, as it was until recently and still is, is simply inadequate to meet these needs. Therefore there remains no alternative but to 'philosophise' within theology itself. We need only observe, on the one hand, that this is in accord with the essence of theology, and on the other hand that it implies no prior judgment with regard to an autonomous secular philosophy nor to questions of the present theological teaching curriculum.

Apart from this question, our first thesis contains a certain protest against a dogmatic positivism and a biblicism, two dangers which seem to me imminent today. There is certainly still a dogmatic positivism today. It *confines* dogmatics to the ordering and structuring of official doctrinal statements and—ultimately—to rendering the latter intelligible by means of the retrospective history of dogma. It does all this *only* within the terms, conceptual models and horizon of understanding provided by these official pronouncements. This positivism will not have been overcome as long as this kind of dogmatics works with the concepts and perspectives of a calmly academic Neo-Scholasticism and so cultivates a certain rational and conceptual skill. Of course, this dogmatic positivism exists nowhere concretely in chemical purity. But it exists.

Perhaps the biblicism against which the same demand is directed is only another form of positivism. However, it must be mentioned separately. Of course it is practically possible to carry on the tasks of exegesis and biblical theology in such a way as to be 'philosophising' in our sense to a more or less satisfactory degree. But if this happens, i.e. if what is aimed at is an understanding of the biblical statements, charged and confronted with the whole of the modern secular understanding of existence and the world, then biblical theology is obliged to burst the bounds of its own nature; not only because in this case official doctrine and the Church's historical development of dogma must be explicitly applied, thereby clearly going beyond the nature and capabilities of biblical theology, but chiefly because the secular understanding of existence and of the world must be the object of critical theological reflection.

Within theology itself, therefore, there must be philosophising, or, more simply, there must be radical thought, radical questioning and radical confrontation. That is at bottom the most edifying theology. For a theology of this kind needs to keep in mind its task of serving the Gospel of Christ; consequently it must not become an 'academic' curiosity, using the data of faith as objects of speculation without being existentially involved. On the contrary. 'Philosophising' goes on in theology as long as man radically confronts the message of the faith with his understanding of existence and of the world, for it is only in this way that the saving message can speak to the whole man as a free person.

A second thesis may perhaps be formulated as follows: *as opposed to earlier times, a 'philosophising' theology is confronted today with a pluralism of philosophies. It must take up its stand vis-à-vis them and work with them, but they cannot be adequately synthesised by each other nor by theology.* Theology today is experiencing perforce what we may be permitted to call its 'gnoseological concupiscence'.

What we have just said by no means implies the relativistic or agnostic thesis that there is quite legitimately a pluralism of mutually contradictory philosophies, fundamentally irreconcilable *'per se'*, or that man may well abandon at the outset the effort of trying to overcome his gnoseologically concupiscent situation by seeking to approach asymptotically an integration of the philosophies and thus a gnoseological integration. But while rejecting this kind of sceptical relativism we must not draw a veil over the unavoidable fact of the contemporary intellectual scene, that today the individual has to exist in an actual pluralism of philosophies, unintegrated and yet mutually coexistent, not separated by a cultural no-man's-land; this pluralism is present and will remain so. Secondary reflection on the matter has produced a new situation and the resultant knowledge has become, in turn, a further factor of the situation. There was certainly a pluralism of philosophies before. But they were either historically separated by the no-man's-land dividing different cultures from each other, or else they came face to face within a common and readily-assumed perspective of understanding as mutually contradictory philosophies, automatically rejecting and excluding each other, or else capable of being integrated and 'transcended' in a wider synthesis. Even when confronted with many philosophies, *one* man could develop *one* philosophy, 'his' philosophy, consciously proclaiming it as 'Philosophy'. If one does *not* have the idea that philosophies are intended for storage in computers and if one remembers that philosophy can only exist concretely in the individual's mind—a fact which no dialogue can change—one is obliged to say that there is today an irreducible pluralism of philosophies, that we are aware of it, and that the fact and the awareness of it are contributory determinants of the theologian's situation and therefore constitute a question for theology.

Therefore our reason for proposing the thesis is not that these philosophies are *per se* irreconcilable. In so far as they *are* irreconcilable they show themselves as false; that creates no new, previously nonexistent problem. Rather, the thesis holds because these philosophies, quite apart from the consideration of their truth-value, can no longer all be appropriated and known by the individual and consequently by the theologian, and because at the same time we know this fact as though in a *philosophia negativa* which is now not merely the consciousness of a materially empty field of awareness, but the consciousness of a historically present reality which has not, however, been mastered and which is in fact intractable. Later on we shall discuss how this 'concupiscent' pluralism of philosophies has arisen; not only from the actual mutual confrontation of the plurality of cultures in a world which has become one and which yet remains unintegrated, not only from the growing differentiation and complexity of the individual philosophies, but at bottom it originates in a pluralism of the human sources of experience, which can never be adequately comprehended. In the plurality of non-philosophical disciplines these sources of experience are ranged, as a matter of historical fact, in a variety of methods, problems and results which it is beyond the individual's capacity to grasp. This means that a comprehensive system of knowledge and education is no longer possible, even if one were to look upon the 'system' as an 'open' one.

Let us look at our first proposition: *today there is inevitably a multiplicity of theologies*. There have always been many schools of theology. This fact was not only tolerated but acknowledged by the Church as an expression of the richness of its life and of the development of the faith within the Church. This recognition is still important today for a right attitude toward the new phenomenon to which we are drawing attention. But the former situation—of the many different schools and approaches in theology—is not the same as what is meant here. The 'schools' of old were either largely separated by a cultural no-man's-land, e.g. the theologies of the West and of the East, or else they existed *within* a milieu which was to a large extent historically, culturally and philosophically homogeneous, common and available to everyone. Or, on the other hand, the 'schools' opposed each other in clear controversy and contradiction, so that one had to *and was able to* decide in favour of one and against another; or else they could be comprehended and marshalled from a common standpoint of the kind we have mentioned, and thus to a large extent could be positively integrated into a higher unity. These former schools and approaches with their demarcated historical outlines do not really exist any longer today.

If we are correct in what we have said about the practical impossibility of integrating the pluralism of philosophies in our historical situation —which we have seen as 'gnoseologically concupiscent'—then there exists today a pluralism of theologies in a much more radical sense, presupposing that we must always 'philosophise' in theology. What present-day theologian seriously has a simultaneous, accurate and sufficiently deep understanding of Scholastic Philosophy and its origins; Transcendental Philosophy in all its profoundly different forms; Existential Philosophy; the various impulses, issues, tendencies, new analyses and perspectives legitimately contributed by Marxist Philosophy; modern Philosophy of Language and hermeneutics; the philosophy which seeks to elucidate theoretically the relation between the plurality of modern sciences; and the philosophies of the East, now appearing on the scene of world civilisation as known but as yet uncomprehended quantities? Above all, who has any knowledge which is at all reliable concerning those particular modes of understanding of the world and of existence which are produced directly by the sciences as such without the mediation of a philosophy, and which are lived out eminently practically and 'unphilosophically', refusing to accept any self-reflection mediated by philosophical theory? Noone. We may say that one must nonetheless know something about all these things. That may be true. But to follow this imperative means in practice that the individual merely acquires a denatured and second-hand version of what really needs to be lived and known. We may say that even today theology together with faith must reflect upon its sphere of origin, which lies deeper and more fundamentally in human existence, *prior* to this plurality of understanding of the world and of existence. Thus theology can and must be seen as the study of faith at a level prior to that of the profane sciences, speaking to man before he 'goes out' into the unintegrable pluralism which is his existence and his world. That may be equally correct, and it may provide the impetus to a new and more original self-interpretation of theology. Theology is then no longer understood primarily as a revealed synthesis and amplification of the profane view of existence, which it surpasses, but as its deeper source and thus also as the slender root which alone makes possible such pluralistic and unintegrable interpretations of existence. The result of this theology is not a synthesis of the pluralistic experiences of existence, but a transferring of them to the intractable mystery of God in humility and hope. It may even be that, starting from this sort of consideration, we may be able to grasp the nature of what is called the 'basic theological course' which is the subject of much discussion, but which is hardly understood at all.

However, all this does not change the fact that, on account of the unintegrable plurality of modern experiences of existence, side by side with each other, mutually acknowledged and yet not really *known,* there are or will be many theologies. It will no longer be possible to apply oneself to clearing up their differences and dissolving them in another synthesis. For ultimately it is in practice impossible to distinguish adequately between what is common to all men's understanding of existence—and there certainly is such a thing—and its plurality of historical appearances. Therefore there cannot be a theology which *only* works with this common material. Every theologian will bring to his theology the particular form, the historical and fragmentary nature of his own given understanding of existence. He will no longer entertain the innocent näiveté of earlier times in thinking that his contribution alone is what is important and decisive, truly metaphysical and supra-historical, and that further distinctions are peripheral and matters of small moment.

In speaking of many theologies we emphatically do not mean that they exist as mutually delimited and separable. In that case they would resemble the old theological schools: one theology is acquainted with the other; they are mutually distinct and contradictory. The modern pluralism of philosophies and theologies consists rather in the fact that no clear, coherent, individual pictures can be formed any longer. Each theology and philosophy knows too much to be merely itself, and too little to become the only Theology or Philosophy.

A second-order situation has arisen in this cultural 'concupiscence': previously what constituted a situation's promise was that there was something in it which remained unreflected, not amenable to objective presentation; today it is precisely what has been once objectified and the subject of reflection which eludes us. Previously it was the as yet unconquered future—nowadays it is the uncontrollable past. If one wishes to say anything 'new' in this field, one does so with the fear that it merely *seems* new because one does not know enough and therefore cannot know that it has already been said somewhere at some time, or because it is unimportant and second-hand erudition. As in a big city: there are *too many* neighbours for any *one* to be a real neighbour. We have a completely new kind of Alexandrinism: in earlier times it was possible to reach the end of a circumscribed culture; thereafter it could only be kept in order; beyond it were only barbarians (i.e. an unfruitful land, its promise as yet only dimly sensed). Nowadays we know that we have come to the limit of all possible kinds of old-style civilization.

We now turn to our second proposition, which draws the practical consequences from the situation we have just described: *the Church's teaching office has been put into a totally new situation as a result of the plurality of theologies.*

Out of this pluralism of theologies arises a new situation for the Church's teaching office, which we shall mention in brief; we cannot deal with its whole range of problems here. It seems to me that the position can be clearly seen if one compares, for instance, 'Human generis' with Ottaviani's letter of July 1966. In the Encyclical we can sense the confident awareness that it is able to formulate the opposing position unequivocally and to demarcate its own official doctrine by positive statements; in the Cardinal's letter we are aware of a certain embarrassment in the face of theological trends which are scarcely tangible and not commonly available or intelligible. Consequently it manages only to ask questions and to give general warnings instead of making doctrinal pronouncements. If we put the matter at its most acute: how is the bearer of teaching authority in the Church to give his verdict on a particular theology if he is *not* and *cannot* really be acquainted with it?—if he cannot really understand it except by knowing the profane presuppositions on which it is based and which he does not share? One may ask whether in the future there should not be ideally as many 'teaching authorities' as there are theologies. To give a very small example, are there in Rome the kind of consultant theologians, fully conversant with the ontological and existential presuppositions which have led to the translation of 'Transubstantiation' into 'Trans-signification' or 'Transfinalisation'? Can such specialised knowledge be expected and required?

We have already referred to a further important factor in the present relationship between philosophy and theology, and we now turn to consider it especially. *In future, theology's key partner-in-dialogue,* to which it will have to relate its 'philosophising' in the sense we have adumbrated, *will no longer be philosophy in the traditional sense at all, but the 'unphilosophical' pluralistic sciences and the kind of understanding of existence which they promote either directly or indirectly.*

This is in many ways a platitude, since it is plain that the historical sciences have already stirred up and changed theology more than modern philosophy has done. The natural and social sciences, too, by creating modern technological man, by their world-picture and the many questions resulting from it, have changed theology's situation to a profound degree. If we observe very little of this in our text-books as yet, it indicates a failure, not a legitimate detachment of theology from science. In spite of this we must inspect our proposition more closely, for it is not as natural and innocent as it at first seems. We do not intend to debate the question of the 'demise of metaphysics'. This 'demise' is indeed proclaimed in the most varied quarters, but in itself it is not a clear thesis at all. What is quite clear is the concrete pluralism of the sciences, which, with all their topics, *a posteriori* methods and wide-open field of activity, do *not* consider themselves as dependent branches of philosophy, however much they may have arisen out of Western metaphysics. These sciences do not acknowledge philosophy as the prescriber of their fields of operation, but rather as one of the factors involved in actual practice and as the necessary spur of criticism. Thus they take their decision about their understanding of existence *before* philosophy is able to have its say. At most it is accepted as reflection on the pluralism of these sciences and their methods, and it is only regarded by them as valid in the role of a formal theory of science.

Even if one submits modern science's understanding of itself to critical examination, questioning the transcendental *a priori* conditions of all science whatsoever, considering the ontological implications of a formal theory of science and thus drawing up an ontology of a particular kind, the fact remains that *earlier theology had as its only standard partner-in-dialogue a* single *philosophy, united in spite of all its internal tensions and controversies*. Although this was in fact the product of history, its historical conditioning had not yet become the subject of reflection by a positive historical science; philosophy had a history, but its history was not something which called philosophy itself in question. To the extent that there already were sciences in the mediaeval 'Universitas litterarum', they had scarcely any theological relevance. Today things are different: there are sciences which consider themselves no longer as tools and handmaids of philosophy, but they are relevant to theology; most important of all, theology no longer lives in the context of a *single* philosophy, established as the primary and autonomous standard. Philosophy may not conceive itself as a 'complete system'; it must be aware that it cannot adequately reproduce man's total potential and therefore cannot be his absolute lord and master. This applies *today* chiefly because the sciences are fellow-contributors to man's understanding of himself without having been empowered to be so by philosophy. They perform this function by *doing things,* reaching out in power and grasping the future, and consequently they exhibit a very problematical relation to the abiding 'essence' of man. How far this view of science is justified, how far it can be called in question by criticism—in turn implying philosophy, which thus enters into a new stage of self-understanding—these matters need not concern us at the moment, for in any case theology must pursue its task in its *actual* situation and can do nothing to alter it immediately. At least in the concrete situation determined by the cultural, intellectual, social and natural sciences, it is science, no longer mediated by philosophy, which constitutes theology's partner-in-dialogue. If this is only visible to a very modest and limited degree in theology as it appears at present—and then mainly in isolated particulars, not in a confrontation with the 'spirit', the 'ethos' of these sciences with their 'openness' towards what cannot be predicted in the world—it says nothing against our thesis but against theology as it actually is in practice. By nature theology ought to be more suited to *this* partner than to philosophy. For theology is primarily concerned with history and the future. Whereas philosophy can really only consider the facts of historicity and orientation towards a future in a *formal* manner, the sciences represent history and future; especially if one remembers that history and future are not *things* but are created by man and his practical awareness, and thus bear 'science' within themselves as an essential factor.

4. The Historicity of Theology*

In a word, if there is a history of revelation, then and only then is there a real history of theology, recognising a real historicity as one of its essential elements. Of course this assertion can be proved directly by reference to historical empirical fact. If it were not true, the theologian would not need to write and to study the history of dogma and of theology. But he does. And yet our assertion can only be proved, in the sense in which it is meant, provided that existing history of dogma and theology itself is not misinterpreted by the theologian.

Here too there is among theologians an unreflected 'model' of the history of dogma and theology beneath the surface which denies its true historicity. It is understood as a system of logical relations and consequences of the basic data of faith (*articuli fidel*), projected separately and in succession on to the stream of time although in reality they are timeless and supra-historical, capable of being reunited as a system. It is certainly the case, if this 'system' exists, that the concrete logical relations and origins of individual statements can be viewed and justified in a deductive theology of this sort. But this applies only if the system exists, only if the particular statement, the new or metamorphosed concept, the new dogmatic formulation already exists. (This is of course always the case in this king of logical, 'timeless' operation, but it does not thereby become automatically 'real'.) One only needs to ask the naïve proponent of such an unhistorical view of the history of civilisation to anticipate the future of theology in the next few millennia by means of his method—which he ought to be able to do if he is right, and yet cannot do—to see the inadequacy of this kind of rationalistic interpretation of the history of dogma and theology.

Our place is in history and it is only in its forward-moving course that we possess the eternal truth of God, which is our salvation. This saving

*From *Theological Investigations*, vol. IX, pp. 69, 71-72.
© 1972 by Darton, Longman & Todd Ltd.

truth is the same within history, but, while remaining the same, it has had and still has a history of its own. This 'sameness' communicates itself to us continually, but never in such a way that we could detach it adequately from its historical forms, in order thus to step out of the constant movement of the flow of history on to the bank of eternity, at least in the matter of our knowledge of truth. We possess this eternal quality of truth in history, and hence we can only appropriate it by entrusting ourselves to its further course. If we refuse to take this risk, the formulations of dogma wrongly claimed to be 'perennial' will become unintelligible, like opaque glass which God's light can no longer penetrate.

In addition, theology must not ignore the fact that on the one hand it must employ already given concepts which it has not itself subjected to exhaustive reflection, but on the other hand these concepts of pre-theological origin continue their history in the extra-theological realm. The content of meaning of the terms used continues to change and thus can lead to deeper insight or to misunderstanding when these concepts and words are employed in theological formulas. Nowadays, for example, on hearing the word 'person' we are bound by an almost inevitable historical conditioning to imagine something which is by no means safely allowable when used in the context of trinitarian and Christological dogma. This is the case even with simple words like 'marriage', 'bread', 'wine'. The subtle theologian may be able to look after himself to some extent in these cases. But what about the ordinary theological 'consumer'? All, however, have to bear the burden of history, which is laid on theology too.

V

Scripture, Tradition, and the Development of Doctrine

1. Inspiration in the Bible*

Rahner's transcendental grounding of the historical and social character of Revelation in Hearers of the Word *supports his theology of scriptural inspiration. The Word of God by becoming man made himself a member of the human species and so identified himself with its history. Therefore he committed his abiding supernatural word of historical Revelation to the supernatural society of his Church, the definitive, indefectible community of salvation which would preserve it until the consummation of human history. Consequently Christ's activity of self-revelation is ontologically identified with his establishment of the Church. For this reason his revealing activity continued until the Church was definitively established with the death of the last apostle.*

God's active inspiring authorship of Sacred Scripture is an intrinsic element in this formation of the primitive Church. Therefore God and the human author are both authors of Sacred Scripture because God's will to establish the Church reaches down into the intellectual, volitional, and spiritual sphere of the human author, enabling him to perceive correctly and judge effectively what should be written. Thus, once God's will to establish the Church definitively had been accomplished, God's inspiration of Scripture came to an end.

In creating through his absolute will the Apostolic Church and her constitutive elements, God wills and creates the Scriptures in such a way that he becomes their inspiring originator, their author. Let it be noted that we say "creating", for we wish to stress that the Scriptures originate not only on the occasion, or in the course of the institution of the Apostolic Church, but that the active, inspiring authorship of God is an intrinsic element in the formation of the primitive Church becoming Church,

*From *Inspiration in the Bible* (*Quaestiones Disputatae* 1), pp. 50-51, 54-60.
© 1961 by Herder KG.

and derives its marks from being this. God wills the Scriptures and himself as their originator. He achieves both because and in so far as he wills himself as the acting and efficient author of the Church. The inspiration of the Scriptures is but simply the causality of God in regard to the Church, inasmuch as it refers to that constitutive element of the Apostolic Church, which is the Bible.

We have not so far entered into the question of whether our proposed thesis could also explain the inspiration of the Old Testament. For reasons of method we have until now used data which referred primarily to the Church and to the New Testament. It could also be thought that the whole theory of inspiration might fail, since the Old Testament has also to be regarded as inspired in the same way as the New Testament. Yet our interpretation of inspiration could not be applied to the Old Testament. Therefore, either a different kind of inspiration has to be assumed for the Old Testament, which is impossible, or inspiration has to be denied, which would be heretical.

Let us first consider some points which are usually overlooked. Although inspiration and canonicity are two conceptually and materially different matters, they are not, therefore, independent of each other. And this not only because canonicity presupposes inspiration of the book which attests for the Church. There is also a certain relation of mutual dependence.

We may say according to our thesis that, inasmuch as God causes the Old Testament as the definitive image of the prehistory of the Church, he inspires the Scriptures and makes them his own as their author. In other words, because the Old Testament belongs *a priori* to the formation of the Church and not only of the Synagogue, as a part of her prehistory and as such remains actual for ever, it can claim the same validity as the New Testament.

Our thesis in regard to the inspiration of the New Testament is thus not abrogated by the fact of the inspiration of the Old Testament. On the contrary, it will be confirmed by showing that the longing for the New Testament belongs from the outset to the nature of the Old Testament and its writings. These books are subject to the same formative law as those of the New Testament.

Assuming that our thesis has been understood, we first intend finally to demonstrate that the essential elements traditionally postulated for divine authorship and inspiration are safeguarded in this conception; second, that we are now in a position to answer those questions which we posed in the first part of our investigation.

1. It follows from the basis of our thesis that God is the originator, the author of the Scriptures. By this we prove, at least, that God's authorship of the Scriptures, which is a truth of faith, is not in contradiction to our theological thesis.

God wills and produces the Scripture by a formal predefinition of a redemptive-historical and eschatological kind as a constitutive element of the foundation of the primitive Church, because and inasmuch as he wills and effects the primitive Church in exactly this manner. But to effect such a book is to be its author in an actual sense, because such an effect upon a book on account of our limited human vocabulary can even be described as authorship when we take into consideration that the divine authorship of the Bible is free from certain characteristics unavoidable in human authorship. The term authorship, therefore, used in regard to God and to man is an analogous concept only. God can thus be said to be the author of the Scriptures of the New Testament.

Regarding the major and minor of the syllogism we would add one remark. We have shown earlier that the current concept of inspiration, as it is explained by acknowledged theologians, may be taken as a very abstract, formal approach. How the elements of the concept of the inspiration are actually to be realized by God has been left open. We have said that, when God by himself only takes care (because he himself wills it in that way) that the human author under his influence should perceive correctly and effectively the judgement of what is to be written (*iudicium speculativum et practicum*), decides to write down what he has perceived, and undertakes his task, we have inspiration and divine authorship, regardless of how the execution of this divine predefinition is thought to be realized. But we may add for the sake of any worried reader that the complete form of the divine realization of the Apostolic Church is, of course, "specified" according to the constituent (for instance, Scripture) in the total effect (Apostolic Church) which at any one time has to be realized. It would certainly not be irreconcilable with our basic idea to require a special kind of divine activity for the realization of a particular constituent (for instance, the composition of the Book of the Church) which are not needed for the realization of another constituent. If then, for some reason, more is thought to be needed for an intelligible concept of inspiration than what we hold to be necessary, this would not contradict our opinion that the divinely inspired authorship is an intrinsic constituent of the divine foundation of the Church. Moreover, this divine impulse, joined to God's will to establish the Church, must always reach down into the intellectual and volitive, spiritual sphere of man, for without such human activity, no Scripture could result. Thus, in this sense it is in any case also correct to hold that there is necessarily an intrinsic inspiration, even if we may leave it open whether or not this divine impulse, which spreads in the human spirit, must necessarily have its starting point within man. The origins of a book are necessarily dependent on its surrounding world. Without it there would not be the intellectual sphere, which is an essential condition for its intelligibility. Indeed, there would be more of a divine inspiration if we allow it to proceed from the redemptive-historical situation, in which the writing took place. The marvellous work of God, who is his own witness in history, is the realm in which the Scriptures emerge. Being Scriptures they originate in a pre-defined manner, and by originating in this realm, they are, *eo ipso*, Scriptures.

2. Finally, we would like to show why this conception is more likely, in our opinion, than others to solve the many questions with which we came into contact in the first part of our investigation. It will then be quite evident that it was not our object to juggle with logic by including a narrower concept (inspiring authorship) in a wider concept (active and predefining composition by the Church), because both concepts have certain formal points in common (*praedefinitio formalis*), and because we would use the trick of considering the former occurrence as part of the latter.

It is, we trust, easier to understand how God and man can both be authors of the same Scriptures. It becomes clear that both authorships are not aimed at the same effect. God does not, as it were, want (*intentione prima et per se*) to be a "writer"; he is one, because his will cannot otherwise be realized. God can achieve his first and last intention only by allowing man to be a writer and an author. In the familiar interpretation of inspiration, God's intention would be achieved even more perfectly if man's function were but a secretary's. In our interpretation, the opposite is the case. A man intends to write a book, and he is to want to do this precisely according to God's ultimate intention. God's will is a super-natural and historical community of redemption, which finds its objective and self-realizing ultimate end in the book. And, as he wills that community effectively and absolutely, historically and eschatologically, and in an historical process beginning anew in himself, God *eo ipso* is, in a real sense, an author. Both authorships thus have a terminative difference and, therefore, they can both be linked with the same book, without either reducing the one or the other to some merely verbal, meaningless concept, or misinterpreting their coexistence as a joint undertaking. When we say that God is the *auctor principalis,* but that men are the *auctores secundarii* and *instrumentales,* we do not here regard inspiration as only one case of a relationship which could occur elsewhere, but we mean one unique relationship. In the writing of a book, we can have no other *auctor principalis,* since any *auctor instrumentalis* would in another case have secretarial functions or conversely any *auctor principalis* could in reality impel or cause the book to be written, but could not be its real author.

We shall also be able to understand more easily why the history of God's authorship has no continuation. In the formal concept of the inspi-ration there is no reason why this should not happen. To rely on God's free and positive will is theology's easiest way out and should be sparingly used. In the mere fact that God's revelation is concluded, there is, in-deed, no reason, for new books could easily be written even about a completed revelation and God could be their author. But if God appears as "author" only where the Church is yet "in growth" and has yet to be formed by divine, redemptive-historical and predefining action, then God's authorship ceases when the establishment of the Church is accomplished.

2. The Development of Dogma.

Transcendental anthropology can also link its understanding of the nature of theology to a coherent account of the development of dogma. On the basis of man's a priori structure as a social and historical hearer of Revelation, the close of Revelation can be linked to the definitive formation of the historical society to which the word of Revelation has been entrusted. Inspired Scripture therefore is the reflection of its human authors on the word of God in the light of their experience in the primitive Church. Consequently there is development of dogma even within Scripture.

Because of its distinction between man's unobjective knowledge of himself and God and the objective knowledge expressed through his universal concepts, transcendental anthropology can explain why the Church's growing understanding of the Revealed Christ is not confined to the rigid progression of a strictly logical conceptual expansion. The presence of the Holy Spirit within the society to which Revelation has been entrusted can account for the Church's infallible fidelity to revealed truth in her development of dogma. Theological anthropology's focus on the a priori conditions of conscious activity and of man's unobjective knowledge of himself, other men, and God enable the contemporary Christian to understand why the authentic development of dogma consists in the thematization of a progressively deeper unobjective penetration of the essential Christian mysteries which deal with man's personal relationship to God rather than in a widening deductive expansion of Revelation's conceptual content.

A. Development of Dogma Within Scripture*

For apologetics, and for the understanding of the history and development of dogma in the Church it is of supreme importance to reflect on the fact that such a development can be already observed within the New Testament. As Catholic theology is normally studied, we are accus-

*From *Theological Investigations*, vol. IV, pp. 6-7.
© 1966 and 1974 by Darton, Longman & Todd Ltd.

tomed, apart from a very few particular problems (perhaps especially in Christology and—naturally—in fundamental theology), to accept unquestioningly the Scriptures, especially the New Testament, as an absolutely homogeneous and undifferentiated quantity, a sort of Summa of revealed statements all laid down at once, like a code of law or a catechism composed in one piece under the same enterprise. We have of course to some extent an indisputable right to this method, which then goes on to prove individual dogmatic assertions of Church doctrine by means of *dicta probantia* chosen more or less at random from the Scriptures. Scripture, the inspired word of God, is for us as a whole and in all its parts an unquestionable authority; we see each of its assertions as dogma and not merely theology, and take each of its assertions as a legitimate starting point for our own theology. True as this may be, and correct as may be therefore the method in question in its positive bearings, it is none the less a one-sided view of Scripture and gives a one-sided method in our dogmatic work. Modern exegesis has taught us that we can no longer reasonably overlook the fact that within what we call one Sacred Scripture, and within the New as well as the Old Testament, the assertions undergo a history and a development. No doubt the contents of Scripture are all dogma, *quoad nos,* and not just debatable theology. But it is equally certain that we must affirm that much of this scriptural dogma, which has for us the quality of inerrant assertions of revelation, is itself derivative theology with regard to a more primordial utterance of revelation. We must not naively imagine that because of inspiration (which for that very reason is not to be confused with new revelation), each sentence of Scripture as such stems from a new original revelation, tributary only to an act of divine revelation which takes place here and now. Not every single sentence of Scripture was heard as it were on its own by a sort of direct telephone connexion to heaven. We may leave aside the difficult question, too little debated from fear of modernist ideas, of how an original revelation of God to the first recipients is to be conceived. But it is imperative to say that not every sentence in Scripture is this type of original revelation. Many assertions, guaranteed as inerrant at once by the Church of apostolic times and by the inspiration of Scripture, are theology derived *from* the original revelation. Since this is so, and since this derivative theology within the Scriptures still makes the just claim on us to be accepted as obligatory doctrine of faith, while it is itself a stage of development with regard to its own origin, there is therefore in Scripture itself a real development of dogma, and not merely of theology.

B. The Development of Dogma*

Now it may at first sight seem that this formulation of the concept of a

*From *Theological Investigations*, vol. I, pp. 46-49, 51-52, 56-57, 63-73.
© 1961, 1965 and 1974 by Darton, Longman & Todd Ltd.

change within a single abiding truth is concerned just with what could be called 'theology' as opposed to revealed faith. We should then be dealing merely with the human understanding of revelation, which as it were circles continually round this fixed point of Scripture and perhaps a few fixed data of (early) Tradition too: at once removed from it and gravitating towards it. Thus we should be dealing all the time with *theology*, with something which could never become the authentic and plenary revealed Word which grasps Revelation itself. Such a relation between Revelation on the one hand, and human understanding (always conditioned by time and situation, and striving to reach perfection) on the other, does undoubtedly exist. In relation to Revelation there is such a thing as theology, the human word which seeks to express and understand the Revealed; so that one can have no certain guarantee from Revelation itself that the attempt has been successful. But there is question not only of a theology which evolves and revolves round the fixed point of a revealed utterance which has been pronounced once and for all. There exists not only a development of theology but also a development of dogma, not only a history of theology but also (after Christ, if only in the same Christ) a history of faith; and this for two reasons. Firstly the Church understands her doctrinal decisions not just as 'theology' but as the Word of faith—not indeed as newly revealed but as the Word which utters Revelation itself truly and with binding force. Secondly this doctrinal Word can be understood within broad limits and at the same time not as a merely external, verbal modification of the original revealed propositions. On the contrary it is very often impossible to say that the new doctrinal utterance is simply the old one 'differently expressed', so that the individual Christian cannot invariably limit its doctrinal content *a priori* to what he himself could recognize as 'identical' with the corresponding declaration made previously.

We shall return later to the question as to how the difference (varying in magnitude, presumably, according to the matter under consideration) between an earlier and a later pronouncement of the magisterium may more exactly be understood *objectively*. For the moment it is sufficient to establish the fact that *quoad nos,* at least, i.e. for the individual and his private theology, such a difference can and in many cases does exist: that is, that at least in this one sense *quoad nos* a development of dogma does in fact exist, as shown in the actual practice of the Church when she proclaims a doctrine.

It is also relatively easy to see that a development of this kind must *necessarily* exist. God's revealing Word is directed through the medium of the historical process at the *total* history of humanity (speaking generally). For this reason the historically conditioned mode in which Revelation is appropriated at any time need not lie absolutely outside this Revelation itself. For the real understanding of what is revealed and its existential appropriation by men is wholly dependent on the transform-

ation of the propositions of faith, as they were originally heard, into propositions which relate what is heard to the historical situation of the men
who hear; it is only then that they become propositions of faith, emerging into the real, historically conditioned world of men as decision and
living deed. If these translating propositions are just theology and nothing
more, 'private interpretations' of the original propositions; if there
were no guarantee that the propostion heard has been correctly understood: then on the one hand the proclamation of faith itself could only be
a monotonous repetition, with a purely material accuracy, of the same
propositions of Scripture (and perhaps of a limited early Tradition as
well); and on the other what we have understood of it, in the situation
which is precisely ours, would be subjective theology—an appropriation of the faith, which is itself faith, would not come to pass.

It is a doctrine of the Church, though not in the strict sense a defined
one, that Revelation 'was closed with the death of the (last) Apostle(s)'
(Denz 2020 s.). What does this proposition mean? It would be false to
interpret it as meaning more or less that when the last Apostle died there
was left a fixed summary of strictly drafted propositions like a legal code
with its clearly defined paragraphs, a sort of definitive catechism, which,
while itself remaining fixed, was going to be for ever expounded, explained and commented upon. An idea like this would do justice neither to
the mode of being proper to intellectual knowledge nor to the fullness of
life of divine faith and its content. When we try to discover the profound
reasons for the completeness of Revelation, we begin to see how we
should approach the interpretation of this proposition. To start with,
Revelation is not the communication of a definite number of propositions,
a numerical sum, to which additions may conceivably be made at will or
which can suddenly and arbitrarily be limited, but an historical dialogue
between God and man in which something *happens,* and in which the
communication is related to the continuous 'happening' and enterprise of
God. This dialogue moves to a quite definite term, in which first the
happening and *consequently* the communication comes to its never to be
surpassed climax and so to its conclusion. Revelation is a saving Happening, and only then and in relation to this a communication of 'truths'. This
continuous Happening of saving history has now reached its never to be
surpassed climax in Jesus Christ: God himself has definitively given himself to the world. Christianity is not a phase or epoch of a history of world
civilizations which could be displaced by another phase, another secular
'Aion'. If formerly, before Christ, something took place in history, it was
and is invariably conditioned, provisional, something with its own limited
range and endurance and thus leading to death and emptiness: one aion
after another. The present always dies in the future. Each age goes by in
successive rise and fall, infinitely far from the true Eternity which abides
beyond: each carries its own death within it, from the moment of its birth:

civilizations, nations, states, or intellectual, political, economic systems. *Before* Christ even God's enterprise in revealing himself to the world was 'open': times and orders of salvation were created and displaced each other, and it was still not apparent how God was going at last to respond to the human answer, usually negative, to his own initiating act: whether the ultimate utterance of his creative Word would be the word of wrath or of love. But 'now' the definitive reality is established, one which can no longer become obsolete or be displaced: the indissoluble, irrevocable presence of God in the world as salvation, love and forgiveness, as communication to the world of the most intimate depths of the divine Reality itself and of its Trinitarian life: Christ. *Now* there is nothing more to come: no new age, no other aion, no fresh plan of salvation, but only the unveiling of what is already 'here' as God's presence at the end of a human time stretched out to breaking-point: the Last and eternally the latest, newest day. It is because the definitive Reality which resolves history proper is already here that Revelation is 'closed'.

Knowledge in faith takes place in the power of the Spirit of God, while at the same time that Spirit is the concrete reality believed: Spirit of the Father and of the Son, Spirit of the Crucified and Ascended, Spirit of the Church and earnest of eternal life, Spirit of justification, holiness and freedom from sin and death. It follows that the object of faith is not something merely passive, indifferently set over against a subjective attitude to it, but simultaneously the principle by which it is itself grasped as object. This statement of course only acquires its full significance on the assumption that the actual support given to faith under the grace of the Holy Spirit is not a merely ontological modality of the act of faith beyond conscious apprehension, but also has a specific effect in consciousness (which is not necessarily to say that it is reflexively distinguishable). This effect makes it possible to apprehend the objects of faith given through the hearing of the external announcement, under a 'light', a subjective *a priori* under grace (the formal object), which is not available to someone without grace. As is well known, this assumption is a controversial topic in Catholic theology. Nevertheless the Thomist view, which does make this assumption, seems to us to be true on Biblical and theological grounds, and we have consequently the right to make this assumption ourselves without being able further to justify it here. But if we do proceed on this assumption, we cannot allow that the unfolding of the Church's consciousness in faith is supported merely by an insight of a conceptual and logical kind and an 'assistentia per se negativa' (i.e. a protection against final error in this work of human, logical understanding) given by the Holy Spirit. It must be insisted upon that between firstly a new revelation, delivering materially new elements, and secondly an *assistentia per se negativa* which contributes nothing to the treasury of faith as it unfolds but only prevents erroneous decisions and *consequently* offers an external guarantee of the validity of decisions in matters of faith, a third possibility is open: and that is a development and unfolding of the original treasures of faith under a positive influence of the light of faith bestowed upon the Church.

If from this point of view we ask what tasks and limits are imposed upon the logical activity which can and does take place upon the original propositions of faith as such (i.e. in so far as the act of grasping them can be distinguished in any way from the possession of the concealed object of faith itself as an apprehended datum, in and through these propositions with the help of the Spirit as light), we come to the following conclusion: the faith of the Church is ever reflected anew in the propositions of faith. It discovers what is implicitly contained in them, the logical and real implications which result from individual propositions or the combination of several. These 'consequences' can be binding even from a purely logical point of view; but they need not necessarily be so.

To clarify the point at issue once again. We have so far tried to show that a development of dogma does *in fact* exist and exist necessarily. Further we have learned to see that it takes place in vital contact with that *res* which is the 'closed' plenitude of revealed reality, in a contact which does indeed include as an intrinsic factor an objective givenness of the *res* in propositions and the possibility of their logical expansion, but is not simply exhausted therein. The 'motive' force which is at work in the development of dogma and guarantees its correctness is not simply to be identified with formal logic. If there does in fact exist a movement from the earlier to the later knowledge in virtue of this force, then we must yet again and more precisely put the question how the earlier and the later knowledge are related to each other. There is of course no doubt that the objective realities grasped in both the knowledge which acts as foundation and that which is founded upon it, are really connected *in themselves,* the only presupposition being that the knowledge which has emerged is a genuine dogmatic truth. But this mere connexion of the (known) *realities* in themselves is not in question: rather it is the connexion of the actual states of knowledge. This connexion must be present. Not only because Revelation was 'closed' with the death of the Apostles, a fact that implies both the abiding plenitude and perfection of the Reality which is the object of faith, and in some sense the continual presence of the plenitude of faith in this reality as well. But also because if there were present only a connexion in the known object itself but not in earlier and later knowledge of it in faith, then there would have to be either a new revelation for the later proposition or an apprehension of the object independent of the earlier divine pronouncements about this object; now both these views are unacceptable.

Summing up what we have seen so far, we may say that the connexion between the original propositions and those reached in consequence of dogmatic development can consist in the connexion between something formally or virtually implicit in a proposition and the explication of this by logical procedures with the support and in the light of the divine Spirit, leaving it open as to whether or not this connexion must be logically compelling in every case 'quoad nos'.

But this does not bring us to the end of our discussion. So far we have with the majority of theologians tacitly assumed that the starting-point of a dogmatic explication is *always a proposition* in the proper sense. But that this should always be the case may by no means be assumed.

In the first place it cannot be doubted that there exists in the natural order a kind of knowledge, which, while it is itself not articulated in 'propositions', is the starting-point of an intellectual process which develops into propositions. Let us suppose that a young man has the genuine and vital experience of a great love, an experience which transforms his whole being. This love may have *presuppositions* (of a metaphysical, psychological and physiological kind) which are simply unknown to him. His love *itself* is his 'experience'; he is conscious of it, lives through it with the entire fullness and depth of a real love. He 'knows' much more about it then he can 'state'. The clumsy stammerings of his love-letters are paltry and miserable compared to this knowledge. It may even be possible that the attempt to tell himself and others what he experiences and 'knows' may lead to quite false statements. If he were to come across a 'metaphysics' of love, he might perhaps understand absolutely nothing of what was said there about love and even his love, although he might know much more about it than the dried-up metaphysician who has written the book. If he is intelligent, and has at his disposal an adequately differentiated stock of ideas, he could perhaps make the attempt, slowly and gropingly, approaching the subject in a thousand different ways, to state what he knows about his love, what he is already aware of in the consciousness of simply possessing the reality (more simply but more fully aware), so as finally to 'know' (in reflexive propositions). In such a case it is not (merely) a matter of the logical development and inference of new propositions from earlier ones, but of the formulation for the first time of propositions about a knowledge already possessed, in an infinite search which only approaches its goal asymptotically. This process too is an explication. Here too there is a connexion *in re* between an earlier knowledge and later explicit propositions. But the starting-point and the procedure are not those of the logical explication of propositions, which we first took as model for the development of dogma.

This case, which we are going to make use of in the field of dogma as a natural analogue for an explication other than that of the logical explication of propositions, must however be examined from a different angle. The lover knows of his love: this knowledge of himself forms an essential element in the very love itself. The knowledge is infinitely richer, simpler and denser than any body of propositions about the love could be. Yet this knowledge never lacks a certain measure of reflexive articulateness: the lover confesses his love at least to himself, 'states' at least to himself something about his love. And so it is not a matter of indifference to the love itself whether or not the lover continues to reflect upon it; this self-reflexion is not the subsequent description of a reality which remains in no way altered by the description. In this progressive self-achievement, in which love comprehends itself more and more, in which it goes on to state something 'about' itself and comprehends its own nature more clearly, the love itself becomes ordered; it has an increasing understanding of what must properly be the foundation of its own activity, mirrors its own nature with increasing clarity, approaches as its goal, with an increasingly clear awareness, what it always has been. Reflexion upon oneself (when it is accurate) in propositions (i.e. in *pensées* which the lover produces about his love) is thus a part of the progressive realization of love itself; it is not just a parallel phenomenon, without importance for the thing itself. The progress of love is a living growth out of the original (the originally conscious) love *and* out of just what that love has itself become through a reflexive experience of itself. It lives at every moment from its original source *and* from that reflexive experience which has immediately preceded any given moment. Original, non-propositional, unreflexive yet conscious possession of a reality on the one hand, and reflexive (propositional), articulated consciousness of this original consciousness on the other—these are not competing opposites but reciprocally interacting factors of a single experience necessarily unfolding in historical succession. Root and shoot are not the same thing; but each lives by *the other*. Reflexive consciousness always has its roots in a prior conscious entering into possession of the reality itself. But just this original consciousness possesses itself later in a new way, such that its life is now the accomplishment of that personal act of reflexive apprehension by which it has enriched itself. Reflexive consciousness would inevitably wither if its life were not rooted in the simpler basic consciousness, or if it were to reproduce this in every particular. The simple basic consciousness would become blind if, because it is richer and fuller, it refused to allow itself to grow out into a reflexive consciousness involving 'pensées' and 'propositions'.

The question now arises whether in the development of dogma there is to be found an interrelationship of types of explication, (analogically) similar to that which has just been indicated by way of example in the natural order. We believe that it is possible to reply in the affirmative.

In the first place it may be supposed that the *Apostles* themselves had a global experience of this kind, lying behind propositions and forming an inexhaustible source for the articulation and explication of the faith in propositions. Christ, as the living link between God and the world, whom they have seen with their eyes and touched with their hands, is the objective content of an experience which is more elemental and concentrated, simpler and yet richer than the individual propositions coined in an attempt to express this experience—an attempt which can in principle never be finally successful. The vivid experience of Christ's relationship to sin, for example, his death, his attitude to Peter and a thousand other experiences of the kind, which the Apostles lived through in an unreflexive and global way, *precede* the doctrinal propositions (at least in many cases, though also *only* in many, not in all cases!) and form a part of the original Revelation, the explication of which, already begun by the Apostles, is not of the same character as the logical explication of propositions. Even in the many cases where our Lord's *spoken* word as such is the necessary starting-point of the Apostles' faith because the actual content of Revelation is available in no other way, these words are heard in the context of a vivid experience of daily life in his company. And so, even in these cases, the concrete experience is an essential presupposition for the true and ever-deepening understanding of the words spoken and heard. These sayings are not in themselves explicit enough; rather they require the complete experience, which in turn becomes continually more explicit and reflexively intelligible as the content of these sayings is unfolded. An explication of this kind, then, is not just a matter of deduction from propositions: it takes a proposition which is offered as a conceptual expression of experience, measures it by the original experience and finds it correct by this standard. Nevertheless this experience depends for its realization upon its actually stating what it knows. The initial degree of self-reflexion in the experience may be slight but it cannot be entirely lacking. Every explication which has been successfully established in propositional form illuminates the original experience, allows it to grow to its proper stature, and becomes an intrinsic factor in the abiding life of this experience itself. Every theological proposition—in St Paul's Epistles, for example—is uttered out of the entirety of this living conscious contact with the incarnate God. *Quoad nos* the 'theology' of the Apostles is original Revelation, because it is guaranteed by the infallibility of prophetic mission and Apostolic inspiration as the new Word intended for us by God. Yet in a certain sense it is also, for the bearers of Revelation themselves, their 'theology', in relation to a more primitive communication made to them before, i.e. it is an explication and an inference from the most primitive data of Revelation. In their case at any rate we have the right to speak of a development of dogma which takes place not just through the logical explication of propositions but through living self-explication within a mind's possession of a given reality. The objective connexion between the new proposition and the old knowledge is not merely that between something logically explicit and something logically implicit in two propositions; it is rather a connexion between what becomes partially explicit in a proposition and the unreflexive, total spiritual possession of the entire *res*, so that the explicit proposition is at the same time more and less than its implicit source. More, because as reflexively formulated it elucidates the original, spiritually simple possession of the reality and in this way enriches it. Less, because it never does more than express reflexively and remotely a part of what was spiritually possessed before. This alone is sufficient to make it clear how one may conceive of the *full* consciousness in faith possessed by the Apostles and the primitive Christian community, and yet avoid anachronisms. It is true that men did not 'know' much then, if we understand by 'knowledge' a form of knowledge which is set up with the help of a reflexive, highly articulated conceptual system. There could have been for the most part so little acquaintance with a system of this kind that we may safely assume that it quite certainly would not have been immediately intelligible at the time, because concepts like this only emerge at a definite point in time and require a definite period of pedagogic activity to become intelligible. Yet at the same time all was known, because men had laid living hold upon the total reality of God's saving Act and now lived in it spiritually. Let us remember that in actual fact (if not in essential principle) greater reflexive articulateness of a spiritual possession is nearly always purchased at the cost of a partial loss in unhampered communication ('naive' in the good sense) with the reality given in faith (and which is still possessed in its entirety). Then we shall see that our more complex and highly differentiated consciousness in faith and the theology which corresponds to it need not fancy themselves 'superior' to the simple faith of Apostolic times! God allots to every age its mode of consciousness in faith. Any romantic desire of our own to return to the simplicity and unreflexive density and fullness of the Apostolic consciousness in faith would only result in an historical atavism. We must possess this fullness in a different way.

It may be urged that in the Apostles we have an exceptional case which can contribute nothing to the explanation of the connexion between old knowledge and new formulation, because the Apostles could only pass on their completed reflexive explication in propositional form and not their original living experience; so that in every age after them only a logical connexion between implicit and explicit in propositions could support the possibility of further development of dogma. But this objection has no force. It is not only propositions about their experience that the Apostles bequeath, but their Spirit, the Holy Spirit of God, the very reality, then, of what they have experienced in Christ. Their own experience is preserved and present together with their Word. Spirit and Word together form the permanent active potentiality of an experience which is in principle the same as that of the Apostles even if, because it is supported on the Apostolic Word handed down in Tradition, it is an experience, resting on that of the Apostles and prolonging *theirs,* which has historical roots and can never continue to live if it is cut off from connexion with the Apostles through Word, Sacrament and the handing down of authority. But just this 'successio apostolica', in a full and comprehensive sense, hands on to the post-Apostolic Church, and precisely with respect to knowledge in faith, not simply a body of propositions but living experience: the Holy Spirit, the Lord, who is ever present in the Church; the keen flair and instinct of faith, the acute sensibility which is a gift of the Spirit, ever alert for the true and the false in the sphere of faith, for what as formulated proposition is or is not homogeneous with the undispersed vitality of truth possessed in innocence. To this extent there exists here too, in post-Apostolic development of dogma, the connexion between what is implicit as a living possession of the whole truth in an unreflexive but conscious way, and what is always only partially explicit in propositions. It is only an explication of this kind that provides both the required bond with earlier explications, already propositional in form, and also the simultaneous passage to a new explication from the original experience through the tradition already formulated; and provides them with greater power and cogency than in the Apostolic age.

If we are properly to appreciate what has been said, we must first make a critical examination of an inadequate way of regarding propositions, all the more active for being tacit. An ordinary statement of everyday life, like those which appear among the propositions of faith too, is tacitly represented under the schema of propositions belonging to mathematics, geometry or formal logic. The latter have in fact—approximately speaking—a fixed content; it is possible—approximately—to *state* unambiguously and exhaustively in a few words (not only to know in an unreflexive and global way) what their concepts mean and what is said with them. Their content, as ascertainable in the form of definitions, is (more or less) identical with what is communicated in them (the object seen through them). It is possible to establish that they state or communicate *this* and *that*, so much and no more. Anything over and above this which it may be possible eventually to infer from them in the way of further knowledge is precisely—newly inferred, precisely then something else. It is possible completely and exhaustively to understand the manifest sense of the initial proposition or propositions and reflexively to exhibit their content without knowing anything about the consequences inferred from them. But this is *not* the case with a normal human proposition. It does indeed have a determinate sense which can be clearly distinguished from the sense of another or contrary proposition. But any attempt reflexively to declare its content comes up against an intrinsic and irreducible marginal indistinctness of this content: its reflexive interpretation does not allow us to state adequately and *exhaustively* all that is concomitantly stated and known in it and all that is not; it is easy to establish unambiguously the minimum but not the maximum of what may in fact be its intelligible content. The proposition is always a kind of window through which a view may be gained of the thing itself and implies in its full sense (as Com-munication) this view of the thing through the proposition (in its 'stated' sense). A proposition of this kind is in the nature of a window that has been opened to give a view of the thing; not of a package with sharply defined contents. For example, if I say, 'N.N. is my mother,' what has been communicated by this? What have I thought of here and *communicated*? The minimum is clear: what would make the proposition false if it did not exist: such-and-such a well-known biological relation. But do we mean by this that the proposition has nothing more to communicate, that when I spoke, I thought of nothing more and had nothing more to state? When I make a statement like this, there can and almost must be an abundance of other things in mind at the same time, globally and implicitly no doubt, but very really (as we have already said). But all this, in excess of the given minimum of propositional content, can concomitantly be heard by the hearer of the proposition: the specifically human character of the motherhood, the relation between mother and son lasting long after the events of generation and birth, and all the other circumstances involved. The hearer too, just like the speaker, looks in and through the proposition with the speaker at the thing itself, and sees what he sees in the things *as* the communication made to one who is taking part as hearer. He rightly hears in the proposition not just its more or less definable minimum content, but concomitantly all that further content of the speaker's unreflexive awareness not yet propositionally objectified; and he hears it *as* something known to the speaker. This state of affairs must not be mistaken for one in which further truths, themselves precisely *not* spoken or communicated, are *inferred* from the propositional content spoken and heard, on the basis of its objective nature and specific cogency. Of course this is sometimes the case, but it need not invariably be so. It would invariably be so only if the proposition spoken and heard were in the nature of a package with clearly definable contents capable of exhaustive enumeration. But if this is not the case for the speaker, whose speech takes place in and with a knowledge, not yet articulated propositionally, of the thing discussed; and if *this* kind of speech, *together with* its 'train' of what is not yet propositionally articulate, is intelligible to the hearer: then it is quite possible for the hearer to hear this knowledge of the thing too *as* the speaker's communicated knowledge, something had in common with the speaker about the thing, although not yet propositionally objectified. Or putting it the other way round, it is quite possible for the speaker to pass this knowledge on in propositions. It will then very often be the case that what seems to be something merely virtually implicit, from the purely logical point of view, will be in fact something formally communicated; it is not merely deducible as new knowledge (not stated) from some other (stated) knowledge, but even regarded as something in mind which is propositionally *not* articulated, it is in fact communicated and so understood; and this is true even if it is only made propositionally objective by the hearer and this operation is exhibited (not, properly speaking, performed) in deductive form. Suppose someone says, 'I, A, sincerely love B'; it is quite possible that this statement should be made with the *fidelity* of the love in mind, and should consequently also be heard precisely as A's express communication of his love's fidelity. Now if C says, 'A has affirmed his sincere love; *atqui* sincere love is faithful: then A is faithful,' it is only in appearance that C's knowledge of A's fidelity (derived from A's first statement) seems to belong to C alone, as a piece of reflexive, propositional explication; it is quite possible that in fact his propositional knowledge is a real ('formal') communication from A, even when it is not stated *as* a proposition.

Now it is not clear why this sort of communication should not be found in the sphere of Revelation: in fact, it must exist there too. Revelation too works with human concepts and propositions. Yet it follows then that we cannot ignore the irreducible distinction between what is explicitly stated on the one hand, and what is co-present in mind and communicated on the other. Its importance is felt, and legitimately so, where propositions and concepts are used to communicate knowledge of a reality to which we could not have access in our present state without verbal information: in Revelation. When, for example, someone says, 'Christ "died" for us', everyone understands what is meant by dying or death in this statement. But what is meant by 'death' in this statement is not (or more prudently: need not be) just a physiological exit. The whole human experience of death can be really *stated* (i.e. com-municated) and heard (not just deduced!) in this word, an experience which neither speaker nor hearer has ever translated adequately and objectively into propositions ('definitions' of death). If the hearer should ever arrive at a reflexive propositional analysis of what the word 'death' has always meant to him, it is then perfectly *possible* (though not in *every* case necessary) that what has been analysed in this way and minted into propositional coin, may still be conceived of precisely *as* communicated by the speaker. And this can still be so even when 'historically' we may grant that the speaker himself has never used a propositionally objective form to clarify his communication 'like this', or indeed if we grant that in his particular situation he *could* never have done so. If we believe a speaker when he says something, then it is still this very speaker whom we believe when what he says has been explicated in propositions, because this is just what he has (or could have) known and *communicated* (though not propositionally).

VI

The Theology of Mystery and Symbol

1. The Concept of Mystery in Catholic Theology*

The concept of mystery which was commonly accepted by theologians after the First Vatican Council cannot do justice to the religious and supernatural character of the strict mysteries of Christian Revelation. According to this concept, a mystery is a revealed truth which, although it cannot be understood in this life, will be understood in Heaven. This understanding of mystery is deficient for several reasons. It cannot adequately account for the religious character of the revealed Christian mysteries. Finally it fails to provide the theological understanding of the intelligible connection of the mysteries with each other which is required to make Christian Revelation a coherent whole.

Theological anthropology can derive from its reflection on human conscious activity a much more satisfactory concept of mystery. Rahner's use of this more adequate understanding of mystery to link the Christian mysteries into an intelligible synthesis is one of the principal structural elements of his system. God, as the Infinite Goal of the human mind, is the Supreme Mystery. Although unobjective knowledge of God is the condition of possibility for every act of human understanding, God himself can never be understood by any finite mind. He must therefore always remain the Holy Mystery even to the blessed souls in Heaven. The Beatific Vision consists in the immediate proximity of the Infinite Mystery, not in the understanding of it.

Even when the human spirit has been elevated to the supernatural order, God remains its mysterious Horizon, whose unobjective presence is necessary for every act of knowledge, but who is never understood himself. God remains the Free Creator who can be known only through the dynamism of the human spirit's loving self-surrender to him. Because God can be known only through an act of loving obedience, the Christian Mystery is essentially religious.

*From *Theological Investigations*, vol. IV, pp. 37-47, 54-55, 71-73.
© 1966 and 1974 by Darton, Longman & Todd Ltd.

Furthermore all the individual mysteries of Christian Revelation are aspects of God's dynamic self-revelation as Infinite Mystery to historical man. Through the Incarnation of the Word, God both revealed his Triune Reality and elevated man to the supernatural order by his self-communication in Uncreated Grace. Man's metaphysical structure as a social, historical, spiritual subject enables us to understand why, when the Word of God joined himself to human history as our Redeemer, he entrusted his Revelation and his grace to the saving community of his indefectible, historical Church.

Since the other Christian mysteries can be ultimately reduced to the mysteries of the Trinity, Incarnation, and grace, the Christian mysteries are not an arbitrary collection of disparate truths. The Incarnation, which is the manifestation of the ontological Trinity, is the ground for both the presence of the economical Trinity in man through Uncreated Grace and for the the continuing presence of the living Christ within his Church. Thus Christianity's three central mysteries are inseparable moments both of the self-communication of the Holy Mystery to historical man and of historical man's return to the Holy Mystery in love.

We start with the conventional notion of mystery as given in the current manuals of dogmatic and fundamental theology. It cannot be our task here to outline the history of the notion, and hence we do not deny that it may once have been richer and more profound than it now appears in the theology of the schools. But when we are trying to see all the problems which the notion presents today we may restrict ourselves without injustice to the average concept as proposed in the schools. There is all the less reason for quarrelling with this procedure because it can be shown that the notion of mystery as now proposed in fundamental and dogmatic theology, is more or less that of the first Vatican Council, which did not go beyond the usual problems of the schools, at least consciously and expressly.

How is the notion of mystery understood in the schools? We begin by noting three remarkable points. First, mystery is regarded from the start as the property of a statement. Then, there are mysteries—in the plural. Finally, this multiplicity of mysteries is comprised of truths which are *provisionally* incomprehensible. Of course, in the language of the Church and of theology, the object expressed by the truth, the thing to which the statement refers, is also called a mystery. This is obvious, and we do not doubt it in the least. But in the ordinary terminology, it is the truths or statements that have the quality of mystery, even though this stems from the object to which they refer. It is the *truths* that are mysterious. This is clear at once from the fact the notion of mystery is orientated from the very start to the 'ratio'. It is something mysterious *to reason*. No one asks whether the relationship which is thus used to clarify the notion is not too narrow and superficial. Without bowing the knee to irrationalism, and without restricting in any way the essential role of *ratio* in religion and theology, we can still ask whether the precise nature of *'ratio'* itself is quite so clear and obvious, and if not, whether such a concept may be used to determine the notion of mystery. And may there not be a more primordial unity of the spirit, whatever its name, prior to the division into the 'faculties' of *ratio and voluntas*—an authentically scholastic question (cf. St. Thomas, S. th., I, q. 16, a. 4)—and may not this primordial unity be the reality to which the mystery is directed and related? In other words, perhaps the will and its freedom have the same essential relation to the mystery as the *ratio,* and the mystery to them, when they are considered in their original state of unity with the *ratio*. Would it be then correct to assume that mystery and mysterious truth are one and the same thing?

Now in the terminology of the schools, mysteries are affirmations whose truth can be guaranteed only by a divine communication and which do not become perspicuous even when communicated by divine revelation but remain essentially the object of faith. This notion of mystery corresponds exactly to the standard notion of revelation, which, in contrast to the biblical theology accepted by Catholics and Protestants, is taken to be the communication of truths, that is, true statements. Revelation is of course and involves essentially the communication of truths. But if we take our concepts from the history of revelation and biblical theology, we shall have to add that it is by his *action* upon us that God imparts truths to us. The wider concept is that of a revelation which is action and event. This follows at once from the fact that in the actual order of things revelation, even as the communication of truth, only comes to us as the salvific action of God's grace in which he must first bestow on us the capacity of hearing his word of revelation and in which he imparts to us the reality of which the word of revelation speaks. The reality is spoken of only in the grace by which the reality itself is communicated, and revelation only expounds it and makes it the object of consciousness. Revelation is not a preliminary substitute for the thing, as if for the moment we had only a message 'about' the thing and not the thing itself.

Revelation, however, as ordinarily discussed in the schools, is purely a verbal communication and the concept of mystery is likewise referred from the start to statement and assertion, which are then distinguished from the truths of natural reason which can be 'seen', 'comprehended' and 'demonstrated'. Thus the special nature of these truths is measured not by the *'intellectus'* which forms a primordial unity with the will, but by the *'ratio'*, which in Vatican I and in theology is taken to be something well known and easily understood, and as the self-explanatory criterion by which these truths are to be measured. Hence it is said that these truths are not accessible to reason, that they surpass the created intellect

(D 1796) and that they remain obscure 'as long as in this mortal life we are on pilgrimage far from the Lord' (cf. D 1676, 1796). The silent presupposition throughout is that we are dealing with truths which should strictly speaking have come within the scope of reason with its power to see and *comprehend,* but in this case do not meet its demands.

The pronouncements of the magisterium in the nineteenth century, and the ordinary theology of mystery, do not go any closer into the notion of this *'ratio'* to which certain doctrinal statements appear mysterious. But its meaning may be gathered from the pronouncements of Pius IX and the Vatican on mystery. It is the faculty which of its very nature is orientated to 'evidence', insight, perspicuousness and strict proof, and seeks a very definite relationship between the mind and its object: the sort of knowledge which was the ideal of the 18th and 19th centuries and stems basically from the ideal of modern science. Now Vatican I and the theologians of the time and after it, do not say that this concept of *ratio* is a relative one, which needs itself to be critically examined, or is too restricted for the character of personal communication which is proper to revelation. They take the concept for granted and go on to affirm that mysteries exist and to define them as well as they can in terms of this problematical norm. In the same way, they take it for granted from the start that if there can be any one such truth which falls within the scope of conceptual assertions, that is, of clear-sighted reason, and yet does not quite meet the demands of reason, there can be *many* such truths or mysteries.

And so the mystery is likewise regarded as, strictly speaking, merely provisional. It is a matter, or so it would seem, of truths obscure and impenetrable for the moment but which will be clarified later on and so finally be adequate to the demands made by human reason for insight and perspicuousness. Both Pius IX and Vatican I state without qualification that these mysteries exist for us 'as long as in this mortal life we are on pilgrimage far from the Lord'. The nature of the mystery as well as its duration are limited to some extent by the *visio beatifica.* With these elementary indications we have not of course exhausted the theology of the schools on the notion of mystery. Much more could be said even on these problematical points, but this is enough for the moment to arouse our astonishment.

So far we have seen that in Vatican I and current theology the criterion of mystery is the *ratio.* Since this criterion is applied to mystery and its nature defined by it, mystery is understood as a statement and therefore as something that can obviously occur in the plural. In the light of this criterion it is also understandable that mystery is given a purely negative definition. It is a truth which cannot for the moment be raised to the level of perspicuous insight which is proper to the *ratio.* It is a truth obscure and veiled, accessible only to faith but not to reason. Theologians are of course prepared to admit that a mysterious truth of faith concerning an important reality is better and more significant than a perspicuous truth of reason concerning some unimportant earthly matter. But the (negative) act by which the more important truth is attained is less highly esteemed than the other.

But what happens when just doubts arise as to the adequacy of the notion of *ratio* presupposed by the theology of the 19th century in its definition of mystery? What if we must take *ratio* itself as basically a spiritual entity of absolute transcendence and therefore as the very faculty by which the presence of the mystery is assured? What if we must take the mystery not as the provisional but as the primordial and permanent, so much so that the absence or disregard of mystery, preoccupation with the seemingly known and perspicuous proves to be the provisional, which dissolves before the gradual revelation of the abiding mystery, as such, to the finite reason? What if there be an 'unknowing', centred on itself and the unknown, which when compared with knowledge, that is, with any knowledge not really aware of itself, is not a pure negation, not simply an empty absence, but a positive characteristic of a relationship between one subject and another? What if it be essential and constitutive of true knowledge, of its growth, self-awareness and lucidity, to include precisely the unknown, to know itself orientated from the start to the incomprehensible and inexpressible, to recognize more and more that only in this way can it truly be itself and not be halted at a regrettable limit? What becomes then of the standard notion of mystery? Can it be evolved *primarily* with reference to reason, the faculty of seeing the evidence of individual truths? Can it be regarded as a merely provisional *deficiency* in a truth? And can there be many mysteries?

It is in fact remarkable that in general the theology of the schools does not confront the notion of mystery with the doctrine of God's abiding incomprehensibility even in the *visio beatifica,* a doctrine obvious in itself and dogmatically assured. God remains incomprehensible, and the object of vision is precisely this incomprehensibility, which we may not therefore think of as a sort of regrettably permanent limitation of our blessed comprehension of God. It must rather be thought of as the very substance of our vision and the very object of our blissful love. In other words, if God is directly seen as the infinite and incomprehensible, and if the *visio beatifica* must then be the permanent presence of the inexpressible and nameless: then, since to possess the absolutely simple in its immediate presence makes it impossible to distinguish between what one comprehends of it and what one does not comprehend, vision must mean grasping and being grasped by the mystery, and the supreme act of knowledge is not the abolition or diminution of the mystery but its final assertion, its eternal and total immediacy. And the concept of mystery receives a new content, which does not contradict the standard notion but becomes for the first time authentic and primordial. It is no longer the limitation of a knowledge which should by right be perspicuous. It is an intrinsic constituent of the very notion of knowledge, and the old, traditional criterion of mystery is basically reduced to a defective mode of a knowledge which is essentially orientated to the mystery as such.

We meet the same type of problem if we take the nature of spirit as our starting-point. Spirit is transcendence. Spirit grasps at the incomprehensible, in as much as it presses on beyond the actual object of comprehension to an anticipatory grasp of the absolute. The 'whither' of this anticipatory grasp—which in the act of grasping the individual and tangible attains the all-embracing incomprehensible—may be called obscure or lucid. Its reality, indescribable because non-objectivated, may be experienced as a divine darkness, or greeted as the light which illuminates all else, since the individual object of knowledge is only present and definable in relation to it. But in any case, this nameless region beyond all categories, on which the transcendence of the spirit lays hold without comprehending, is not an accessory or a preliminary sphere of darkness which is to be gradually lit up. It is the primordial and fundamental which is the ultimate transcendental condition of possibility of knowledge. It alone makes categorical clarity possible in the distinct knowledge of contours.

If then the reason which gives shape and contour to the object lives by the indefinable; if the lucidity of the spirit comes from its being open to the divine and truly super-luminous darkness—what are we to think of mystery? Can it be regarded as a defective type of another and better knowledge which is still to come? Is *ratio*, understood in the standard sense, just incidentally and secondarily the faculty of mystery, precisely because of its almost too taut tension? Or is it, in spite of the obscurity cast by the standard terminology, the very faculty which is originally and basically the faculty of mystery, and only derivatively *ratio* in the ordinary sense of the word, as supposed by Vatican I and the theology of the schools?

We are met by the same challenge when we consider the nature of spirit as being *one* in the '*perichoresis*' (circumincession) of knowledge and love. The positivism which places knowledge and love merely *de facto* beside one another in an unreconciled dualism must be excluded. For one thing—no one knows why—the same existent thing is both knowing and loving. Hence, in spite of a real multiplicity of faculties and acts, this one being must have a primordial and total relationship to itself and absolute being: a basic act, whose components are the interrelated and interdependent acts of knowing and willing, of insight and love, as we call them empirically. But this must ultimately mean that while guarding the distinction between knowing and willing, we must understand the act of knowing in such a way that it will explain why knowledge can only exist in a being when and in so far as that one being realizes itself by an act of love. In other words, the self-transcendence of knowledge, the fact that it comes to be only *in so far* as it passes over into something else, must be understood in this way: knowledge, though prior to love and freedom, can only be realized in its *true* sense when and in so far as the subject is more than knowledge, when in fact it is a freely given love. This is only possible if knowledge is ultimately a faculty ordained to an object attainable only because the object is greater than the faculty. And what but the incomprehensibility of mystery can be such an object of knowledge, since it forces knowledge to surpass itself and both preserve and transform itself in a more comprehensive act, that of love?

It is the mystery that forces knowledge either to be more than itself or to despair. For as distinct from love it is the faculty which grasps the object to submit it to its *a priori* laws, the faculty of weighing and judging, of seizing and comprehending. But in so far as the reason is more than reason, when it is understood as a potentiality only to be actuated in love, then it must indeed be the faculty which welcomes the greater sight unseen, the faculty of simple rapture, of submissive dedication, of loving ecstasy. But this it can only be if its most proper object is that sovereign and all-embracing exigence which cannot be mastered, comprehended or challenged: in a word, the mystery. And mystery is not merely a way of saying that reason has not yet completed its victory. It is the goal where reason arrives when it attains its perfection by becoming love.

This consideration is not an attack upon a well thought out Thomistic intellectualism which is also Christian. For such intellectualism cannot deny that man as spirit is ultimately *one,* and that its plurality is therefore only intelligible by reason of a prior unity: *non enim plura secundum se uniuntur*—the multiple is not one by virtue of that by which it is multiple. So there must be one last key-word which conjures up the essence of man, not two or three. And this Thomist intellectualism cannot deny that in Christianity the last word is with love and not knowledge. For we are not saved by knowledge but by love, and this can only mean that the act of loving can be the entrance-fee to a life whose essential perfection is centred on something else than that by which it was attained. If one really wishes to be true to Thomist intellectualism, one must understand the intellect in such a way that love is the perfection of knowledge itself. If so, the object, even initially, must contain something which constrains knowledge to become love, under pain of betraying its own nature. Merely to say that love is aroused when the intellect discloses the goodness and appetibility of the object, would be to fail to establish a true perichoresis and to leave the two faculties without any fundamental unity. For, to use the language of St Thomas, either the truth would then be the good of the intellect, or the intellect's function would merely be to propose an object to be loved by the will, the intellect as such being unable to function further on the object. But then of course the question would arise as to how the intellect could even know the good as such, if it cannot as such be comprised by the formal object of the intellect. The mystery, being essential to the 'object' to which the intellect is primarily ordained, forces it either to consume itself in protest or to transform itself in the self-surrender by which it accepts the mystery as such, that is, in love, and so to attain its proper perfection. Thus the nature of spirit also shows that mystery is not just a provisionial limit of thought, as it usually appears in the theology of the schools.

These are merely the most general and formal aspects under which the problems posed by the standard concept of mystery may be envisaged. Much more could be said on particular points, but we restrict ourselves to the following brief remarks. There is nothing in the concept of mystery as usually put forward in theology which assigns it essentially to the *religious* sphere, which seems however to be its proper place. Mystery is usually defined as a truth which one could only hear from God, that is, from another, and as a truth in which the inner compatibility of the terms is not perspicuous either before or after revelation. But it makes no difference to the truth of a statement and my acceptance of it, whether the truth is presented to me by an encounter with the thing itself or by a communication from another. To learn certain truths, it may be necessary that they be communicated to me by another; and it may be impossible to deduce the truth of an affirmation by inspection of its contents. But this does not really prove that the truths in question are of such a nature that they are entitled to the name of mystery. We do not hold that two terms are certainly and finally non-contradictory simply because we do not see any trace of an eventual contradiction, that is, we do not hold the rationalistic view that a mere lack of contradiction in concepts is proof of a real ontological compossibility. There are therefore many items of purely positive knowledge where the *de facto* compossibility of the terms is known directly or indirectly, but without any really clear insight into the ontological compossibility and without any note of mystery being attached to them. Neither lack of insight into the compatibility of the terms nor the circumstance that they must be communicated by another makes a truth a mystery, nor does a combination of these factors.

This can hardly be gainsaid. For otherwise, to take an example, the statement that there was a river XY in Australia would be a mystery, because not being an Australian, I can only know about it if I am told. Or again, the statement 'It is possible to have a mountain of gold as big as the Matterhorn' would be a mystery, because I might well deny that the ontological possibility of this affirmation is really known and evident. Or at least the statement, 'In Australia there is a mountain of gold as big as the Matterhorn' would be a mystery for me. But this does not really make sense. Such concepts miss the actual phenomenon of 'mystery'.

And the distinction between natural and supernatural mysteries does not take us any further. For the so-called natural mysteries, when regarded clearly, are either not real mysteries at all, or they raise again the question of what makes them mysterious. Is the note of mystery sufficiently justified by the fact that they need to be communicated by another or that the compossibility of their terms is not apparent or by both together? But in any case there are many assertions which on close inspection fulfil exactly the conditions laid down by the standard definition of mystery and which still do not necessarily have that character of the *numinous* which is ascribed to the mysteries of faith in the strict sense. We are not therefore bound to say that the ordinary definition of mystery is positively wrong. But we can say that it does not work out clearly the difference between such statements as are normally termed 'natural mysteries' and the 'mysteries strictly so-called', which must obviously be kept well apart from 'natural mysteries'. The difference cannot originally be constituted by the simple fact that they derive from different sources. The nature of the truth and our relationship to it need some other foundation than the fact that the real mysteries must either be revealed by God or remain entirely unknown. We should at least be told why some truths can be known only by revelation and why this confers on the truths *themselves* a character which does not belong to the 'natural mysteries', explaining why the *mysteria stricte dicta* are not constituted as such by the mere lack of positive insight into the compossibility of the terms. For, as we have said, the same impossibility of insight exists also in a whole field of statements which derive either from experience or from a communication which is not a divine revelation.

And the case is not really advanced if we say that the *mysteria stricte dicta* surpass even the angelic reason. Even if we prescind from the fact that we should be told expressly and clearly why this is true even of the loftiest created intellect imaginable—and so given a definition of mystery based on the special nature of the truth itself and not on its *de facto* relationship to various sorts of intelligences—my own relationship to a truth said to be a mystery is no way altered by the fact that it remains a mystery even for another and perhaps higher intelligence. We have not explained why and in what sense something is a mystery to me, simply by saying that it is also incomprehensible to others.

Further, the ordinary concept of mystery, starting as it does always with mystery as a statement, gives no idea of why the communication of the mystery must always be a *grace*. But obviously there must be some relationship between the mystery and its communication to a subject elevated by divine grace, who responds to the mystery under the inspiration of grace. One relationship, as Vatican I says, is that the revelation of mysteries in the form of truths is necessary if man is called ontologically to a supernatural goal: grace demands the communication of mysteries.

But we must go on to affirm that the relationship also exists the other way round. The communication of mystery can only take place in grace; mystery demands, as the condition of possibility of its being heard, a hearer divinized by grace. But this relationship is obscured in the ordinary definition, which does not make it clear why a truth in which the actual objective connexion of the terms and the compatibility of the concepts involved can be known only from revelation, while remaining otherwise inaccessible to man, can and may be imparted only in grace. To say that this holds good only for the divine mysteries, and not for other such statements would be to admit implicitly that by demarcating the *mysteria stricte dicta* from so-called perspicuous truths nothing has been said about the real nature of the mysteries.

The problems raised by the ordinary concept of mystery, which starts with the proposition and so with propositions in the plural, can be seen still more clearly when we reflect on the silent pre-supposition that there can be *many* propositions in the nature of *mysteria stricte dicta*. From the ordinary standpoint there seems to be no possible doubt about it: if there can be any mystery at all—which may be granted for the moment—why could there not be many such? Why can there not be many propositions whose correctness can be known only by revelation and which remain obscure even after revelation?

However: a multiplicity of mysteries presupposes that each proposition has its own distinct content. They cannot all affirm the same thing, if they are really to constitute a number of propositions, each existing in its own right and different from the others. But if they are to have a really different content by which they are distinguished from one another *as* mysteries, then their sphere of reference can only exist where such primordially distinct contents, that is, distinct realities, occur: in the non-divine sphere. Even if we admit that man cannot express the absolutely simple reality of God except in plural terms, the basis of the mysteriousness of such a plurality of affirmations about God would still remain the same. It would still be the essentially mysterious Godhead of God. And the question would still be, whether the one and the same godhead of these many mysteries could really be the objective basis for *so* primordial a plurality and differentiation as is pre-supposed in the ordinary concept of mystery: a concept which more or less silently assumes that God could reveal as many mysterious propositions as he liked.

Let us suppose on the other hand that the multiplicity of mysteries was based on the multiplicity of really distinct and therefore created realities. The question then arises whether there can ever be a reality among created beings which by virtue of its natural constitution strictly as such can supply a proposition which is really a mystery. This question must be answered with a decided negative in any truly Thomistic metaphysic of being and spirit. By its very nature, any created reality must be such that some ontologically comparable intellect could be ordained to it: and for such an intellect, it would not be an absolute mystery. In other words, if being and consciousness, as Thomistic epistemology holds, grow in the same measure, there can be absolutely no created reality which would not be all the more conscious, all the more intelligible to itself, all the less a mystery to itself, the higher the level of its being. Mystery can therefore only exist where it is a matter of the relationship of God, strictly as such, to the created intellect.

Man, elevated by grace, is the spiritual being which is ontologically directed to the beatific vision. Grace, being strictly supernatural, is ultimately the beatific vision or its ontological presupposition. If then grace orientates its spiritual subject towards an immediate grasp of God, where knowledge of God no longer comes through objects and categories derived from created things, this essential quality of grace cannot mean that this immediacy eliminates the transcendental necessity whereby God is essentially the holy mystery. We already pointed out in our first lecture that God remains incomprehensible in the beatific vision, and that this incomprehensibility, because of the absolute simplicity of God and the relationship between knowledge and love in the creature, cannot be just a marginal negative phenomenon of the intuitive knowledge of God. The knowledge of the incomprehensibility of God must rather be one of the positive attributes of such intuitive knowledge. The beatific vision is not contrasted with pilgrim knowledge of God in the way that knowledge of the revealed and hence perspicuous is contrasted with that of the concealed and hence only vaguely suspected. The contrast is between immediate sight of the mystery itself and the merely indirect presence of the mystery after the manner of the distant and aloof. Grace does not imply the promise and the beginning of the elimination of the mystery, but the radical possibility of the absolute proximity of the mystery, which is not eliminated by its proximity, but really presented as mystery. Pilgrim man, still a stranger to the vision of God, can be deceived about the character of absolute mystery in God, because he knows the holy mystery only as the distant and aloof. When he sees God, God's incomprehensibility is the content of his vision and so the bliss of his love. It would be a foolish and anthropomorphic misunderstanding to think that the proper object of vision and bliss was something perspicuous, comprehensible and perfectly well understood, merely surrounded as it were by an obscure margin and a limit set by the finitude of the creature who must resign himself to this. What is comprehended and what is incomprehensible are in reality one and the same thing. The incomprehensible has of course its positive side. It has a blessed content which can be known even though it cannot really be expressed. Otherwise the incomprehensibility of God would be only a blank unintelligibility, the mere absence of a reality. But the knowledge in question would not bear on God if he were not grasped precisely as the incomprehensible. Knowledge as clarity, sight and perception, and knowledge as possession of the incomprehensible mystery must be taken as the two facets of the same process: both grow in like and not in inverse proportion. Grace and the beatific vision can only be understood as the possibility and the reality, respectively, of the immediate presence of the holy mystery as such.

Thus the first of the three mysteries which we have named, the Trinity, appears—if we may say so—as the God-ward aspect of the two absolute self-communications of God in the hypostatic union and in the grace which grows into glory. The truly immanent 'in itself' is identically the two-fold 'for us' which, because it is really self-communication of God in formal causality and not natural efficient causality, must be something of God himself.

If what we have just said, giving indeed only the briefest of indications, is really true, we may draw the following conclusions with regard to the main theme. The three mysteries, the Trinity with its two processions, and the two self-communications of God *ad extra* in a real formal causality corresponding to the two processions, are not 'intermediate mysteries'. They are not something provisional and deficient in the line of mystery which comes *between* the perspicuous truths of our natural knowledge and the absolute mystery of God, in so far as he remains incomprehensible even in the beatific vision. Nor are they as it were mysteries of the beyond, which lie or lay still further on behind the God who is for us the holy mystery. But they signify the articulation of the one single mystery of God, being the radical form of his one comprehensive mysteriousness, since it has been revealed in Jesus Christ that this absolute and abiding mystery can exist not only in the guise of distant aloofness, but also as absolute proximity to us, through the divine self-communication. The mysteries of Christianity, in the plural, can be then understood as the concrete form of the one mystery, once the presupposition is made—which can however be known only by revelation —that this holy mystery also exists, and can exist, as the mystery in absolute proximity. This of course we only know in so far as this absolute proximity has already always been granted us in the concreteness of the incarnation and grace. To this extent, the thesis here put forward does not necessarily include the affirmation that we could start with the abstract notion of the absolute proximity and self-presentation of the holy mystery, and deduce from it the incarnation and the possibility of a divinization of man by grace. The abstract notion of the absolute proximity and self-communication of God, if it is to be ontologically valid and not merely a logical and notional possibility, is and can only be attained in the experience of the incarnation and grace. But in this way it is still possible to recognize that these mysteries are really intrinsically connected, in their character of communication of the abso-

lute proximity of the primordial mystery. And thence it can be shown
(though we cannot go into it now) that the canon of the three absolute
mysteries, first arrived at by an *a posteriori* listing, is on principle incapable of further extension. There are these three mysteries in Christianity, no more and no fewer, and the three mysteries affirm the same
thing: that God has imparted himself to us through Jesus Christ in
his Spirit as he is in himself, so that the inexpressible nameless mystery
which reigns in us and over us should be in itself the immediate blessedness of the spirit which knows, and transforms itself into love.

2. The Theology of the Symbol*

*Another structuring element in Rahner's theology is his metaphysics of
the symbol. Rahner finds this metaphysics at work in those cases in which
a being reaches the fulness of its own perfection by "expressing itself" in
its "other" or its "real symbol." The "real symbol" is a distinct being
which, although it retains its proper ontological autonomy, is united to its
expressive producer's own ontological reality. Philosophical anthropology provided Rahner with his basic model of the real symbol. The human
knower, as we have seen, is a form received in matter. Therefore, if the
human soul is to reach its own proper perfection as the eliciting principle
of discursive knowledge, the soul must effect the emanation of its intellectual and sensible faculties from its own being through an exercise of
active causality. This exercise of the soul's active causality, which St.
Thomas calls* causalitas resultantiae, *is a prime instance of what Rahner
means by symbolic "self-expression." The other in which the soul expresses itself are the proper accidents which constitute its faculties.
The soul is present in its faculties through its active, emanating causality.
Nevertheless, the faculties are genuinely "other," since they retain their
proper autonomy as accidents, distinct principles of being. The soul
reaches its perfection in them, since only through them can the soul
exercise its specific activities of knowing and loving. Furthermore, the
soul is not only present in the accidental faculties through its emanating*
causalitas resultantiae. *As their substantial subject it ceaselessly sustains
them by uniting them to its own being through the exercise of its material
causality.*

*Thus the substance-accident relation between the human soul and its
faculties is by no means the static juxtaposition imagined by Locke. On
the contrary, the soul and its faculties constitute a dynamic unity which
can be held in being only through the continuous exercise of a multiplex*

*From *Theological Investigations*, vol. IV, pp. 224-30, 234-42.
© 1966 and 1974 by Darton, Longman & Todd Ltd.

causality. Nevertheless, the source and ground of this dynamic multiplicity is the soul, the human substantial form, which brings itself to its own perfection in the proper accidents which it sustains. Once Rahner's philosophical anthropology had established the dynamic circle of causality which binds the unitary human soul to the multiplicity of its faculties in the dynamic unity of a single nature, he was able to account for the ontological unity of sensation and intellection in the single act of human knowledge.

Rahner's theological anthropology extends his metaphysics of the symbol to a number of other cases in which a being expresses itself in the "other" which is its "real symbol." Through his manifold applications Rahner reveals the great potentialities which the metaphysics of the symbol possesses as a heuristic and ordering principle in systematic theology. In The Theology of the Symbol *Rahner gives an exposition of the metaphysics of the symbol and makes a summary presentation of its theological possibilities. He briefly describes how it can be used in the theology of the Trinity, the Incarnation, grace, the Church, and the sacraments. Subsequent chapters will show in more detail the fruitful results to which it can lead in a number of these areas.*

Our first statement, which we put forward as the basic principle of an ontology of symbolism, is as follows: all beings are by their nature symbolic, because they necessarily 'express' themselves in order to attain their own nature.

We should already be dealing with merely derivative modes of symbolic being if we started with the fact that two realities, each of which is supposed to be already constituted in its essence and intelligible of itself, 'agreed' with one another on a certain point, and stated that this 'agreement' made it possible for each of them (more particularly the better known and more accessible of the two, of course) to refer to the other and call attention to it, and hence be used by us as a symbol for the other, precisely by reason of the 'agreement'. Symbols would then only vary, and be distinguishable from one another, by the degree and precise mode, of this subsequent similarity between the two realities. Since in the long run everything agrees in some way or another with everything else, to start the analysis of symbols this way would make it impossible to distinguish really genuine symbols ('symbolic realities') from merely arbitrary 'signs', 'signals' and 'codes' ('symbolic representations'). Anything could be the symbol of anything else, the orientation from the symbol to the thing symbolized could run the other way round or be determined merely accidentally, from a view point extrinsic to the matter itself, by the human observer, who finds one aspect more telling than another. Such derivative, secondary cases of symbolism do of course exist, so that it is not easy to say where the function of being merely a sign and indicator so predominates over the 'function of expressiveness' that a symbol loses its 'overplus of meaning' (Fr. Th. Vischer) and sinks to the level of a sign with little symbolism. The margins are fluid. One need only recall that our numbers once had a religious and sacral character. Indeed it often happens that in a vocabulary more attentive to history of art and aesthetics 'symbol' represents a very derivative case of the symbolic. It is a feature of such terminology that the symbol (an anchor, a fish and so on) indicates a lower degree of the symbolic than for instance a religious image. We shall not discuss these matters further now. Our task will be to look for the highest and most primordial manner in which one reality can represent another—considering the matter primarily from the formal ontological point of view. And we call this supreme and primal representation, in which one reality renders another present (primarily 'for itself' and only secondarily for others), a symbol: the representation which allows the other 'to be there'.

To reach the primary concept of symbol, we must start from the fact that all beings (each of them, in fact) are multiple, and are or can be essentially the expression of another in this unity of the multiple and one in this plurality, by reason of its plural unity. The first part of this assertion is axiomatic in an ontology of the finite. Each finite being as such bears the stigma of the finite by the very fact that it is not absolutely 'simple'. Within the permanent inclusive unity of its reality (as essence and existence) it is not simply and homogeneously the same in a deathlike collapse into identity. It has of itself a real multiplicity, which is not merely a mental distinction and division extrinsic to the reality and only due to the limited intelligence of the external and finite observer, who only explicitates for himself the absolutely simple fullness of the being in question by using several terms (presuming that it would be thinkable at all under these circumstances).

In saying this, however, we do not mean to assert that an intrinsic plurality and distinction must *always* be merely the stigma of the finiteness of a being. We know, on the contrary, from the mystery of the Trinity—we are doing theological ontology, which need not be afraid of adducing revealed data: that there is a true and real—even though 'only' relative—distinction of 'persons' in the supreme simplicity of God, and hence a plurality, at least in this sense. Let us now further consider—in keeping with a theology of the 'traces' and 'reflexions' of the inner-trinitarian plurality—that it is quite thinkable that the pluralism of the finite creature is not merely a consequence and indicator of its finiteness, as a merely negative qualification, but also a consequence—even though not naturally recognizable as such—of that divine plurality which does not imply imperfection and weakness and limitation of being, but the supreme fullness of unity and concentrated force: then we may say candidly, though also cautiously, that being is plural in itself, and formulate this as a general principle without restrictions. On this supposition, we do not need to take it as merely part of the ontology of the finite as such. Even where it is applied to a plurality of the finite as such, we can take it as an assertion which understands even the plurality of the finite as an allusion—disclosed only in revelation—to a plurality which is more than an indistinguishable identity and simplicity. We should of course have to think of it so, if even our sublimest ontological ideals were not further directed by the self-revelation of the God who is still loftier than these ideals, and who by thus surpassing our always approximate metaphysical ideals comes once more, suddenly and strangely, that is, miraculously and mysteriously, close to us. It is therefore true: a being is, of itself, independently of any comparison with anything else, plural in its unity.

But these plural moments in the unity of a being must have an inner agreement among themselves on account of the unity of the being, even though the plurality of moments in a being must be constituted by the reciprocal diversity of these moments. And they cannot have this agreement as the simple juxtaposition, so to speak, of moments which are there as such originally. This would imply a denial of the unity of the being in question: unity would be the subsequent conjunction of separate elements which once stood only on their own. This would be to betray the profound principle of St Thomas: *non enim plura secundum se uniuntur*: there can be no union of things which are of themselves multiple. A plurality in an original and an originally superior unity can only be understood as follows: the 'one' develops, the plural stems from an original 'one', in a relationship of origin and consequence; the original unity, which also forms the unity which unites the plural, maintains itself while resolving itself and 'dis-closing' itself into a plurality in order to find itself precisely there. A consideration of the Trinity shows that the 'one' of unity and plurality, thus understood, is an ontological ultimate, which may not be reduced to an abstract and merely apparently 'higher' unity and simplicity: it cannot be a hollow, lifeless identity. It would be theologically a heresy, and therefore ontologically an absurdity, to think that God would be really 'simpler' and hence more perfect if there were no real distinction of persons in God. There exists therefore a differentiation which is in itself a 'perfectio pura' and which must be taken into consideration from the very start of a theological understanding of being. It is not provisional, but something absolutely final, an ultimate of the self-communicating unity itself as such, which constitutes this unity itself: it does not half destroy, so to speak, this unity. Being *as* such, and hence *as* one (*ens* as *unum*), for the fulfilment of its being and its unity, emerges into a plurality—of which the supreme mode is the Trinity. The distinct moments deriving from the 'one' which make for the perfection of its unity stem essentially, i.e. by their origin in and from another, from this most primary unity: they have therefore a more primary and basic 'agreement' with it than anything produced by efficient causality.

But this means that each being, as a unity, possesses a plurality

—implying perfection—formed by the special derivativeness of the plural from the original unity: the plural is in agreement with its source in a way which corresponds to its origin, and hence is 'expression' of its origin by an agreement which it owes to its origin. Since this holds good for being in general, we may say that each being forms, in its own way, more or less perfectly according to its degree of being, something distinct from itself and yet one with itself, 'for' its own fulfilment. (Here unity and distinction are correlatives which increase in like proportions, not in inverse proportions which would reduce each to be contradictory and exclusive of the other.) And this differentiated being, which is still originally one, is in agreement because derivative, and because derivatively in agreement is expressive.

That that which is derivatively in agreement, and *hence* one with the origin while still distinct from it, must be considered as the 'expression' of the origin and of the primordial unity needs some further explanation. The agreement with its origin (by reason of its derivation) of that which is constituted as different within the unity is at once, in a certain sense, the constitution of the derivative *as* an *expression*. For there is an agreement which is explained by the relation of being originated. We may therefore prescind from the question as to whether we must always consider such a derivation as the formal constitution of the agreement as such and hence whether we must always think of it formally *as* expression. Whether and when and why this is so in certain cases may be left without misgivings to a special ontology concerned with certain spheres. We shall meet such cases in the (second) theological consideration of the matter. But prescinding from this question, we may already affirm: every being as such possesses a plurality as intrinsic element of its significant unity; this plurality constitutes itself, by virtue of its origin from an original unity, as the way to fulfil the unity (or on account of the unity already perfect), in such a way that that which is originated and different is in agreement with its origin and hence has (at least in a 'specificative', if not always in a 'reduplicative' sense) the character of expression or 'symbol' with regard to its origin. But this brings us to the full statement of our first affirmation: being is of itself symbolic, because it necessarily 'expresses' itself. This affirmation needs some further explanation in the light of what has been said, and then its applicability to some well-known themes must be demonstrated.

Being expresses itself, because it must realize itself through a plurality in unity. This plurality is often, and in many respects, an indication of finiteness and deficiency, but it can also be something positive, of which at least a 'trace' remains even in the plurality which is given formally with the finiteness of a being. The self-constitutive act whereby a being constitutes itself as a plurality which leads to its fulfilment or rather (in certain circumstances) which is a reality given with the perfection of the being, is however the condition of possibility of possession of self in knowledge and love. *In tantum est ens cognoscens et cognitum, in quantum est ens actu*. This statement also holds good of course if inverted: the degree of '*reditio completa in seipsum*' is the indication of its degree of being. 'Being present to itself' is only another way of describing the actuality, that is, the intrinsic self-realization of the being. But then it follows that a being 'comes to itself' in its expression, in the derivative agreement of the differentiated which is preserved as the perfection of the unity. For realization as plurality and as possession of self cannot be disparate elements simply juxtaposed in a being, since possession of self (in knowledge and love) is not just an element, but *the* content of that which we call being (and hence self-realization). And it comes to itself in the measure in which it realizes itself by constituting a plurality. But this means that each being—in as much as it has and realizes being—is itself primarily 'symbolic'. It expresses itself and possesses itself by doing so. It gives itself away from itself into the 'other', and there finds itself in knowledge and love, because it is by constituting the inward 'other' that it comes to (or: from) its self-fulfilment, which is the presupposition or the act of being present to itself in knowledge and love.

A symbol is therefore not to be primarily considered as a secondary relationship between two different beings, which are given the function of indicating one another by a third, or by an observer who notes a certain agreement between them. The symbolic is not merely an intrinsic propriety of beings in so far as a being, to attain fulfilment, constitutes the differentiation which is retained in the unity, and which is in agreement with the original originating unity and so is its expression. A being is also 'symbolic' in itself because the harmonious expression, which it retains while constituting it as the 'other', is the way in which it communicates itself to itself in knowledge and love. A being comes to itself by means of 'expression', in so far as it comes to itself at all. The expression, that is, the 'symbol'—as the word is now to be understood in the light of the foregoing considerations—is the way of knowledge of self, possession of self, in general.

To sum up and propound once more the results arrived at up to this, we may invert the first assertion which we put forward as the fundamental principle of an ontology of the symbol, by affirming as a *second assertion*: The symbol strictly speaking (symbolic reality) is the self-realization of a being in the other, which is constitutive of its essence.

Where there is such a self-realization in the other—as the necessary mode of the fulfilment of its own essence—we have a symbol of the being in question. One might ask for whom does this self-realization in the other express the being and make it present, and who possesses the being in such a symbol—the being in question itself or another; one might ask in what (essentially different) degrees and in what ways this self-realization in the symbol and this presence are realized, in a self-discovery which is really knowledge and love or in a way relatively deficient compared to this. But these are secondary questions which, in comparison with these two first principles, enquire into distinctions which are secondary in relation to this general ontology of the symbol. They arise because the concept of a being is 'analogous', that is, it displays the *various* types of self-realization of each being, and being in itself, and hence also the concept and reality of the symbol are flexible. But because these are necessarily given with the general concept of beings and being—as the 'unveiled' figure of the most primordial 'truth' of being—the symbol shares this *'analogia entis'* with being which it symbolizes.

When we were working out the ontology of the symbol, we took no great pains to formulate it so that it would be immediately applicable to the theology of the Trinity in blameless orthodoxy. Even now we shall not try to establish expressly the convergence of this ontology and the theology of the Trinity (especially the theology of the Logos). It is enough for our purpose to point out very simply that the theology of the Logos is strictly a theology of the symbol, and indeed the supreme form of it, if we keep to the meaning of the word which we have already worked out, and do not give the term quite derivative meanings, such as the ordinary language of popular speech attributes to it. The Logos is the 'word' of the Father, his perfect 'image', his 'imprint', his radiance, his self-expression. Whatever answer is to be given to the question of how binding the psychological theory of the Trinity, as put forward by St Augustine, may be—whether the Father utters the eternal Word *because* he knows himself or *in order to* know himself, two items at any rate must be retained. One, the Word—as reality of the immanent divine life—is 'generated' by the Father as the *image* and *expression* of the Father. Two, this process is necessarily given with the divine act of self-knowledge, and without it the absolute act of divine self-possession in knowledge cannot exist. But if we retain these two elements, which are traditional in theology—not to give them a higher qualification—then we may and must say without misgivings: the Father is himself by the very fact that he opposes to himself the image which is of the same essence as himself, as the person who is other than himself; and so he possesses himself. But this means that the Logos is the 'symbol' of the Father, in the very sense which we have given the word: the inward symbol which remains distinct from what is symbolized, which is constituted by what is symbolized, where what is symbolized expresses itself and possesses itself.

It is because God 'must' 'express' himself inwardly that he can also utter himself outwardly; the finite, created utterance *ad extra* is a continuation of the immanent constitution of 'image and likeness'—a free continuation, because its object is finite—and takes place in fact 'through' the Logos (Jn 1:3), in a sense which cannot be determined more closely here. But it is not our intention to go into this difficult subject here. But it has to be mentioned, even if only in passing, because we could hardly omit this link between a symbolic reality within and without the divine, since it has also been noted to some extent in tradition.

If a theology of symbolic realities is to be written, Christology, the doctrine of the incarnation of the Word, will obviously form the central chapter. And this chapter need almost be no more than an exegesis of the saying: 'He that sees me, sees the Father' (Jn 14:9). There is no need to dwell here on the fact that the Logos is image, likeness, reflexion, representation, and presence—filled with all the fullness of the Godhead. But if this is true, we can understand the statement: the incarnate word is the absolute symbol of God in the world, filled as nothing else can be with what is symbolized. He is not merely the presence and revelation of what God is in himself. He is also the expressive presence of what—or rather, who—God wished to be, in free grace, to the world, in such a way that this divine attitude, once so expressed, can never be reversed, but is and remains final and unsurpassable.

To continue on these lines, and to give greater clarity to the inexhaustible content of the truth of faith which expresses the incarnation, one could take up here the Thomistic doctrine, that the humanity of Christ exists by the existence of the Logos. But when putting forward this thesis, one should be clear that this existence of the Word is again not to be thought of as the reality which—merely because of its being infinite —could bestow existence on any thinkable 'essence', as if it could offer any essence a ground of existence which in itself was indifferent to this essence rather than that or to which manner of existent being arose thereby. The being of the Logos—considered of course *as* that which is received by procession from the Father—must be thought of as exteriorizing itself, so that without detriment to its immutability in itself and of itself, it becomes *itself* in truth the existence of a created reality—which must in all truth and reality be predicated of the being of the Logos, because it *is* so. But then, starting from these Thomistic principles, we arrive at considerations and insights which show how truly and radically the humanity of Christ is really the 'appearance' of the Logos itself, its symbolic reality in the pre-eminent sense, not something in itself alien to the Logos and its reality, which is only taken up from outside like an instrument to make its own music but not strictly speaking to reveal anything of him who uses it. However, these considerations have already been put forward in an earlier chapter on the mystery of the incarnation. The humanity of Christ is not to be considered as something in which God dresses up and masquerades—a mere signal of which he makes use, so that something audible can be uttered about the Logos by means of this signal. The humanity is the self-disclosure of the Logos itself, so that when God, expressing himself, exteriorizes himself, that very thing appears which we call the humanity of the Logos. Thus anthropology itself is finally based on something more than the doctrine of the possibilities open to an infinite Creator—who would not however really betray *himself* when he created. Its ultimate source is the doctrine about God himself, in so far as it depicts that which 'appears' when in his self-exteriorization he goes out of himself into that which is other than he. However, we must refer to the earlier chapter for these considerations.

It follows from what has been said that the Logos, as Son of the Father, is truly, in his humanity as such, the revelatory symbol in which the Father enunciates himself, in this Son, to the world—revelatory, because the symbol renders present what is revealed. But in saying this, we are really only at the beginning of a theology of the symbol, in the light of the incarnation, not at the end.

When we say that the Church is the persisting presence of the incarnate Word in space and time, we imply at once that it continues the symbolic function of the Logos in the world. To understand this statement correctly, we must consider two points. One, where a reality which is to be proclaimed in symbol, is a completely human one, and so has its social and existential (freely-chosen) aspect, the fact that the symbol is of a social and hence juridically determined nature is no proof that the symbol is merely in the nature of arbitrary sign and representation, and not a reality symbolic in itself. Where a free decision is to be proclaimed by the symbol and to be made in it, the juridical composition and the free establishment is precisely what is demanded by the very nature of a symbolic reality in this case and what is to be expected. A *non*-existential reality cannot express itself in this free and juridically constituted way, where the symbol is likewise a symbolic reality which contains the reality of the thing symbolized itself, because it has realized itself by passing over into the 'otherness' of the symbol. This would be contrary to the nature of the non-existential reality. But exactly the opposite is true when it is a matter of something which has been freely constituted by God himself and which has a social structure. When such a reality renders itself present in a freely constituted symbolism formed on social and juridical lines, the process is merely what its essence demands and is no objection to the presence of a symbolic reality. But the Church, even as a reality tributary to the Spirit, is a free creation of the redemptive act of Christ and is a social entity. When therefore it is constituted along juridically established lines, the result does not contradict the fact that it is the symbolic reality of the presence of Christ, of his definitive work of salvation, in the world and so of the redemption. Secondly, according to the Church's own teaching, especially as voiced by Leo XIII and Pius XII, the Church is not merely a social and juridical entity. The grace of salvation, the Holy Spirit himself, is of its essence. But this is to affirm that this symbol of the grace of God really contains what it signifies; that it is the primary sacrament of the grace of God, which does not merely designate but really possesses what was brought definitively into the world by Christ: the irrevocable, eschatological grace of God which conquers triumphantly the guilt of man. The Church as indefectible, as Church of infallible truth and as Church of the sacraments as *opus operatum* and as indestructibly holy as a whole, even in the subjective grace of men—by which it is not merely object but even motive of faith—really constitutes the full symbol of the fact that Christ has remained there as triumphant mercy.

The teaching *on the sacraments* is the classic place in which a theology of the symbol is put forward in general in Catholic theology. The sacraments make concrete and actual, for the life of the individual, the symbolic reality of the Church as the primary sacrament and therefore constitute at once, in keeping with the nature of this Church a symbolic reality. Thus the sacraments are expressly described in theology as 'sacred signs' of God's grace that is as, 'symbols', an expression which occurs expressly in this context. The basic axioms of sacramental theology are well known: *Sacramenta efficiunt quod significant et significant quod efficiunt*. If these axioms are taken seriously, they point to that mutually supporting relationship which in our notion of the symbol intervenes between it and what is symbolized. Hence too in recent times theological efforts have been multiplied which try to explain the causality of the sacraments in terms of the symbol. Theologians try to show that the function of cause and the function of sign in the sacraments are not linked merely *de facto* by an extrinsic degree of God, but that they have an intrinsic connexion by virtue of the nature of things—here, their symbolic character, rightly understood. *As* God's work of grace on man is accomplished (incarnates itself), it enters the spatio-temporal historicity of man as sacrament, and *as* it does so, it becomes active with regard to man, it constitutes itself. For as soon as one sees the sacraments as the action of *God* on man—even though it takes place through someone who acts as 'minister' by divine mandate and gives body to the action done to man and so renders it concretely present and active—then the question no longer arises as to how the sacramental sign 'works on' God, and it is no longer possible to ask whether this sign produces grace by 'physical' or 'moral' causality. For at no stage can the sign be seen apart from what is signified, since it is understood *a priori* as a symbolic reality, which the signified itself brings about in order to be really present itself. But we can on the other hand see that the sacrament is precisely 'cause' of grace, *in so far as* it is its 'sign' and that the grace—seen as coming from God—is the cause of the sign, bringing it about and so alone making itself present. So the old axioms receive their very pregnant sense; *sacramenta gratiam efficiunt, quatenus eam significant*—where this *significatio* is always to be understood in the strict sense as a symbolic reality. So too: *sacramenta significant gratiam, quia eam efficiunt.* In a word, the grace of God constitutes itself actively present in the sacraments by creating their expression, their historical tangibility in space and time, which is its own symbol. That the juridically established structure of the sacraments does not run counter to this view of the sacraments as symbolic realities has already been explained equivalently, when the same objection was eliminated in the question of the Church as symbolic reality of the grace of God.

VII

The Triune God

The God of the New Testament is not the God whose metaphysical attributes engage the attention of the classical theologians. He is the free Triune God whose salvific interventions in human history culminated in his bestowal of himself on man in Christ. He is the God who has entered into fellowship with us by sending his Spirit into our hearts to make us his children by our supernatural participation in the eternal sonship of his only begotten Son. The New Testament God is God the Father, the First Person of the Blessed Trinity. In the New Testament the unity of God is the consequence of the fact that the Father has communicated his nature to the Son and, through the Son, to the Holy Spirit.

Unfortunately the profound awareness of the Triune God which characterized New Testament piety has practically disappeared from Christian piety today. Psychologically, if not dogmatically, contemporary Christians have become unitarian monotheists. They do not dispute the fact that the blessed in heaven will contemplate the Blessed Trinity in the Beatific Vision. Apart from that admission, however, the Trinity remains an arcane doctrine which has little or no influence on their daily life and thought.

Nevertheless, a proper understanding of the Trinity will show that it is still the central doctrine of Christianity and that an authentically Christian response to reality should be profoundly affected by it. Rahner has tried to restore the Trinity to its rightful place in Christian consciousness by restructuring his theology around this doctrine. The Word of God is the "real symbol," the "other" in whom the Father expresses Himself. Since the Word is the personal expression of the Father, he is the only Person through whom God could express himself as man in the Incarnation. Therefore God's eternal decree of creation is inseparably connected with a possible Incarnation of the Word. So a necessary connection links the procession of the Word from the Father within the immanent Trinity with the procession of the world from God through the divine act of creation. Thus the true significance of the relation between the world and God cannot be appreciated without some understanding of the inner life of its Triune Source.

Furthermore, historical creation proceeded from a divine decree which ordered it to the actual Incarnation of the Word. Therefore creation has been in the order of grace from its beginning. Grace, however, is primarily Uncreated Grace, or the actual indwelling of the three Persons of the economical Trinity within the justified soul. Historical man comes from the Trinity, lives a supernatural life which relates him personally to each of the Persons of the Trinity, and is ordered to eternal personal union with the Trinity as his beatifying goal. Far from being a metaphysical abstraction the Trinity is the mystery of his personal salvation.

Transcendental anthropology's theology of the procession of the Son and the Holy Spirit from the Father enables us to see why they are truly Persons, even though they are not separate centers of consciousness in the modern sense of person. It also provides a more fruitful understanding of the missions of these two divine Persons.

Contemporary Christians will not be able to overcome their psychological unitarianism unless theology becomes more consciously Trinitarian than it has been. Systematic theology should begin with a doctrine of God in which the immanent Trinity is not overshadowed by a metaphysical theology of the divine nature. Its theology of the Incarnation and grace should be built upon the identity of the immanent Trinity with the economical Trinity of Uncreated Grace. Restructured in this way, systematic theology can give a more satisfactory explanation of the intrinsic links between its theology of the immanent Trinity and its soteriology, theology of grace and eschatology.

1. OBSERVATIONS ON THE DOCTRINE OF GOD*

Even historically speaking, the relationship between the general doctrine of God (De Deo uno) and the doctrine of the Trinity is problematical. One cannot elicit a unified conception of this relationship from a study of the history of Catholic theology. The order of the treatises which is almost universally accepted today—first De Deo uno, then De Deo trino—has probably become general custom only since Peter Lombard's Sentences were ousted by Thomas' Summa Theologica. The Apostles'

*From Theological Investigations, vol. IX, pp. 130-31, 134.
© 1972 by Darton, Longman & Todd Ltd.

Creed with its trinitarian structure would only provide a clue to solving
the problem of the unity and diversity of these two treatises if one were to
understand—in common with the ancient θεως terminology—the word
'God' as the Father of the trinitarian confession, and, taking a Greek kind
of trinitarian theology (linear with respect to the world), to discuss in
addition the whole 'being' of God in the first chapter concerning the
Father. It is noteworthy that Peter Lombard subsumes the general doctrine of God under his doctrine of the Trinity, which M. Grabmann, for
instance, regards as one of Lombard's 'chief errors'. Noteworthy is also
the fact that we do not yet find a clear division in the *Summa Alexandri*
either, whereas Thomas, for reasons which have not yet really been
explained—whether in opposition to the Arabic systems or from apolo-
getic or pedagogic motives—clearly follows the Augustinian and Latin
method: he does not treat the general doctrine of God as the doctrine of
God the Father, the sourceless origin in the Godhead, but, by way of
anticipation, as the doctrine of the nature of God which is common to all
the Persons. Only after that does he commence his doctrine of the Trinity. And so it has remained in general right up to today. For example the
new Spanish Jesuits' Dogmatics gives an uncompromising and explicit
defence of this method. In still more recent times, for instance in the case
of Anselm Stolz and M. Schmaus, one can sense this problem again. M.
Schmaus subsumes the treatise De Deo uno as the doctrine of 'the fulness
of life of the three-personal God' under the first section of his dogmatics
which deals with 'God the Three in One'.

The mere *sequence* of the treatises De Deo uno and De Deo trino, as if
the second treatise were only supplementary to the first, and as if only the
second contained affirmations going beyond metaphysics (even though of
a metaphysics requiring to be confirmed and secured), is apt to obscure
the concrete history of theology, i.e. the two possibilities which present
themselves in the orthodox conception of the doctrine of the Trinity itself,
and it presupposes wrongly that the history of revelation itself followed
such a sequence, i.e. from the revelation of God's being to the revelation
of the Trinity. One could just as well say—indeed it would be more
correct to say—that the history of revelation first of all shows God as a
Person without origin, the Father, who has then revealed himself (as we
say in technical terms) within this relationship with the world as a self-
communication, as the source of divine life-processes, capable of creating
persons. These life-processes reveal their divine immanence characteristically in the economic trinitarian relationship of God in Christ and in his
Spirit which is given to us. So the sequence whereby the treatise De Deo
uno precedes the doctrine of the Trinity is not *necessarily* to be seen as
the result of the infiltration of philosophy. Thus the question seems to be
more didactic than fundamental whether and in which order the two
treatises should follow one another, or whether they should be assimi-

lated to each other. But on the other hand it is most important, if the general doctrine of God is placed first, not to present it as though there were no doctrine of the Trinity at all (as occurs in standard Catholic dogmatics). If the creation of what is not divine is understood dogmatically at the outset as a factor and a condition for the possibility of God's absolute self-communication, in which absolute Love gives its very self and not something other than itself, creation as the freely uttered Word of the unfathomably Inconceivable is then seen as the beginning and the 'grammar' of the divine self-expression communicated into the void. Thus it is the beginning of the trinitarian self-revelation.

2. *Theos* in the New Testament*

When we say that God is love, and that this is what finally characterizes God's free, historical behaviour in the fullness of time, in the *kairos* of the New Testament, we mean to say two things. Firstly, this is in fact a free *act* of God in Christ, an Event, not an attribute: the coming to pass of the New Testament in Christ. Secondly, it is the event in which God's inmost life is communicated to men, in his love for them, fully and without restraint. A genuinely personal love always has these two marks. Love is not the emanation of a nature but the free bestowal of a person, who possesses himself, who can therefore refuse himself, whose surrender therefore is always a wonder and a grace. And love in the fully personal sense is not just any relationship between two persons who meet in some third thing, whether this *tertium quid* is a task, a truth or anything else. it is the ceding and the unfolding of one's inmost self to and for the other in love.

That God is Love, that he has received man to the most intimate communion with himself in love—this has become manifest in the Sending and Incarnation, in the Cross and Glorification, of his only begotten *Son*. It has become manifest not merely in the sense that the Christ-reality may be taken as a particular instance, from which may be read off what attitude God has necessarily adopted with regard to man; but it has become manifest in the sense that all God's free activity in the whole history of salvation has been directed to this event from the very beginning and thus rests on this single decision; and that this free purpose of entering into unrestricted personal communication with man first became finally irrevocable and unconditional through God's act in Christ.

Nowhere in the New Testament is there to be found a text with

*From *Theological Investigations*, vol. I, pp. 123, 143-44, 146.
© 1961, 1965 and 1974 by Darton, Longman & Todd Ltd.

ὁ θεός which has unquestionably to be referred to the Trinitarian God as a whole existing in three Persons. In by far the greater number of texts ὁ θεός refers to the Father as a Person of the Trinity. It should be noted here that in the texts in which ὁ θεός is used without its being absolutely clear from the immediate context who precisely is meant, the expression never contains anything which is not said of God in other texts; and in just these other texts, this God may be recognized (directly or indirectly) as Father in the Trinitarian sense. Besides this there are six complete texts in which ὁ θεός is used to speak of the Second Person of the Trinity, but still in a hesitant and obviously restricted way (the restriction is concerned of course not with the reality but with the use of the word). In addition, ὁ θεός is never used in the New Testament to speak of the πνεῦμα ἅγιον. These findings are sufficient in themselves to justify the assertion that when the New Testament speaks of ὁ θεός, it is (with the exception of the six texts mentioned) the Father as First Person of the Trinity who is signified. ῾Ο θεός signifies him and does not merely stand suppositionally for him, because a constant and practically exclusive suppositional use of a word is proof that this word also signifies the thing for which it stands suppositionally, especially when it stands for the thing as subject and not just as a predicative name. The few exceptional uses of θεός, where the linguistic form itself marks them as exception, do not justify the view that in the usage of the New Testament ὁ θεός is an expression which signifies the Trinity in the unity of its proper nature, and so has always stood suppositionally for each of the three divine Persons in like manner.

When in consequence of all this we say that ὁ θεός in the language of the New Testament signifies the Father, we do not of course mean that it always signifies him *precisely in so far as* he is Father of the only begotten Son by an eternal generation. All that is meant is that when the New Testament thinks of God, it is the concrete, individual, uninterchangeable Person who comes into its mind, who is in fact the Father and is called ὁ θεός; so that inversely, when ὁ θεός is being spoken of, it is not the single divine nature that is seen, subsisting in three hypostases, but the concrete Person who possesses the divine nature unoriginately, and communicates it by eternal generation to a Son too, and by spiration to the Spirit.

It may easily be seen that this result is nothing more than a more precise demonstration of the fact that the conception of the Trinity, customarily (if inexactly) known since de Régnon as the Greek view, is closer to Biblical usage than what de Régnon called the Latin or scholastic view. The latter proceeds from the unity of God's nature (one God in three Persons), so that the unity of the divine nature is a *presupposition* of the whole doctrine of the Trinity; while the former begins with the three

Persons (three Persons, who are of a single divine nature) or better, with the Father, who is the source from which the Son, and through the Son the Spirit, proceed, so that the unity and integrity of the divine nature is conceptually a *consequence* of the fact that the Father communicates his whole nature. Associated with this Greek view of the Trinity is the fact that the Father is regarded as God κατ' ἐξοχήν.

3. Remarks on the Treatise "De Trinitate"*

Here and there in religious literature one may undoubtedly see that efforts have been made to link Christian piety more expressly and more vitally with this mystery. Theology too has shown instances of writers who are more consciously and keenly aware of the obligation of presenting the doctrine of the Trinity in such a way that it can become a reality in the concrete religious life of Christians—one thinks of the dogmatic theology of M. Schmaus and of the writings of G. Philips. One notes also in the history of devotion that in spite of a mystical cult of the supremely one, undifferentiated and nameless God of this mystery, the mystery has not remained the preserve of abstract theology. There has also been, no matter how rare and diffident, a true mysticism of the Trinity. We may mention in this matter St Bonaventure, Ruysbroek, St Ignatius of Loyola. St John of the Cross, Mary of the Incarnation, perhaps Bérulle and some moderns such as Bl. Elisabeth of the Holy Trinity and Anton Jans.

But this does not hide the fact that Christians, for all their orthodox profession of faith in the Trinity, are almost just 'monotheist' in their actual religious existence. One might almost dare to affirm that if the doctrine of the Trinity were to be erased as false, most religious literature could be preserved almost unchanged throughout the process. And it cannot be objected that the *Incarnation* is such a theologically and *religiously* central element in Christian life that on that account the Trinity is always and everywhere irremovably present. For when the Incarnation of God is spoken of, theological and religious intention is today concentrated on the fact that 'God' has become man, that 'a' person of the Trinity has assumed flesh—but not on the fact that this person is precisely that of the Word, Logos. One could suspect that as regards the catechism of the head and the heart, in contrast to the catechism in books, the Christian idea of the Incarnation would not have to change at all, if there were no Trinity. God, as one person, would have become man, and the average Christian who professes faith in the Incarnation does not go

*From *Theological Investigations*, vol. IV, pp. 78-82, 87-88, 91-92, 94-97, 100-02.
© 1966 and 1974 by Darton, Longman & Todd Ltd.

any farther in his express understanding of the doctrine. There are proba-
need pay no express attention to the fact that the satisfaction was given
precisely by the Word incarnate, and not simply by the *Deus-homo;* that
therefore one could imagine another divine person as man offering a
satisfactio condigna to the triune God; and that indeed, we could conceive of such satisfaction even if there were no question of the Trinity as
the condition or presupposition at all.

In the same way, the treatise called *'De gratia Christi'* gives a doctrine
of grace which is in fact monotheistic and not trinitarian, from the *consor-
tium divinae naturae* to the *visio beata essentiae divinae*. It is affirmed, of
course, that the grace was 'merited' by Christ. But as this grace is explained at best as the grace of the 'Dei-hominis', not as the grace of the
Word incarnate as Logos, and as this grace appears only as the restoration of a grace which in its supralapsarian condition is mostly treated
bly several modern, scientific and extensive Christologies which pay no
particular attention to *which* precisely of the divine hypostases has taken
on human nature. The average theological text-book today operates in
fact with the abstract concept of a divine hypostasis—a concept which is
however a very analogous and precarious unity. It does not operate with
the concept of exactly the second person in God as such. It asks what it
means that God became man, but not what it means in particular that the
Logos, precisely as himself in contradistinction to the other divine persons became man. And this state of affairs is not at all surprising. For
since St Augustine, contrary to the tradition preceding him, it has been
more or less agreed that each of the divine persons could become man.
From which it follows that the Incarnation of the second person in particular throws no light on the special character of *this* person within the
divine nature.

It is not surprising therefore that piety draws no more in fact from the
doctrine of the Incarnation than that 'God' became man and finds therein
no clear assertion about the Trinity. And hence the existence of a clear
and conscious faith in the Incarnation is far from being a proof of the fact
that the Trinity means something in the normal piety of Christians. And
there are other consequences, which show once more how popular piety
is reflected in dogmatic theology, and how little the contrast is felt to the
fixed, sacral formulas of the ancient liturgy. Theology for instance almost
takes it for granted that the 'Our Father' is directed in the same way to the
Holy Trinity, to all three divine persons, without any basic distinction
whatsoever; that the sacrifice of the Mass is offered to all three divine
persons in the same way; that the ordinary contemporary doctrine of
satisfaction (and therefore redemption), with its theory of a double moral
person in Christ, conceives of an act of redemption which is directed
essentially in the same way to all three divine persons; that this doctrine

merely as *gratia Dei,* not of the Word, and still less of the Word to be made flesh: the treatise on grace is only very vaguely a theological and religious introduction to the mystery of the Trinity.

The same anti-trinitarian timidity affects theologians when treating of the relationship between man and the three divine persons which is set up by grace. Exceptions like Petavius and Thomassinus, Scheeben, Schauf and so on merely confirm the rule. It is always taken to be a relation founded on 'created grace', a grace brought about by efficient causality, and the relationship is merely 'appropriated' in a different manner by each of the three divine persons. The sacraments and eschatology are naturally treated in the same way. In the doctrine of creation also, as treated today, the Trinity is hardly mentioned—in contrast to the way it was handled by the great theologians of former times like St Bonaventure. This silence is supposed to be justified by the doctrine that the works of God *ad extra* are performed so much in common by the divine nature that the created world can bear in itself no real sign of the divine inner-trinitarian life. Without of course saying so expressly, theologians consider the ancient classical doctrine of the *vestigia* or *imago Trinitatis* in the world more or less as a pious speculation, to be indulged in when the essential doctrine about the Trinity has been learnt elsewhere. Such speculations are not considered to add anything important to what is already known independently of the Trinity or of created reality.

As a result of all this, the treatise on the Holy Trinity remains rather isolated in the structure of dogmatic theology as a whole. To put it crudely (and of course with some exaggeration and generalization): once this treatise has been dealt with, it does not recur again in dogmatic theology. Its general function with regard to the whole is only vaguely seen. The mystery appears to have been revealed merely for its own sake. Even after the revelation, the *reality* of the mystery remains entirely centered on itself. Statements are made about it, but the reality itself has really nothing or almost nothing to do with us ourselves. We might summarize the average theological opinion as follows, without fear of being charged with exaggerating: in Christology, only one hypostatic function of 'one' divine person is considered and it could just as well be exercised by any other divine person; the only thing considered important in the concrete for us is that Christ is 'a' divine person, and which he is does not matter; in *De Gratia,* only strictly appropriated relationships are considered between man and the divine persons; objectively, only the efficient causality of the One God is considered; and this is as much as to say soberly but expressly that we ourselves have really nothing to do with the mystery of the Trinity, beyond receiving some revelation 'about' it.

The only objection to be considered is that it will be our blessedness later on to see this triune God face to face, which means being 'absorbed' into the inner divine life itself, and so attaining our most real perfection, and that this is the reason why the mystery is already revealed to us. But then we must ask how can all this be true if one denies any ontologically real relationship between man and each of the divine persons, and confines it all to appropriations. We must ask whether the vision even of the supreme reality can really make us blessed when, as in the supposition which we are criticizing, it is considered to be absolutely *unrelated* to us in the real ontological order.

In recent Catholic apologetics, the normal thing is to reject sharply any effort at discovering presentiments of this mystery outside the New Testament. And this is unquestionably logical. For if this theology does not admit the Trinity, as reality, into this world and the history of salvation, then it is to say the least unlikely that even the slightest knowledge of it should be found there. Hence before the question is asked *a posteriori* whether such traces exist or not (a question which of course cannot be answered affirmatively *a priori*), it is tacitly assumed, more or less, that there *can* be no such traces. There is at any rate very little inclination to give *positive* value to hints and analogies in the history of religion or in the Old Testament. Practically all the emphasis is placed on the difference between the doctrines inside and outside of Christianity.

The very isolation of the treatise on the Trinity proves at once that something is wrong: the thing is impossible! For the Trinity is a mystery of *salvation*. Otherwise it would never have been revealed. But then it must be possible to see why it is a mystery of salvation. And then it must be possible to show in *all* dogmatic treatises that the realities of salvation with which they deal cannot be made comprehensible without recurring to this primordial mystery of Christianity. If the intrinsic connexion between the various treatises does not constantly appear, this can only be a sign that in the treatise on the Trinity or in the other treatises attention has not been paid to the points which show that the Trinity is a mystery of salvation in our regard and hence confronts us wherever our salvation is spoken of—that is, in the other dogmatic treatises.

The basic thesis which constitutes the link between the treatises and shows the reality and not just the doctrine of the Trinity as a mystery of salvation for us may be formulated as follows: the Trinity of the economy of salvation *is* the immanent Trinity and vice versa. This assertion must be explained, proved as far as possible and applied to Christology, so that its importance for the latter may be clearly seen. These tasks are so much interwoven and condition each other so thoroughly that they must be undertaken together and not one after another.

The Trinity of the economy of salvation *is* the immanent Trinity: this assertion is a defined truth of faith at one point, in one case, for Jesus is not simply God in general, but the Son; the second divine Person, the Logos of God is man, and he alone. So there is at least one 'sending', one presence in the world, one reality in the economy of salvation which is not merely appropriated to a certain divine person, but is proper to him. Thus it is not a matter of saying something 'about' this particular divine person in the world. Here something takes place in the world itself, outside the immanent divine life, which is not simply the result of the efficient causality of the triune God working as one nature in the world. It is an event proper to the Logos alone, the history of one divine person in contrast to the others. (This is not changed by saying that the causation of this hypostatic union is the work of the whole Trinity.) There is an assertion with regard to the history of salvation which can only be made of one divine person. But if this is true *once*, then it is always *false* to say that there is nothing in the history or 'economy' of salvation which cannot be predicated in the same way of the triune God as a whole and of *each* person in particular. And the converse is also false: that in the doctrine of the Trinity, meaning what is said of the divine persons in general and particular, there can only be assertions which describe the immanent divine life. And it is certainly correct to say that the doctrine of the Trinity cannot be adequately distinguished from the doctrine of the economy of salvation.

Is it correct to affirm that *each* divine person can become man? Our answer is that this pre-supposition is both not proved and false. It is not proved: the most ancient tradition, before St Augustine, never thought of the possibility and really pre-supposed the contrary in its theological reflexions. The Father is by definition the unoriginated who is essentially invisible and who shows and reveals himself only by uttering his Word to the world. And the Word, by definition, is both immanently and in the economy of salvation the revelation of the Father, so that a revelation of the Father without the Logos and his incarnation would be the same as a wordless utterance. But the pre-supposition is also false: one cannot deduce from the mere fact that one divine person became man that this 'possibility' exists for another. Such a deduction supposes: 1. that in God, '*hypostasis*' is a univocal conception with regard to the three divine persons; and 2. that the unbridgeable difference between the way each divine person is a person—which is indeed so great that it is only the loosest of analogies that allows us to apply the same notion of person to all three —does not stand in the way of the other two persons entering into a hypostatic union with a created reality, by virtue of their own special and unique way of being a person, in the same way as the second person did. But what is supposed in 1. is false and what is supposed in 2. is not simply proved. The thesis which we here oppose is false. For if it were true, and if it occurred anywhere except on the fringes of theological thought and were really taken seriously, it would throw the whole of theology into confusion. There would be no longer any real and intrinsic connexion between the mission of a divine person and the immanent life of the Trinity. Our sonship in grace would have absolutely nothing to do with the sonship of the Son, since it would have been absolutely the same if it could have been based on any other incarnate person of the Godhead. There would be no way of finding out, from what God is to us, what he is in himself as the Trinity. These and many other similar conclusions which would follow from the thesis in question are quite contrary to the inner movement of Sacred Scripture. This can only be denied if one does not submit one's theology to the norm of Scripture but only allows it to say what is already known from one's scholastic theology and dissolves the rest away in clever and cold-blooded distinctions.

The Trinity of the economy of salvation *is* the immanent Trinity—that is the statement which we have undertaken to explain here. We have now shown that this axiom is verified in at least one case which is dogmatically incontrovertible. But that this case is really a precedent or instance can only be proved when we reflect on the doctrine of grace. This is a case of non-appropriated relationships of the divine persons to the justified. The problem and the different opinions to which it has given rise among theologians are well known and need not be expounded again here. But in any case, and to say the least, the thesis of proper, nonappropriated relationships is a free theological opinion and not in conflict with dogma. We pre-suppose it here, and merely try to develop the well-known and widespread—thought not undisputed— doctrine in the line of our thesis.

The thesis, which we pre-suppose as justified here, is, when understood rightly and taken seriously, not a piece of scholastic subtlety but a simple and straightforward statement. It is that each of the three divine persons communicates himself as such to man, each in his own special and different way of personal being, in the free gift of grace. This trinitarian communication (the 'indwelling' of God, the 'uncreated grace', to be understood not merely as the communication of the divine 'nature' but also and indeed primarily as communication of the 'persons', since it takes place in a free spiritual personal act and so from person to person) is the real ontological foundation of the life of grace in man and (under the requisite conditions) of the immediate vision of the divine persons at the moment of fulfilment.

We can now consider the relationship between immanent and salvific Trinity the other way round. The one God imparts himself as absolute self-utterance and absolute gift of love. This communication—the absolute mystery, which is only revealed in Christ—is however *self*-communication. God does not merely give his creature a 'share' 'in himself' (indirectly) by creating and donating finite realities through his all-powerful *efficient* causality: but he gives *himself*, really and in the strictest sense of the word, in a *quasi-formal* causality. But this *self*-communication of God to us has, according to the testimony of revelation in the Scripture, a three-fold aspect. It is a self-communication in which that which is imparted remains the sovereign and incomprehensible, and which even as something received continues to be unoriginated and not at the disposal or within the grasp of anyone. It is a self-communication in which the God who reveals himself 'is there', as self-expressive truth and as free directive power acting in history. And it is a self-communication in which the God who imparts himself brings about the acceptance of his gift, in such a way that the acceptance does not reduce the communication to the level of merely created things. But this three-fold aspect of the self communication must not be considered, in the dimension of the communication, as a merely *verbal* development of a communication which is of itself undifferentiated. In the dimension of the economy of salvation, the distinction is truly 'real': the origin of the self-communication of God, his radically self-revealing and self-expressing 'existence', the acceptance, which he himself brings about, of the self-communication, are not simply one and the same thing which is merely described by different words. In other words, according to the self-understanding of the experience of faith, as attested in Scripture, the Father, the Word (Son) and the Spirit—no matter how infinitely inadequate all these words are and must be—indicate a true difference, a double mediation within this self-communication.

In principal, there is no precise and permanent difference between the three elements. God's presence by the Word in the Spirit must be different from himself, the eternal mystery: and yet it cannot be other than himself, something that would stand before him and veil him. If the *absolute* nearness of the God 'who comes' is to be realized with regard to the convenant in which he really and truly imparts himself to his partner, then the dynamism of this historical process leaves only two courses open. Either the Word of God and the Spirit just disappear as created things, like the many prophets and their many words, in face of the unsurpassable and overwhelming presence of God himself, which is now revealed as the secret object of all partnership with God at all times. Or these two 'communications' remain, and are then at once revealed as being themselves truly divine, that is, as God himself, one with and distinct from the God who is to be revealed, in a unity and distinction which therefore belong to God himself. On this basis, the Old Testament must be understood to contain a genuine secret pre-history of the revelation of the Trinity. And this pre-history—which no one can totally deny—no longer gives the impression of dealing with antique concepts which are suddenly used in the New Testament, and still more in early Church history, to make assertions utterly remote from their genuine contents. When the unity of the salvific and immanent Trinity is thus invoked, another danger may be banished which, when all is said and done, remains the real danger of the doctrine, not so much in the abstract theology of the schools as in the average understanding of the normal Christian. It is that of a crude tritheism, not of course explicit but nonetheless very deeply embedded, which is a much greater danger than a Sabellian modalism. It is undeniable that the doctrine of the three persons in God evokes the almost unavoidable danger, which is usually countered far too late by express correctives, of thinking of three different consciousnesses. The danger is increased in the usual scholarly approach to the doctrine of the Trinity. It begins with a concept of 'person' taken from experience and philosophy and develops it independently of the revealed doctrine of the Trinity and the history of its revelation. The resulting notion is then applied to God and used in the proof that three *such* persons exist in God. The treatise then generally goes on to reflect on the relationship between unity and triune 'personality' in God, during which no doubt the needful is said about the more exact and correct understanding of these three 'persons'. The process is a sort of after-thought, in which—without, to be sure, admitting it—one makes the necessary modifications and restrictions with regard to the concept of person with which one began this spiritual Odyssey in the ocean of the mystery of God. But in all honesty, one must ask oneself with some embarrassment at the end what right one has to call the surviving remnant of the triune 'personality' in God a person, if one has had to eliminate from these three persons precisely what one began by thinking of as person. And then, when the more subtle distinctions of theology have been returned to oblivion, one notices that one is probably back with the false and basically tritheistic position, in which the three persons are thought of as three personalities with different centres of action.

But why not operate from the very start with a concept and a word —call it 'person' or anything else that seems fitting—which can be more easily adapted to the matter in hand and can render it with less risk of misunderstanding? This is not to affirm with Karl Barth that the word 'person' is not apt when speaking of the reality in question and that it should be replaced by some less ambiguous word in Church terminology. We may however concede that the development of the word 'person' outside the theology of the Trinity, after the definitions of the fourth century, took a very different direction from its originally near-Sabellian tone. It developed the existential meaning (as in Hermes) of the ego which is opposed to every other person in independent, proper and distinctive freedom. The ambiguity of the word was thereby increased. However, there it is, sanctioned by the usage of more than fifteen hundred years, and there is no other word which would be really better, more generally understandable and less exposed to misconceptions. We must therefore continue to use the word, even though we know there is a history behind it and that strictly speaking it is not altogether suitable to express what is meant and has no great advantages. But if one is definite and systematic in approacing the mystery of the Trinity from the standpoint of the economy of salvation, there is as little need to operate with the notion of 'person' from the beginning as in the history of revelation itself. Starting from the presence of God the Father himself, communicated in the economy of salvation through the Word in the Spirit, one could show that the differentiation in the 'God for us' is also that of the 'God in himself', and go on simply to explain that this three-fold quality of God in himself may be called triune 'personality'. Thus we shall on principle confine the notion of 'person' in this context to what may be affirmed of it from this starting-point, which is that offered by the testimony of Scripture. All difficulties would not disappear, because in non-theological contexts the concept of person today has in fact another meaning. But the difficulties could be rendered less acute and the danger of a tritheistic misunderstanding lessened.

Finally, this approach to the mystery would allow us to re-state the question of the relationship, connexion and difference between the two treatises *De Deo Uno* and *De Deo Trino*. It is not so easy to distinguish them as it has been supposed to be since St Thomas set the example. For if the title *De Deo Uno* is taken seriously, we are not dealing merely with the essence and attributes of God, but with the unity of the three divine persons. It is the unity of Father, Son and Spirit and not merely the unicity of the godhead, the mediated unity, of which the Trinity is the proper fulfilment, and not the immediate unicity of the divine nature which if considered as one numerically is of itself far from providing the foundation of the three-fold *unity* in God. But if one begins with the treatise *De Deo Uno* and not with *De Divinitate Una*, one is concerned at once with the Father, the unoriginated origin of the Son and the Spirit. And it is then strictly speaking impossible to place one treatise after the other in the disjointed fashion which is still so common today.

VIII

The Incarnation

1. On the Theology of the Incarnation*

Far from being an anthropocentrism, Rahner's theological anthropology is theocentric and Trinitarian in its focus. A genuine anthropology, Rahner also insists, must open out into a Christology. Theological anthropology leads to a clearer understanding of the Hypostatic Union. Human nature is the only spatio-temporal nature ordered to reach its intrinsic ontological perfection through loving self-surrender to the word of God. In other words, the free human knower is the mystery whose defining characteristic is a drive to personal union with the Infinite Mystery. The highest form of personal union is Hypostatic Union. If then the Word of God, who alone is capable of doing so, is to unite himself to a creature hypostatically, God must create a "real symbol," a finite "other" in whom the Word can express himself through personal union. Man alone can be this "real symbol," for no other spatio-temporal nature can reach the perfection of its own reality through personal union with God. No person except the Word can "express" himself hypostatically; no nature except human nature can be the "grammar" of that expression.

When the Word expresses himself in human nature He really becomes. Classical Scholastic theology restricted this ontological "becoming" to Christ's human nature. The Infinite Immutable Divine Nature of the Word could not undergo change. In one of his most controversial statements–and one in which he differs most sharply with classical Scholastic tradition–Rahner says unequivocally that the Divine Word really becomes. Change is not predicated of the Word simply by communicatio idiomatum. *God himself undergoes change in the Incarnation. Nevertheless God changes not in himself but in his other, the real symbol which is his human nature. On the basis of this "dialectical" position Rahner claims that God really suffers in the Crucifixion and that*

*From Theological Investigations, vol. IV, pp. 107, 109-17, 119-20.
© 1966 and 1974 by Darton, Longman & Todd Ltd.

God really changes through his involvement in the evolution of human history. Rahner's Christology which, contrary to classical Thomism, insists that God is really related to the world, has clear affinities to process theology, although Rahner insists on the infinity of God. It also manifests the extent to which he has been influenced by the philosophy of Hegel. Both God's expression in his "other" and the intrinsic connection between the divine creation of the world and the Incarnation of the Logos are Thomistic adaptations of well-known Hegelian themes.

The Word of God became *man*. What does it mean: 'became *man*'? We are here omitting entirely the question of what it means when we say that this Word 'became' something. We are considering only *what* it became: man. Do we understand that? It could indeed be affirmed that 'man' is easily the most intelligible element of this assertion. Man is what *we* are, what we experience every day, what has been tried out and interpreted a billion times already in the history to which we belong, what each of us knows inside himself and outside himself in his environment. One could go further and say: This is so well known that we can recognize its basic constituents and distinguish its essential contents from accidental modifications on the one hand and from an ultimate self-hood on the other. We can then give the name of 'nature' to the ultimate constituent and content and say that that is 'what' it is. Thus our assertion will mean: the Word of God has assumed an individual human nature and so has become man. But do we really know from what has been said what man is and so what 'human nature' is?

We begin to understand more clearly—always of course within the framework of the basic mystery which is God and we—what it means to say: God takes on a human nature as his own. The indefinable nature, whose limits—'definition'—are the unlimited reference to the infinite fullness of the mystery, has, when assumed by God as *his* reality, simply arrived at the point to which it always strives by virtue of its essence. It is its *meaning*, and not an incidental activity which could perhaps be left aside, to be that which is delivered up and abandoned, to be that which fulfils itself and finds itself by perpetually disappearing into the incomprehensible. This is done in the strictest sense and reaches an unsurpassable pitch of achievement, when the nature which surrenders itself to the mystery of the fullness belongs so little to itself that it becomes the nature of God himself. The incarnation of God is therefore the unique, *supreme*, case of the total actualization of human reality, which consists of the fact that man *is* in so far as he gives up himself. For what does the *potentia oboedientialis* mean for the hypostatic union? What does it mean when we say that human nature has the possibility of being assumed by the person of the Word of God? Correctly understood, it means that this *potentia* is not one potentiality along with other possibilities in the constituent elements of human nature: it is objectively identical with the essence of man. But once this is understood, it is impossible to contest on grounds of scholastic theology that one is justified in describing this essence in such a way that it appears precisely *as* this potentiality. And that is precisely what we have tried to indicate in the simplest possible outline.

This effort does not mean, 1. that the possibility of the hypostatic union can be strictly perspicuous as such *a priori,* that is, independently of the revelation of its *de facto* existence. And it does not mean, 2. that such a possibility must be realized in every man who possesses this nature.

1. The transcendence of man makes it clear that it would be wrong to define him, to delimit and put bounds to his possibilities. At least a hypothetical extension and culmination of the possibilities given with his trancendence are justified. But any type of fulfilment whatever remains within the bounds of the hypothetical as long as (and it will undoubtedly be impossible here) it is not proved that the transcendence would lose all meaning if it did not find precisely this fulfilment. And this transcendence means being immeasurably open with regard to the *freedom* of the mystery, and being utterly abandoned to the necessity of allowing oneself to be disposed of. We can therefore deduce from the transcendence no exigency of such fulfilment. And hence a strict knowledge of its possibility, including aspects which perhaps remain hidden to us, is not possible.

2. Hence it follows that the potentiality need not be realized in every man. And the fact of our being simply creatures, the fact of our sinfulness and of our radical peril, shows us, when our situation is brought to light in the word of God, that the possibility has not in fact been actualized in us. And yet we can say: God has taken on a human nature, because it is essentially ready and adoptable, because it alone, in contrast to what is definable without transcendence can exist in total dispossession of itself, and comes therein to the fulfilment of its own incomprehensible meaning. Man has ultimately no choice. He understands himself as a mere void, which one can encompass only to note with the cynical laughter of the damned, that there is nothing behind it. Or—since he is *not* the fullness which can repose contentedly in itself—he is found by the infinite and so becomes what he is: one who never succeeds in encompassing himself because the finite can only be surpassed by moving out into the unfathomable fullness of God.

But if this is the essence of man, he attains his supreme fulfilment, the gratuitous fulfilment of his essence to which through his own ways of perfection he is always tending, only when he adoringly believes that somewhere there is a being whose existence steps so much out of itself into God, that it *is* just the question about the mystery utterly given over to the mystery. He must believe that there is a being who is the question which has become unquestioning, because it has been accepted as his own answer by him who answers. And then we may perhaps say that it is not so strange, since this strange element already floats before the mind of man in the pure mystery of his primordial understanding, along with the perfected whole. The more difficult question is *how* and *where* and *when* one may give an earthly name to him who is such a being. But if one seeks *him*, to whom one can bring the eternal mystery of the pure fullness of one's own being for fulfilment, one can see very simply, if one seeks 'quietly', that is, in meekness and with the eyes of innocence, that it is only in Jesus of Nazareth that one can dare to believe such a thing has happened and happens eternally. The rest of us are all farther from God, because we always have to think that we are the only one to understand ourselves. But he *knew* that only the Father knows his mystery, and so he knew that only he knows the Father.

To avoid misunderstanding, we must note that the Christology outlined above is not a 'Christology of consciousness' in contrast to an ontological Christology affirming the substantial unity of the Logos with his human nature. It is based on the metaphysical insight, derived from a strict ontology, that true being is the spirit as such itself. It tries to formulate the necessary ontological counterpart to the ontic statements of tradition, so that we may reach a better understanding of what is meant, and in order that the true traditional affirmations do not give the impression that God has wrapped himself in the disguise of a human nature which only clings to him exteriorly and has come to his earth to set things right because they could not be managed from heaven. And there is another remark to make. It might be imagined that this God-becoming-man takes place as often as men come into existence and that the incarnation is not a unique miracle. This would imply that the historicity and personality in question was reduced to the level of the nature which is everywhere and always the same: and this would be nothing short of mythologizing the truth. It would also ignore the fact that the humanity of God—in which he is there as an individual for each individual man, not having come to divinize nature—can be and is *in itself*[1] favoured with nothing essentially more or less in the line of closeness to and encounter with God, than that which is in fact provided for *each* man in grace: the beatific vision.

[1] The words in itself should be noted. All Catholic theologians are familiar with the view that the hypostatic union of the humanity of Christ with the Logos has as a necessary consequence the *intrinsic* divinization of this human nature. Thought it is a consequence of the hypostatic union which is morally and indeed ontologically necessary, it is distinct from the union, and through it alone is the humanity of Christ sanctified and divinized in itself —and (though in a unique measure of intrinsic holiness) is precisely that which is to be bestowed on all men as grace of justification.

The Word of God has *become* man: this is the assertion which we are trying to understand better. We take the word 'become'. Can God 'become' anything? This question has always been answered in the affirmative by pantheism and all other philosophies in which God exists 'historically'. But it leaves the Christian and all really theistic philosophers in a difficult situation. They proclaim God as the 'Unchangeable', he who simply *is—actuus purus*—who is blessed security, in the self-sufficiency of infinite reality, possesses from eternity to eternity the absolute, unwavering, glad fullness of what he is. He has not first to become, he has not first to acquire what he is. And precisely because we have received for our part the burden of history and change, as a grace and a distinction, we necessarily proclaim *such* a God, because it is only because he is the infinite fullness that the processes of spirit and nature can be more than the pointless self-awareness of absolute emptiness which collapses into its own void. And hence the acknowledgement of the unchanging and unchangeable God in his eternally perfect fullness is not merely a postulate of philosophy, it is also a dogma of faith. Nonetheless, it remains true: the Word *became* flesh.

And we are only truly Christians when we have accepted this. It will hardly be denied that here the traditional philosophy and theology of the schools begins to blink and stutter. It affirms that the change and transition takes place in the created reality which is assumed, and not in the Logos. And so everything is clear: the Logos remains unchanged when it takes on something which, as a created reality, is subject to change, including the fact of its being assumed. Hence all change and history, with all their tribulation, remain on this side of the absolute gulf which necessarily sunders the unchangeable God from the world of change and prevents them from mingling. But it still remains true that the Logos *became* man, that the changing history of this human reality is *his* own history: our time became the time of the eternal, our death the death of the immortal God himself. And no matter how we distribute the predicates which seem to contradict one another and some of which seem incompatible with God, dividing them up between two realities, the divine Word and created human nature, we still may not forget that one of these, the created reality, is that of the Logos of God himself. And thus, when this attempt at solving the question by the division and distribution of predicates has been made, the whole question begins again. It is the question of how to understand the truth that the immutability of God may not distort our view of the fact that what happened to Jesus on earth is precisely the history of the Word of God himself, and a process which *he* underwent.

If we face squarely the fact of the incarnation, which our faith testifies to be the fundamental dogma of Christianity, we must simply say: God can become something, he who is unchangeable in himself can *himself* become subject to change *in something else*.[1] This brings us to an ontological ultimate, which a purely rational ontology might perhaps never suspect and find it difficult to take cognizance of and insert as a primordial truth into its most basic and seminal utterances: the Absolute, or more correctly, he who is the absolute, has, in the pure freedom of his infinite and abiding unrelatedness, the possibility of himself becoming that other thing, the finite; God, in and by the fact that he empties *himself* gives away *himself, poses* the other as his own reality. The basic element to begin with is not the concept of an assumption, which pre-supposes what is to be assumed as something obvious, and has nothing more to do than to assign it to the taker—a term, however, which it never really reaches, since it is rejected by his immutability and may never affect him, since he is unchangeable, when his immutability is considered undialectically and in isolation—in static concepts. On the contrary, the basic element, ac-

---

[1] One can confine oneself to saying that the created thing is the humanity of the Word in itself, and the therefore something has happened, a change has taken place. But if one sees the event as taking place only on this side of the boundary which separates God and the creature, one has seen and said something which is true, but missed by a hairbreadth and omitted what is really the point of the whole statement: that this even is that of God himself. This has not yet been expressed if one speaks for instance merely of the 'inconfused' human nature! To call it then a 'change' does not really matter: it is a reality (namely, that God *himself* has become flesh, through the fact that something has taken place in this human dimension), even though one fights shy of the term 'change'. If we do call it a change, then, since God is unchangeable, we must say that God who is unchangeable in himself can change in another (can in fact become man). But this 'changing *in* another' must neither be taken as denying the immutability of God in himself nor simply be reduced to a changement *of* the other. Here ontology has to orientate itself according to the message of faith and not try to lecture it. The formal truth of the oneness of God is not denied by the doctrine of the Trinity. But this oneness, such as we can conceive it (and which is a dogma) cannot be used to determine what the nature of the Trinity may be. So too here. We must maintain methodologically the immutability of God, and yet it would be basically a denial of the incarnation if we used it alone to determine what this mystery could be. If, to expedite the mystery, one transferred it into the region of the creature alone, one would really abolish the mystery in the strict sense. For in the finite alone as such there can be no absolute mysteries at all, because one can always conceive a finite intellect proportionate to any finite thing and able to fathom it. The mystery of the incarnation must lie in God himself: in the fact that he, though unchangeable 'in himself,' can become something 'in another.' The immutability of God is a dilectical truth like the unity of God. These two truths only—*de facto*—retain their validity for us when we think at once of the two other truths (of the Trinity and the incarnation). But *we* cannot and may not think of either as prior to the other. We learn from the doctrine of the Trinity that radical unity (as we might conceive it, were our thinking it out not dominated from the start by divine revelation) is not an absolute ideal. Even in the Most High it is a Trinity because he is absolute perfection. In the same way we learn from the incarnation that immutability (which is not eliminated) is not simply and uniquely a characteristic of God, but that in and in spite of his ummutability *he* can truly *become* something. He himself, he, in time. And this possibility is not a sign of deficiency, but the height of his perfection, which would be less if in addition to being infinite, he could not become less than he (always) is. This we can and must affirm, without being Helegians. And it would be a pity if Hegel had to teach Christians such things.

cording to our faith, is the *self*-emptying, the coming to be, the κένωσις and γένεσις of God himself, who can come to be by *becoming* another thing, derivative, in the act of constituting it, without having to change in his own proper reality which is the unoriginated origin. By the fact that he remains in his infinite fullness while he empties himself—because, being love, that is, the will to fill the void, he has that wherewith to fill all—the ensuing other is his own proper reality. He brings about that which is distinct from himself, in the act of retaining it as his own, and vice versa, because he truly wills to retain the other as his own, he constitutes it in its genuine reality. God himself goes out of himself, God in his quality of the fullness which gives itself. He can do this. Indeed, this power of subjecting himself to history is primary among his free possibilities. (It is not a primal must!) And for this reason, Scripture defines him as love—whose prodigal freedom is the indefinable itself. What then is his power of being creator, his ability to keep himself aloof while constituting, bringing out of its nothingness, that which in itself is simply something else? It is only a derivative, restricted and secondary possibility, which is ultimately based on the other primal possibility—though the secondary could be realized without the primal.

It follows—and this truth is now situated on a profounder level than before—that the creature is endowed, by virtue of its inmost essence and constitution, with the possibility of being assumed, of becoming the material of a possible history of God. God's creative act always drafts the creature as the paradigm of a possible utterance of himself. And he cannot draft it otherwise, even if he remains silent. For this self-silencing always presupposes ears, which hear the muteness of God. Though we cannot go into it here, this truth might be the key to understanding why precisely the Logos of God became man and why he alone becomes man. The immanent self-utterance of God in his eternal fullness is the condition of the self-utterance of God outside himself, and the latter continues the former. It is true that the mere constitution of something other than God is the work of God as such, without distinction of persons. Yet the ontological possibility of creation can derive from and be based on the fact that God, the unoriginated, expresses himself in himself and for himself and so constitutes the original, divine, distinction in God himself. And when this God utters himself as himself into the *void*, this expression speaks *out* this immanent Word, and not something which could be true of another divine person.

And now we can understand better what it means to say: the Logos of God *becomes* man. There are of course men who are not the Logos himself. There could of course be men, if the Logos had not become man. The lesser can exist without the greater, though the lesser is always founded on the possibility of the greater and not vice versa, as an unworthy, resentful and proletarian type of thinking would have it, all too often and readily—a type of thinking which from sheer force of habit makes everything grow out of a lower stage. But when the Word becomes man, his humanity is not prior. It is something that comes to be and is constituted in essence and existence when and in so far as the Logos empties himself. This man is, as such, the self-utterance of God in its self-emptying, because God expresses *himself* when he empties himself. He proclaims *himself* as love when he hides the majesty of this love and shows himself in the ordinary way of men. Otherwise his humanity would be a masquerade in borrowed plumes, a signal that tells of the existence of something but reveals nothing of what is there. That there are other men, who are not this self-utterance of God, not another way of being God himself, does not affect the issue. For 'what' he is is the same in him and us: we call it human nature. But the unbridgeable difference is that in his case the 'what' is uttered as his self-expression, which it is not in our case. And the fact that he pronounces as his reality precisely that which we are, also constitutes and redeems our very being and history. He says openly into the freedom of God what we are: the truth in which God could express himself and expose himself to the empty nothingness which necessarily surrounds him. For he is love, and therefore necessarily the miracle of the possibility of the free gift, or better: as love, he is the incomprehensible obvious.

We could now define man, within the framework of his supreme and darkest mystery, as that which ensues when God's self-utterance, his Word, is given out lovingly into the void of god-less nothing. Indeed, the Logos made man has been called the abbreviated Word of God. This abbreviation, this code-word for God is man, that is, the Son of Man and men, who exist ultimately because the Son of Man was to exist. If God wills to become non-God, man comes to be, that and nothing else, we might say. This of course does not mean that man is to be explained in terms of his ordinary everyday life. It means that man is brought back home to the region of the ever incomprehensible mystery. But he is such a mystery. And if God himself is man and remains so for ever, if all theology is therefore eternally an anthropology; if man is forbidden to belittle himself, because to do so would be to belittle God; and if this God remains the insoluble mystery, man is for ever the articulate mystery of God. He is a mystery which partakes for ever of the mystery on which it is founded, and must always be accepted in blissful love as the undecipherable mystery, even in the eternity where the provisional is past and done with. For we may not think that we could completely understand God's expression of himself outside himself, which is man, so that it, and we too, could become tedious to us. We do not think that we could see what is behind man except by seeing through him into the blessed darkness of God himself and then really understanding that this finite being is the finitude of the infinite Word of God himself. Christology is the end and beginning of anthropology. And this anthropology, when most thoroughly realized in Christology, is eternally theology. It is the theology which God himself has taught, by speaking out his Word, as our flesh, into the void of the non-divine and sinful. It is also the theology which we pursue in faith, unless we think that we could find God without the man Christ, and so without man at all.

Man is a mystery. Indeed, he is *the* mystery. For he is mystery not merely because he is open in his poverty to the mystery of the incomprehensible fullness of God, but because God uttered this mystery as his own. For supposing God wills to speak himself out into the void of nothingness, supposing he wills to call out his own Word into the mute desert of nothingness—how else could he do it than by creating the inward acceptance of this Word and by uttering his word to be accepted? And so it is all one: the self-utterance of God's Word and its acceptance. That this takes place at all is a mystery. A mystery is something that is totally unexpected and incalculable, something that is at once blissfully, mortally amazing and yet obvious—but obvious only because in the last resort the mystery makes the conceivable understandable and not vice versa. And so the incarnation of God is the absolute and yet the obvious mystery. One could almost think that what is strange, historically contingent and hard about it is not the thing in itself but the fact that the obviously absolute mystery has taken place precisely in Jesus of Nazareth, there and now. But when the longing for the absolute nearness of God, the longing, incomprehensible in itself, which alone makes anything bearable, looks for *where* this nearness came—not in the postulates of the spirit, but in the flesh and in the housings of the earth: then no resting-place can be found except in Jesus of Nazareth, over whom the star of God stands, before whom alone one has the courage to bend the knee and weeping happily to pray: 'And the Word was made flesh and dwelt amongst us'.

2. Christ the Mediator: One Person and Two Natures*

Despite the great differences between the medieval and the modern conception of the person, the Chalcedonian doctrine of the one divine person subsisting in two natures can be made quite credible to modern man. Although the Incarnation may appear to be a strange, almost magical, event in some of its classical presentations, Rahner's metaphysics of

* From *Theological Investigations*, vol. I, pp. 158-63, 180-82.
© 1961, 1965 and 1974 by Darton, Longman & Todd Ltd.

the Trinity explains how the Incarnation of the Logos is the only intelligible way in which the Triune God could personally unite himself to the history of the evolving world which he created. Creation therefore entails the possibility of the Incarnation. Furthermore, Rahner's metaphysics of the symbol enables his reader to understand more readily how a divine person can unite himself to a human nature in such a way that the very union constitutes that human nature a center of genuine psychological freedom. Only the intrinsic creativity of God is capable of constituting, by God's own act as such, a being which, by the very fact of being radically dependent (because wholly *constituted in being by God), acquires autonomy with respect to the God who constitutes it.*

Is it possible from the basic Chalcedonian doctrine itself actually to evolve the account given us above in reply to the question how far Jesus can be the Mediator between us and God? Although this requirement is not strictly necessary, it seems nevertheless to be justified, because in fact the formula 'One Person and two natures' is the basic formula of Christology. If it is replied that we are quite certainly bound to take into account the fact that other truths, witnessed to in Scripture, must be *added* to this basic formula for a full understanding of the Lord as Mediator, although strictly speaking they are not found in this basic formula and cannot be *derived from* it—then the question with which we began arises *implicite* with even more urgency. Is it in fact possible to *derive from* the formula 'One Person—two natures in the possession of the one Person' that characteristic relationship to God in the sphere of Jesus' human reality, a relationship apparent in Scripture and indispensable for the understanding of Christ's function as Mediator (for it makes it possible for him to act freely towards and before God)? That is to say, is it possible to recognize this relationship as contained in the formula *implicite*? Or is it in fact open to one to doubt this? It is well known that at the last moment it was decided to make an omission, verbally slight but theologically important, from the text of the Encyclical on Chalcedon: instead of rejecting a doctrine which held that there were two subjects in Christ 'saltem psychologice', the Encyclical rejected the (Nestorian) doctrine of two (ontological) subjects, by omitting the phrase 'saltem psychologice'. One thing at least becomes clear from this little episode in the history of the Encyclical's redaction: that there were and are theologians who cannot see that the doctrine of two natures involves a duality of even a merely psychological and relative kind between an existentially independent I-centre (*Ichzentrum*) in the man Jesus and the Logos; indeed they believe that anything of the sort is excluded. And there are theologians who hold that something of the kind is a fact which can be demonstrated theologically and historically. But what must be granted is that the concept of *person* is always at least in danger of being understood in such a way that the 'independence' in view here seems to be excluded. It is not merely since the nineteenth century, with Günther's modern concept of *person* and Existentialist philosophy, that this has been the case. The concept of *person* as the ontological principle of a free active centre, self-conscious, present to itself and through itself in being, is a concept which, in the sense just indicated, has always played round the edge of the most static and objective concept of *person*. We cannot prove this here. But if it were not the case, monothelitism would have been quite inconceivable; for it was not just a political device for making a concession to monophysitism, but persisted with such vigour that today it is still a widespread 'heresy' among Christians—all verbal orthodoxy notwithstanding. In the customary teaching about sin, untouched by any kind of Existentialism, a distinction is made between *peccatum personale* and *peccatum naturae*; in this terminology too we see that existential ideas about the *person* are simultaneously at play. If these come to the fore, a connexion obtrudes itself upon the mind: where there is a *single* person, there is a *single* freedom, a *single* unique personal active centre, in relation to which any other reality (=nature, natures) can only be in this person the material and the instrument, the recipient of commands and the manifestation of this single, personal centre of freedom. But this is precisely not the case with Jesus. Otherwise he would only be the God who is active among us in human form, and not the true man who can be our Mediator with respect to God in genuine human freedom. It would of course be utterly false to say that the conceptual pair 'Person-nature' *involves* this monothelite interpretation (it would be better and clearer to say today 'mono-existentialist conception'). But the concept of *person*, as it is in actual fact understood,[1] in fact insistently suggests this interpretation, and it is again and again taken unreflexively in this sense, though the interpretation is never reflexively thought out and formulated (for that would be heretical). Inevitably the question then arises: how can the whole complex of Christological dogma be formulated so as to allow the

[1] We shall later have to discuss at some length why it is that such a misconception or the danger of it cannot be removed simply by terminological exactitude. Clearly it can be laid down that by 'person' we shall understand only the ultimate substantial unity and completeness of a subject which is incommunicable and whose reality as one in this sense can only be expressed by this subject itself. But as soon as the concrete person understood in this way exhibits a plurality in its real being, the question must arise as to how and in virtue of what the plurality is combined with the personal unity: what is sought is just the unique unifying center of this plural unity, the unique point prior to the instituted plural unity; we want to make clear to ourselves *in terms of its actual content* what the function of this prior unity is in establishing unity in plurality, not just in terms of the *communicatio idiomatum*, which is only a *consequence* of this unity. Consequently when we are thinking, in connexion with this unity, of a person as *ens rationabile*, we tend to think that the function of the person which consists in establishing unity is not the actual, centralized, existential control and direction of the plural realities of the person, but rather their ontological foundation, which most clearly emerges to view *in* this control and direction. How little permissible it is simply

Lord to appear as Messianic Mediator and so as true Man, as soon as possible, or at any rate with sufficient clarity? As true Man, who, standing before God on our side in free human obedience, is Mediator, not only in virtue of the ontological union of two natures, but also through his activity, which is directed to God (as obedience to the will of the Father) and cannot be conceived of *simply* as God's activity in and through a human nature thought of as purely instrumental, a nature which in relation to the Logos would be, ontologically and morally, purely passive? The ordinary doctrine of two natures just by itself is quite insufficient as a ground from which to derive this insight into Christ's mediation as something which arises from the inner tendency of the doctrine. For if someone says that a human nature has a free will and that *eo ipso* this gives us all that is required, he overlooks the point that the question arises just here as to how freedom can belong to someone[1] with whom it is not identical, whose intrinsic core it does not constitute; why this freedom is neither subjugated to the 'person' distinct from it nor in a position to rebel against it.[2]

It is easy to see from all this that only a *divine* Person can possess as its own a freedom really distinct from itself in such a way that this freedom does not cease to be truly free even with regard to the divine Person possessing it, while it continues to qualify this very Person as its ontological subject. For it is only in the case of God that it is conceivable at all that he himself can constitute something in a state of distinction from

to exclude this position out of hand may be seen from the defined doctrine that Christ's 'human nature,' on account of the *unio hypostatica,* is wholly subject in its freedom to the Logos, and thus was essentially sinless. But once again, how little this doctrine offers us by way of an answer to the problem with which we are concerned, may be seen by putting the following question. Is it the case *either* that the *unio hypostatica* just in itself as such is the *immediate* real ontological ground for the realization of this sinless subjection of the humanly free spontaneity of Christ's human nature to the other will (that of the Logos)? *Or* is it only the mediately operative requirement in order that the Logos should effect this subjection by the use of means which elsewhere in the domain of creatures God is also capable of using as sovereign master over creaturely freedom, without thereby injuring it—indeed precisely realizing it? Or finally does the question itself in its disjunctive form show itself to be false one, once the *unio hypostatica* is set quite generally in the wider context of the ontological relationship between God and the free creature?

[1] A person in the tradition ontological sense.

[2] There is no need to spend any time here in showing that the following approach provides no solution. Someone might say: The will is an accident of the substance of the soul (= nature), and freedom is its modality; consequently this cannot be conceived of in such a way that the question should ever arise as to how the freedom could be 'eccentric' to the person. The starting-point of this answer is sound enough in certain respects; yet 'frreedom' remains in its intrinsic ontological root supremely central to the person, and thus the question we have tried to put remains. If anyone doubts this, he should consider the fact that this modality of the second act of this accident is simply speaking master of the destiny and the decision of the *whole* reality of the free being, and that the free act can thus never be made 'central' enough.

himself. This is precisely an attribute of his divinity as such and his intrinsic creativity: to be able, by himself and through his *own* act *as such,* to constitute something in being which by the very fact of its being radically dependent (because *wholly* constituted in being), also acquires autonomy, independent reality and truth (precisely because it is constituted in being by the one, unique *God*), and all this precisely with respect to the God who constitutes it in being. God alone can make something which has validity even in his own presence. There lies the mystery of that active creation which is God's alone. Radical dependence upon him increases in direct, and not in inverse, proportion with genuine self-coherence before him. Measured against God, the creature is precisely *not* to be reduced unambiguously to the formula of merely negative limitation. Our problem here is only the supreme application of this basic truth concerning the Creator-creature relationship (a truth which at least historically has never been reached in non-Christian philosophy). And it immediately follows once again that the purely *formal* (abstract) schema *nature-person* is inadequate. We must conceive of the relation between the Logos-Person and his human nature in just this sense, that here *both* independence *and* radical proximity equally reach a unique and qualitatively incommensurable perfection, which nevertheless remains once and for all the perfection of a relation between Creator and creature. But in view of the fact that this simultaneous perfection can only be realized in a creature with regard to *God*, it becomes even clearer that the abstract concept of a 'person who has a nature' is not enough to allow us to infer this characteristic feature of Christ's human liberty with respect to God, a feature which is of such decisive significance for him and which characterizes him as Man and Mediator. This liberty is possible only when the person who has this free nature is either identical with this nature or is the *divine* Person as divine.

Our discussion of the problems of the Chalcedonian formula cannot set out to offer a precise and detailed answer to the question which has been raised; we shall merely make a few brief observations. Obviously what we should have to do would be to work out a fresh concept of unity (of a substantial, hypostatic kind, clearly). This concept would not *merely* analyse the unity in terms of a logical predication of idiomata (however indispensable this may be), because by itself this would either only be understood 'monophysitically' in the form of a cryptogamic heresy (*sit venia verbo!*), as we have pointed out above; or, while the immutability of the Logos and the Chalcedonian ἀσυγχύτως remained clear, the emptily formal abstractions of the unity (for all its being hypostatic[1]) would

---

[1] We repeat: anyone who is tempted by our speaking of a formal emptiness of the unity to maintain that on the contrary, the unity in question is a *hypostatic* one, and thus a perfectly 'full' and close unity, must be warned that the should consider what precisely it is that he is saying. He will then realize (supposing that he has taken the average Christology as his

take on no real fullness of meaning for us. We cannot escape from this trap by looking at the unity as the (even merely logically) subsequent unity of two things to be united, already existing independently as two prior to the unity. The Logos may be regarded in this way; but as soon as the humanity is so conceived of too, the position becomes untenable. It is not enough to say that the humanity has never existed apart from the hypostatic unity *in fact,* that is to say temporally. Nor is it permissible to suppose that it may *merely* be conceived of as always combined *in fact,* on the grounds that its nature is the same as ours, and we certainly exist apart from the hypostatic unity and yet as 'men'.[1] The only way in which Christ's *concrete* humanity may be conceived of in itself as diverse from the Logos is by thinking of it *in so far as* it is united to the Logos. The unity with the Logos must constitute it in its diversity from him, that is, precisely as a human nature; the unity must itself be the ground of the diversity. In this way, the diverse term as such is the united[2] reality of him who as prior unity (which can thus only be God) is the ground of the diverse term, and therefore, while remaining 'immutable' 'in himself', truly comes to be *in* what he constitutes *as* something united (*geeinte*) with him *and* diverse from him.[3] In other words, the ground by which the diverse term is constituted and the ground by which the unity with the

---

starting-point) that his explanation of the hypostatic unity is conceived of in terms of a *communicatio idiomatum.* And then he will have to ask himself what it means for the Logos to remain 'unchanged' by this unity, when any sort of history which it implies takes place on this side of the abyss between God and creature, and what is more, without confusion. He is bound to indicate what remains of the former given the latter. If he says that this is just the mystery (and that we ought not to let go of one end of the famous chain because we don't know how it is linked with the other end, which we also hold), then we must ask with all moderation whether this mystery might not permit of being formulated more clearly, so as to come before the eye of faith as a whole; in this way the impression would not arise that the one truth must be utterly blotted out 'quoad nos' when we turn to look at the other.

[1] It will appear from what follows that this consideration is at any rate lacking in force. Everyone who is a Thomist in Christology must grant this. Further, it must be borne in mind that a purely *de facto* unity in the strict sense would be an accidental one.

[2] *Geeinte.* Fr Rahner gives *einen* (to unite) the sense of an act by which one of the two terms of a unity is the cause of this unity. It is difficult to make the English 'to unite' bear this sense: in English it is usually some *third* term which unites the other two, a suggestion which would be quite unsuitable here. *Einen* here means simply and solely 'to one'.—Tr.

[3] It follows from this statement that the assertion of God's 'immutability', of the lack of any real relation between God and the world, is in a true sense a dialectical statement. One may and indeed must say this, without for that reason being a Hegelian. For it is true, come what may, and a dogma, that reason being a Hegelian. For it is true, come what may, and a dogma, that the Logos himself has become man: thus that he himself has become somthing that he had not always been *(formaliter);* and therefore that what has so become is, as just itself and of itself, God's reality. Now if this is a truth of faith, ontology must allow itself to be guided by it (as in analogous instances in the doctrine of the Trinity), must seek enlightenment from it, and grant that while God remains immutable 'in himself', he can come to be 'in the other', and that *both* assertions must really and truly be made of the same God as God. that *both* assertions must really and truly be made of the same God as God.

PASSIONIST FATHERS
ST. GABRIEL'S RESIDENCE
Marbel, Koronadal, South Cotabato
Philippines 9708

Joe — Written assignment — for
Rahner — due Monday
Oct. 11 —

Questions — (Ref — Rahner Reader +
Hearers of the Word)

① How can there be a
revelation of God that is not
anticipated in human ~~experience~~
transcendental experience?

② How does Rahner arrive in
the affirmation of freedom in
God & in humanity, & what are
some of the implications?

③ What is the meaning of
obediential potency?

Buy — 6×4 index card —

Due Mon. Oct. 11
Oct. 18 Pannenberg — 2PM LSTC — no class.
Fr. Nonito B. Adorable, C.P.

diverse term is constituted must as such be strictly the same. But if what makes the human nature ek-sistent as something diverse from God, and what unites this nature with the Logos, are *strictly* the same, then we have a united which (a) cannot, as uniting unity *(einende Eienheit)*, be confused with the united unity *(geeinte Einheit)* (this is not permissible); (b) which unites *precisely by* making existent, and *in this way* is grasped in a fullness of content without any relapse into the empty assertion of the united unity; and finally (c) which does not make the ἀσυγχύτως look like a sort of external counterbalance to the unity, always threatening to dissolve it again, but shows precisely how it enters into the *constitution* of the united unity as an intrinsic factor, in such a way that unity and distinction become mutually conditioning and intensifying characteristics, not competing ones.

3. The Knowledge and Self-Consciousness of Christ*

Rahner's theological anthropology allows for greater historical development in Christ's human consciousness than the older Scholastic theologians were willing to permit. Neither the perfection of Christ's human nature nor his possession of the Beatific Vision through the grace of union excludes the possibility of ignorance and of progressive growth in his human knowledge. On the contrary, one of the conditions of possibility for the exercise of human freedom is a certain degree of nescience in the human subject. Therefore, unless there were some ignorance in his human knowledge, Christ—contrary to the Greek ideal of perfection —could not really be a perfect man. Furthermore, the distinction between objective and unobjective human knowledge makes it manifest that neither the grace of union nor the Beatific Vision are incompatible with ignorance. Christ's human spirit, ontologically united to the World, was aware of God unobjectively, in a manner analogous to the awareness which other human spirits have of their own purely human spirit and of its Infinite Horizon. The ordinary human subject needs time and the experience of life in order to thematize this unobjective knowledge in objective concepts. Christ too needed time and experience to thematize the unobjective knowledge which he possessed because of the ontological union of his human spirit with the Word of God. This progressive thematization and clarification of Christ's knowledge in objective concepts was a

* From *Theological Investigations*, vol. V, pp. 199-211.
© 1966 by Darton, Longman & Todd Ltd.

genuine growth in knowledge. As such, it required human experience of the world, and it was in no way incompatible with doubt or with suffering.

In preparing for our reflections proper, it should be stated first of all that knowledge has a multi-layered structure: this means that it is absolutely possible that in relation to these different dimensions of consciousness and knowledge something may be known and not known at the same time. We state this because one gets the impression that the explanation of the knowledge of Christ usually starts with the tacit presupposition that man's knowing consciousness is the famous *tabula rasa* on which something is either written or not, so that this simple 'either-or' is the only possibility with regard to the question of something being written or not written on it. Yet this does not correspond to the facts. Human consciousness is an infinite, multi-dimensional sphere: there is reflex consciousness and things to which we attend explicitly; there is conceptual consciousness of objects and a transcendental, unreflected knowledge attached to the subjective pole of consciousness; there is attunement and propositional knowledge, permitted and suppressed knowledge; there are spiritual events in consciousness and their reflex interpretation; there is non-objectified knowledge of a formal horizon within which a determined comprehended object comes to be present, and this sort of knowledge is an objectified, conscious *a-priori* condition of the object comprehended *a-posteriori;* and finally there is the knowledge about this object itself.

The second preparatory remark consists in a critique of the Greek ideal of man in which knowledge is simply the yard-stick of human nature as such. In other words, a Greek anthropology cannot but think of any ignorance *merely* as a falling short of the perfection towards which man is orientated. Nescience is something which has simply to be overcome, it is not regarded as having any possible positive function. Anything which through nescience is not present is simply something which fails to take place, but this absence is not seen as an opening out of space for freedom and action, which can be more significant than the mere presence of a certain reality. Living at the present time, we cannot think as undialectically as that about knowledge and ignorance. And we have objective reasons for this. It is impossible here to develop the positive nature of nescience—of the *'docta ignorantia'*—in every direction. We would merely draw the reader's attention to the following fact. A philosophy of the person and of the freedom of a finite being, a philosophy of history and of decisions, could undoubtedly show with comparative ease that the fact of challenge, of going into the open, of confiding oneself to the incalculable, of the obscurity of origin and the veiled nature of the end—in short, of a certain kind of ignorance—are all necessary factors in the very nature of the self-realization of the finite person in the historical decision of freedom. It could be shown quite easily that freedom also always demands the wisely unobstructed area of freedom and its willingly accepted emptiness, as the dark ground of freedom itself and as the condition making it possible. In other words, there is certainly a nescience which renders the finite person's exercise of freedom possible within the still continuing drama of his history. This nescience is, therefore, more perfect for this exercise of freedom than knowledge which would suspend this exercise. There is, therefore, undoubtedly a positive will for such a nescience. That there is a place for nescience is always already affirmed and this precisely in the will for absolute transcendence into the infinite and incomprehensible being as such. And in so far as the nature of the spirit is directed towards the mystery of God—in so far as all the clarity of the spirit is founded on the ordination to the eternally Incomprehensible as such, and this even still in the *visio beatifica,* which does not consist in the disappearance of the mystery but in the absolute nearness of this mystery as such and in its final beatifying acceptance—it becomes once more manifest, from the point of view of the final perfection of the spirit, that one must be very careful when one is tempted to qualify nescience as something merely negative in man's life. Whether this consideration has any contribution to make to our subject—and if so, what contribution—is something which will become clear only later on.

We come now very quickly to the very heart of our reflections. These reflections are of a dogmatic kind. Hence we ask: for what reasons must one, together with Catholic text-book theology and the *magisterium,* ascribe to Jesus even during his life on earth the kind of direct vision of God which is the basis and centre of the beatific vision of God enjoyed by the blessed in heaven? If we put the question this way, it is because we wish to indicate even in the way we put the question, that right from the beginning one ought not to speak here of a 'beatific vision'. For one thing, it is far too easily taken for granted as self-evident that direct contact with God must always be beatific. Without necessarily adopting the Scotist view about the manner of beatitude, it may nevertheless be asked why absolute nearness and immediacy to God, understood as the direct presence to the judging and consuming holiness of the incomprehensible God, should necessarily and always have a beatific effect. Furthermore, is it certain that what is meant, in the tradition of theology, by the consciousness of Jesus is really intended to convey an idea of beatitude by direct union with God over and above this union itself? In view of the data provided by the historical sources regarding Christ's death-agony and feeling of being forsaken by God in his death on the Cross, can one seriously maintain—without applying an artificial layer-psychology—that Jesus enjoyed the beatitude of the blessed, thus making of him someone who no longer really and genuinely achieves his human existence as a '*viator*'? If one may reply to these questions in the negative, then the problem occupying us at present is simply a question of determining what valid theological reasons could be brought forward to convince us that we are quite correct in attributing a direct union of his consciousness with God, a *visio immediata,* to Jesus during his earthly life, but this without qualifying or having to qualify it as 'beatific'.

We regard the *visio immediata* of God as an intrinsic element of the Hypostatic Union and hence regard it as simply given bound up in this Union and as something which also cannot be abandoned. Thus in this view, it is not at all necessary to find a proper direct proof for this in the tradition of all ages. Furthermore—and this is a decisive point for our reflections—it follows in this view that this vision can be determined more exactly from the nature of the Hypostatic Union, in such a way that the consequences of this nature for the *visio beatifica* must also be affirmed, and whatever does not follow from it must also be denied theologically, whenever one cannot support it by any other certain and theologically binding additional tradition, which presumably will not be the case.

We must now explain the meaning of this answer more fully and—for reasons of time—this will have to be done in as brief a speculative reflection as possible, without even attempting to find any confirmation of it in the history of theology. We start then from the axiom of the thomistic metaphysics of knowledge according to which being, and self-awareness, are elements of the one reality which condition each other immanently. Hence, something which exists is present to itself, to the extent in which it has or is being. This means that the intrinsically analogous and inflective nature of being and of the power of being, is in absolutely clear and equal proportion to the possibility of being present to oneself, to the possibility of self-possession in knowledge, and the possibility of consciousness. Let us presuppose this axiom—without being able to develop its meaning and justification more exactly here—and let us apply it now to the reality of the *Unio hypostatica*. The Hypostatic Union implies the self-communication of the absolute Being of God—such as it subsists in the Logos—to the human nature of Christ which thereby becomes a nature hypostatically supported by the Logos. The Hypostatic Union is the highest conceivable—the ontologically highest—actualization of the reality of a creature, in the sense that a higher actualization would be absolutely impossible. It is the absolutely highest manner of being there is apart from God's. The only other form of being which might be comparable with it, is the divine self-communication by uncreated grace in justification and in glory, in so far as both forms of being do not come under the notion of an efficient causality but rather of a quasi-formal causality, since it is not a created reality which is communicated to a creature but the uncreated being of God himself. In as much as the Hypostatic Union involves an ontological *'assumptio'* of the human nature by the person of the Logos, it implies (whether formally or merely consequently need not be investigated here) a determination of the human reality by the person of the Logos and is therefore at least also the actualizing of the *potentia obedientialis,* i.e. of the radical capacity of being 'assumed', and hence is also something on the part of the creature, particularly since—as is stressed by scholastic theology—the Logos is not changed through the Hypostatic Union, and anything happening (which is the case here in the most radical way) takes place on the side of the creature. But according to the previously stated axiom of the thomistic metaphysics of knowledge, this highest ontological determination of the created reality of Christ (i.e. God himself in his hypostatic, quasi-formal causality), must of necessity be conscious of itself. For, according to this axiom, what is ontologically higher cannot be lower on the plane of consciousness than what is ontologically lower. Thus, given that this self-consciousness is a property of the human reality, then this ontological self-communication of God is also—and, indeed, specially and primarily—a factor in the self-consciousness of the human subjectivity of Christ. In other words, a purely ontic *Unio hypostatica* is metaphysically impossible to conceive. The *visio immediata* is an intrinsic element of the Hypostatic Union itself.

When we hear about Christ's direct vision of God, we instinctively imagine this vision as a vision of the divine essence present before his mind's eye as an object, as if the divine essence were an object being looked at by an observer standing opposite it, and consequently as if this divine essence were brought into Christ's conscoiusness from without and occupied this consciousness from without and hence in all its dimensions and layers. Once we have adopted this imaginative scheme (naturally we do not do this reflectively, but for that very reason this schematic representation determines our notion of the vision of God all the more profoundly) then we pass equally unconsciously and naturally to the thought that this divine essence offering itself and viewed in this way as an object of vision from without, is like a book or mirror offering, and putting before Christ's consciousness, more or less naturally all other conceivable contents of knowledge in their distinct individuality and propositionally formulated possibility of expression.

But then we have arrived at the problem with which we started: can such a consciousness have been that of the historical Jesus as we know him from the Gospels—the consciousness of the one who questions, doubts, learns, is surprised, is deeply moved, the consciousness of the one who is overwhelmed by a deadly feeling of being forsaken by God? Precisely this schematic image requiring an immediate conscious union with God and forcing itself upon us as if it were self-evident is not only not demanded but is also proved to be false if we start (as we have tried to indicate briefly above) from the only dogmatic basis we have for the recognition of the fact of this conscious, direct vision of God. For it follows from this that the direct presence to God, considered as a basic condition of Christ's soul, must be thought of as grounded in the substantial root of his created spiritual nature. For this direct presence to God is the plain, simple self-awareness—the necessary self-realization—of this substantial union with the person of the Logos himself . . . this and nothing more. This means, however, that this really existing direct vision of God is nothing other than the original unobjectified consciousness of divine sonship, which is present by the mere fact that there *is* a Hypostatic Union. For this consciousness of divine sonship is nothing more than the inner, onto-logical illumination of this sonship—it is the subjectivity of this objective sonship necessarily present as an intrinsic factor of the actual objective condition. But for this very reason, this awareness of sonship, which is an intrinsic element of the objective sonship, must not be conceived as a being-faced-with an object-like God to which the intentionality of the human consciousness of Jesus would then be referred as to the 'other', the 'object' facing it. This consciousness of sonship and of direct presence to God (which is not something merely known by starting from outside it, but consists in a direct presence to God which is at once—and absolutely identically—both the reality itself and its inner illumination) is therefore situated at the subjective pole of our Lord's consciousness. The best and objectively most correct way of understanding it is to compare its characteristic nature with the intellectually subjective basic condition of human spirituality in general. This basic condition of man—his spiritual nature, his transcendence and freedom, his unity of knowledge and action, and his freely activated understanding of self—is consciously present in him not only when he thinks about it, when he reflects on it, when he forms propositions about it, or weighs up the various interpretations of this reality. Whenever and wherever he is and acts as a spirit—in short, wherever he occupies himself intentionally with the most commonplace external realities—this 'looking away from himself' towards external objectivity rests on this unformed, unreflective, perhaps never actually reflected knowledge about himself; it rests on a simple self-awareness which does not 'reflect' or objectify itself but which—looking away from itself—is always already present to itself by way of this apparently colourless, basic condition of a spiritual being and by way of the horizon within which all traffic with the things and notions of daily life takes place. This inescapable, conscious and yet in a sense not-known state of being lit up to oneself, in which reality and one's consciousness of reality are still unseparated from each other, may never be reflected upon; it may be given a false conceptual interpretation; it may be—and indeed always is—attained only very inadequately and never completely; it may be interpreted from the most variant possible and impossible view-points, using most assorted terminologies and systems of concepts, so that man may systematically tell himself what he has already always known ('known' in that unformed attunement which is the unembraceable ground of his whole knowledge, the permanent condition of the possibility of all other knowledge, its law and gauge, and its ultimate form). This all-pervading basic condition is present and is conscious even in a person who declares that he has never noticed it.

To this innermost, primitive and basic condition on which rests all other knowledge and activity, there belongs in Jesus that direct presence to God which is an intrinsic subjective element of the hypostatic 'assumption' of the human spiritual nature of Jesus by the Logos. And this conscious, direct presence to God shares in the characteristics of the spiritual, basic condition of a man, for it belongs to it as an ontic factor of that substantial basis whose self-presence constitutes this basic condition. This direct and conscious presence to God must not be understood in the sense of the vision of an object. This fact does not make this direct presence any the less ontically and ontologically fundamental and unsurpassable. But it means that this direct presence is the same kind of presence as is meant by the *'visio immediata'*, except that it excludes the element of 'standing opposite' an object, an element which is usually associated with it as soon as one forms an image of 'vision'; we can quite rightly speak of a vision even in this case, as long as we exclude from our notion of vision this particular element of an objective, intentional counter-pole. A direct presence to God belongs to the nature of a spiritual person, in the sense of an unsystematic attunement and an unreflected horizon which determines everything else and within which the whole spiritual life of this spirit is lived. This direct presence to God belongs to the nature of a spiritual person as the ground which, though not allowing us to grasp it completely in a reflex manner, is nevertheless the permanent basis for all other spiritual activities and which, on this account, is always more 'there' and less objectively 'there' than everything else. This presence belongs to the nature of a spiritual person as the tacit factor in self-awareness which orders and explains everything but cannot be explained itself, since a basis is always the clear but inexplicable factor. If we take what has just been said above about the characteristic nature of Christ's conscious, direct presence to God, and connect it up with what was said in our first introductory remark, then we may say that the basic condition of direct presence to God is not only reconcilable with, but moreover demands, a genuinely human spiritual history and development of the man Jesus. After all, this basic condition is itself of such a nature as to demand a fixed form and a spiritual, conceptual objectification, without it itself having such a form as yet, though leaving all the necessary free room for it in the *a-posteriori*, objective consciousness of Christ. In spite of Man's always already-given basic condition *as* a spiritual being, and in spite of the attunement (*Gestimmtheit*) which is always present in the very ground of his existence (but which has nothing at all to do with a 'mood' or '*Stimmung*'), a man must first 'come to himself', i.e. only in the course of long experience can he learn to express to himself what he is and what indeed he has always already seen in the self-consciousness of his basic condition. In other words, just as there is this objectively reflex-ive process of becoming conscious of what has always been already understood consciously but without knowing it and in an unsystematic and unobjectified manner, so it is also in the case of Christ's conscious-ness of divine sonship and his basic condition of direct presence to God. This consciousness in Christ realized itself only gradually during his spiritual history, and this history does not consist only, or even first and foremost, in being occupied with this or that fact of external reality but consists rather in the never quite successful attaining of what and who one is oneself, and this precisely as what and whom one always already pos-sessed oneself in the depths of one's existence. Hence it is absolutely meaningful, and no cheap trick of a paradoxical dialectic, to attribute to Jesus at the same time an absolute, basic state of being directly present to God from the very beginning and a development of his original self-consciousness of the created spiritual nature being absolutely handed over to the Logos. For this development does not refer to the establish-ment of the basic state of direct presence to God but to the objective, humanly and conceptually expressed articulation and objectification of this basic state; this basic condition is not a fully formed and position-ally differentiated knowledge, nor is it an *objective* vision.

4. Christology Within an Evolutionary View of the World*

The Incarnation of the Word provides the theological key to a proper understanding of world history. The decree of creation ordered the uni-verse from its beginning to the historical Incarnation of the Word. Thus the order of creation has been under the grace of Christ from its very start. World history has always been identical with salvation history. From the dawn of creation evolution has been moving toward the emergence of human nature, the real symbol through which God could unite the material world and its history with his own Being. The culmina-tion of human history with which God has identified himself through

* From *Theological Investigations*, vol. V, pp. 173-78, 181-84.
© 1966 by Darton, Longman & Todd Ltd.

Christ living in his Church will be reached at Christ's Second Coming. Christ is the Absolute Future of human history. At Christ's Second Coming the community of the human race, which has been making progress toward its goal, with the help of God's grace, through the trials and triumphs of human history, will reach its definitive state. In and through Christ world history and salvation history will have reached their term.

We presuppose that the goal of the world consists in God's communicating himself to it. We presuppose that the whole dynamism which God has instituted in the very heart of the world's becoming by self-transcendence (and yet not as that which constitutes its nature) is really always meant already as the beginning and first step towards this self-communication and its acceptance by the world. In exactly what way are we then to conceive this self-communication of God to the spiritual creature in general and to all those subjects in which the cosmos becomes conscious of itself, of its condition and of its basic cause? To understand this, it must first of all be pointed out that these spiritual subjectivities of the cosmos signify freedom. We can only state this baldly here and must abstain from going into the transcendental reasons for it. Once we presuppose this, however, we presuppose also that this history of the self-consciousness of the cosmos is always necessarily also a history of the inter-communication of these spiritual subjects. For the fact that the cosmos becomes conscious of itself in the spiritual subjects must mean above all and necessarily that these subjects—in which the whole is present to itself each time after the manner proper to that subject—become more closely associated with each other, as otherwise the 'becoming present to itself' would separate and not unite. God's self-communication is, therefore, communication of freedom and inter-communication between the many cosmic subjectivities. Hence this self-communication necessarily turns in the direction of a free history of the human race, and can only happen in *free* acceptance by these free subjects and in a *common* history. God's communication of himself does not suddenly become uncosmic —directed merely to an isolated, separate subjectivity—but is given to the human race and is historical. This event of self-communication must therefore be thought of as an event which takes place historically in a specifically spatio-temporal manner and which then turns to everyone and calls upon their freedom. In other words, this self-communication must have a permanent beginning and must find in this a permanent guarantee of its reality so that it can rightly demand a free decision for the acceptance of this divine self-communication. (In this connection it should be mentioned briefly that this free acceptance or refusal on the part of individual free beings does not really determine the actual event of self-communication but, more exactly, only determines the attitude adopted by the spiritual creature towards it; of course, normally only that is called self-communication which is accepted freely and hence beatifies, i.e. only the successful, accepted self-communication of God.)

From this there follows first of all the explanation of the notion of Saviour. We give the title of Saviour simply to that historical person who, coming in space and time, signifies that beginning of God's absolute communication of himself which inaugurates this self-communication for all men as something happening irrevocably and which shows this to be happening. This notion does not imply that God's self-communication to the world in its spiritual subjectivity begins *in time* only with this person. This does not need to be the case at all; it can quite easily be conceived as beginning before the actual coming of the Saviour, indeed as co-existent with the whole spiritual history of humanity and of the world—as was actually the case according to Christian teaching. The historical person whom we call Saviour is that subjectivity in whom this process of God's absolute self-communication to the spiritual world is *irrevocably* present as a whole; through him this self-communication can be clearly recognized as something irrevocable, and in him it reaches its climax, in so far as this climax must be thought of as a moment in the total history of the human race and in so far as this climax is not simply identified with the totality of the spiritual world subject to God's communication of himself (which is a different, though absolutely legitimate notion of the climax of the divine self-communication). For, in so far as this self-communication must be conceived as free on the part of God and of the history of the human race which must accept it, it is quite legitimate to conceive of an event by which this self-communication and acceptance attains an irrevocable and irreversible character in history—an event in which the history of this self-communication realizes its proper nature and in which it breaks through—without it thereby becoming necessary that this history of God's self-communication to the human race has already simply found its end and conclusion both in its extension and in regard to the spatio-temporal plurality of the history of humanity. It must be noted in this connection that this moment in which the irreversible character of this historical self-communication of God becomes manifest refers equally to the communication itself and to its acceptance. Both these factors are included in the notion of the Saviour. In so far as a historical movement already lives in virtue of its end even in its beginnings—since the dynamism of its own being desires its end, carries its goal in itself as that towards which it is striving and really unveils itself in its own proper being only in this goal—it is absolutely legitimate, and indeed necessary, to think of the whole movement of God's communication of himself to the human race (even when it takes place during the time *before* the event which makes it irrevocable in the Saviour) as something based on this event—in other words, as something based on the Saviour. The whole movement of this history lives only for the moment of arrival at its goal and climax—it lives only for its entry into the event which makes it irreversible—in short, it lives for the one whom we call Saviour. This Saviour, who represents the climax of this self-communication, must therefore be at the same time God's absolute pledge by self-communication to the spiritual creature as a whole *and* the acceptance of this self-communication by this Saviour; only then is there an utterly irrevocable self-communication on both sides, and only thus is it present in the world in a historically communicative manner.

Seen in this light, it now becomes possible to understand what is really meant by the doctrine of the Hypostatic Union and of the Incarnation of the divine Logos and how, following quite naturally from what has been said, it fits into an evolutionist view of the world. In the first place, the Saviour is himself an historical moment in God's saving action exercised on the world. He is a moment of the history of God's communication of himself to the world—in the sense that he is a part of this history of the cosmos itself. He must not be merely God acting on the world but must be a part of the cosmos itself in its very climax. This is in fact stated in the Christian dogma: Jesus is true man; he is truly a part of the earth, truly a moment in the biological evolution of this world, a moment of human natural history, for he is born of woman; he is a man who in his spiritual, human and finite subjectivity is just like us, a receiver of that self-communication of God by grace which we affirm of all men—and hence of the cosmos—as the climax of development in which the world comes absolutely into its own presence and into the direct presence of God. Jesus is the one who—by what we call his obedience, his prayer and the freely accepted destiny of his death—has achieved also the acceptance of his divinely given grace and direct presence to God which he possesses as man. All this is Catholic Dogma. If one is not to fall into a false belief or heresy, one must not think of the God-man as if God or his Logos had put on a kind of livery for the purpose of his saving treatment of man, or as if he had disguised himself, as it were, and had given himself merely an external appearance to enable him to show himself in the world. No, Jesus is truly man. He has absolutely everything which belongs to the nature of man; he has (also) a finite subjective nature in which the world becomes present to itself and which has a radical directness to God which, like ours, rests on that self-communication by God in grace and glory which we too possess. It must also be underlined in this connection that the statement of God's *Incarnation*—of his becoming *material* —is the most basic statement of Christology. The divine Logos himself both really creates and accepts this corporeality—which is a part of the world—*as his* own reality; he brings it into existence as something other than himself in such a way, therefore, that this very materiality expresses *him*, the Logos himself, and lets him be present in his world. His taking hold of this part of the one material-spiritual world-reality may quite

legitimately be thought of as the climax of that dynamism in which the
Word of God who supports everything, supports the self-transcendence
of the world as a whole. For we are quite entitled to conceive what we call
creation as a part-moment in that process of God's coming-into-the-world
by which God actually, even though freely, gives expression to himself in
his Word become part of the world and of matter; we are perfectly entitled
to think of the creation and of the Incarnation, not as two disparate,
adjacent acts of God *'ad extram'* which in the actual world are due to two
quite separate original acts of God, but as two moments and phases in the
real world of the unique, even though internally differentiated, process of
God's self-renuniciation and self-expression into what is other than himself. For such a conception can certainly appeal to a most ancient Christian tradition of 'Christocentricity' as found in the history of Christian
theology, and it does not deny in any way that God *could* have created a
world without an Incarnation, i.e. that he could have denied the final
climax of grace and Incarnation to the self-transcendence of the material
in the spirit and towards God by His own dynamism inherent in the world
(without thereby becoming constitutive of its being). For every such essential self-surpassing always stands in a relationship of grace—the unexpected and the gratuitous—to its lower stage, even though it is the 'goal'
of this movement.

The thesis towards which we are working purports to show that, even
though the Hypostatic Union is in its proper nature a unique event
and—when seen in itself—is certainly the highest conceivable event, it
is nevertheless an intrinsic factor of the whole process of the bestowal
of grace on the spiritual creature in general. Why is this so? We have already pointed out that, if this total event of the divinizing sanctification
of humanity attains its consummation, it must be a concrete, tangible
phenomenon in history (in other words, it must not suddenly become
a-cosmic) and hence must be an event in such a way as to spread out
spatio-temporally from one point (in other words, it must not destroy the
unity of mankind and men's essential community and intercommunication
but must on the contrary come into existence within these very factors); it
must be an irrevocable reality in which God's self-communication proves
itself not merely as a temporary offer, but as an absolute offer accepted by
man; it must (in accordance with the nature of the spirit) become conscious of itself. Whenever God—by his absolute self-communication
—brings about man's self-transcendence into God, in such a way that
both these factors form the irrevocable promise made to all men which
has already reached its consummation in this man, there we have a hypostatic union. When we think of 'hypostatic union', we must not simply
remain attached to the imagined model of any sort of 'unity' or connection. To grasp the proper nature of this particular unity, it is also not
enough simply to say that, on account of this unity, the human reality

must also be attributed in all truth to the divine subject of the Logos. For this is precisely the question:—*why* is this possible, and *how* are we to conceive this unity which justifies such a statement of the 'communication of idioms'? This 'assumption' and 'unification' has the nature of a self-communication; there is 'assumption' so that God's reality may be communicated to what is assumed, viz. the human nature (and in the first place the human nature of Christ). But this very communication which is aimed at by this 'assumption' is *the* communication by what we call grace and glory and the latter are intended for all. It must not be objected that *this* (latter) communication is possible even without a hypostatic union, since it does in fact occur without it in our own case. For in us this communication is possible and effected precisely by this union and acceptance as it occurs in the Hypostatic Union. And, theologically speaking at least, there is nothing against the assumption that grace and hypostatic union can only be thought of together and that, as a unity, they signify one and the same *free* decision of God to institute the supernatural order of salvation. In Christ, God's self-communication takes place basically for all men, and there is 'hypostatic union' precisely in so far as this *unsurpassable* self-communication of God 'is there' irrevocably in a historically tangible and self-conscious manner. Once more we ask: why? Apart from the case of the Beatific Vision (and perhaps even this is no different in this respect from other cases, but we cannot deal with this here), every self-manifestation of God takes place through some finite reality—through a word, an event, etc., which belongs to the finite realm of creatures. As long as this finite mediation of the divine self-manifestation, however, is not in the strictest sense a divine reality itself, it is basically transitory and surpassable (since it is finite) and is not in this finiteness simply the reality of God itself; and thus can be surpassed by God himself simply by positing a new finite reality. Hence, if the reality in which God's absolute self-communication is pledged and accepted for the whole of humanity and thus becomes 'present' for us (i.e. Christ's reality) is to be really the final and unsurpassable divine self-communication, then it must be said that it is not only posited by God but is God himself. The pledge itself cannot be anything else than a human reality which has been absolutely sanctified by grace. For a mere word would not be the actual event of self-communication but would merely tell us about it: in other words, it would not be in any sense (since the event itself in its openness, and not a word *about* it, is the primary proclamation of itself) the *actual* and really primary communication addressed to us about this self-communication made to us. If this is so, and if this pledge must be truly and absolutely God himself, then it must be a human reality which belongs absolutely to God—in other words, exactly what we call 'Hypostatic Union'. Hence, if we may put it this way, the Hypostatic Union does not differ from our grace by what is pledged in it, for this is grace in both cases (even in the case of Jesus). But it differs from our grace by the fact that Jesus is our pledge, and we ourselves are not the pledge but the recipients of God's pledge to us. But the unity of the pledge, and the inseparability of this pledge from the one who pledges (indeed, pledges *himself to us*!) must be conceived in accordance with the peculiar nature of the pledge. If the real pledge made to us is precisely the very human reality itself which has been given grace and in which and through which God pledges himself to us in his grace, then the unity of the one who pledges and the pledge cannot be considered as a merely 'moral' one—as for instance the unity between a human 'word' (or something similar which is merely a sign) and God—but must be conceived as an *irrevocable* unity between this human reality and God making a separation between the proclamation and the giver of this proclamation impossible—which, in other words, makes of the really humanly proclaimed and the pledge given to us, a reality of God himself. And this is precisely what is meant by hypostatic union. It means this and, properly speaking, nothing else: in the human reality of Jesus, God's absolute saving purpose (the absolute event of God's self-communication to us) is simply, absolutely and irrevocably present; in it is present both the declaration made to us and its acceptance—something effected by God himself, a reality of God himself, unmixed and yet inseparable and hence irrevocable. This declaration, however, is the pledge of grace to us.

IX
Grace

1. Nature and Grace*

The theology of grace of the standard neo-Scholastic manuals regarded grace as a purely entitative elevation of human nature. Grace was in no way perceptible to human consciousness. In general neo-Scholastic theologians also took an extrinsicist approach to grace. Man's elevation to the supernatural order was considered to be the juridical effect of a divine decree which, although it ordered man to a supernatural end, produced no ontological effect on his human nature. Thus man without grace in the historical order differs from man in the state of pure nature sicut spoliatus a nudo. *There is no ontological difference between them, although there is an all important juridical one. Furthermore the link between grace and the Incarnation in the standard manuals was a purely* de facto *one. True, all grace was the grace of Christ. Nevertheless, the ontological ground for that fact was simply the positive will of God which required the death of Christ as the price of man's redemption. There was no intrinsic link between grace and the self-communication of God to man through the Incarnation of the Logos. Finally the run-of-the-mill theology of grace, which made created grace the primary cause of justification, refused to admit that the indwelling of the economic Trinity through sanctifying grace grounded a proper personal relation between the justified soul and each one of the Divine Persons.*

This theology of grace made the supernatural order a region remote from human experience which had little practical significance for Christian living. Since conscious moral activity would be the same, as far as awareness went, in the natural or the supernatural order, the values and goals for which men strive would be the same whether a supernatural order existed or not. Christ might be the exemplary cause of the Christian's redemption by furnishing a model for religious imitation. But

*From *Theological Investigations*, vol. IV, pp. 166-69, 174-84.
© 1966 and 1974 by Darton, Longman & Todd Ltd.

Christ's connection with a non-experienced order of grace was difficult to understand. The ordinary Christian found little in it to promote his self understanding or to motivate his Christian living.

Rahner's theology of grace bridges the gap between the grace of Christ and Christian experience, which remained unbridged in standard neo-Scholastic theology. His theological anthropology enabled him to see that, contrary to the manuals' purely entitative understanding of grace, grace must have a perceptible effect on human consciousness. Thomists have always held that an entitatively supernatural act must have a different formal object than an entitatively natural act. A different formal object for the conscious striving of the human spirit, however, means an entitatively different Ultimate Horizon. If then the human spirit has been transformed by grace so that its intrinsic dynamism has been reordered to a strictly supernatural goal, the Ultimate Horizon of its striving must now be the God of grace and glory. One of the fundamental theses of theological anthropology is that the human spirit has an implicit, unobjective awareness of its Ultimate Horizon. Consequently its entitative elevation to the supernatural order must result in a change of its implicit awareness of itself and God. Albeit implicitly and unobjectively, grace cannot fail to be conscious. In every justified man there is a consciousness of grace, even though he may not be objectively aware of it as grace. Indeed there can be a consciousness of grace even before justification. Actual grace is also an entitatively supernatural act. Therefore its inspirations, which involve an ontological elevation of the human spirit, also have an effect on human consciousness.

God's offer of grace is an offer of himself. Justifying grace is primordially Uncreated Grace, the indwelling of the economical Trinity within the justified soul. Because of the inseparable connection between God's decrees of creation and of the Incarnation, Uncreated Grace has been offered to man since the beginning of human history as the grace of Christ. It is the initial stage of the same ontological possession of God whose fully developed stage will be reached in the Beatific Vision. Run-of-the-mill scholastic theology cannot provide an adequate understanding of this offer which God has made of himself in Christ. If created grace is considered simply in terms of efficient causality, it cannot be the ground of a presence of God in the human soul which is essentially different from God's causal presence in the rest of his creation. The relation of created grace to God as an efficient cause terminates at the common divine nature. Therefore it cannot ground a proper relation to each of the Divine Persons but only a relation of appropriation. On this view it is hard to explain the ontological identity between God's presence in the justified soul through grace and the presence of the Trinity in the Beatific Vision. For a satisfactory explanation of God's presence in the graced and glorified human soul the theologian must turn to the metaphysics of for-

mal and material causality. In justification, as in the Beatific Vision, the Holy Trinity communicates its own divine reality to the human soul as Uncreated Grace. Since this communication is the communication of God's own divine reality, it can only be understood in terms of quasi-formal causality. Uncreated Grace is therefore the primordial grace. Created grace is not the efficient cause of Uncreated Grace. Created grace is rather its material cause, the ultimate disposition which renders the human spirit apt to receive God's quasi-formal communication of himself.

Although the presence of the economical Trinity in the human soul through quasi-formal causality is the cornerstone of Rahner's theology of grace, this thesis was by no means unknown to Thomists before his writing on the subject. Maurice de la Taille had proposed it earlier in the century. Although de la Taille's thesis had won wide acceptance among French Thomists, Rahner was not familiar with it until it was called to his attention subsequent to his own articles on Uncreated Grace. Thus both Rahner and de la Taille came to the same conclusion independently. Rahner has cheerfully admitted the similarity of his own theological position to the thesis proposed by the French theologian Edmond Brisbois in the mid-Thirties.

What then has been the average concept of the relationship of nature and grace in neo-Scholasticism? To see the peculiar elements of this concept, which was not strictly speaking clear to the theologians themselves, we must start by discussing a position which is apparently only a marginal one in the doctrine of supernatural grace. This grace by which man is justified, and by which he is enabled to perform salutary acts, was taken to be something totally beyond the region of consciousness. In itself, this is merely a scholastic opinion, which was always in fact disputed. For Thomistic theology always maintained that a supernatural act had a formal object which could never be attained by a purely natural act. But the opposite opinion was predominant in the schools and determined the average mentality: supernatural grace is a reality of which one knows something through the teaching of faith but which is in itself completely inaccessible and gives no sign of its presence in the conscious, personal life of man. Once taught of its existence by faith, man must of course refer to it, take care to possess it (by moral acts and the reception of the sacraments), treasure it as the divinization of his being and the pledge and presupposition of eternal life. But the space where he comes to himself, experiences himself and lives, is, as regards the data of consciousness, not filled by this grace. His experience of his spiritual and moral acts in their proper reality (in contrast to their proposed objects, which are distinct from the acts) remains exactly what it would and could be, if there were no such thing as a supernatural 'elevation' of these acts. Thus grace, of itself, according to this very common opinion, is a superstructure beyond the realm of consciousness, with regard to the mental experience of the moral being, though it is of course a conscious object of faith and acknowledged to be the most sublime and divine element in man, his only salutary possession.

This view also seems to be the only possible and the obvious one. One can know nothing of one's state of grace, or at most, one can make deductions about it, more or less probable, using certain indications. But one does not 'notice' grace at all, or at the very most, only some of the 'healing' graces which help to fulfil the natural law and are of themselves natural aids. Simple experience and the teaching of Trent (Denzinger 802; 805; 825; 826) seem to confirm this opinion which anyway presents itself as the obvious one. Once it is accepted, the region where we know ourselves as active spiritually and morally seems to be naturally identifiable with the dimension of 'nature'. Indeed, this state becomes the very definition of what we mean by nature: that which we know about ourselves without the word of revelation—for that is nature and *merely* nature. And vice versa; nature alone and its acts are the components of the life which we experience as our own. We use the elements of natural concepts, attitudes etc, to construct the acts in which we refer ourselves by our intention to the realities of the revealed mysteries of God, acts which we know to be 'ontologically' elevated to the supernatural plane—but only 'ontologically'. Supernatural 'enlightenment', moral 'impulse' and 'inspiration' to good acts, the 'light' of faith, the breath of the Spirit and other similar concepts from Scripture and tradition (the unction, the signing of the Spirit etc.), are reduced either to this purely entitative elevation of our natural moral acts, or to a natural influence of a psychological type —which is however considered to be providentially directed to our supernatural salvation. In a word, the relationship between nature and grace is conceived in such a way that they appear as two layers so carefully placed that they penetrate each other as little as possible.

In the same way, the orientation of 'nature' to grace is conceived of in as negative a way as possible. Grace is, it is true, an unsurpassable perfectioning of nature; God as the Lord of this nature can command man to submit to his *de facto* will and to be receptive to his grace, which direct man to a supernatural life and end. But of itself nature has only a '*potentia obedientialis*' to such an end, and this capacity is thought of as negatively as possible. It is no more than non-repugnance to such an elevation. Of itself, nature would find its perfection just as readily and harmoniously in its own proper realm, in a purely natural end, without an immediate intuition of God in the beatific vision. When it finds itself in immediate possession of itself—as is part of the essence of the spirit '*reditio completa in seipsum*'—it meets itself as though it were 'pure nature'. According to the well-known axiom (which is a matter of opinion), it is distinguished from pure nature only *'sicut spoliatus a nudo'*. And this 'state of being despoiled' is silently considered as a merely extrinsic element with regard to the absence of sanctifying grace: a deprivation due to a divine decree (which demands the possession of grace) and to an historical fact of the past (the guilt of Adam). But we do not usually think that the lack of grace might be different in the two cases, that of pure nature and that of fallen nature.

This popular view cannot be absolved from a certain 'extrinsicism', as it has been called, if it can be shown that all the data of official Church teaching on the relationship of nature and grace can be maintained untouched even if the relationship is held to be closer than it is described in this current opinion. And it cannot be denied, though it is distasteful to some to admit it, that the current view is not without danger in practice. For if it is correct, the known spiritual life of man must take place within the region of his pure nature, which has two sectors: the 'purely natural' which is totally confined to its own dimensions, apart from an 'elevation' which is outside consciousness, and then a number of acts of knowledge which are (subjectively) composed of purely natural elements (in matters of the spiritual as such) and are referred to the supernatural only by their objects (by faith, by a pure intention etc.). If this is true, then it is not surprising—though not of course justifiable—that man should take very little interest in this mysterious superstructure of his being. After all, he does not find grace where he finds himself, in the immediate activation of his spiritual being. And one could have the impression—not objectively justifiable—that something originally called grace had come to be considered, in the course of the medieval evolution of dogma, as an act produced by nature's own capacity (e.g. its possibility of loving God above all things); after which, to conceal the process, this same act was once more placed above nature as the 'supernatural'. And then this supernatural was displaced into a region beyond consciousness, as an unconscious modality of what was spiritual and moral in nature, so that it was very hard to say what use it was at all. Let us think, for instance, of the distinction (correct in a certain sense) between a natural and a supernatural 'love of God above all things'. How are these two acts to be distinguished *as acts of love, that is, spiritually,* if the supernaturalness of supernatural love *only* consists of its entitative 'elevation'? Is it *totally* misguided, to see modern naturalism as having *some* connexion with this theory? Is it quite wrong to suggest that the modern lack of interest in the supernatural can only have developed on the basis of such a view of grace, which must be to some extent nominalist?

One may well think that the question of 'uncreated grace' may be taken further. In the encyclical *'Mystici Corporis'* Pius XII indicated that there were open questions here, which were deliberately left open by the magisterium. If, as Pius XII emphasizes, grace and glory are two stages of the one divinization of man; if, as classical theology has always emphasized, glory means a self-communication of God to the created spirit which is not a created quality or entity distinct from God, produced by efficient causality, but God's imparting himself to man by means of quasi-formal causality: then this notion can be applied far more explicitly to grace than has been customary hitherto in theology. 'Uncreated grace' will then no longer appear to be merely a consequence of the creation of 'infused' habitual grace, regarded as a 'physical accident'. It will be rather seen as what is truly central in grace—which will explain much better the strictly mysterious character of grace, since a purely created entity, strictly as such, can never be an absolute mystery. God communicates himself to man in his own proper reality. That is the mystery and the fullness of grace. Starting from here, it will be much easier to find the link with the mystery of the Incarnation and that of the Trinity.

It seems indeed to be true that the opinion maintained by Petavius, Scheeben and others, each in their own way, is gaining ground: that grace founds a relationship between man and each of the three divine persons which is not an appropriation, but something proper to each divine person. If one supposes that the immediate vision of God can only be based on a quasi-formal self-communication of God in vision, and not (adequately) on a created quality in the spirit of man; and if one recalls the obvious truth, that each of the three divine persons is the object of immediate intuition in his personal propriety: then that entitative (ontic) quasiformal communication of God, which takes the place of a *species impressa* as the ontological foundation of man's possession of God in knowledge, must include a non-appropriated relationship of each of the three divine persons to man. On this basis, the relation of the 'immanent' to the 'redemptive' Trinity could be thought out anew. And the supreme mystery of the Christian faith could appear more clearly as a reality with which man has to do not merely conceptually (and through the incarnation of the Logos) but also really, in the exercise of his life of grace. It could be seen that God is not only trinitarian in himself, but also communicates himself in a trinitarian way, in grace, which means more than efficient causality on the part of God in the line of *creatio ex nihilo* outside himself—though it remains true that where God exercises *efficient* causality, the work is to be attributed to the whole Trinity as one single cause.

One may and perhaps must go still further. As a rule, the connexion between the Incarnation and grace is thought of as merely *de facto*: God has in fact decreed that the order of grace should depend on the Incarnate Word. It is implicitly supposed that things could be otherwise. But is this supposition clear and certainly correct? Both the order of grace and the Incarnation derive from God's free grace. But does it follow that both these objects of God's gracious will, in both of which he communicates himself, as himself, *ad extra,* though in different ways, are really *two* different acts of his freely exercised love? Is there anything in Catholic principles to prevent us taking the Scotist point of view and considering the primal act of God, in which everything else is in fact given, as the self-exteriorization of God who is the love which gives itself in the incarnation? And then the order of grace would already be instituted, which would (probably) be unthinkable without such a decree of God with regard to his personal communication. Are there any valid arguments against the position which holds that the *possibility* of creation rests on that of the Incarnation, even though the fact of creation (as nature) does not necessarily imply the actual realization of the self-exteriorization of God in the Incarnation? Let us assume this position, which is recommended by its lofty simplicity, not to mention its more positive support in the Logos-theology of pre-Nicene and pre-Augustinian theology. Then grace has a much more radically Christological character. The Logos who has become part of the world is not merely the *de facto* mediator of grace by his merit—which only became necessary because Adam had cast this grace away—he is also the person who by his free Incarnation creates the order of grace and nature as his own presupposition (nature) and his milieu (the grace of the other spiritual creatures). This would enable us, as we have already said, to reach a deeper understanding of the immanent Trinity. The Logos would not be merely one of the divine persons who could become man if they wished: he would be *the* person in whom God communicates himself hypostatically to the world. The Incarnation would mirror the personal propriety of the second divine person, the Logos as such. The Trinity of the economy of redemption would enable us to have some insight into the immanent Trinity. This is not impossible, because the axiom that the efficient causality of God *ad extra* is common to the one God without distinction of persons cannot be applied to this quasi-formal causality. This invites us to re-consider the speculation of pre-Nicene theology and of the Greeks in general. It will appear that on this point St Augustine had too little understanding of the most ancient theology, which held that it is the Logos who appears and must appear if God wishes to show himself personally to the world.

With a more exact concept of 'uncreated grace' in mind, we can also see more clearly how the Catholic theology of grace, on its own proper principles (grace is not just pardon for the poor sinner but 'participation in the divine nature'), can go beyond the notion of a *merely* entitative, created state and the merely 'ontic' and non-existential element of a 'physical accident'. Grace is God himself, the communication in which he gives himself to man as the divinizing favour which he is himself. Here his work is really *himself,* since it is he who is imparted. Such grace, from the very start, cannot be thought of independently of the personal love of God and its answer in man. This grace is not thought of as a 'thing'. It is something that is only 'put at man's disposal' in that act of 'letting oneself be disposed of' which is the proper gift of the freest grace, the miracle of love. Ontic categories are only maintained here (even by Catholics) because and in so far as a Catholic philosophy does hold that the real (and what could be more real and effective than the love of God?) must be thought of as 'real' and 'being', that the highest must be expressed in the most abstract words, and that therefore the act of divine love towards us—God's act, not ours, though enabling us to act, and not just submit —previous to our act, must be considered as that which renders possible our moral and religious decisions. It cannot therefore be expressed except in categories of being such as state, accident, habit, infusion etc. Such expressions are not confusing if properly understood, and they need not distort one's view of the fact that grace is always the free action of divine love which is only 'at the disposal' of man precisely in so far as he is at the disposal of this divine love. One must indeed always remember that God is not diminished by our becoming greater. And in the last resort, Christianity is not the religion whose basic attitude is fear of its going to our head—and not into our grateful heart—if we extol the greatness to which God has raised man in order that he might praise God. This is true of Mariology. And it is also true of grace, of which Mariology is merely the most beautiful part of the doctrine.

This grace affects our conscious life, not just our being but our existence. The Thomistic doctrine of the specific object of the act entiatively elevated to the supernatural, an object which, as formal, cannot be attained by any natural act, must be fully considered once more and again be given a predominant place. For in such a context 'object' does not mean 'something present like other objects, distinguishable from them and placed beside them by reflexion'. A formal object is neither a datum of knowledge nor an abstract and merely consequent summing up of what is common to many individual objects. It is the *a priori* horizon given in consciousness, under which, in grasping the individual *a posteriori* object, everything is known which is grasped as an object strictly speaking. If we understand aright the old scholastic doctrine of the formal object as the *a priori* 'light' under which and in which all single objects are grasped, no one can object to the old Thomistic doctrine of the formal supernatural object by appealing to 'experience', which is supposed to know nothing of such a formal object—meaning in fact material object! It must only be noted that the *a priori* formal object of an act is not the same thing conceptually as a formal object which is clearly *distinguishable* by reflexion from another formal object. For a metaphysics of knowledge, there is no great difficulty in recognizing that transcendence towards being in general, the natural openness for being as a whole, cannot be clearly distinguished in subsequent reflexion from the supernatural transcendence, the openness of the soul informed by grace, which is directed in all its supernaturally elevated acts towards the God of eternal life, towards the immediate experience of the (triune) absolute being. And this is true although both modes of transcendence, the formal object of the natural spirit and the formal object of the supernaturally elevated spirit, are both given in consciousness. Such considerations, taken from a metaphysics of the spirit, though barely indicated here, show that the ancient Thomistic doctrine is perfectly defensible.

It has in its favour that it is a transposition into metaphysical and theological terms of a conviction which is voiced in the Scriptures. Let us take the doctrine of Scripture as it is, honestly and without prejudice, and without correcting it in the light of the silent presupposition that it cannot have said something, because this something is supposed to be impossible. Then we must say that for Scripture, the communication of the Spirit (the divine *pneuma*) is not just a trans-conscious entitative 'elevation' of the conscious moral acts of man, which remain existentially the same and are only changed extrinsically by the *fides ex auditu*. It is 'life', 'unction', 'consolation', 'light', the inexpressible co-intercession of the Spirit, *pneuma* which is more than *nous*, an inward attraction, testimony given by the Spirit etc. It would be well if the doctrine of Scripture were carefully examined in the light of this scholastic controversy. If this were done, one would gradually rid oneself of the unavowed opinion that in an objectively serious and religiously important question one is already certain *a priori* that no more light is to be had from Scripture if the subject is controverted in the schools, because otherwise the question would have been settled long ago. Once all the schools are of the opinion that supernatural actual graces are to be described as 'lights' and 'inspirations', this doctrine of tradition must be taken seriously. It may not be so interpreted in anti-Thomistic teaching that nothing of it in fact remains. For an entitatively elevated act which remains from the point of view of consciousness a natural act, cannot be characterized as an inward illumination and inspiration without doing violence to language. The fact that that the anti-Thomistic (Molinist) thesis still holds on to this characterization and tries to do justice to it, shows how strongly tradition is convinced that the act due to supernatural grace is even spiritually different from the natural act. The difference is felt to be conscious and existential, and not confined to an entitative modality.

Here we must note something else, which should be borne more clearly in mind than is usually the case. Acts inspired supernaturally by grace are not confined to the justified. There are stirrings of grace which precede the act of accepting justification in a free act of faith and love. There is also grace outside the Church and its sacraments. The offer of grace to a man who has reached in his spiritual development the immediate possibility of an existentaal decision is not intermittent, restricted to some very definite occasions and 'actual' in this momentary sense. There is no stringent theological reason for thinking it should be so. 'Actual' means that grace is given prior to an existential decision, as an 'offer' and 'possibility' (of a free salutary act). In this sense, the moral freedom of man to dispose of himself always exists in the prior possibility of supernatural acts, a possibility effected by grace. If this is so, then we may say that the supernatural transcendence is always present in every man who has reached the age of moral reason. That does not necessarily mean that he is justified. He may be a sinner and an unbeliever. But where and in so far as he has the concrete possibility of a morally good act, he is in fact constantly within the open horizon of transcendence towards the God of the supernatural life, whether his free act is in accord or in conflict with this prior state of his supernaturally elevated spiritual existence. *If* in every moral act he takes a positive or negative attitude to the *totality* of his *de facto* existence (a supposition whose reality we need not examine here): *then* we must say: every morally good act of man is, in the actual order of salvation, also in fact a supernaturally salutary act. We should *then* have arrived at the well-known point of view maintained by Ripalda. This conclusion need not terrify us. First of all, the thesis of Ripalda, though rarely maintained, is exposed to no theological censure. And secondly, one could still hold the basic position outlined here, even if the supposition which brought us to the thesis of Ripalda were contested, which would avoid the position of Ripalda. However that may be, the notions which we have outlined show clearly that it is quite conceivable that the whole spiritual life of man is constantly affected by grace. It is not a rare and sporadic event just because grace is unmerited. Theology has been too long and too often bedevilled by the unavowed supposition that grace would be no longer grace if it were too generously distributed by the love of God! Our whole spiritual life is lived in the realm of the salvific will of God, of his prevenient grace, of his call as it becomes efficacious: all of which is an element within the region of our consciousness, though one which remains anonymous as long as it is not interpreted from without by the message of faith. Even when he does not 'know' it and does not believe it, that is, even when he cannot make it an individual object of knowledge by merely inward reflexion, man always lives consciously in the presence of the triune God of eternal life. God is the unexpressed but real 'Whither' of the dynamism of all spiritual and moral life in the realm of spiritual existence which is in fact founded, that is, supernaturally elevated by God. It is a 'purely *a priori*'. Whither, but always there, present to consciousness without being in the nature of an object, but nonetheless there.

We do not need to insist on the existence of such an *a priori* of a supernatural nature in spiritual existence, even though it can only be clearly expounded and translated into objectivated knowledge in the light of the word of revelation which comes from without. It manifests itself as the mysterious activation of individual and collective spiritual life in countless ways, which would not exist if this mysterious activation and dynamism were not at work. It follows that even outside the process of official revelation the history of religion is not merely a product of natural reason and sin. Precisely in its consciously tangible results, in its objective spirit, it is the product of the natural spirit, grace and sin. Thus when man is summoned by the message of faith given by the visible Church, it is not the first time that he comes into spiritual contact with the reality preached by the Church: such conceptual knowledge of it is not primary. The call only makes him consciously aware of—and of course forces him to make a choice about—the grace which already encompassed him inarticulately but really as an element of his spiritual existence. The preaching is the express awakening of what is already present in the depths of man's being, not by nature, but by grace. But it is a grace which always surrounds man, even the sinner and the unbeliever, as the inescapable setting of his existence.

We are now in a position to face the real problem of 'nature and grace' in the strict sense and to pose it properly. It is clear that by living out his spirtual existence, man always attains his 'nature', even in the theological sense, where this concept is opposed to that of grace and the supernatural. For in every question which he poses about himself, in every judgment where he contrasts himself with an object and grasps it in the perspective of an unlimited transcendence, he experiences himself as something which he must necessarily be, as something that is a unity and a totality which cannot be dissolved into variables, which either is there as a whole or is not there at all. He grasps his metaphysical being: spirit in transcendence and freedom. And on the basis of this initial transcendental analysis of what is implicitly asserted about man in each of his human acts, much more could probably be affirmed as 'essential' to him: his existence in a world, his having a body, his belonging to a society of his fellows. In a word, there is such a thing as a metaphysical knowledge of man, his essence and nature, by the light of his reason, which means here primarily independently of the word of revelation; but it also means knowledge through the means (his reason) which is itself an element of the essence so grasped. But it also follows from the theological data already given that this *de facto* human nature, as it knows itself here, and in view of all its experiences (especially when this human experience is viewed in the light of the whole history of mankind, where alone its development is fully realized) cannot and need not be considered as the reflexion of that 'pure' nature which is distinguished in theology from everything supernatural. Our actual nature is *never* 'pure' nature. It is a nature installed in a supernatural order which man can never leave, even as a sinner and unbeliever. It is a nature which is continually being determined (which does not mean justified) by the supernatural grace of salvation offered to it. And these 'existentials' of man's concrete, 'historical' nature are not purely states of being beyond consciousness. They make themselves felt in the experience of man. By simple reflexion on himself, in the light of natural reason, he cannot simply and clearly distinguish them from the natural spiritual activity which is the manifestation of his nature. But once he knows from revelation that there is an order of grace, not due to him and not belonging to the necessary constitutives of his being, he becomes more cautious. He must allow for the fact that much of his concrete experience which he is almost automatically tempted to attribute to his 'nature' may perhaps in fact be the effect in him of what he must recognize as unmerited grace in the light of theology.

This does not mean that he is now quite ignorant of what is natural to him. The nature of a spiritual being and its supernatural elevation are not opposed to each other like two things which lie side by side, so that they must be either kept separate or confused. The supernatural elevation of man is, though not due to him, the absolute fulfilment of his being, whose spiritual quality and transcendence towards being as such prevents its being 'defined', that is 'delimited' in the same way that sub-human entities can. For these are 'defined' by the fact that it is their essence to be restricted to a certain realm of reality. (It is therefore impossible, for instance, for them to be 'elevated' to a supernatural fulfilment: such an elevation would destroy their being which is essentially limit.) The 'definition' of the created spirit is its 'openness' to being as such: as created, it is open to the fullness of reality; as spirit, it is open to absolute reality in general. It is not therefore surprising that the grandeur of the (varying) fulfilment of this openness (which does not of itself imply necessarily an absolute and unsurpassable fulfilment and yet, as absolute openness, still has a sense without such fulfilment) cannot be recognized at once as 'due' or 'undue'. And yet the basic essence of man, his nature as such openness (transcendence) can be perfectly well established. The initial elements of such fulfilment are already present: the experience of infinite longings, of radical optimism, of unquenchable discontent, of the torment of the insufficiency of everything attainable, of the radical protest against death, the experience of being confronted with an absolute love precisely where it is lethally incomprehensible and seems to be silent and aloof, the experience of a radical guilt and of a still abiding hope etc. These elements are in fact tributary to that divine force which impels the created spirit—by grace —to an absolute fulfilment. Hence in them grace is experienced *and* the natural being of man.

For the essence of man is such that it is experienced where grace is experienced, since grace is only experienced where the spirit naturally is. And vice versa: where spirit is experienced in the actual order of things, it is a supernaturally elevated spirit.

2. Relationship Between Nature and Grace: The Supernatural Existential*

There is no such thing as a purely natural act in the historical order. Human nature is a "remainder concept." The philosopher, who reflects on the historical human nature which men experience, has no knowledge of human nature's "metaphysical essence." Only the theologian, who knows of its elevation through Revelation, can work out a metaphysical concept of pure human nature. Contrary to the extrinsicist position of the manuals, God's decree elevating man to the supernatural order produces an intrinsic ontological effect on man's human nature. For, if that decree is to be a real offer of grace, it must make human nature capable of accepting it. Therefore God's real offer of his grace produces a "supernatural existential" in the human soul. This "existential" is a permanent modification of the human spirit which transforms its natural dynamism into an ontological drive to the God of grace and glory. The supernatural existential is not grace itself but only God's offer of grace which, by ontologically modifying the soul, enables it to freely accept or reject grace. The pain of loss is the effect of the free rejection of grace in the damned soul. In fact, the soul is damned precisely because its inbuilt longing, elevated by the supernatural existential, cannot be satisfied without the Beatific Vision of which it is forever deprived.

The supernatural existential enables Rahner to hold that all men are in the supernatural order without seeming to compromise the gratuity of the supernatural, as de Lubac was accused of doing in his Surnaturel. *The term "existential" is used by Heidegger to designate a fundamental structure of* Dasein, *the subject whose intentionality is directed toward the world and Being. Rahner's critics have frequently complained of his failure to clarify the exact ontological status of his supernatural existential.*

How am I to know that everything I in fact encounter in my existential experience of myself (the ultimate yearning, the most profound inner dispersion, the radical experience of the universally human tragedy of concupiscence and death) does in fact fall within the realm of my 'nature', and would also exist, exist in just this form, if there were no vocation to supernatural communion with God? There is no way of providing a justification for this tacit presupposition starting from man, nor is it really proved by any theological argument. And this for the simple reason that the possibility of experiencing grace and the possibility of experiencing grace *as* grace are not the same thing. If this is not assumed beforehand or

*From *Theological Investigations*, vol. I, pp. 300–02, 310–15.
© 1961, 1965 and 1974 by Darton, Longman & Todd Ltd.

taken for granted, is it so easy to say what belongs to human 'nature', and what is more not merely to the contingently factual nature of this concrete economy but to 'pure' nature, in such a way that if it were lacking man would cease to be man? How could one give this question a precise answer philosophically, without recourse to Revelation? It may with justice be said that man is an *animal rationale*. But do we know whether the subsistent object actually envisaged in terms of this formula would really be just such as we actually experience it, if this man were not called to eternal communion with the God of grace, were not exposed to the permanent dynamism of grace and were not to feel its loss a mortal wound on account of being continuously ordained to it in his inmost depths? One may have recourse to a transcendental deduction in order to ascertain the irreducible quiddity of man, i.e. take that for man's purely natural essence which is simultaneously posited in first asking the question about this essence at all. But even then one does not know whether one may not have introduced too little into this concept of man, or whether in the very act of asking the question, contingently but for us unavoidably, a supernatural element may not have been at work in the questioner which could never in actual fact be bracketed off, and so would prevent one from laying hold *purely* of man's natural essence in the concept. A *precise* delimitation of nature from grace (supposing it were possible at all) and so a really pure concept of pure nature could thus in every case only be pursued with the help of Revelation, which tells us what in us is grace and so provides us with the means of abstracting this grace from the body of our existential experience of man and thus of acquiring pure nature (in its *totality*) as a 'remainder'.

We should like to try to suggest in a few brief words how we ourselves conceive of the relationship between man and grace. God wishes to communicate himself, to pour forth the love which he himself is. That is the first and the last of his real plans and hence of his real world too. Everything else exists so that this one thing might be: the eternal miracle of infinite Love. And so God makes a creature whom he can love: he creates man. He creates him in such a way that he *can* receive this Love which is God himself, and that he can and must[1] at the same time accept it

---

[1]Two things are meant by this 'can and must'. Firstly, merely the *fact*: God wishes so to communicate himself that his self-communication to the creaturely subject is unexacted. Hence he must create man just 'so' that he can receive this self-communication only as grace; thus he must not only give him an essence but also constitute him as a 'nature' (as opposed to an unexacted supernatural). But this formula is intended to convey a second point: the self-communication simply *cannot* be other than unexacted, i.e. the will to a 'purely' *unexacted* self-communication is not only a fact but a *necessity*: there is no essence of a creaturely kind which God could constitute for which this communication could be the normal, matter-of-course perfection to which it was compellingly disposed. This is indeed (against Ripalda) the general teaching of theology today: grace and glory are simply speaking supernatural. But then one would have to draw the consequence of this proposition, more

for what it is: the ever astounding wonder, the unexpected, unexacted gift. And let us not forget here that ultimately we only know what 'unexacted' means when we know what personal love is, not *vice versa*: we don't understand what love is by knowing the meaning of 'unexacted'. Thus in this second respect God must so create man that love does not only pour forth free and unexacted, but also so that man as real partner, as one who can accept or reject it, can experience and accept it *as* the unexacted event and wonder not owed to *him,* the real man. As unexacted, not only because he does not deserve it as *sinner,* but further because he can also embrace it as unexacted when, already blessed in this love, he is allowed to forget that he was a sinner once. That is all we have to say on this matter 'kerygmatically'. It will appear that one need not discourse at such great length about nature and the supernatural in one's proclamation of the Gospel as one has been accustomed to do in this connexion.

Now if one quite rightly sets about transposing these simple propositions, which every Christian can in a true sense make his own, into 'theology', because this transposition is necessary for the theologian and the preacher if he is to be preserved from the danger of misinterpreting them or rendering them innocuous, the following points may be made.

1. Man should be *able* to receive this Love which is God himself; he must have a congeniality for it. He must be able to accept it (and hence grace, the beatific vision) as one who has room and scope, understanding and desire for it. Thus he must have a real 'potency' for it. He must have it *always*. He is indeed someone always addressed and claimed by this Love. For, as he now in fact is, he is created for it; he is thought and called into being so that Love might bestow itself. To this extent this 'potency' is what is inmost and most authentic in him, the centre and root of what he is absolutely. He must have it *always*: for even one of the damned, who has turned away from this Love and made himself incapable of receiving this Love, must still be really able to experience this Love (which being scorned now burns like fire) as that to which he is ordained in the ground of his concrete being; he must consequently always remain what he was created as: the burning longing for God himself in the immediacy of his own threefold life. The capacity for the God of self-

---

clearly than is usually the case: this grace is only then conceived of in its true essence when it is recognized to be not just the *created* 'accidental' reality produced by God's efficient causality 'in' a (natural) substance, but includes 'uncreated grace' in its own concept in such a way that this may not be conceived of purely as a consequence of created grace. For it is difficult to see from an ontological point of view why it should not at least be *possible* for a created accident (however 'divinizing' it may be thought to be) to be ordered to a natural substance connatural with it, i.e. it is difficult to see how a purely created, accidental reality could be supernatural *simpliciter*.

bestowing personal Love is the central and abiding existential of man as he really is.[1]

2. The real man as God's real partner should be able to receive this Love as what it necessarily is: as free gift. But that means that this central, abiding existential, consisting in the ordination to the threefold God of grace and eternal life, is itself to be characterized as unexacted, as 'supernatural'. Not because man first of all—'obviously'—has a fixed, circumscribed nature in the sense that measured by it (as a fixed quantity known beforehand) grace, which is to say ultimately God himself, appears to be out of proportion and must therefore be called supernatural. But because the longing for, the ordination to, God's Love, this existential for supernatural grace, only allows grace to be unexacted grace when it is itself unexacted, and at the moment when, fulfilled by grace, it becomes conscious of itself *as* supernatural, i.e. shines forth as unexacted by the real man, not owed to him. Man is not to recognize himself merely as part of God's free creation; because he exists and although he exists already, he is to accept God's Love as gift and unexpected wonder. But if he were in a certain sense nothing but this existential, and were *this*—here there arises the *theological* word 'nature' for the first time—simply his nature, i.e. were it in absolutely no way capable of being dissociated from what he is otherwise and from what he could understand himself to be, then he could certainly as a free agent always continue to behave contrary to this nature in the despite of Love; but he could not accept this Love as bestowed gratuitously and without exaction upon him, God's really existent partner. Were he simply this existential, and were this his nature, then it would be unconditional in its essence, i.e. once it has been given, the Love which is God would 'have to' be offered by God.

3. Thus the man who receives this Love (in the Holy Spirit and thanks to the Word of the Gospel) will know this very existential for this Love as not owed to him, unexacted by him the real man. *This* knowledge is what allows him to distinguish and delimit what he always is (his concrete, indissoluble 'quiddity') into what is this unexacted real receptivity, the supernatural existential, and what is left over as remainder when this

[1]The theologian must seriously ask himself how it is possible to explain the *poena damni* without adopting such an abiding supernatural existential foreordained to grace. In fact it cannot otherwise be explained. For the loss of a good which is possible, but not the object of an ontological ordination prior to free endeavour ('voluntas ut res'), can only be felt as a painful evil when the loser wills it *freely* (but the damned have no use for this and do not do it). But the decisive argument for the existence of the supernatural existential is that already indicated above: even prior to grace man's binding, indissoluble ordination to the supernatural end is a real determination of man himself, and not merely a divine intention, a decree 'in God's will'. To make of this a purely 'juridical', purely 'moral' entity is nothing but a nominalism which has not taken cognisance of itself.

inmost centre is subtracted from the substance of his concrete quiddity, his 'nature'. 'Nature' in the theological sense (as opposed to nature as the substantial content of an entity always to be encountered in contingent fact), i.e. as the concept contraposed to the supernatural, is consequently a remainder concept (*Restbegriff*). By that is meant that starting as we have done, a reality must be postulated in man which remains over when the supernatural existential as unexacted is subtracted, and must have a meaning and a possibility of existence even when the supernatural existential is thought of as lacking (for otherwise this existential would necessarily be demanded precisely by the postulated reality, and it could only be unexacted with respect to a purely possible man, as an element in creation in general). But this 'pure' nature is not for that reason an unambiguously delimitable, de-finable quantity; no neat horizontal (to use Philipp Dessauer's way of putting it) allows of being drawn between this nature and the supernatural (both existential and grace). We never have this postulated pure nature for itself alone, so as in all cases to be able to say *exactly* what in our existential experience is to be reckoned to its account, what to the account of the supernatural. Where life is a matter of concrete yearning for eternal Truth and pure and infinite Love, of the inescapability of a free decision before God, of the pangs of birth, of concupiscence, labour, toil and death (hence of man's real essence and its achievement), all this is unquestionably experienced by a man who (consciously or unconsciously) is subject to the influence of the supernatural existential (if not of grace). Thus there is no way of telling *exactly* how his nature for itself alone would react, what precisely it would be for itself alone. This is not to deny that in the light of experience and still more of Revelation it might not be possible in some determinate respect to use a transcendental method to delimit what this human nature contains. 'Animal rationale' may still in this respect be an apt description. Certainly the philosopher has his own well-grounded concept of the nature of man: the irreducible substance of human being, established by recourse to human experience independently of verbal revelation. This concept may largely coincide with the theological concept of man's nature, in so far as without Revelation the greater part of what goes beyond this theological 'nature' is not experienced, and at any rate is not recognized *as* supernatural without the help of Revelation to interpret it. But in principle the content of this philosophical concept of man need not simply coincide with the content of the theological concept of man's 'pure nature'. It can in concrete fact contain more (i.e. something already supernatural, though not as such). When therefore one undertakes to state with precision what exact content is intended by such a concept of a pure nature, in particular as regards God and his moral law, the difficulties, indeed the impossibility, of a neat horizontal once again become apparent for us, as the history of theology shows only too clearly. But these difficulties lie precisely in the nature of things: man can experiment with himself only in the region of God's supernatural loving will, he can never find the nature he wants in a 'chemically pure' state, separated from its supernatural existential. Nature in this sense continues to be a remainder concept, but a necessary and objectively justified one, if one wishes to achieve reflexive consciousness of that unexactedness of grace which goes together with man's inner, unconditional ordination to it. Then in fact this unconditional ordination must itself be grasped as unexacted and supernatural; man's concretely experienced quiddity differentiates itself into the supernatural existential as such and the 'remainder'—the pure nature.

3. The Order of Creation and the Order of Redemption*

From the beginning of human history all men have received the real offer of Uncreated Grace, the indwelling of the economic Trinity. The order of creation and the order of redemption historically are one and the same. There has never been a purely natural order. Nevertheless the natural order has its own proper autonomy within the supernatural order. Nature and supernature are not simply juxtaposed as the extrinsicist theologians seemed to think. The order of creation is the "real symbol" in which the order of grace and redemption expresses itself, just as Christ's autonomous human nature was the "real symbol" in which the Word expressed himself as man. The order of grace requires the development of the natural order for its own expansion. Far from requiring the absorption or the neglect of the natural order, the metaphysics of grace and nature demand that both orders should grow together. God's self expression through grace requires the autonomous development of the natural order.

Therefore the natural ideals for which men strive have an ontological connection with the growth of the economic Trinity. Their progressive realization is part of God's real history in the world whose ground is the "becoming other" of the Word in his human nature and whose goal is the final union of a developed creation with the Trinity at Christ's second coming. Far from being an esoteric doctrine remote from human experience, the doctrine of Uncreated Grace, understood in the light of its ontological connection with world and salvation history, provides powerful motivation for moral and social action.

*From *The Christian Commitment*, pp. 44-53.
© 1963 by Sheed and Ward Ltd.

These considerations and distinctions, made here purely at the conceptual level, show how necessary it is to be careful about terminology. We cannot treat all the terms appearing down one side of our series of pairs as interchangeable, if we want to speak with any accuracy. We must have a care about this if we do not want to involve ourselves in difficulties arising not from the matter in hand but from bad terminology.

With these preliminaries stated, we come now to the matter in hand, though the first section has inevitably anticipated some of what now has to be said. Our subject is the fact and the more precise nature of the unity of the orders of redemption and creation.

(a) First let us make some formal ontological observations on the unity of a complex entity. Difficult though it may be for formal ontology and logic to deal with, the created intellect is faced with the fact that there are entities which are really *one* and yet, within this unity and without ceasing to have it, do include factors really distinct from each other. Unless we think of this unity in a merely superficial way, on the imaginative pattern of different things placed side by side and spatially continuous, we have a real logical and ontological problem: The different factors really are different within the "one thing," and not deducible from each other; to pose one of them is not simply and self-evidently to pose another, or they would have to be simply identical; and yet these different factors must form a real unity, and hence there must be within this one thing a single principle constituting an ultimate unity, which both maintains the separateness of the many in the one and really and truly unites them in the primal unity. We have got to be able to understand the different individual factors, in their difference and their relative opposition, by means of one unitary principle of plurality.

These ontological relations vary essentially, of course, according to what particular plural unit is involved. The "one thing" which consists of quantitative parts; the one human being consisting of body and soul; the one spirit with its plurality of powers, etc., are all very different cases, in which this ontological mystery of a plural unity recurs analogically in very different ways. Let us merely indicate at this point, abstractly and formally, one case of an ontological unity-plurality dialectic, because this is the quickest way of obtaining a particular conceptual tool which we need here. I mean that plural unity in which something, in order to be able to be itself, calls into being something else, distinct from and presupposed to itself, sets it up over against itself and maintains it in unity with itself as a differentiated thing.

This is very abstract, but such a situation does plainly exist, and can surely be traced, as an ontological relation, at very various levels of being. To take just one example: Concrete bodiliness is certainly distinct from the spiritual. But it is not, in the concrete, simply something added, complete in itself, to the spiritual being, so that the question would then arise of how these two entities could be united as from outside them both. Anyone who has really understood the Church's teaching on the soul as the actualizing formal principle of the body knows what we mean when we say that the soul itself creates this bodiliness, which is other than itself, as something distinct from and yet united with itself, in order to achieve its own being, its own essential fulfilment as spirit; when we say that bodiliness is not accidental, but an essential presupposition which the soul creates for itself, distinct from itself, and thus, from its very origins, maintains in unity with itself. The usefulness of this concept to our present discussion will soon become evident.

(b) There is no doubt that creation, including man and his history, material and spiritual together, is, as originally conceived by God, a unity such that each thing in it is relevant to all the rest, and all the rest to each thing. This mutual interdependence, which is the ground of the unity of creation, is of course of the most various kinds, since within the unity *of* creation there exist the most various entities which, being essentially different from each other, cannot have simply the same functions in relation to each other. But we must say radically, and from the start, that Christianity knows nothing of *creations*, only of one *creation*, since the entities which God has created do not merely connect with each other in so far as they all go back to one and the same origin, but are also in communion with each other, and this applies to all of them.

But within this one world there exists not only mutual relationship but also order, i.e. an objective gradation of degrees of being, of the worth and the effective power of each individual being within this one world. This order too is willed by God, or it would not exist. Now we have to say, on the one hand, that the totality of this one creation is willed by God as a totality, and hence that each individual (as is shown by the way its very nature is directed towards others) is willed by God only in so far as it is also a factor (though perhaps an absolutely irreplaceable and unique factor) in and for the one world: it is possible to say of every single thing, in a true sense, "This would not be if that were not also willed, and everything, great and lofty though it may be, exists for the sake of the rest." But because this single totality is willed as an ordered thing, the relation between the gradations of being, worth and significance can also be expressed by saying that everything lower exists for the sake of the higher, and so that everything in creation exists for the sake of the highest thing in this world. For we must always bear in mind that the creative action of God, which is in its divine origin absolutely and identically *one,* wills that the world should have, in the concrete, precisely this order of subordination and superiority, and the structure (if we may call it so) of the divine action can be read from the structure of what that action produces. We can then confidently say that God wills the whole of creation for the sake of the highest being in creation; and this proposition is not simply an application of the one we stated first, which is also true, namely that in this one world, in order that it shall be one, each thing must necessarily exist for all else, and all else for each thing, our second proposition expresses the equally important truth, as an effect of the action of God, that this one world is hierarchically ordered.

If we apply these formal considerations to the world in the concrete, we then have to say: within God's creation there is not only existence constituted as created by God out of nothing, infinitely different from and other than God; within this world there takes place the miracle of divine love, the self-communication of God to what he has created, when God himself, coming forth from himself in person, takes a created reality to himself as his own in the hypostatic union, and so truly empties himself and becomes a creature. If by creation we understand everything which exists externally to the inner divine life, then God's self-expression in that which is other than God (the incarnation of the Word of God) is the highest of God's creative acts. It is of this, then, that we must say that everything else in this one and hierarchically ordered world exists for its sake. We do not need to embark on the question of whether God would have become man if there had been no sin. This world, in the concrete, which God has willed, and has willed as one thing (without our needing to imagine, anthropomorphically, a series of divine decrees all, from God's side, depending on each other)—this world is a world in which God has allowed sin to exist and hence one in which the incarnation of the Word of God necessarily took place because of sin and for our salvation. But it is also a world in which this incarnation is the highest of the acts of God, to which all other entities essentially refer, and for whose sake everything else, including nature, the secular sphere and sheer matter, is willed by God.

Hence we can also say that the order of creation, even considered *as natural,* belongs to the order of redemption seen as the self-communication of God in that act in which the Word of God became a creature; that it belongs to it as a presupposition, distinct from redemption, which redemption itself creates for itself in order to be able to be itself; that therefore redemption graces the order of creation—precisely *this* creation—with itself, laying creation open to itself in all its dimensions and potentialities and giving to everything in it an ultimately supernatural meaning, but at the same time confirming it in its true and permanent naturalness and seeking to heal it wherever it is damaged.

(c) We need to say something further about this inner openness of the natural creation towards the divine self-communication in grace. It is not only that we can speak of such an openness in every natural creature towards grace, towards divine self-communication, towards a sharing in divine life, in so far as the whole of creation manifests, in the nature of angels and of men, a *potentia obedientialis* for grace; meaning that, if God wills, it can be the subject of a supernatural conferring of grace. We can speak of it, beyond this, in the sense that in the concrete order of supernatural divine self-communication as in fact willed by God, every natural created entity is ordered to this grace in such a way that it cannot remain really whole and healthy in itself, nor achieve the completion required by its own nature, except as integrated into the supernatural order of grace. In the concrete order, then, nature itself can find its way to its own completion only if it realizes that it is actually a factor within the all-embracing reality of grace and redemption. The "relative autonomy" of the natural physical and cultural spheres never extends, in catholic teaching, to the implication that they can achieve even the significance which is their own and immanent to them, except through the grace of God in Jesus Christ. To miss supernatural salvation means missing natural salvation as well. Anyone who wants to persevere in keeping the natural moral law in its entirety needs the grace of Christ, even though this may need, in the first instance, to be only "entitatively natural."

This, in the light of what has been said already, precisely does not mean an alienation of the natural from the law of its own immanent being, nor an authorization to Christians to bypass this law immanent in nature for the sake of any directly supernatural and religious aim. We have said that it is precisely the natural in its natural structure that is presupposed and affirmed, in its natural validity, by the redemptive order as the very condition of the latter. The validity of natural structures of a secular, pre-religious, pre-moral and extra-ecclesial kind is precisely a requirement of redemption, which must be taken into account; it must be respected for the sake of the redemptive order itself. But precisely because, and in so far as, the natural order is the presupposed condition for the very possibility of the supernatural order, set apart from itself by the supernatural order itself, natural existence has, within the concrete order of total creation, an inner openness to grace and a real crying need for grace. But it follows from this that everything natural, if fully and freely experienced, accepted and realized as what it really is (i.e. necessarily supernatural in its ultimate goal) is actually always, at every stage, more than purely natural. For if one tries to achieve the "purely natural" in this concrete order, simply in its "purity," what results is not the purely natural but the guilt-laden merely natural, closed, to its own undoing, against grace.

What is a quite different question, of course, is whether and how far and in what way this quality in natural things of having a supernatural end needs to be consciously appreciated by the human beings who are experiencing natural things and giving them their realization. In a case, for instance, where the natural moral law is *de facto* being observed, the healing grace of God is *de facto* being given even if the person concerned does not know it and has not expressly desired it. But we Christians, at least, ought to be aware of this openness within all natural things directing them towards the ordering of grace. We ought not merely to be stating it as a theoretical fact, here and there, once in a way; we ought to be experiencing it more and more, in the concrete, in everyday life, and putting it into detailed practice. We need to be gradually waking up to the fact that the detailed events and actions of concrete human existence are always in fact, even in their very naturalness, something more than merely natural.

When, for example, a concrete human being (and whether he is aware of it or not is, in the first instance, immaterial) experiences genuine, personal love for another human being, it always has a validity, an eternal significance and an inexpressible depth which it would not have but that such a love is so constituted as to be a way of actualizing the love of God as a human activity springing from God's own act. Death, however much just a "natural death," when suffered by man is always *in concreto* a death which happens only because of the death of Adam the sinner and of Christ on the cross. The only reason why we take man so absolutely seriously, the only reason why we *can,* and the reason why (whether we like it or not) we *must,* is that God, in the Word who became man, has taken man so absolutely seriously that it is only possible to take God seriously if we take him seriously as man, and man, with a divine seriousness, in him. All human realities have in fact, even as natural, an unexpressed, perhaps merely potential, but nevertheless truly Christian quality, and we can indeed address to all earthly existence the words of St. Paul to the Athenians (Acts 17, 23): "What you worship [we might say: actualize.] I preach to you"—namely, the God in whom everything exists and lives and who is the God of redemption precisely as being the God of creation, and *vice versa*.

God has not created two realities needing subsequently to be, so to speak, harmonized. Rather, he has constituted the whole of reality distinct from himself, to which he communicates himself, according to one ultimate, primordial intention, so that it all has a primordial unity and every difference in it springs from that unity as a mode of the unity itself, the unity preceding the differences which arise from it and which must precisely for its sake be respected. So if we want to formulate the relation of the supernatural to the natural order, we can equally well speak of the redemptive order within the created order or of the created order within the redemptive order. I mean that we can use each of these two concepts either as a term for the totality of God's world as concretely existing or as standing for one distinct factor within that whole order; and according to which way we mean it, we can either say: The redemptive order must develop within the created order as its all-informing, healing, elevating and divinizing principle, even though it is (as grace) more than the mere affirmation of the world and its immanent natural structures; or else we can formulate it as: The created order remains included within the redemptive order (using this for the totality of the divine order), in so far as it is a distinct, necessary factor within the redemptive order, having its own task in it and attaining to a share in the salvation of the whole order of things.

4. The Experience of Grace*

Because of the supernatural existential, produced in the human soul by God's real offer of his grace, the strivings of the human spirit which all men experience are the strivings of elevated nature. Even the non-Christian and the atheist have an experience of grace in the love, the longings, the emptiness, the loneliness, which accompany a genuine loving commitment to true human values. In their fidelity to true human values, despite discouragement and disillusionment, they are serving the "absent God," whom they experience through his grace, although they cannot find him in the world with which they deal explicitly through their objective concepts. This experience of grace, Rahner believes, can be the basis of a "mystagogy" through which Christians can explain to their non-Christian neighbors how man's most genuinely human experience lies in the mystery of God's grace.

Have we ever actually experienced grace? We do not mean by this some pious feeling, a sort of festive religious uplift, or any soft comfort, but precisely the experiencing of grace, i.e. of that visitation by the Holy Spirit of the triune God which has become a reality in Christ through his becoming man and through his sacrifice on the Cross. Is it possible at all to experience grace in this life? Would not an affirmative answer to this question mean the destruction of faith, of that semi-obscure cloud which envelops us as long as we are pilgrims on this earth? The mystics do indeed tell us—and they would testify to the truth of their assertion by laying down their lives—that they have already experienced God and hence also grace. But this empirical knowledge of God in mystic experience is an obscure and mysterious matter about which one cannot speak if one has not experienced it, and about which one will not speak if one has. Our question, therefore, cannot be answered simply *a priori*. But perhaps there are steps in the experience of grace, the lowest of which is accessible even to us?

*From *Theological Investigations*, vol. III, pp. 86-89.
© 1967 and 1974 by Darton, Longman and Todd Ltd.

Let us ask ourselves to begin with: have we ever experienced the *spiritual* in man? (What is meant here by spirit is itself a difficult question which cannot be answered simply and in a few words.) We will perhaps answer: of course, I have experienced this and in fact experience it every day. I think, I study, I make decisions, I act, I enter into relationships with others, I live in a community which is based not only on biological but also on spiritual factors, I love, I am happy, I enjoy poetry, I possess cultural, scientific, artistic values, etc. In short, I know what spirit is. Yet it is not quite as simple as that. Everything we have stated is perfectly true. But in all these things the 'spirit' is (or can be) merely, as it were, the ingredient which is used for making this earthly life human, beautiful and in some way meaningful. Yet it does not follow that we have thereby already experienced the spirit in its proper transcendence. This does not mean, of course, that spirit as such is to be found only where one speaks and philosophizes about the transcendence of the spirit. Quite the contrary: that would merely be a derived and secondary experience of that spirit which does not govern the life of man merely as one of its inner moments. Where then lies the real experience? At this point we would like to say from the very start: let us try to discover it for ourselves in our experience; and to aid this, one can merely tentatively and cautiously point out certain things.

Have we ever kept quiet, even though we wanted to defend ourselves when we had been unfairly treated? Have we ever forgiven someone even though we got no thanks for it and our silent forgiveness was taken for granted? Have we ever obeyed, not because we had to and because otherwise things would have become unpleasant for us, but simply on account of that mysterious, silent, incomprehensible being we call God and his will? Have we ever sacrificed something without receiving any thanks or recognition for it, and even without a feeling of inner satisfaction? Have we ever been absolutely lonely? Have we ever decided on some course of action purely by the innermost judgment of our conscience, deep down where one can no longer tell or explain it to anyone, where one is quite alone and knows that one is taking a decision which no one else can take in one's place and for which one will have to answer for all eternity? Have we ever tried to love God when we are no longer being borne on the crest of the wave of enthusiastic feeling, when it is no longer possible to mistake our self, and its vital urges, for God? Have we ever tried to love Him when we thought we were dying of this love and when it seemed like death and absolute negation? Have we ever tried to love God when we seemed to be calling out into emptiness and our cry seemed to fall on deaf ears, when it looked as if we were taking a terrifying jump into the bottomless abyss, when everything seemed to become incomprehensible and apparently senseless? Have we ever fulfilled a duty when it seemed that it could be done only with a consuming sense of really betraying and obliterating oneself, when it could apparently be done only by doing something terribly stupid for which no one would thank us? Have we ever been good to someone who did not show the slightest sign of gratitude or comprehension and when we also were not rewarded by the feeling of having been 'selfless', decent, etc.?

Let us search for ourselves in such experiences in our life; let us look for our own experiences in which things like this have happened to us individually. If we find such experiences, then we have experienced the spirit in the way meant here. For the experience meant here is the experience of eternity; it is the experience that the spirit is more than merely a part of this temporal world; the experience that man's meaning is not exhausted by the meaning and fortune of this world; the experience of the adventure and confidence of taking the plunge, an experience which no longer has any reason which can be demonstrated or which is taken from the success of this world.

To proceed: once we experience the spirit in this way, we (at least, we as Christians who live in faith) have also already *in fact* experienced the *supernatural*. We have done so perhaps in a very anonymous and inexpressible manner. Probably we have experienced it in such a way even that we were unable to turn round—and did not dare to do so—to look the supernatural straight in the face. But we know—when we let ourselves go in this experience of the spirit, when the tangible and assignable, the reliable element disappears, when everything takes on the taste of death and destruction, or when everything disappears as if in an inexpressible, as it were white, colourless and intangible beatitude—then in actual fact it is not merely the spirit but the Holy Spirit who is at work in us. Then is the hour of his grace. Then the seemingly uncanny, bottomless depth of our existence as experienced by us is the bottomless depth of God communicating himself to us, the dawning of his approaching infinity which no longer has any set paths, which is tasted like a nothing because it is infinity. When we have let ourselves go and no longer belong to ourselves, when we have denied ourselves and no longer have the disposing of ourselves, when everything (including ourselves) has moved away from us as if into an infinite distance, then we begin to live in the world of God himself, the world of the God of grace and of eternal life. This may still appear strange to us at the beginning, and we will always be tempted again to take fright and flee back into what is familiar and near to us: in fact, we will often have to and will often be allowed to do this. But we should gradually try to get ourselves used to the taste of the pure wine of the spirit, which is filled with the Holy Spirit. We should do this at least to the extent of not refusing the chalice when His directing providence offers it to us.

The chalice of the Holy Spirit is identical in this life with the chalice of Christ. This chalice is drunk only by those who have slowly learned in little ways to taste the fullness in emptiness, the ascent in the fall, life in death, the finding in renunciation. Anyone who learns this, experiences the spirit—the pure spirit—and in this experience he is also given the experience of the Holy Spirit of grace. For this liberation of the spirit is attained on the whole and in the long run only by the grace of Christ in faith. Where he liberates this spirit, however, he liberates it by supernatural grace which introduces the spirit into the life of God himself.

5. Grace and Concupiscence*

God's communication of himself in grace is not only elevating, it is also sanating (healing). Grace enables the human spirit's power of self-determination, which Rahner calls his "person," to extend its control over the other dynamisms in the human subject which escape its domination. These other dynamisms, which Rahner calls man's "nature," are necessary conditions for the existence and exercise of freedom in man, yet they resist domination by it. This resistence of man's "nature" to control by man's "person" is what is meant by concupiscence in the proper theological sense of the term. Because Adam had the gift of integrity, his "person" could dominate his whole "nature" by its free decision. The "person" of fallen man has lost this dominating power. Nevertheless, concupiscence can work to the spiritual advantage of fallen man. Concupiscence prevents fallen man from committing himself totally to evil by the irrevocable determination of his whole being, of which angels are capable since they are pure spirits. The good habits which a virtuous life have ingrained in man's "nature" resist an evil choice to which his "person" is tempted and enable the "person" to reverse such an evil choice more readily. This distinction which Rahner draws between "person" and "nature" in his theology of concupiscence permits him to elucidate the operation of sanating grace. With the help of sanating grace man's "person" can gradually eradicate the evil habits ingrained in his "nature" and implant the virtues which help the human subject to commit himself more thoroughly and firmly to a life of Christian virtue.

Concupiscentia in the *narrowest* (theological) sense.

We give first of all (ignoring the distinction between sensitive and spiritual desire) the usual description of concupiscentia in the narrowest sense (= concupiscence, *Begierlichkeit*). On this account concupiscence

*From *Theological Investigations*, vol. I, pp. 360-66, 368-69.
© 1961, 1965 and 1974 by Darton, Longman and Todd Ltd.

is man's spontaneous desire, in so far as it precedes his free decision *and resists it*.

If we are to understand this description of concupiscence aright, we must go rather further back. We ask: what can be meant by saying that concupiscence anticipates the free decision and resists it? With this in mind we begin first of all with a phenomenology (if we may so call it) of man's free decision. This free decision firstly is obviously a spiritual act. But this spirituality must not be conceived of as though it were a *purely* 'spiritual' act. For such an act does not exist in man. It is necessarily accompanied in man by a sensitive process, and therefore necessarily has its influence also on the sensitive sphere in man. The essential feature of the free decision is thus what is personal and free, as opposed to that spontaneous act of the appetite which, because of its non-free character is essentially pre-moral.

Now such a free decision in man permits of being more closely qualified in two ways. First of all it is an act through which man is explicitly or implicitly set before God, the absolute Good, and comes to a decision in his regard. This is true in so far as God is comprehended at least implicitly in every free decision in virtue of falling under the concept of the good simply speaking, for the individual finite good can only be freely assented to or rejected in the dynamism of a movement towards the good simply speaking. The spontaneous, involuntary act, on the other hand, is always referred to a finite (or finitely presented) good, for only such a good can be immediately set before man's cognitive and appetitive powers and thus call forth the spontaneous act.[1]

In the second place, man's free decision is an act by means of which he disposes of himself as a whole. For originally and ultimately moral freedom is not so much a decision with regard to an objectively presented individual value-object as a decision with regard to the freely operative subject himself. For in the last resort, on account of the first aspect of the moral act just mentioned, the morally free agent comes to a decision not so much with regard to his attitude to the finite good presented to his mind as to his relationship to God's absolute reality as value. Because man can

---

[1]This is not of course to deny but rather to affirm by implication that through the spontaneous, involuntary act (so far as it is a spiritual one), the unlimited horizon of spiritual aspiration is already opened up in a movement of transcendence towards being and the good in general, and that precisely by this means the necessity of having to decide freely in this way or that is for the first time disclosed. And conversely what has been said must not be taken to mean that the free spirit always comes to a decision before God (for or against him) in such a way that God himself is the express, objectively presented object of the free decision. Transcendence towards being and the good in general is disclosed as conscious (in receptive knowledge and spontaneous aspiration) through the finite object, which gives itself by being what it is; and in the free act the free spirit, through the finite object, adopts an attitude to the absolute good, which is simultaneously affirmed in voluntary transcendence.

only be free in regard to the finite good in virtue of his dynamic orientation to the infinite good, every free decision is a disposition made by man in respect of his situation before God, not only in virtue of a juridical or moral interpretation of this act but on the ground of its metaphysical structure. In this way the free decision tends of itself to dispose of man as a whole. For the spiritually knowing and willing subject necessarily brings to completion in every objective act of knowledge and decision a return upon itself as well (*reditio completa subiecti in seipsum, Summa contra Gentiles* IV, 11), and in this way is present to itself and itself acts as something so present to itself. In this way the free operation, as a genuine operation and not just a passive experience, arises from the inmost core of the subject and exercises a determining influence upon this subject. For otherwise the operative subject, in so far as it is identical with this personal centre, would merely undergo the free decision passively and not actively posit it. But that is in contradiction to the inmost essence of the free operation, inasmuch as the operative subject is really responsible for it. Now the operative subject itself can only be and remain responsible for the free decision if it posits this decision in such a way that the decision becomes a qualification of the operative subject itself. Thus the free decision is essentially a disposal of himself made by man, and one which proceeds from the inmost centre of his being. Now if man's free decision is the shaping (or in the terms of modern existential philosophy, the 'self-comprehension') of his own being proceeding precisely from its *inmost* core—from that core, that is to say, from which man's whole metaphysical essence arises and is compacted—then the free decision also tends essentially to shape and modify this whole essence arising from the centre of the person. Thus the free decision tends to dispose of the operative subject as a whole before God.

The question now arises as to how far the freely operative subject when he makes his decision succeeds in actually extending this tendency totally to dispose of himself throughout the whole extent of his being. And here we simply lay it down *a posteriori*—the metaphysical justification of this fact will be briefly touched on later—that this tendency within man's ordinary free decision never completely succeeds in making its way. There always remains in the nature of things a tension between what man is as a kind of entity simply present before one (as 'nature') and what he wants to make of himself by his free decision (as 'person'): a tension between what he is simply passively and what he actively posits himself as and wishes to understand himself to be. The 'person' never wholly absorbs its 'nature'.

The metaphysical discussion of this fact can only be briefly indicated here. It presents special difficulty in that it is based upon two interdependent factors which not even a metaphysical anthropology has ever really succeeded in distinguishing in detail in a clear and concrete way. Cer-

tainly in one essential respect the dualism of person and nature just indicated has its metaphysical root in the finitude of man; thus ultimately in
the distinction between essence and existence, in virtue of which the
essence, in its complete unfolding, always remains an ideal capable of
being attained only asymptotically by the concretely existent being, even
as regards the freedom through which it makes itself what it is. But on the
other hand it is equally a matter of course for an anthropology on the basis
of Thomist metaphysics, that just as essential an element of the dualism of
person and nature, of the resistance of the entity given prior to the free
decision counter to the tendency of the free subject totally to dispose of
its whole subsistent reality, arises from the materiality of the human
being, from the real differentiation of matter and form, which prevents the
form from bringing itself fully to manifestation in the 'other' of matter.

Here too is to be found the nucleus of truth in that otherwise too crude
distinction between the spirit as the freely operative principle and the
sensibility as the principle which resists this free decision. In reality of
course the whole 'nature' given prior to freedom offers resistance to the
'person's' free and total disposition of himself, so that the boundary between 'person' and 'nature' stands as it were vertically in regard to the
horizontal line which divides spirituality from sensibility in man.

The specifically *human* form of the distinction between person and
nature (as distinguished, for example, from a like dualism which has to be
supposed for the angels as well) is explained by the dualism of matter and
form in man, regarded as each possessing its own consistency
(*insichständig*); thus in the concrete experience of life this human dualism
finds its sharpest expression—no one will contest this—in the resistance
of the sensitive to the spiritual part of man.

From what has been said it follows that the spontaneous act of desire
(*actus indeliberatus*) belongs to the 'nature' in the sense indicated by our
distinction above. For to the nature (as opposed to the person) belongs
everything which must be given prior to the person's free decision, as a
condition of its possibility. Now as we have just shown, the spontaneous
act of desire, arising from the bare dynamism of nature and directed to a
wittingly apprehended object, is one of the metaphysically necessary presuppositions of a concrete free decision made by a finite subject.

It is now possible to arrive by stages at a statement of what is meant by
concupiscence in the theological sense. As we have said, the free decision
tends to the end that man should dispose of himself as a whole before
God, actively make himself into what he freely wishes to be. Thus the end
to which the free decision is orientated is that everything which is in man
(nature), hence the involuntary act as well, should be the revelation and
the expression of what man as person wishes to be; thus that the free
decision should comprehend, transfigure and transfuse the spontaneous
act, so that its own reality too should no longer be purely natural but
personal.

In connexion with this personal entry into and shaping of naturally spontaneous desire, we must not think straight away simply of those spontaneous acts which can be a hindrance to one of man's morally *good* decisions. Because a spontaneous act precedes every personal act of man, whether it be directed to good or evil, and because in every one of them the person never wholly absorbs and personally assumes what it is on the basis of its spontaneous acts and what is given prior to it, it follows that the dualism of nature and person in its specifically human form, which we call concupiscence, is something which is at work both in the case of a good decision of man's freedom against the spontaneous desire of nature for a morally negative good, and also in the case of a bad free decision against a natural inclination to something morally good. Both the good and the bad moral decision encounter the resistance, the solidity and the impenetrability of nature. Concupiscence in the theological sense shows itself for instance just as much when a man blushes in the act of lying as when the 'flesh' refuses to follow the willingness of the 'spirit' for the good.

It is now possible to see what is the essence of desire in the narrowest (theological) sense, the essence of concupiscence. In the concrete man of the present order free personal decision and self-determination are not capable of perfectly and exhaustively determining the operative subject throughout the whole extent of his real being. The free act does indeed dispose of the whole subject, in so far as it is as free act an act of man's personal centre, and so, by the root as it were, draws the whole subject in sympathy with it. And yet man's concrete being is not throughout its whole extent and according to all its powers and their actualization the pure expression and the unambiguous revelation of the personal active centre which is its own master. In the course of its self-determination, the person undergoes the resistance of the nature given prior to freedom, and never wholly succeeds in making all that man is into the reality and the expression of all that he comprehends himself to be in the core of his person. There is much in man which always remains in concrete fact somehow impersonal; impenetrable and unilluminated for his existential decision; merely endured and not freely acted out. It is this dualism between person and nature, in so far as it arises from the dualism of matter and spirit and not from man's finitude, the dualism of essence and existence and the real distinction of his powers given with it, that we call concupiscence in the theological sense. While it does indeed find its concrete experiential expression in a dualism of spirituality and sensibility, it is not identical with the latter. Thus concupiscence does not consist in any conceivable givenness of the spontaneous act prior to the free one; nor does it in every case necessarily consist in a capacity of the spontaneous act to be despotically expunged by freedom nor precisely in the fact that the spontaneous act drives towards what is morally impermissible contrary to the direction of the free decision. Concupiscence consists essentially in the fact that man in this regime does not overcome even by his free decision the dualism between what he is as nature prior to his existential decision and what he becomes as person by this decision, not even in the measure in which it would absolutely speaking be conceivable for a finite spirit to overcome it. Man never becomes wholly absorbed either in good or in evil.

X

Faith, Hope, and Charity

1. A Short Formula of Christian Faith*

The Christian who lives in our contemporary pluralistic society does not receive the social support for his faith which Christians received in former times. His faith must be a personal commitment. Therefore Christians need a short formula of their faith in which its fundamental doctrines are arranged as a coherent whole in a form which is both credible to modern man and useful to him in the interpretation of his experience. Rahner believes that the main elements of his theological synthesis (Trinity, Incarnation, grace, Church, sacraments) can be presented to the ordinary Christian in such a short formula of faith. In the selection printed below he endeavors to present this kind of "modern confession of faith."

In order to be effective *vis-à-vis* modern unbelief the mission of the Church calls for a kind of witness to the Christian faith which can be really intelligible to modern man. This truism implies a demand, however, which is by no means easily fulfilled and is often neglected. For this message must be so expressed that what is essential is clearly distinguished from everything of secondary importance and can be actually 'realised'. Otherwise a modern 'pagan' is not able to distinguish this essence of Christianity from the Church's often uninviting and repellent appearance (in sermons, religious practice, social conditions, etc.), and consequently applies his—partially justified—opposition towards Christians to Christianity itself. Thus the Christian message must be such that it clearly criticises Christians and concrete Christianity. This message must be able to express what is essential *in brief* to today's highly preoccupied men, and it must go on saying it. Such repetition is not wearisome so long as it is really concerned with what is decisive and essential, not as an 'ideology' which impinges on man from outside (and which changes no-

* From *Theological Investigations*, vol. IX, pp. 117–18, 121–26.
© 1972 by Darton, Longman and Todd Ltd.

thing as far as the 'facts' are concerned), but as the experienced and lived reality of man's life itself. Such a 'short formula' is especially urgently required in our *pluralist* society. In earlier times a homogeneous society itself 'lived' Christianity, at least as a 'religion', even if perhaps not always as a personal 'faith'. In a situation where one was already impregnated with Christianity as social custom and 'ideology' *before* being capable of and compelled to a personal decision of faith, it was possible to be unconcerned as to the doctrinal mode of communication of Christianity. This kind of 'postponement' was true of Baptism and also to a certain extent of life in general. It was not necessary to be very concerned about the correct proportions of what was said; secondary things could be communicated more urgently as if they were primary; one could permit oneself rather to neglect that *single whole* of Christianity as such, whereas nowadays it is precisely this 'whole' which is the precondition for a correct understanding and realisation of the 'particular' within it. Nowadays the baptised person too, even if he is born into a Christian family, lives in a situation of existence which largely does not communicate Christianity. Simply from the fact of the situation in which he finds himself, even a baptised person is in many respects more 'pagan' than ever anyone has been since Constantine. He must understand sufficiently clearly what is particular and really distinctive in Christianity, those things by which he is to be distinguishable from his environment.

In what follows we shall present an attempt at this kind of 'modern' confession of faith. It is indeed no more than an attempt. The emphasis could be placed differently and it could be longer or shorter. Naturally it can only be intelligible to educated western man, if at all. But I do not find this in itself a drawback: ought we to try to make a thing suitable for everyone by rendering it not really acceptable to anyone? Was not the ancient Creed 'generally intelligible' as a traditional sacral formula by being suitable for only a very small cultural field? If anyone says that he finds this attempt useless we shall certainly not take offence at his opinion, provided that he himself knows better how to communicate just *what* we Christians actually believe to an 'unbeliever' of our own time, in his own environment, and can state it briefly. How would it be if the new Secretariat for Unbelievers in Rome were to produce examples of a short catechism for unbelievers? These examples would follow the teaching of the Decree on Ecumenism that there is a very important distinction between the 'fundamentals' of the faith and other truths, and they would underline the abiding value of the ancient formulas not by repeating the latter but by explaining them. And must this decidedly necessary process of explanation (which even the most stubborn defender of the abiding validity of the ancient formulas recognises as justified and necessary) always be very much longer than the formulas it is supposed to be explaining? Why? If this is not the case, even our stubborn defender must be able to produce a short 'creed' containing the ancient abiding truth and yet expressing it in a different way as compared with traditional formulas. As we have said, the present attempt is to be understood in this sense. Its only purpose is to enable many other people to do the same thing more quickly and better.

Whether he is consciously aware of it or not, whether he is open to this truth or suppresses it, man's whole spiritual and intellectual existence is orientated towards a holy mystery which is the basis of his being. This mystery is the inexplicit and unexpressed horizon which always encircles and upholds the small area of our everyday experience of knowing and acting, our knowledge of reality and our free action. It is our most fundamental, most natural condition, but for that very reason it is also the most hidden and least regarded reality, speaking to us by its silence, and even whilst appearing to be absent, revealing its presence by making us take cognisance of our own limitations. We call this God. We can ignore him, but even in an act which professes to be unconcerned about him, God is once more affirmed as the sustaining fundamental of such an act, just as logic is still operative even in an act which denies the validity of logic, or just as an action which affirms absolute meaninglessness considers itself more meaningful than the acceptance of a meaning for existence, thus explicitly affirming once again that meaning is fundamental to reality. In its capacity as the very ground of the individual absorbed in knowing and acting, the holy mystery we call God is at once what is most internal to ourselves and also what is furthest from our manipulation and has no need of us. Our proper response to it is reverence and worship. Where these are present, where man accepts his being in an attitude of absolute responsibility, seeking and awaiting this ultimate meaning in trust, he has already found God, whatever name he may give him. For his ultimate name can only be uttered, finally, in loving silence before his incomprehensibility.

However hard and unsatisfactory it may be to interpret the deepest and most fundamental experience at the very bottom of our being, man does experience in his innermost history that this silent, infinitely distant holy mystery, which continually recalls him to the limits of his finitude and lays bare his guilt, yet *bids him approach;* the mystery enfolds him in an ultimate and radical love which commends itself to him as his salvation and as the real meaning of his existence (provided only that he allows its possibilities to be greater than his own finitude and guilt). This love —experienced at the ground of being, which is nothing other than God's absolute self-communication, in which God gives himself and not only what is finite, in which he becomes the infinitely wide horizon of our being—we call divinising grace. It is offered to everyone as light and as the promise of eternal life, working freely and graciously in every man,

208 A RAHNER READER

welling up from the origin of his existence and—even though perhaps not named as such—appearing everywhere where in the history of man courage, love, faithfulness to the light of conscience, endurance of darkness by faith in the light, or any other witness to the ground of his being is at work and is made plain as the holy mystery of the loving nearness of God. That history which reveals more and more clearly God's pledge of himself in radical self-communication to man, accepted in faith, hope and love, we call salvation and revelation-history. It is the 'categorial' historical form in which God's self-communication, 'transcendentally' given from the very beginning in the ground of man's being (by virtue of the deification of man through grace, effected by this self-communication), becomes more and more apparent. It is true that this history is often marred and darkened by the history of the guilt by which humanity shuts itself off from the grace of God in the mystery of self-refusal and wishes to understand itself from within itself alone. But in spite of this it is always and everywhere present, since the mystery of the God who reveals and communicates himself in love is more powerful than the mystery of human guilt.

This history of man's self-discovery as one who is (at least as far as God's offer is concerned) divinised in the ground of his existence, the history of the concrete expression in space-time of this self-discovery in God (both always by virtue of the divine self-pledge, called grace) reaches its historical apogee and unsurpassable goal—which secretly sustained this whole historical movement from the very beginning—in the one in the midst of divinised humanity whom we call simply the God-man. It is he whom everyone seeks, not expressly but in reality all the same, in wishing the ultimate question (of one's own being and of one's destiny in death) and the ultimate acceptance (of this question by God) to appear together, experienced in the concrete terms of one's own history, and thus be completely existent and finally affirmed. To this extent every man who is true to this conscience is for us an Advent Christian, looking forward to the *one* Man in whom his own question (we do not merely *put* questions; we *are* questions) and God's acceptance have become one and have finally appeared in one person. As Christians we have the courage to believe that this looked-for one is found. He is Jesus of Nazareth.

The man who has experienced God in Christ in this way wants to and must confess him. Not as though he thought that the others, who are not able to call the consummation of their secret experience by name, are not embraced by God's mercy (by which he gives himself to us, provided only that we do not refuse him). But the man who has found Christ must bear witness to him before his brethren. In the first place that simply means that he obediently accepts life and death as they are. In this way he meets Him. Further, it means looking towards God and the continually renewed acceptance of His forgiveness, and finally the explicit confession of His Name, of the hope we find in Him.

Christ is the one in whom God's self-communication to man and man's acceptance of him have become materially and existentially 'One' by the action of God. In him, God is unsurpassably and irrevocably *present* where we are, and in him man exists not only as the question in respect of God, but, as God's pledged acceptance, has become God himself in appearance: *the* Son of Man, the Son of God in the true and unconditional sense of the word. The Christian recognises in faith that the historically concrete realisation of this goal of salvation-history, which sustains and perfects the latter and causes it to triumph irrevocably over the history of evil, is given in Jesus of Nazareth. Throughout its whole history humanity looks for the God-man as the fulfilment of its own salvation-history; it has found no-one but Jesus of Nazareth in whom it is able to recognise the God-man; by his wonderful life, his death and resurrection he shows himself to be this God-man, the presence of God himself in the history of mankind. In him, God is irrevocably the one who has accepted us in love and has made us possessors of his infinite wealth of truth, life and eternity. The Christian believes in the death of Jesus, in which mankind has delivered itself with its own ground and goal to the grace of God, and in the complete perfection of the man Jesus (called his Resurrection), in which mankind has already begun to possess the life of God himself directly, breaking the bounds of its space-time history.

In so far as God, in his self-communication, still remains the holy and inconceivable mystery who, in giving himself away, does not lose his divinity, we call him Father. In so far as God communicates himself to us as our most real and eternally valid life by the means of divinising grace at the ground of our being, we call him Holy Spirit. In so far as the genuine truth of our being appears in history in the God-man, we call him the Word and the Son of God. In so far as these two mutually sustaining and determining ways of God's self-communication actually communicate God himself and not a creaturely, finite representation of God, we acknowledge that in his own life God himself, while remaining one, is distinguished as Father, Word and Spirit, so that we call him the threefold God, or the Three Persons: Father, Son and Spirit, one God.

The community of those who come together in faith around Jesus, in hope waiting to participate in his perfection and in him bound together in love with the Father and with each other by his Spirit—this community we call the Church. He himself founded this Church in the persons of his first disciples and provided it with his Spirit in the 'twelve' messengers to whom he entrusted his commission. He united this apostolic community in Peter as its head and gave it a constitution which these authorised messengers had authority to hand on. Thus he gave the Church the task and the powers of representing him and witnessing to him throughout history until its end, so that he should remain God's self-committal to the world in the dimension of historical concreteness, and as such should be continually at work. In this way, in its origin in and in its witness to

Christ, the Church is the historical sign of God's victorious will for Salvation, conquering all man's guilt. To this extent the Church is the 'sacrament' (i.e. the holy, effectual sign) in which the world's divinisation appears and, in appearing, establishes itself. As the historical presence of God's unrevoked pledge of himself in Christ, the Church's testimony, wherever it is expressed in a definitive witness on the part of its authoritative teaching office, is protected from slipping from God's truth; and in so far as the word spoken by the Church by means of holy symbols communicates grace (which lives in the Church) in its full measure to the individual in the decisive situations of his life, it is an effectual word, carrying with it what it signifies: this word is itself a sacrament.

Just as man in his personal life is familiar with words which involve him totally and which reveal precisely what is happening *while* they are being said—for instance, words of ultimate love or of forgiveness—so in a similar way the Church is acquainted in its own field with words by which it pledges itself to man as what it actually is: the sign of mercy and of the love of God to all.

Seven of these effectual words of grace are known to the Church: the sign of grace (called Baptism), in which the sinful human being is dedicated to the triune God by the rite of washing and is also accepted into the Church as a member—in the concrete historical dimension—by the forgiveness of his sinfulness and by sanctifying by God's Spirit; the express promise of the Spirit in conjunction with the imposition of hands (Confirmation), enabling and empowering the baptised person to be a witness by life and testimony to the fact that God loves the world, even in the presence of those who think they are unable to believe in his love; the word of judgment and forgiveness (Penance), in which the Church reconciles the culpable person to herself and to God; the word by which the Church commends the baptised person in imminent danger of death to the God of eternal life (Holy Unction); the word (Ordination) by which the Church imparts to one of her members by the imposition of hands a share (in three stages) in her authority and the power of that authority; the word (in the Sacrament of Matrimony) which lays the foundation for the marriage bond and at the same time reveals it as the reflection of the unity and fertility of the love of God toward human kind gathered into the Church in Christ. In addition to these six signs of sanctifying grace there is the seventh and greatest in the holy meal of the community of Christ, in which the latter is mindful of the death and resurrection of its Lord as its salvation and is united anew with Him in the rite of the meal under the signs of bread and wine: the Sacrament of the Altar. Thus the Chruch is at the same time the visible community of the redeemed and also the sign by which God's Spirit effects the world's salvation and renders it visible in concrete history.

To the extent that the Christian is united with his Lord by his Spirit in faith, hope and love, he knows that he has already been set free from all intramundane forces and powers (sin, law, death) into the infinity and finality of the life of the true and living God. But he also knows that he must share with his Lord his destiny of death, until he too, at the point where his life and death seem to enter the most extreme degree of forsakenness by God, the ultimate darkness of guilt, lays his existence into the hands of the living God. He knows that his life must be an act of unconditional love to God and his fellow men, which far exceeds the fulfilment of all law. He confidently looks forward to the end of his life and the end of the history of mankind, when what is already present now in faith and lowliness will appear unveiled and perfected to all who have loved: the life of God, who is all in all.

2. Anonymous Christians*

Christians must realize, however, that, besides the explicit faith which they profess as believing members of the visible Church, there is an implicit faith which is also salvific. Through this implicit faith, men who have never accepted or even encountered Christian Revelation become, not just anonymous theists, but anonymous Christians. In other words, they place an act of conscious, though implicit, faith in the Triune God of Christian Revelation.

Rahner's theology of the anonymous Christian is an extension of his theology of the supernatural existential. Through the supernatural existential the unobjective Horizon of the human spirit has become in the historical order the Triune God of grace and glory. By his Incarnation the Word has become the ground of man's elevation to the supernatural order and has also become God's historical revelation of himself to men. Therefore when the human spirit, elevated by the supernatural existential, makes its loving surrender to the Horizon of its world, man receives the justifying grace of Christ. The surrender of the human spirit is a surrender in which both knowledge and love unite themselves in a single dynamic process. For, as we have seen in Hearers of the Word, *love is the lamp of knowledge. A salutary surrender of the human will to the Triune God is an implicit act of charity. A salutary surrender of the intellect to the Triune God, who, in and through the Word, is ontologically God's Revelation, is an implicit act of faith. It follows therefore that, if the human subject's free response to his world includes in its intentionality an act of loving surrender to the world's Absolute Horizon,*

* From *Theological Investigations*, vol. VI, pp. 390–91, 393–95.
© 1969 and 1974 by Darton, Longman and Todd Ltd.

the human subject has made an implicit act of salutary Christian faith. Ontologically, and not just metaphorically, he has become an anonymous Christian.

Rahner's theology of the anonymous Christian is one of the most fruitful elements of his system and one of the most widely known. It is also one of the clearest examples of the pastoral consequences which flow from Rahner's systematic theology. For Rahner's theology of the anonymous Christian is a systematic conclusion which rests on a number of his previous positions: the indwelling of the economical Trinity through Uncreated Grace; the conscious, though unobjective, presence of God in the human spirit as its Absolute Horizon; the union of knowledge and love in man's response to the world and its infinite ground; and, of course, the supernatural existential. Philosophers and theologians who have problems with these fundamental elements of Rahner's philosophical theology will also have problems with his theology of the anonymous Christian and with the further theological conclusions which follow from it.

The Christian is convinced that in order to achieve salvation man must believe in God, and not merely in God but in Christ; that this faith is not merely a positive commandment from which one could be dispensed under certain conditions; that membership of the one true Church does not constitute a merely extrinsic condition from which it would be appropriate for someone to be freed by the mere fact that he does not and cannot know about it and its necessity. On the contrary, this faith is in itself necessary and therefore demanded absolutely, not merely as a commandment but as the only possible means, not as a condition alone but as an unavoidable way of access, for man's salvation is nothing less than the fulfilment and definitive coming to maturity of precisely *this* beginning, for which therefore nothing else can substitute.—In this sense there really is no salvation outside the Church, as the old theological formula has it.

It is true that before Christ no philosopher ever recognised in man's self-interpretation these depths of the human reality, but as a historical being man is one who in the concrete comes to be and to know what he is only in the unfolding of his history. Now that his thinking is illuminated by the light of the revelation which has in fact been made in the historically accomplished reality of Christ, he can recognise this unapproachable height as that perfection of his own being which can be effected by God, not in order that in a rationalistic fashion man may have it under his control but in order that he may more fully recognise the fact that he is ordained to this mystery. Bestowal of grace and incarnation as the two basic modes of God's self-communication can therefore be conceived as the most radical modes of man's spiritual being, beyond his powers to compel and yet precisely as such eminently fulfilling the transcendence of his being.

The believer will then also grasp that this absolute eminence is not an optional adjunct to his reality; that it is not given to him as the juridical and external demand of God's will for him, but that this self-communication by God offered to all and fulfilled in the highest way in Christ rather constitutes the goal of all creation and—since God's word and will *effect* what they say—that, even before he freely takes up an attitude to it, it stamps and determines man's nature and lends it a character which we may call a 'supernatural existential'. A refusal of this offer would therefore not leave man in a state of pure unimpaired nature, but would bring him into contradiction with himself even in the sphere of his own being. This means positively that man in experiencing his transcendence, his limitless openness—no matter how implicit and incomprehensible it always is—also already experiences the offer of grace—not necessarily expressly *as* grace, as distinctly supernatural calling, but experiences the reality of its content. But this means that the express revelation of the word in Christ is not something which comes to us from without as entirely strange, but only the explicitation of what we already are by grace and what we experience at least incoherently in the limitlessness of our transcendence. The expressly Christian revelation becomes the explicit statement of the revelation of grace which man always experiences implicitly in the depths of his being.

If man accepts the revelation, he posits by that fact the act of supernatural faith. But he also already accepts this revelation whenever he really accepts *himself completely,* for it already speaks *in* him. Prior to the explicitness of official ecclesiastical faith this acceptance can be present in an implicit form whereby a person undertakes and lives the duty of each day in the quiet sincerity of patience, in devotion to his material duties and the demands made upon him by the persons under this care. What he is then taking upon himself is therefore not merely his basic relationship with the silent mystery of the Creator-God. Accordingly, no matter how he wants to understand and express this in his own reflective self-understanding, he is becoming thereby not merely an anonymous 'theist', but rather takes upon himself in that Yes to himself the grace of the mystery which has radically approached us. 'God has given himself to man in direct proximity': perhaps the essence of Christianity can be reduced to this formula.

In the acceptance of himself man is accepting Christ as the absolute perfection and guarantee of his own anonymous movement towards God by grace, and the acceptance of this belief is again not an act of man alone but the work of God's grace which is the grace of Christ, and this means in its turn the grace of his Church which is only the continuation of the mystery of Christ, his permanent visible presence in our history.

It is true that it would be wrong to go so far as to declare every man, whether he accepts the grace or not, an 'anonymous Christian'. Anyone who in his basic decision were really to deny and to reject his being ordered to God, who were to place himself decisively in opposition to his own concrete being, should not be designated a 'theist', even an anonymous 'theist'; only someone who gives—even if it be ever so confusedly —the glory to *God* should be thus designated. Therefore no matter what a man states in his conceptual, theoretical and religious reflection, anyone who does not say in his *heart*, 'there is no God' (like the 'fool' in the psalm) but testifies to him by the radical acceptance of his being, is a believer. But if in this way he believes in deed and in truth in the holy mystery of God, if he does not suppress this truth but leaves it free play, then the grace of this truth by which he allows himself to be led is always already the grace of the Father in his Son. And anyone who has let himself be taken hold of by this grace can be called with every right an 'anonymous Christian'.

This name implicitly signifies that this fundamental actuation of a man, like all actuations, cannot and does not want to stop in its anonymous state but strives towards an explicit expression, towards its full name. An unfavourable historical environment may impose limitations on the explicitness of this expression so that this actuation may not exceed the explicit appearance of a loving humaneness, but it will not act against this tendency whenever a new and higher stage of explicitness is presented to it right up to the ultimate perfection of a consciously accepted profession of Church membership. Here alone does this belief find not merely its greatest support and source of confidence but also its proper reality and that peace which St Augustine likened to repose in being: peace and repose which do not mean stagnation and flight but the capacity of casting oneself all the more resolutely into the inexorable will of the mystery of God, since now, as St Paul says, one knows whom one believes and to whom one fearlessly submits in radical trust.

3. Christianity and the Non-Christian Religions*

The theology of the anonymous Christian gives theological support to the positive pastoral attitude which the Church adopted toward non-Christian religions in Vatican II. Non-Christian religions can be genuinely salvific. Their objective doctrines can be the categorical thematization of the implicit faith of the justified anonymous Christians whose response to God took those religious forms. Nevertheless, non-Christian religions should not be accepted uncritically and placed on a par with Christianity. Since the doctrines of non-Christian religions are the utterances of men who are fallen and sinful, they are not exclusively

* From *Theological Investigations*, vol. V, pp. 118, 121–25, 127, 131–32.
© 1966 by Darton, Longman and Todu Ltd.

the thematization of implicit faith and charity. They can also be the thematization of the human ignorance, weakness, and malice from which none of us is free. Since the Church has the help of Christian Revelation and is protected from error by the assistance of the Holy Spirit, she cannot evade her responsibility to test what is of God in non-Christian religions.

1st Thesis: We must begin with the thesis which follows, because it certainly represents the basis in the Christian faith of the theological understanding of other religions. This thesis states that Christianity understands itself as the absolute religion, intended for all men, which cannot recognize any other religion beside itself as of equal right. This proposition is self-evident and basic for Christianity's understanding of itself. There is no need here to prove it or to develop its meaning.

2nd Thesis: Until the moment when the gospel really enters into the historical situation of an individual, a non-Christian religion (even outside the Mosaic religion) does not merely contain elements of a natural knowledge of God, elements, moreover, mixed up with human depravity which is the result of original sin and later aberrations. It contains also supernatural elements arising out of the grace which is given to men as a gratuitous gift on account of Christ. For this reason a non-Christian religion can be recognized as a *lawful* religion (although only in different degrees) without thereby denying the error and depravity contained in it. This thesis requires a more extensive explanation.

We must first of all note the point up to which this evaluation of the non-Christian religions is valid. This is the point in time when the Christian religion becomes a historically real factor for those who are of this religion. Whether this point is the same, theologically speaking, as the first Pentecost, or whether it is different in chronological time for individual peoples and religions, is something which even at this point will have to be left to a certain extent an open question. We have, however, chosen our formulation in such a way that it points more in the direction of the opinion which seems to us the more correct one in the matter although the *criteria* for a more exact determination of this moment in time must again be left an open question.

The thesis itself is divided into two parts. It means first of all that it is *a priori* quite possible to suppose that there are supernatural, grace-filled elements in non-Christian religions. Let us first of all deal with this statement. It does not mean, of course, that all the elements of a polytheistic conception of the divine, and all the other religious, ethical and metaphysical aberrations contained in the non-Christian religions, are to be or may be treated as harmless either in theory or in practice. There have been constant protests against such elements throughout the history of Christianity and throughout the history of the Christian interpretation of the non-Christian religions, starting with the Epistle to the Romans and following on the Old Testament polemics against the religion of the 'heathens'. Every one of these protests is still valid in what was really meant and expressed by them. Every such protest remains a part of the message which Christianity and the Church has to give to the peoples who profess such religions. Furthermore, we are not concerned here with an *a-posteriori* history of religions. Consequently, we also cannot describe empirically what should not exist and what is opposed to God's will in these non-Christian religions, nor can we represent these things in their many forms and degrees. We are here concerned with dogmatic theology and so can merely repeat the universal and unqualified verdict as to the unlawfulness of the non-Christian religions right from the moment when they came into real and historically powerful contact with Christianity (and at first only thus!). It is clear, however, that this condemnation does not mean to deny the very basic differences within the non-Christian religions especially since the pious, God-pleasing pagan was already a theme of the Old Testament, and especially since this God-pleasing pagan cannot simply be thought of as living absolutely outside the concrete socially constituted religion and constructing his own religion on his native foundations—just as St Paul in his speech on the Areopagus did not simply exclude a positive and basic view of the pagan religion. The decisive reason for the first part of our thesis is basically a theological consideration. This consideration (prescinding from certain more precise qualifications) rests ultimately on the fact that, if we wish to be Christians, we must profess belief in the universal and serious salvific purpose of God towards all men which is true even within the post-paradisean phase of salvation dominated by original sin. We know, to be sure, that this proposition of faith does not say anything certain about the *individual* salvation of man understood as something which has in fact been reached. But God desires the salvation of everyone. And this salvation willed by God is the salvation won by Christ, the salvation of supernatural grace which divinizes man, the salvation of the beatific vision. It is a salvation really intended for all those millions upon millions of men who lived perhaps a million years before Christ—and also for those who have lived after Christ—in nations, cultures and epochs of a very wide range which were still completely shut off from the viewpoint of those living in the light of the New Testament. If, on the one hand, we conceive salvation as something specifically *Christian,* if there is no salvation apart from Christ, if according to Catholic teaching the supernatural divinization of man can never be replaced merely by good will on the part of man but is necessary as something itself given in this earthly life; and if, on the other hand, God has really, truly and seriously intended this salvation for all men—then these two aspects cannot be reconciled in any other way than by stating that every human being is really and truly exposed to the influence of divine, supernatural grace which offers an interior union with God and by means of which God communicates himself whether the individual takes up an attitude of acceptance or of refusal towards this grace. It is senseless to suppose cruelly—and without any hope of acceptance by the man of today, in view of the enormous extent of the extra-Christian history of salvation and damnation—that nearly all men living outside the official and public Christianity are so evil and stubborn that the offer of supernatural grace ought not even to be made in fact in most cases, since these individuals have already rendered themselves unworthy of such an offer by previous, subjectively grave offences against the natural moral law. If one gives more exact theological thought to this matter, then one cannot regard nature and grace as two phases in the life of the individual which follow each other in time. It is furthermore impossible to think that this offer of supernatural, divinizing grace made to all men on account of the universal salvific purpose of God, should in general (prescinding from the relatively few exceptions) remain ineffective in most cases on account of the personal guilt of the individual. For, as far as the gospel is concerned, we have no really conclusive reason for thinking so pessimistically of men. On the other hand, and contrary to every merely human experience, we do have every reason for thinking optimistically of God and his salvific will which is more powerful than the extremely limited stupidity and evil-mindedness of men. However little we can say with certitude about the final lot of an individual inside or outside the officially constituted Christian religion, we have every reason to think optimistically—i.e. truly hopefully and confidently in a Christian sense—of God who has certainly the last word and who has revealed to us that he has spoken his powerful word of reconciliation and forgiveness into the world. If it is true that the eternal Word of God has become flesh and has died the death of sin for the sake of our salvation and in spite of our guilt, then the Christian has no right to suppose that the fate of the world—having regard to the whole of the world—takes the same course on account of man's refusal as it would have taken if Christ had not come. Christ and his salvation are not simply one of two possibilities offering themselves to man's free choice; they are the deed of God which bursts open and redeems the false choice of man by overtaking it. In Christ God not only gives the *possibility* of salvation, which in that case would still have to be effected by man himself, but the actual salvation itself, however much this includes also the right decision of human freedom which is itself a gift from God. Where sin already existed, grace came in super-abundance. And hence we have every right to suppose that grace has not only been offered even outside the Christian Church (to deny this would be the error of Jansenism) but also that, in a great many cases at least, grace gains the victory in man's free acceptance of it, this being again the result of grace. Of course, we would have to show more explicitly than the shortness of time permits that the empirical picture of human beings, their life, their religion and their individual and universal history does not disprove this optimism of a faith which knows the whole world to be subjected to the salvation won by Christ. But we must remember that the theoretical and ritualistic factors in good and evil are only a very inadequate expression of what man actually accomplishes in practice. We must remember that the same transcendence of man (even the transcendence elevated and liberated by God's grace) can be exercised in many different ways and under the most varied labels. We must take into consideration that whenever the religious person acts really religiously, he makes use of, or omits unthinkingly, the manifold forms of religious institutions by making a consciously critical choice among and between them. We must consider the immeasurable difference— which it seems right to suppose to exist even in the Christian sphere—between what is objectively wrong in moral life and the extent to which this is really realized with subjectively grave guilt. Once we take all this into consideration, we will not hold it to be impossible that grace is at work, and is even being accepted, in the spiritual, personal life of the individual, no matter how primitive, unenlightened, apathetic and earth-bound such a life many at first sight appear to be. We can say quite simply that wherever, and in so far as, the individual makes a moral decision in his life (and where could this be declared to be in any way absolutely impossible —except in precisely 'pathological' cases?), this moral decision can also be thought to measure up to the character of a supernaturally elevated, believing and thus saving act, and hence to be more in actual fact than merely 'natural morality'. Hence, if one believes seriously in the universal salvific purpose of God towards all men in Christ, it need not and cannot really be doubted that gratuitous influences of properly Christian supernatural grace are conceivable in the life of all men (provided they are first of all regarded as individuals) and that these influences can be presumed to be accepted in spite of the sinful state of men and in spite of their apparent estrangement from God.

Our second thesis goes even further than this, however, and states in its second part that, from what has been said, the actual religions of 'pre-Christian' humanity too must not be regarded as simply illegitimate from the very start, but must be seen as quite capable of having a positive significance. This statement must naturally be taken in a very different sense which we cannot examine here for the various particular religions. This means that the different religions will be able to lay claim to being lawful religions only in very different senses and to very different degrees. But precisely this variability is not at all excluded by the notion of a 'lawful religion', as we will have to show in a moment. A lawful religion means here an institutional religion whose 'use' by man at a certain period can be regarded on the whole as a positive means of gaining the right relationship to God and thus for the attaining of salvation, a means which is therefore positively included in God's plan of salvation.

We must therefore rid ourselves of the prejudice that we can face a non-Christian religion with the the dilemma that it must either come from God in everything it contains and thus correspond to God's will and positive providence, or be simply a purely human construction. If man is under God's grace even in these religions—and to deny this is certainly absolutely wrong—then the possession of this supernatural grace cannot but show itself, and cannot but become a formative factor of life in the concrete, even where (though not only where) this life turns the relationship to the absolute into an explicit theme, viz. in religion. It would perhaps be possible to say in theory that where a certain religion is not only accompanied in its concrete appearance by something false and humanly corrupted but also makes this an explicitly and consciously adopted element—an explicitly declared condition of its *nature*— this religion is wrong in its deepest and most specific being and hence can no longer be regarded as a lawful religion—not even in the widest sense of the word. This may be quite correct in theory. But we must surely go on to ask whether there is any religion apart from the Christian religion (meaning here even only the Catholic religion) with an authority which could elevate falsehood into one of its really essential parts and which could thus face man with an alternative of either accepting this falsehood as the most real and decisive factor of the religion or leaving this religion.

3rd Thesis: If the second thesis is correct, then Christianity does not simply confront the member of an extra-Christian religion as a mere non-Christian but as someone who can and must already be regarded in this or that respect as an anonymous Christian. It would be wrong to regard the pagan as someone who has not yet been touched in any way by God's grace and truth. If, however, he has experienced the grace of God—if, in certain circumstances, he has already accepted this grace as the ultimate, unfathomable entelechy of his existence by accepting the immeasurableness of his dying existence as opening out into infinity —then he has already been given revelation in a true sense even before he has been affected by missionary preaching from without. For this grace, understood as the *a-priori* horizon of all his spiritual acts, accompanies his consciousness subjectively, even though it is not known objectively. It is not thereby denied, but on the contrary implied, that this explicit self-realization of his previously anonymous Christianity is itself part of the development of this Christianity itself—a higher stage of development of this Christianity demanded by his being—and that it is therefore intended by God in the same way as everything else about salvation. Hence, it will not be possible in any way to draw the conclusion from this conception that, since man is already an anonymous Christian even without it, this explicit preaching of Christianity is superfluous. Such a conclusion would be just as false (and for the same reasons) as to conclude that the sacraments of baptism and penance could be dispensed with because a person can be justified by his subjective acts of faith and contrition even before the reception of these sacraments. The reflex self-realization of a previously anonymous Christianity is demanded (1) by the incarnational and social structure of grace and of Christianity, and (2) because the individual who grasps Christianity in a clearer, purer and more reflective way has, other things being equal, a still greater chance of salvation than someone who is merely an anonymous Christian.

4. Atheism and Implicit Christianity*

As there are anonymous Christians in the non-Christian religions, there are also anonymous Christians among contemporary atheists. Christians must distinguish between the atheism which consists in culpable refusal of loving surrender to the world's Absolute Horizon and the atheism which stems from inculpable inability to understand or accept the formulated doctrine of the Christian religion. Although the first type of atheism is incompatible with implicit faith, the second type is quite compatible with it. When society was thoroughly Christian it may have been a good working hypothesis that most atheists were of the first type. In today's irreligious society it is safer to assume that they are of the second. Pastorally we should deal with contemporary atheists on the assumption that they are anonymous Christians.

For the sake of full conceptual clarity we must emphasise this: By virtue of God's desire for universal salvation, the 'objective redemption' constituting a fundamental factor in every man's 'subjective' state of salvation, the 'supernatural *existentiale*' and the continual offer of the grace of God's supernatural saving activity, even the unbaptised person (in the state of original sin as well) is in a unique situation. Prior to any existential attitude which he takes up, whether in faith and love or unbelief and sin, he is in a different position (and he himself is different too) from what would be the case if he were only the result of his 'nature' and his original sin. He can never be simply a 'natural' man and a sinner. By virtue of the grace of Christ (as possibility and obligation), which is at least a constant offer, he is always in a Christ-determined situation, whether he has accepted this grace or not.

Terminologically, however, it is better not to call this existentially (but not *existentiell*) 'Christian' position on the part of every man 'implicit' or 'anonymous' Christianity straight away . Otherwise we obscure the radical distinction between grace merely offered and grace existentially accepted in faith and love.

* From *Theological Investigations*, vol. IX, pp. 146–47, 151–52, 155–56.
© 1972 by Darton, Longman and Todd Ltd.

The basic thesis of this study is that even an atheist may possess this kind of 'implicit' Christianity.

This basic thesis is by no means self-evident. For it must be said that right up to most recent times official text-book theology has fairly unanimously supported the view (in spite of various theological qualifications) that it is impossible for a normal responsible human being to entertain a 'positive atheism' for any considerable time without becoming personally culpable. Since in this context there is no sense in weakening this culpability as though it were only 'venial', the official view involves a denial of the possibility of 'implicit Christianity' for any length of time in an adult atheist.

On the one hand one is obliged to appreciate the weight of the official view: in scripture God's knowability seems so clearly *given* and atheism seems to give evidence so definitely of being man's most terrible aberration, that it was only thought possible to understand it as a *sin* in which a man *freely* turns away in the *mysterium iniquitatis,* evilly suppressing the truth which everywhere impinges on him (Rom 1:18).

On the other hand it must be said that until now neither text-book theology nor scripture has been confronted with the experience of a world-wide and militant atheism, confident of its own self-evident nature and because of this it was possible to regard the earlier, ubiquitous, theistic 'common opinion' as something necessarily so, as an eternally valid quality of human nature. This was a mistake: it led to the official text-book view we mentioned being taken as self-evident.

Next, for the sake of brevity, it will be simplest if we have recourse to the doctrine of the Second Vatican Council in order to illustrate our basic thesis theologically. The texts concerned are Nos. 19–21 of the first chapter of the first part of *Gaudium et spes,* the fifth paragraph of No. 22 of the same chapter, No. 16 in Chapter 2 of *Lumen gentium* and finally— since what has been said about the polytheistic religions of mission lands also holds good in the case of atheism as the product of a different historical and sociological situation—No. 7 of the Decree on the Church's Missionary Activity.

It emerges from our definition of 'implicit' Christianity that the basic thesis can be suitably demonstrated in two stages:

1. According to Vatican II not every instance of positive atheism in a concrete human individual is to be regarded as the result and the expression of personal sin.

2. Such an atheist can be justified and receive salvation if he acts in accordance with his conscience.

In the first place, therefore, although it is relatively exhaustive in its treatment of atheism, the Council makes no reference to the traditional text-book view that positive atheism cannot be entertained for any considerable period of time by a fully developed person of normal intelligence without involving blame on his part. Furthermore it is safe to say that the Council not only left this thesis alone, but actually *assumed a contrary thesis*, i.e. that it is possible for a *normal adult to hold an explicit atheism for a long period of time*—even to his life's end—*without this implying moral blame* on the part of such an unbeliever. It is true, however, that this view is not taught explicitly.

These declarations have rendered obsolete even the earlier, *moderately* optimistic interpretations of the situation of non-Christians and heathen and atheists too which were to be found in text-book theology. According to the latter, such people outside the jurisdiction of Christianity were recognised as capable of attaining a 'natural' salvation (similar to that which the text-books acknowledged in the case of children dying without being baptised) but excluded from a really *supernatural* salvation. The Decree on the Church's Missionary Activity (No. 7) expressly states that these people too, by the grace of God and in ways not known to us, can reach a real *saving* faith even without having accepted the explicit preaching of the Christian Gospel. And wherever the word 'salvation' occurs in the other texts we have quoted, what is meant is genuine supernatural salvation, more particularly since it is expressly declared that all men have only *one* vocation to salvation, and since the attainment of this salvation is understood as participation in Christ's Easter mystery.

Thus according to the teaching of Vatican II it is possible for an atheist to be living in the grace of justification, i.e. possessing what we have called 'implicit Christianity'. In this short investigation it cannot be our business to show how this conciliar doctrine is deduced from the genuinely original sources of revelation, nor how it is defended against the seemingly weighty objections which could be brought against it by Scripture and Tradition. The Council itself only gives a very brief and general justification for its approach. To a certain degree the Council makes its own case—the possibility of the unbaptised non-Christian's salvation without contact with the Gospel (thus including the atheist)—more difficult to defend by requiring a real supernatural faith even in such a case, i.e. not escaping the issue by saying that such a person attains supernatural salvation at the end of his life on the basis of a mere 'natural' morality.

In connection with the Council's teaching our basic thesis implies:

1. the thesis of God's will for the salvation of all men in Christ (the will is understood as 'infralapsarian'), and the availability of his grace, and the doctrine that there is only *one* supernatural goal for all men; and

2. the conviction that not every individual atheist can be regarded as a gravely culpable sinner.

We have already seen that the Decree on the Church's Missionary Activity (No. 7) teaches the possibility of salvation for all men, and we have included atheists too in this category in so far as they are without blame. But the Decree expressly says that the people referred to attain salvation in so far as they come—by paths known only to God—to a saving *faith*.

If we adopt these assumptions (which we have really only touched upon here) we can draw up a sort of table of the fundamental types of man's relationship with God. In doing so it must always be borne in mind that a conscious or known reality present to man's mind may exist in the mode of free acceptance or free rejection, since man is not merely a being who is intellectually knowing, but is also always a free being.

First possibility: God is present in man's transcendental nature and this fact is objectified in a suitably and correctly explicit and conceptual theism, and moreover is also freely accepted in the moral affirmation of faith (in the practice of living). In this case we have what constitutes simply correct theism, what we might call transcendental *and* categorial theism, accepted and affirmed by man's freedom in both these dimensions. In this way it represents in every respect a proper relationship between man and God such as we may assume in the case of a justified Christian.

Second possibility: Both transcendental and categorial theism are present; man knows of God in his transcendental experience and also his reflection upon the latter is correct, but in his moral freedom he rejects this knowledge, whether as a sinner, denying God, or going on to reject the God whom he has correctly 'objectified' conceptually in real free unbelief. This is the category in which the 'atheist' was thought of previously in religious and in specifically Christian matters. It was assumed that he had an objectified and more or less correct idea of God but rejected him in sin or freely turned away from him either in a merely practical 'godlessness' or in theoretical atheism as well.

Third possibility: The transcendental experience of God is present of necessity and is also freely accepted in a positive decision to be faithful to conscience, but it is incorrectly objectified and interpreted. This inadequate, false (and under certain circumstances totally lacking) *idea of God* as such can be again the object of free acceptance or rejection in various ways, but we need not concern ourselves with that in any greater detail here. For instance, consider the case of a polytheist who, in the dimension of free reflection, freely 'believes' this polytheism or freely and 'atheistically' rejects it, without replacing it by a correctly conceived theism. In either case this third instance is the sort of atheism which is innocent in the sense of Vatican II. It is atheism on the plane of categorical reflection, coexisting in the subject with a freely affirmed transcendental theism. There can be such a thing as innocent atheism because of the difference between subjective transcendentality and categorial objectification in concepts and sentences, producing this coexistence of transcendental theism and categorial atheism. For the said 'difference' is necessarily present in every act of the mind. The components of this innocent atheism are: *one the one hand* the subject's continual transcendental dependence on God and the free acceptance of this dependence, especially in the moral act which respects absolutely the demands of conscience—i.e. a transcendental theism 'in the heart's depths'—an *on the other hand* the free rejection the objectified concept of God, i.e. a categorial atheism in the forefront of conscious reflection, a rejection which cannot in itself be regarded as culpable.

Fourth possibility: The transcendental dependence on God is present; objectively it is interpreted falsely or insufficiently correctly in a categorial atheism, and this transcendental dependence on God is itself simultaneously denied in a free action by gravely sinful unfaithfulness to conscience or by an otherwise sinful, false interpretation of existence (as being 'totally absurd' or of no absolute significance, etc). In this case the free denial does not refer merely to the categorial interpretation of man's transcendental nature, but to existence and thus to God himself. Here we have culpable transcendental atheism, which excludes the possibility of salvation as long as it persists.

5. On the Theology of Hope*

Run-of-the-mill Scholastic theology has difficulty in justifying the unique, original, and independent status of hope as a theological virtue. A theological virtue is an attitude freely adopted by a subject endowed with intellect and will yet supported by God's self-bestowal in grace. However the Persons of the Trinity are constituted by only two processions, the procession of knowledge by which the Logos proceeds from the Father and the procession of love through which the Holy Spirit proceeds from the Father and the Son. Furthermore, there are only two basic spiritual intentionalities through which the human subject can express his response to God. These are knowledge and love. If then faith corresponds to knowledge and charity to love, what can be the third procession within the Trinity or the third intentionality in the human subject to which the third theological virtue of hope can correspond?

The standard theological manuals endeavor to solve this problem by virtually reducing hope to a transient mode of faith and charity. Hope becomes the provisional form which knowledge and love of God assume during man's earthly journey toward his heavenly salvation. This standard theology of hope, however, suffers from two defects. It ignores the Pauline teaching that hope abides as a distinct and irreducible theologi-

* From *Theological Investigations*, vol. X, pp. 245–59.
ⓒ 1973 by Darton, Longman & Todd Ltd.

cal virtue even in heaven, and it fails to do justice to the special and radical uniqueness of hope even in this life.

This deficiency is a very serious one because faith and love can be seen in their true nature only when they are conceived in the light of the original and independent status of hope. Rahner insists that hope cannot be treated simply as a transient modality of supernatural knowledge and love of God during man's earthly life. Hope is the abiding radical attitude which remains the source and interior ground of all salvific knowledge of God in this life and the next. For hope is the radical attitude which draws us "out of ourselves" into that which is utterly beyond our control. Hope does not disappear in heaven because, as we have already seen, the Beatific Vision is never the comprehension of God but simply the immediate proximity of the Absolute Mystery who freely chooses to communicate his inner life to the blessed. Thus the Beatific Vision must be experienced as a grace which is utterly beyond the control of the blessed in heaven. Far from being simply the reaction of man's free will to his knowledge of God's promises through faith, hope is the inner unifying structure of man's salutary knowledge and love of God during this life. For the theoretical knowledge of God's promises which faith provides is not sufficient to ground the conviction of the individual Christian that the God, who can be the God of grace or wrath, has actually become the God of grace for him individually by the free and utterly undeducible concession of his efficacious grace.

This accurate understanding of the role of hope as the unifying source of man's loving surrender to God is urgently needed today. Our age is characterized by its extensive scientific and social planning for the future of the world. It is future-oriented, often in a revolutionary way. The Christian's attitude toward the world, structured by his hope, is also an attitude which is orientated toward the future. The Christian's Absolute Future, however, is the Christ of the Second Coming. Therefore the Christian realizes that the world's Absolute Future is not under the control of even the most perfect human planning. The Absolute Future is the Uncontrollable God to whom men can only commit themselves in hope. Nevertheless, since Christ's Second Coming will be the culmination of the order of creation within the order of grace, the Christian's hope in the Absolute Future should not dampen his enthusiasm for the scientific and social planning which he realizes is required for the successful evolution of God's creation.

On the other hand, however, the Christian's hope in the Absolute Future will be his protection against the fascination of the inner-worldly revolutionary ideologies whose hope to achieve human fulfilment through a secular planned society is doomed to frustration.

Rahner's theology of hope is a further development of the theology of the Beatific Vision which he first worked out in his reflections on the *concept of mystery in Catholic theology. The metaphysics of knowledge which supports it is the familiar metaphysics of love as the lamp of knowledge which Rahner claims is always operative in any genuine knowledge of the world's free Creator. Given Rahner's theology of man's knowledge of the world's free Creator, it follows that man's salutary knowledge and love of God must, of its very nature, be structured by hope.*

Although Rahner's reflections on Christ as the world's Absolute Future are an expansion of his earlier reflections on Christology within an evolutionary view of the world, they have also been influenced by the more recent European theology of hope. Rahner's use of his theology of hope as a critique of contemporary secular ideologies will remind his readers of Jürgen Moltmann's Theology of Hope, *inspired by the latter's reaction to the Marxist philosopher, Ernst Bloch. Rahner's introduction of his theology of hope into his later writings on eschatology and political theology follows the same general pattern which a number of other German theologians have followed in their reaction to Bloch's* The Principle of Hope.

A first attempt to penetrate somewhat more deeply into the nature of hope must now be made, and in order to do this we shall take as our starting-point the classic principle of Catholic theology that hope is a special *theological* virtue which must be assigned a place together with and between faith and love.

At first this statement seems to be readily understandable. A theological virtue is an attitude freely adopted by the subject endowed with intellect and will, yet supported by God's self-bestowal in grace. It is an attitude which is related not, as with the moral virtues, to a particular finite moral value which can be defined in 'this-worldly' categories, but bears upon God himself as he is 'in and for himself', and as such becomes, in a direct sense through this act of self-bestowal in grace, our absolute good. In this way, therefore, God becomes radically and effectively 'God for us'. But hope bears precisely upon God in this sense, God who has promised himself to us in this dimension of his nature and who constitutes our absolute future. This seems to be enough to enable us to understand the fact that hope is one of the three theological virtues and why it should be so. In fact, however, not everything is *ipso facto* clear, especially if we are to understand that hope is not merely a preliminary and provisional form of faith and love, not merely faith and love 'on the way' and before they have attained their goal, not merely, therefore, a form conditioned by that situation in human existence in which we are still making pilgrimage and therefore in danger. On the contrary hope is to be thought of as a unique theological virtue in its own right, and one which cannot be reduced to the other two. This, however, is not clear immediately or without further explanation.

In order to recognise the obscurity here we must consider the following factors. In the doctrine of the Trinity we know of *two* 'processions', in other words two modes of mediation through which God as ungenerated (the Father) utters himself and possesses himself in love, so that three modes of subsistence in the one God are constituted, the 'procession' as Word and also as 'breathing forth love'. In conformity with this, in any Christian interpretation of man, we must hold fast, in spite of many contrary tendencies of recent times, to the fact that there are two basic modes of human (transcendental) self-realisation: awareness of, and reflection upon the self through knowledge and through free love, corresponding to the two basic transcendentals *Verum* and *bonum,* in which the one *(unum)* being *(ens)* imposes itself. These two basic transcendentals, then, are such that we cannot at will add any others to them on the same plane. Thus it appears that from what we know both of God and of man it is natural to expect two basic attitudes to be involved in man's right realisation of his own nature, two basic virtues which correspond to this original transcendental duality inherent in man. This is all the more true in view of the fact that a 'divine' or theological virtue is sustained precisely by God's self-bestowal, and the response of the creature who has personal status and is endowed with spiritual faculties to this divine self-bestowal is precisely made possible and effective by the divine self-bestowal itself. Now there are only two such modes or—better—aspects in this *one* divine self-bestowal: the first aspect is constituted by the *Logos* and the second by the divine *Pneuma*. It is precisely through these two aspects that God as ungenerated, God the 'Father' (not, therefore, an abstract divinity!), who is incomprehensible and never loses his incomprehensibility even through his act of divine self-bestowal, imparts himself. Because of this we cannot imagine that the Trinity in the modes of subsistence in the one God implies *ipso facto* that there is also a trinity in the response by which we accept this self-bestowal of the Father in *Logos* and in *Pneuma*. The fact that there is only *one* act of self-bestowal in which the 'Father' imparts himself in *Logos* and *Pneuma* implies that in the response, i.e. the 'theological' virtue, of man which is itself upheld by this divine self-bestowal, only a single act is conceivable with *two* modalities: faith and love, to correspond to the Word and the Love of the Father.

It also seems to be in conformity with this that in the theology of the bible the twofold combination of faith and love is earlier than our threefold combination of faith, hope and love, even though in not a few passages in the New Testament itself ἐλπίς has been inserted between πίστις and ἀγάπη. Thus hope is intended to figure primarily as a mere formal aspect of faith and love taken together, the power and the mode in which man, while still in peril, lovingly yearns for God as the absolute essence of truth as apprehended by his faith, and as the absolute essence of all that is good as the goal of his love, reaching out for him under these aspects as a salvation that is still to be attained in the future, but is, nevertheless, promised. Hence it is that hope does not figure so very clearly as a distinct attitude in its own right with an independent status of its own and a nature of its own somewhere between faith and love. Nor can we evade the question arising from this merely by pointing out first that hope is appropriate to the nature of this present life considered as a pilgrimage, as provisional, as lived in *statu viatoris,* seeing that later it is to be left behind, abrogated, once we 'possess' God, and second that this is also proper to faith, which ceases and gives way to the vision which is 'face to face'. For in one passage in which he is dealing with all three of the theological virtues which he mentions in 1 Cor 13 Paul ascribes to them a definitive permanence, a $\mu\acute{\epsilon}\nu\epsilon\iota\nu$ that is absolute. Thus he does not recognise any total abrogation of $\pi\acute{\iota}\sigma\tau\iota\varsigma$ or $\dot{\epsilon}\lambda\pi\acute{\iota}\varsigma$. On the other hand, however, and *e converso*: If we follow the traditional interpretation, and regard hope as coming to an end with 'possession', just as faith comes to an end with 'vision', then this 'possession' of God would be constituted precisely by a vision and a love which unites, and hope would once more appear as the mere mode in which man for the time being, and in his *statu viatoris* strives for this possession of God as truth and love. Hope as such would be abrogated in a far more radical manner than faith, which is raised to the level of vision. In comparison with faith or vision and with love, whether as still in process of development or in its definitive form, we would constantly be in a position where we could not yet ascribe this status to hope as of the same origin as these other virtues and as 'enduring' like them as that in which the basic fulness of human life is achieved in the attainment of God. Thus at this stage it seems as though we can only construct a triad of divine virtues by postulating an interrelationship of initially disparate concepts which is relatively superficial, and only in such a triad can hope be considered one of the three theological virtues. Now despite all appearances to the contrary this problem is not a question of subtle, and ultimately superfluous playing with concepts. On the contrary, the process of finding the answer to it will bring us perforce to a deeper understanding of the nature of hope, and thereby of man and even of God himself. This is why we have dwelt upon this problem in all its acuteness. But what is the solution to it?

It would certainly be false for us to seek to find a solution to the problem by contesting the statements which have been made, as for instance by holding that ultimately speaking what is being postulated is a third basic power to which hope would correspond as its appropriate virtue. In fact we do not need to conceive of the triad of the theological virtues as such that it necessarily presents us with three virtues together, unified by a strict principle of distinction which is common to them all in the same sense and at the same level, so that they have precisely the *same* relationship *among themselves*. We do not necessarily need to argue against the correctness of regarding these three virtues as constituting a triad. We do not need to adopt this approach even though 'hope' is regarded as the mid-term and the common factor between the two other virtues. Admittedly in saying this we are assuming that it is not regarded merely as a *transient* modality of the two other virtues and of the 'powers' corresponding to these, but rather as that property which endures in them, and which draws both equally together into one. We must not regard hope merely as standing 'between' the two other virtues. Rather we must think of it as constituting the original and unifying medium between them. If we can show this then we are justified in speaking of a triad, but at the same time we do not have to conclude from its existence that hope must be related to faith and love in precisely the same way as these two are related to each other. Nor is it, ultimately speaking, of decisive importance whether the basic modality of the relationship to God as understood here is that which is called 'hope' in the common parlance of everyday, or whether rather there is something which lies concealed behind this term, but which, nevertheless, this term is used to point to because there is no better one for it.

It is common practice in scholastic theology to replace the vision of this quality of hope which is so obscurely pointed to by the conceptual model according to which hope is dissolved by 'possession', by the 'attainment of the goal'. This conceptual model is drawn from everyday experience, and from the experience of 'hope' at the profane level. Initially, for instance, we 'hope' for a position in life which we have not yet attained to. But once this has been achieved, once we 'have' it, then we no longer need to 'hope', but at most hope to retain that which we have achieved, though in that case we experience or interpret this attitude as something quite different from 'hope'. But what is to be said of precisely *that* basic act in which (it is called theological hope) we reach out towards God? Can we interpret this basic act too as a mere provisional attitude which will be dissolved once we have attained to that state of 'possession' which itself in turn is constituted by 'vision' and unifying 'love'? In that case hope will be abolished as something that belongs to the past, because now there is nothing more that has to be 'hoped for', but rather everything is already in our possession, and we do not even have to fear that we may lose what has been attained to, in other words we do not even have to hope that this will continue permanently. But is this line of thought correct?

In fact, however, it is questionable in the extreme—in other words basically inadequate—to take as our guide the conceptual model of 'possession' in order to understand the definitive consummation of man's life, and on this basis to conceive of hope as that which is merely provisional. This conceptual model in fact distorts the special quality of man's final consummation as consisting in vision and love, and thereby too that basic modality belonging to this final consummation which is both expressed and concealed at the same time in the term 'hope'. This basic modality only constitutes the authentic nature of *that* theological hope in so far as it is present in the life of the pilgrim here below—and here admittedly it has a certain provisional quality. The act of attaining to God as truth in the 'vision' of God in fact allows for the transcendence of this God as the incomprehensible. The event in which this takes place, inasmuch as it is made possible by the divine self-bestowal, is not the act in which the absolute mystery which is God is finally overcome and solved, but rather the act in which this truly unfathomable mystery in all its finality and its overpowering acuteness is no longer able to be suppressed, but must be sustained and endured as it is in itself without any possibility of escape into that which can be comprehended and so controlled and subordinated to the subject and his own nature as it exists prior to any elevation by grace. The act of attaining to love as love is the response to, and acceptance of, a love which, totally independent of any element in ourselves, is rather freedom in its most radically incalculable form. The intelligibility of this love is not to be found in any prior quality in ourselves which makes us 'worthy to be loved' (even though the love itself does confer this). On the contrary, it always depends totally and eternally on this freedom of God which is based on nothing else than itself alone. In this radical sense the love we are speaking of is, and remains eternally, 'grace'. The 'possession' of God—if in spite of what has been said we may still use this term—is that radical transcendence of self and surrender of self which is entailed in the act of reaching out for truth into the unfathomable mystery, and it is also the radical self-surrender and self-transcendence of that love which cannot charm love from the beloved through any act of self-surrender on its part, but lives totally by the love of that which is beloved as based on nothing else than itself. It is pure act of reception and *as such* sustains the mutual interplay or *commercium* of the love involved, but is not itself upheld by this *commercium*.

These qualities inherent in the response to and acceptance of God as truth and as love have an interior unity and a common source in the one radical attitude which draws us 'out of ourselves' into that which is utterly beyond our control. This 'letting of one's self go' is certainly the essence of man, rightly understood *in the concrete* as already bearing 'grace' within itself. Once he has discovered this nature of his and freely assented to it, man has attained to freedom in the true sense, which consists in realising himself and fulfilling the meaning of his life. And precisely this fulfilment of his nature is that 'outwards from the self' attitude of the finite subject reaching out into the incomprehensibility and incircumscribability of God as truth and as love. In the word 'hope' this one unifying 'outwards from the self' attitude into God as the absolutely uncontrollable finds expression. Hope, therefore, represents this unifying medium between faith or vision and love (still on the way and also, even when it has achieved its 'goal'). *'Hence "hope" does not, in this most ultimate sense, express a modality of faith and love so long as these are at the provisional stage. On the contrary, it is a process of constantly eliminating the provisional in order to make room for the radical and pure uncontrollability of God. It is the continuous process of destroying that which appears, in order that the absolute and ultimate truth may be the intelligible as comprehended, and love may be that which is brought about by our love.* We would like to be those who set up God for ourselves through that which we ourselves do, acting (morally) as free and intelligent beings, and thereby having him as ours to dispose of as we will. But hope is the name of an attitude in which we dare to commit ourselves to that which is radically beyond all human control in both of man's basic dimensions, that, therefore, which is attained to precisely at that point at which the controllable is definitively transcended, i.e. in the ultimate consummation of eternal life. Taken in this sense hope is that which 'endures'. And this means that it also shares in this character of 'enduring' which is involved in the definitive finality of the relationship to absolute truth. Hence Paul can say that faith itself 'endures', even when vision has been attained to. A further point also becomes clear in the light of this, namely that the love of eternity can only rightly be understood if it is thought of as carrying the quality of 'hope', so that we can just as truly speak of a *fides* and *caritas spe formata* as of a *fides* and *spes caritate formata*. Hope implies the one basic character which is the common factor in the mutual interplay of truth and love: the enduring attitude of 'outwards from self' into the uncontrollability of God. Conversely we can say: where hope is achieved as the radical self-submission to the absolute uncontrollable, there alone do we truly understand what, or still better *who* God is. He is that which of its very existence empowers us to make this radical self-commitment to the absolute uncontrollable in the act of knowledge and love. One might almost say our radical self-commitment to the 'absurdity' of truth and love, because both derive their true essence—quite otherwise to what we would have thought at first sight—from the incomprehensibility and uncontrollability of truth and love in themselves.

This means that radically speaking hope is not the modality of the historical process by which we pass through time to that state which is definitive and eternal, but rather the basic modality of the very *attitude to the eternal* which precisely as such sets the true advance towards eternity 'in train'. In the light of this both presumption *and* despair are, at basis, the refusal of the subject to allow himself to be grasped by the uncontrollability and to be drawn out of himself by it. Clearly all that has been said with regard to the ultimate nature of hope does not imply any denial of the fact that it itself, in the *status viatoris* it bears certain properties which can no longer be ascribed to it in the eternal life in which it achieves its consummation. But these properties—the striving for the finite *within* that process in which the encounter with the provisional is still taking place —conceal more than they unveil the innermost essence of hope. For this encounter, even when we rise above it in our hope for the future, always gives rise to the impression that that which is definitive and final too will one day be possessed in the same way as now we comprehend, dominate and so dispose of the provisional and temporary benefits available to us.

We must now adopt a second approach, and attempt thereby to penetrate still more deeply into the absolute essence of hope. In this we must once more take as our starting-point certain familiar theological data. In this way it will be sought to clarify still further the unique and original nature of hope which, perhaps, even after our first approach, still continues to be understood as a modality of faith and love in *such a way that* it is not sufficiently made clear how faith and love too themselves only appear rightly in their true nature when they are conceived of in the light of the original and independent status of hope.

In the average Catholic theology hope appears almost as an inevitable consequence of faith. Faith is the assent and apprehension not merely of the theoretical statements in which divine revelation is formulated, but also of God's promises which are proclaimed in this revelation, the promises of grace, of forgiveness and of eternal life. Once these promises are apprehended and are present by *faith* itself, then—so the average theology of hope appears unreflectingly to suppose—everything is clear and simple. These promises which are present and apprehended by faith itself considered as *fides historica et dogmatica* apparently set hope in train of themselves. Hope as a reaction on the part of the free will appears to be the simple consequence of the *assensus intellectualis* of faith considered as the act by which revelation is initially accepted, but it is this only provided that this freedom is not used to block the way in an incomprehensible and nonsensical refusal of these promises as theoretically apprehended, to which faith has already given its assent and which it offers to the free will as a subject on which to exercise its power.

This conception of hope, unreflecting for the most part but nonetheless real, is of course only the reflection of a more general theoretical intellectualism, according to which the 'will' is almost reduced to the status of the executive power for attaining to that good which is the *verum* of the intellect as *ipso facto* attained to, and which, therefore, in its original essence as the final consummation of knowledge as such, also signifies its beatitude. In saying this we have no intention of entering into the questions raised in the traditional controversy between Thomism and Scotism, or of supporting an option in favour of will, freedom and love as against 'intellect', if from both points of view the matter is conceived of as a choice between two 'powers'. Both historically speaking and of their real natures, the factors involved are not so simple. On the contrary, what has just been said is intended to be understood as an indication of a prior and more radical unity of knowledge and will, which the word 'hope' is precisely inteded to represent in its status as a prior medium or common factor between faith and love, and therefore between knowledge and will.

But let us notice in greater detail the misunderstanding indicated above, in which hope is interpreted as a simple consequence of faith. On the one hand what does faith offer in the way of promise if it is understood in the traditional sense of *assensus intellectualis* as put forward by the Council of Trent and the First Vatican Council? And what promise is it, on the other hand, that becomes the object of hope as such? We can and must answer this question in the following terms: in both cases it is far from being precisely the same promise, however much the second too, though not in isolation, may be based upon the first and depend upon it. From this a fresh insight can be obtained into the special quality and radical uniqueness of hope. Faith—viewed more in its 'theoretical' nature (including in this the dogmatic and historical specifications)—can only proclaim the 'metaphysical' kindness and holiness of God, the universal and fundamental meaningfulness of existence, God's universal will to save all men as 'prior' to man's response and conditioned by it, the existence of 'sufficient grace' for all and the existence of 'efficacious grace' for 'those in whom its presence cannot be recognised', so that we can never know precisely to whom this efficacious grace is *de facto* to be attributed. Faith in this sense, therefore, can only express a universal 'promise'. *This* faith as such cannot tell me that God has conferred this efficacious grace precisely on *me* in particular and is thus bringing about my salvation in the concrete.

Now if it were sought to object to this point that it is only through some inexcusable *fault* that a given individual can forfeit salvation in general and so *his* salvation, which is set before him as something that is possible and actually offered to him precisely through this faith and the universal promise of freedom which it contains, then we must rejoin that, without prejudice to the fact of the inexcusable fault on the individual's part, the distinction between 'sufficient' and 'efficacious' grace is prior to this as established *by God himself,* so that the presence or otherwise of this efficacious grace does not simply depend upon his fault. Faith in its theoretical aspects, therefore, cannot overcome this difference which is established by the freedom of choice of God's grace, and so not subject to any influence of ours. It cannot remove this difference according to which there is a distinction between the universal promise and the concrete and particular promise which intends and brings about the salvation of me as a concrete individual through this 'efficacious' grace. Certainly grace as formulated in dogmatic terms only realises its authentic nature and attains its true purpose when it is subsumed and transcended, when the theoretical promise which is proper to it is transformed into the specific and particular promise in which it is applied to the individual. But this takes place precisely in virtue of the fact that faith is transformed into hope. The free subject recognises that in spite of his freedom, and precisely *in* it he himself is subject to God's control, even though it still remains true that this cannot diminish his personal responsibility before God. Where-ever and whenever he exercises his freedom to receive the salvation that is offered to him, this acceptance is itself in turn the effect of the grace of God which as such is unmerited and *'effective'*, not merely 'sufficient'. The will of God is 'prior' to the decision of man in his freedom. And this will of God is as such distinct from God himself and not merely from man, so that it is beyond our powers to discern even so far as theoretical faith is concerned. Does this will of God, even at that level at which it is prior to my free decision, *de facto* represent the ultimate and definitive meaning of existence for me in particular in such a way as to exclude all other possible meanings? This is a question which no-one can answer by turn-ing the fundamental statement of theoretical faith with regard to the gen-eral promise of God's will to save all men into an absolute statement. But although such a statement is not possible *theoretically* speaking, and though we cannot achieve any positive knowledge of the meaning of existence or of our salvation in the concrete, nevertheless we must find another way of making this assertion to ourselves, because a positive decision of this kind is necessary for the subject himself who takes the initiative: I must hope.

Hope, then, is an act in which we base ourselves in the concrete upon that which cannot be pointed to in any adequate sense at the theoretical level, that which ultimately speaking is absolutely beyond our power to control, namely upon God who, in himself, can be the God of grace *or* the God of anger, but who in this case is apprehended as the God of grace and under no other aspect. And it is apparent from what has been said that hope in this sense is a basic modality of human existence. Hope, there-fore, is not merely a function which follows manifestly from knowledge, including in this the factor of theoretical faith. Certainly it can be demon-strated 'in theory' and 'in principle' that there must be hope. But this does not make hope a secondary function of the insight provided by theoretical faith. For the concrete hope of each individual in particular for *his* salva-tion is, in a certain sense, authorised even prior to any theoretical judg-ment precisely by this theoretical insight and by his knowledge of the general promise. But while this is true, still this hope cannot be consti-tuted by these factors alone. They cannot provide the actual *basis* for this concrete hope. This can only be the 'efficacious' will of God to save as applied to the concrete individual case, and it proceeds from God alone and remains hidden in him. This 'basis' is not something that faith pro-vides for hope, but rather something that is grasped solely by hope as such. As providing the basis for hope the will of God to save in the concrete is only present and attained to in hope itself and as such. It is the hope that is not derived from something other than itself, i.e. from faith, unless indeed we are to understand faith—with Luther—as being itself *fides fiducialis* and as such already including hope within itself. But this would be to obliterate the sound and permanent distinction between theoretical and practical awareness.

Hope, therefore, appears as *that* act in which the uncontrollable is made present as that which sanctifies, blesses and constitutes salvation without losing its character as radically beyond our powers to control, precisely because this salvific future is hoped for but not manipulated or controlled. However true it may be that hope has its basis in the special, but uncontrollable promise of God, it still can and must be said without any cheap attempts at paradox, that it is only hope itself that provides its own basis and in this sense creates that basis. For this special and particular promise takes place only *for* the individual who hopes as such, and only in hope itself as such. Hope alone is the *locus* of God as he who cannot be controlled or manipulated, and so of God as such.

This does not mean that the function of hope as the medium of the theological virtues is removed. The *perichoresis,* the mutual interaction between the three theological virtues by which they condition one another and permeate one another, is not disrupted. But what we have said does, perhaps make plainer that in hope which is irreducibly unique and underived: we only know who God is and who man is when we hope, i.e. when we take as our basis that which is incalculable and uncontrollable as the blessed which as such, and only in this guise, makes itself present to us in hope. The expression 'the incalculable and uncontrollable as the blessed' here is to be taken as the expression of a closer identification, although one that presents it more as having the nature of an event. For he who commits himself to the absolutely incalculable and uncontrollable is committing himself to the blessed one and to salvation. Presumption *and* despair both entail the same basic refusal to commit oneself and so to abandon oneself to the incalculable and the uncontrollable.

This does not mean that the status of Christ as the fundamental promise of hope is done away with in favour of a hope which, by its sheer radical quality, is based upon itself. For precisely this radical quality inherent in the 'outwards from self' movement into the absolute incalculability and uncontrollability of God as our absolute future, is based upon that grace of God which finds its unique historical manifestation in Christ precisely as *crucified,* and thereby as surrendering himself in the most radical sense to the disposing hand of God. It is in this historical manifestation that the grace we are considering here definitively establishes itself in the world. But precisely this takes place in the death of Christ as the most radical act of hope ('into *thy* hands I deliver up my life').

Whatever divisions there may be in human powers, in theory and practice, in knowledge and in free love, they are all subsumed alike in respect of what is common to all and what is peculiar to each of these elements, under the single factor of their common creaturehood and their orientation to God who, in his act of self-bestowal, makes himself the absolute future of man. And to this extent the act of hope stands revealed as the acceptance of this orientation towards the incalculability and uncontrollability of God. This act comprehends and unifies all these divisions even though, in order to be realised in the concrete, it has itself to be distinguished into faith and love. For, even allowing for this, this orientation must come from God and find its consummation in attaining to him.

In order to allay the suspicion that up to now we have been speaking of hope too much in terms of individual salvation, our considerations must now be supplemented by a third line of approach. Certainly it is not possible to include a full treatment of all that contemporary theology and existential ontology has to say with regard to the cosmic and social dimensions of hope, with regard to hope as exercised by the people of God on pilgrimage as such and in the course of its journey, with regard to the exodus which this people is constantly undertaking afresh, quitting all situations which have become 'frozen' and static in all dimensions of human existence.

Let us concentrate simply upon a single small passage in the Dogmatic Constitution on the Church, *Lumen gentium* (cf. C. IV, No. 35) which has for the most part gone unnoticed. There it is stated with regard to the laity that they should not conceal their eschatological hope in the innermost depths of their hearts (*in interioritate animi*), but should rather give it concrete expression ('exprimant') in the complexities and in the framework (*per structuras*) of secular life (*vitae saecularis*). This admonition is found in the context of the prophetic function of the laity in the Church and in the world. Surely it would be to misunderstand it if we sought to interpret it merely as a moralising conclusion of a secondary kind, following from the nature of that hope which the 'sons' of *the* 'promise' (*ibid.*) could ultimately speaking have lived by even without 'informing' the secular framework of the world with their hope in this way. Contrary to this view, the admonition contains a statement about an element which is essential to hope itself. The process by which this becomes an achieved reality involves a permanent transformation of the framework of secular life. Abstracting for the moment from the fact that 'revolution' is an extremely indeterminate and ambiguous concept, we might go so far as to say that the significance of this admonition is that Christian hope is at basis a continually revolutionary attitude on the part of Christians in the world. If we interpret the significance of Christianity aright, and if Christians themselves have a right understanding of the real significance of their own commitment, then the position is the diametrical opposite of what is generally thought both within and without the Christian body. The hope that is directed towards the absolute future of God, towards that eschatological salvation which is God himself as absolute, is not entertained in order to justify an attitude of conservatism which, from motives of anxiety, prefers a certain present to an unknown future and so petrifies everything. It is not the 'opium of people' which soothes them in their present circumstances even though these are painful. Rather it is that which commands them, and at the same time empowers them, to have trust enough constantly to undertake anew an exodus out of the present into the future (even within the dimension of this world).

In reality man as physical and as belonging to the historical dimension actually fulfills the ultimately transcendental structures of his own nature not in the abstract 'interiority' of a mere attitude of mind, but in intercourse with the world, the world made up of his own environment and of his fellow men. 'Practice' in the real sense, and as opposed to, and radically different from, theory, is, moreover, not confined solely to the mere execution of what has been planned and so is merely theoretical, but rather consists of an opening of the sphere of action in general and an attitude in which we dare to enter upon that which has not been planned, so that it is only in practice itself that any genuine possibility is given of what we have been bold enough to commit ourselves to. Planning may be necessary and justified in the manipulation of our environment (by technical measures), of the society we live in (by social measures), and of man himself. But all this does not derogate from the element of the unplanned which presses in upon us, and does not reduce it to a mere remnant of the contents of our lives which we have 'not yet' worked out. On the contrary such planning increases the element of that which is unplanned and has the effect of causing it to stand out still more sharply as the outcome of practice itself. Man himself, in the very process of breaking down the factor of the incalculable already present *beforehand* in his life, actually builds up those incalculable factors which are produced by *himself*. Now the effect of these two elements is that in the very act of venturing upon the future which is unforeseen and incalculable in 'this worldly terms' in his practical life as understood here, man realises, and necessarily must realise, his eschatological hope as a commitment 'outwards from self' to that which is incalculable and uncontrollable in an absolute sense. The Christian must, therefore, impress the form of his hope upon the frame-work of the world he lives in. Of course this does not mean for one moment that certain specific and firm structures of the secular world he lives in could ever be such that they could constitute the enduring objective realisation of his eschatological hope (in the sense of being established as this once and for all). On the contrary, every structure of secular life, whether present *or still to come* in the future, is called in question by hope as that in which we grasp at the incalculable and uncontrollable, and in this process of being called in question, the act of hope is made real in historical and social terms. Admittedly this is not the only way in which this is achieved. The Christian also accepts in the 'form of the world' as it passes over him those factors for which he himself is not responsible, and which he merely has to endure. He accepts these as part of the individual lot of his own personal life in death and in the renunciations which prepare for this, and it is no less true that he makes his hope real and living in this process too. A wildly revolutionary attitude, taken by itself, can be one of two things: either it implies that an absolute value is accorded to the form which the world is about to assume in the immediate future, in which case it is the opposite of hope, namely a form of presumption which only recognises that which can be controlled and manipulated, or which treats that which is not subject to our control or calculations as though it were so. Alternatively this attitude signifies despair, a state in which nothing more is hoped for, and therefore everything is absolutely negated because there is nothing final or definitive, or because nothing of this kind exists at all. But to subject the structures of this world too to constant reappraisal and criticism is *one* of the concrete forms of Christian hope which, as the courage of self-commitment to the incalculable and uncontrollable, must never hold fast to anything in this worldly life in such a way that it is as though without it man would be cast headlong into an absolute void. Hope commands man in the very moment in which, far more clearly than hitherto, he actually becomes the fashioner of his world, not only to let go of that which is taken away from him, but more than this actively to renounce that which, in the light of the limitless future which hope opens up to him, he recognises as provisional, and which, because of this, he can also understand to be dispensable already in this present time.

It is strange that we Christians, who have to achieve the radical commitment of hope in which we venture upon that which is incalculable and uncontrollable in the absolute future, have incurred the suspicion both in the minds of others and in our own that so far as we are concerned the will to guard and preserve is the basic virtue of life. In reality, however, the sole 'tradition' which Christianity precisely as the people of God *on pilgrimage* has acquired on the way is the command to hope in the absolute promise and—in order that thereby this task may not remain at the level merely of a facile ideology of ideas—to set out ever anew from the social structures which have become petrified, old and empty. Precisely *in what* this hope is to be brought to its fulness in the concrete in an exodus which is constantly renewed in this way, precisely *what* the Christian is to hold firm to (for this too is in fact possible)—because his hope also divests the future, even within the temporal dimension, of any false appearance of being the absolute future—this is something which 'theoretic' faith cannot answer as a simple deduction following from its own tenets. This concrete imperative is not merely the result of applying the theory of faith in practice. It would be just as wrong to hold this as to say that faith as such, and by itself, transforms the general promise into that special and particular one which is only realised in the original and underivable act of hope. But this hope summons the Christian and Christianity to venture upon this imperative, underivable in each case, in which they have constantly to decide anew between whether they are to defend the present which they alread possess, or to embark upon the exodus into the unforeseeable future. This is something which hope can do, for hope itself has in fact already all along achieved something which is even greater. In it man has surrendered himself to that which is absolutely and eternaily uncontrollable and incalculable by any powers of his. In the power of this greater hope he also possesses the lesser hope, namely the courage to transform the 'framework of secular life', as the Council puts it, and the converse too is no less true. In this lesser hope the greater one is made real.

There remain, therefore, faith, hope and love—these three. But the greatest of these is love. So says Paul. But we could also translate this: 'Faith, hope and love constitute that which is definitive and final.' Perhaps it has been shown that hope is not simply the attitude of one who is weak and at the same time hungering for a fulfilment that has yet to be achieved, but rather the courage to commit oneself in thought and deed to the incomprehensible and the uncontrollable which permeates our existence, and, as the future to which it is open, sustains it. Perhaps it has also been shown that such courage has the power to dare more than what can be arrived at merely by planning and calculations. Perhaps it has been shown that in the final and definitive consummation hope still prevails and endures, because this definitive consummation is God.

6. Unity of the Love of Neighbor and Love of God*

The anonymous Christian makes his act of implicit surrender to God through the categorical knowledge of the world which structures his individual acts. Nevertheless, a basic intentionality, a fundamental option, runs through the categorical acts by which the human subject responds to the people and things which he encounters in his world. His fundamental choice may be to respond to these people and things as they deserve. On the other hand, his fundamental choice may be to subject them to his own egotism and make them simply instruments for his own selfish satisfac-

* From *Theological Investigations*, vol. VI, pp. 236–38, 245–47.
© 1969 and 1974 by Darton, Longman & Todd Ltd.

tion. The first basic choice contains in its perduring intentionality a loving surrender to a transcendent order of truth and value whose ground is God. The second basic choice is the fundamental choice of self, that fundamental rejection of the true order of values which Augustine calls concupiscentia *or self-love.* Concupiscentia *is the contrary of Augustinian* caritas *which is a loving response to the universal order of values and its founder, the Word of God.*

Once we have understood the intentionality of these two fundamental choices of attitude, we can see that genuine love of our neighbor is implicitly love of God. Furthermore, we can also recognize that our explicit love of our neighbor rather than our implicit love of God holds the primary place in our attention. Thus our conscious love of our neighbor is the explicit act through which our implicit love of God is exercised.

As many contemporary phenomenologists have done, Rahner has seen in the Augustinian two-fold love the basic exercise of freedom through which the historical human subject chooses himself in his choice of attitude toward the realm of values. Since the realm of values is the realm of truth, the human subject can only choose himself authentically by loving submission to the order of values. With Augustine, Rahner can say that man's love is the weight by which he is borne wherever he is borne—amor meus pondus meum. For response to the realm of values unites man to the world and to God, while refusal of this response separates man from both in selfish isolation. Furthermore, since Rahner holds that the economic Trinity dwells in the justified soul as Uncreated Grace, Rahner can say with Augustine that a genuine response to the realm of values comes from the love of God living and working in his heart.

Rahner's theology of charity has combined the phenomenological ontology of Heidegger's authentic human subject, who lets the world of being manifest itself through his authentic self-choice, with the metaphysics of the love of God which Rahner inherited from Augustine and Bonaventure.

The tradition of the schools in Catholic theology has already held fast for a long time and this unanimously to the fact that the specific Christian love of neighbour is both in potency and in act a moment of the infused supernatural theological virtue of *caritas* by which we love God in his Spirit for his own sake and in direct community with him. This means, therefore, that the love of neighbour is not merely the preparation, effect, fruit and touchstone of the love of God but is itself an act of this love of God itself; in other words, it is at least an act within that total believing and hoping surrender of man to God which we call love and which alone justifies man, i.e. hands him over to God, because, being supported by the loving self-communication of God in the uncreated grace of the Holy Spirit, it really unites man with God, not as He is recognised by us but as

He is in Himself in His absolute divinity. Three things must not be over-looked in connection with this thesis of scholastic theology which iden-tifies the love of God and neighbour at least in their supernatural potency of the one infused supernatural theological virtue of *caritas*. (1) Scholastic theology does *not* overlook (in principle quite correctly) the fact that such a *caritas* can be also a mere impulse for certain modes of relationship to others by personal love which are not themselves formally acts of charity but merely its *actus imperati* restricting themselves more to a merely human dimension. (2) Scholastic theology, when giving a more precise interpretation of its radical thesis, will presumably often fall short of it, especially when it tries to give reasons for it; it will realise this thesis and will give reasons for it in such a way that it really remains a thesis in words only, and it will not really catch up with the existential, ontological presuppositions of this thesis. (3) If scholastic theology were asked ex-plicitly whether this identity is absolutely valid, it would no doubt answer that every act of charity towards our neighbour is indeed formally, even though perhaps only implicitly, love of God since the act is done after all by definition 'for the sake of God loved with a supernatural love'; but scholastic theology would probably deny that conversely every act of the love of God is formally also a love of neighbour (even though it naturally includes also the *readiness* for this). Above all, most theologians today would still shrink from the proposition which gives our fundamental thesis its ultimate meaning, its real clarity and inescapable character, viz. that wherever a genuine love of man attains its proper nature and its moral absoluteness and depth, it is in addition always so underpinned and height-ened by God's saving grace that it is also love of God, whether it be explicitly considered to be such a love by the subject or not.

Yet this is the direction in which the understanding of the thesis of identity as it is meant here leads us, since we hold it to be objectively correct and of basic significance for the Christian self-understanding of the future. What is meant by this requres a more detailed even though unavoidably still very summary explanation.

LOVE AS A REFLECTED AND EXPLICIT MODE OF ACTION AND AS AN UNCONCEPTUALISED TRANSCENDENTAL HORIZON OF ACTION

If we are to keep our ideas clear and avoid the most gross misunderstand-ings of the envisaged thesis from the very start, it is first of all necessary to distinguish in a human spiritual act between its explicit object rep-resented in a determined concept and category, which is envisaged in a systematic way both by the intellect and will, on the one hand, and the *a priori* formal object, the transcendental horizon or 'space' within which a determined individual object is encountered, on the other hand. The transcendental horizon is, on the one hand, the subjective possibility for the individual object to show itself at all; it is, as it were, the system of co-ordinates within which the classified object is given its place and which makes it comprehensible. On the other hand, the transcendental horizon is that which is itself given only in the encounter with the object of a concretely historical experience (it itself in transcendental experience), which of course does not mean that this experienced transcendental hori-zon of the categorised individual experience must be for this reason al-ready systematically, explicitly and objectively represented and named. The latter is, of course, not usually the case. Indeed, even where this transcendental horizon objective knowledge is reflected on and where it is therefore systematised, conceptually represented and named, and hence is itself made the explicit object of knowledge, this happens once more in virtue of this same horizon which as such must once more be given in an unconscious manner. The representation of its concept cannot dispense with this horizon itself in its unconscious exercise.

This distinction being presupposed, it must be said, of course, that not every act of the love of God is also a formal act of love of neighbour, if and in so far as the love of neighbour means an act in which our neighbour is envisaged and loved as the conscious object in its categorised and conceptual representation. If one relates oneself explicitly by prayer, trust and love to God, then this is in *this* sense an act of love of God and not an act of love of neighbour. Moreoever, measured by the object, such an act of love of God has, of course, a higher dignity than an act of reflected love of neighbour. Yet where the whole 'transcendental' depth of interhuman love is realised and represented (which, as has been said, *can* at least be *caritas,* as is quite certain from tradition), there such a love is also necessarily a conscious love of God and has God as its reflex motive (even though this is of course true once more in very different degrees of clarity). In this case our neighbour, and he himself, must then also be really loved and must be the formal object and motive of this love, no matter how one may explain the unity of the two then given motives. (The neighbour, through God's love for him, is 'one' with God, etc.) Yet this still leaves open the other question which also occupies us here, viz. whether all interhuman love, provided only that it has its own moral radicality, is also *caritas* (i.e. love also of God), since it is orientated towards God, not indeed by an explicitly categorised motive but (and this is the question) by its inescapably given transcendental horizon, which is given gratuitously by God's always prevenient saving grace.

The (naturally and supernaturally) transcendental experience of God which is also the necessary presupposition of the historical revelation of the Word and both is and remains its supporting ground, is possible only in and through man who has *already* (in logical priority) experienced the human Thou by his intramundane transcendental experience (of his *a priori* reference to the Thou) and by his categorised experience (of his concrete encounter with the concrete Thou) and who only *in this way* can exercise the (at last) transcendental experience of his reference to the absolute mystery (i.e. God). The classical thesis of scholastic theology (against ontologism and the innate idea of God) which maintains that God can be known only *a posteriori* from the created world, does not ultimately mean to imply (if it is properly understood) that man merely comes upon God like any object given to him purely accidentally (e.g. this flower or Australia) with which he might just as well not be concerned (from the point of view of the *a priori* structure of his knowledge) but it does mean that the transcendentally original *a priori* experience of his original reference to God and thus of God himself (an experience which must in some measure also be objectified in categories) can be made only in an always already achieved going-out into the world which, understood as the world of man, is primarily the people *with whom* he lives. Precisely because the original reference towards God is of a transcendental kind and hence does not fall into any cateogry but is given in the infinite reference of the spirit of man beyond every mere object of his personal and material surroundings, the *original* experience of God (as distinct from his separating representation in an individual concept) is always given in a 'worldly' experience. This, however, is only present originally and totally in the communication with a 'Thou'.

Since every conceptual reflection on the transcendental conditions of the possibility of knowledge and freedom is itself based once more on these same conditions then even the *explicit* religious act in which God becomes the reflex theme of knowledge and love is once more underpinned and taken up by that act which offers a transcendental, inclusive experience of God (of a natural-supernatural kind) and this *by the fact* that this act—in our turning towards the people we live with, and therefore in our explicit communication with them—lets us also experience unreflectedly the transcendental conditions of this act (i.e. the transcendental reference to God and the transcendental openness to the human Thou).

The act of love of neighbour is, therefore, the only categorised and original act in which man attains the whole of reality given to us in categories, with regard to which he fulfils himself perfectly correctly and *in which* he always already makes the transcendental and direct experience of God by grace. The reflected religious act as *such* is and remains secondary in comparison with this. It has indeed, as has already been said, a higher dignity than the reflected act of love of neighbour, if and in so far as the latter is measured by the particular explicit, conceptually represented object of the act in question. Measured by its 'horizon' or its transcendental possibility, it has the same dignity, the same 'draught' and the same radicality as the act of explicit love of neighbour, since both acts are necessarily supported by the (experienced but unreflected) reference both to God and to the intramundane Thou and this by grace (of the infused *caritas*), i.e. by that on which the explicit acts both of our relationship to God and of our love of neighbour 'for God's sake' reflect. Yet this does not alter the fact that the primary basic act of man who is always already 'in the world' is always an act of the love of his neighbour and *in this* the original love of God is realised in so far as in this basic act are also accepted the conditions of its possibility, one of which is the reference of man to God when supernaturally elevated by grace.

LOVE OF NEIGHBOUR AS THE PRIMARY ACT OF LOVE OF GOD

We are now in a position to give a direct answer to the basic question of our whole reflections. This was the question about the identity of the love of God and the love of neighbour. More exactly, it was the question about whether the love of neighbour understood as *caritas* is ultimately only a secondary moral act (one among many) which more or less proceeds objectively from the love of God as an *'actus imperatus'*. In other words, does the love of neighbour have God for its 'motive' (just as in the explicit love of God) in such a way that this love of neighbour really 'loves' God alone and hence, in accordance with the will of God who is really loved, is well disposed towards its neighbour and does good to him? *Or* is there a more radical unity between the love of God and of neighbour (taken as *caritas*) in such a way that the love of God itself is always also already love of neighbour in which our neighbour is really loved himself? We can now answer: the categorised explicit love of neighbour is the primary act of the love of God. The love of God unreflectedly but really and always intends God in supernatural transcendentality in the love of neighbour as such, and even the explicit love of God is still borne by that opening in trusting love to the whole of reality which takes place in the love of neighbour. It is radically true, i.e. by an ontological and not merely 'moral' or psychological necessity, that whoever does not love the brother whom he 'sees', also cannot love God whom he does not see, and that one can love God whom one does not see only *by* loving one's visible brother lovingly.

XI

Moral Theology

1. A Formal Existential Ethics*

Although Rahner rejects situation ethics as a "massive nominalism,"
he admits that its impact on Catholic moral theology has been beneficial
in many respects. The situationists' attack on universal moral norms has
forced the Catholic moralists to reexamine the grounding both of the
universal prescriptions of the natural law and of the Church's right to
impose universal obligations on the faithful.

Transcendental anthropology can ground a number of natural law pre-
scriptions on the unrevisable a priori structure of conscious human ac-
tion. Nevertheless, the number of natural law prescriptions which are
capable of such transcendental grounding is by no means coextensive
with the number of prescriptions which moral theology has traditionally
considered to be unrevisable prescriptions of the natural law.

Furthermore, although the Church's essential connection with Christ's
salvific and revealing mission justifies her right to impose universal moral
obligations, there is more to moral theology than the grounding and
clarification of the Church's general moral teaching. The situationists'
stress on the importance of individual moral decisions has forced
Catholic theologians to admit that the traditional manuals have practi-
cally ignored the theology of uniquely individual moral obligations. Moral
theologians have been content simply to subsume individual acts under
universal laws as typical "cases." They have given practically no consid-
eration to strictly individual commands, manifesting the divine will con-
cerning either individual acts or concrete modalities of acts which, while
not constituting a universal law, possess a genuinely obligatory character
for the concrete moral agent to whom they are communicated.

Transcendental anthropology can readily show how these strictly indi-
vidual divine commands are possible. The human subject's knowledge of

*From *Theological Investigations*, vol. II, pp. 218-22, 224-29, 231-34.
© 1963 by Darton, Longman & Todd Ltd.

God is not restricted to the categorical knowledge of God derived from universal concepts. God is present to each individual as the implicit and unobjective Horizon of his spiritual dynamism. This unobjective awareness of God, which coexists in the human mind with the categorical knowledge derived from universal concepts, can be the source of the uniquely individual obligations which come to the moral agent in addition to the general obligations imposed on him by the universal precepts of natural and positive law.

Christian morality can no longer be presented simply as a morality of general rules and ecclesiastical directives. In order to clarify the way in which uniquely individual divine commands can be discerned by the Christian conscience, moral theology must work out a formal existential ethics. This formal existential ethics will restore God's individual commands to their rightful place in moral and pastoral theology. One badly needed consequence of this restoration will be a clearer understanding of the relation of the charismatic individual to the hierarchical Church. Another consequence will be a renewed appreciation of the true nature of the vow and virtue of obedience and of the discernment of spirits in religious life. The practical conclusions which Rahner drew from his theology of individual commands for pastoral theology and religious life drew great popular attention to his writings in the period immediately before and after Vatican II.

The following are the theoretical foundations of situation ethics: on the one hand, an extreme existentialist philosophy, and on the other hand, a Protestant repugnance to the validity of a 'law' within a Christian way of human existence. What situation ethics implies in consequence of this is easily understandable: it denies the universal obligation (and one which remains valid in every case) of material universal norms in the concrete individual case, it being quite immaterial whether these norms be conceived as a natural law or as a positive divine law. Norms are universal, but man as an existent is the individual and unique in each case, and hence he cannot be regulated in his actions by material norms of a universal kind. Man is the believer; and faith sets free from the Law. There remains then as 'norm' of action only the call of each particular unique situation through which man must pass successfully, be it before the inappellable judgement of his free decision as a person, or be it before God, whose immediateness to the situation, conscience and faith must not be thought of as mediated by a universal law. A law can therefore only have the function of making man always face up again to each situation peculiar to him, or forcing him to believe, but it cannot be that which has to be fulfilled. How such a situation ethics is then established more in detail, whether it is in fact always advocated in the extreme form we have just outlined and whether every theory which calls itself 'situation ethics' adopts this extreme position—all these are questions which need not occupy us here. When we speak here of an (extreme) situation ethics, we mean the explicit or implicit denial of the absolute validity of material norms for the human person as such or the believer as such—the denial of norms which can state something which is also binding in the concrete situation.

That such a situation ethics is unacceptable to a Catholic hardly needs any lengthy proof, however much the practice of many Catholics in the present age is in danger of favouring such a situation ethics unconsciously. This kind of situation ethics comes in the last analysis to the same thing as a massive nominalism; it basically denies the possibility of any universal knowledge which has objective significance and truly applies to concrete reality. It turns the human person into an individual who is absolutely and in every respect unique (which the human person, considered as created and material, is not), and (what is far more important still) it also comes into conflict with divine revelations as given in the Scriptures and *magisterium* of the Church. It is not our intention to expound and establish all this more closely here. All this has, after all, been impressed once more on Catholic theologians in most recent times by 'Humani generis'. Yet we must nevertheless add one thing even to this: one may get the impression that we sometimes make the proof for this rejection too easy for ourselves. For the question is—among other things—the following: *How* do we determine, for instance, the eternal, universal and unchanging nature of man? Is it by a transcendental deduction (and in that case, how and with what results)? Or can this notion of the nature be found in a purely *a-posteriori* empirical fashion? Or partly in the former, partly in the latter way? However, is the *a-posteriori* determined condition of man really unchangeable? How do I recognize in it what really belongs to the nature? Is what we have (until now) been able to find always and everywhere a sure and sufficient criterion for this condition? Can this existence (investigated *a posteriori*), *may* it (morally), be changed by man himself who achieves himself freely? What would follow in this case as to what concerns the moral norms? What would then be the peculiar structure of the knowledge concerning this sort of essential make-up of man (which is first of all effected and delivered in and through freedom) and the moral norms drawn from it? Of what kind would then be the 'necessity' indicated in such norms? What sort of relationship is there basically between law, faith, grace and freedom according to St Paul? There will no doubt be few theologians who can remember from their school years in theology ever having heard anything really exact about these questions. Yet, as has been said, none of these questions are up for discussion here. We have referred to situation ethics at the beginning of our reflections merely because, on the one hand, what we are going to call 'formal existential ethics' must not be confused with the (outlined) situation ethics, and because, on the other hand, this existential ethics is in our opinion the core of truth which is also found in the false situation ethics.

Let us take a determined material imperative for a particular person in a concrete situation: here and now, this particular thing with this particular material content is to be done by you. Now how, according to the common conception of our present-day moral teaching, does such a concrete and materially determined imperative come about for the individual man in his particular determined situation? Surely it does so by the fact that the application of universal moral norms to the concrete situation results *ipso facto* in the concrete imperative. Naturally this conception knows also that in the concrete individual case there may possibly be several things which can be lawfully done (I may, for instance, in certain circumstances choose to go for a walk *hic et nunc* or say my breviary). Yet this does not alter anything in this way of understanding things as far as the basic conviction is concerned that the concrete imperative arises out of a universal norm and the concrete situation simply given as a matter of fact. Simply, this imperative is in the case just mentioned merely a concrete permissiveness of several possibilities. This permissiveness itself is in this case the norm which arises out of the general norms plus the given situation.

It is not essential for us to know here how these universal norms are founded and how they are recognized. We can presuppose as given that they exist and that they are recognized by the acting subject as being obligatory for him. The question in this common conception is merely as to what is the given situation here, and what application of determined universal norms is demanded by this situation. The situation, as it were, gives the cue for the choice of the universal norms to be considered here and now. What is carried out and applied, are the universal norms and they alone. The situation is conceived tacitly and as a matter of course as *simply pre-existent* to the finding of the norm and the making of one's decision. The coincidence of this simply objective situation and the general norm results, according to the common opinion, in the concrete imperative in this situation, and this quite unambiguously, in such a way that apart from these two factors nothing more is required for the finding of the concrete imperative. Or put in another way: according to the common teaching, ethics is a syllogistic, deductive ethics. I.e., the major premise contains a universal principle: in this situation, under these presuppositions this or that is to be done. It must be noted in this connection that in such a major even the situation is something abstract—something of which it is tacitly presupposed that it can in principle happen often and that it can, therefore, be (adequately) expressed in a universal notion and in a universal proposition. The minor premise of this syllogism then asserts the fact that the presuppositions, the situation is given *hic et nunc*.

The conclusion finally converts the major into a concrete and clear imperative. Conscience, accordingly, is conceived exclusively as that mental-moral function of the person which applies the universal norm to the concrete 'casus'. The difficulty in discovering the moral imperative in the concrete is accordingly seen to lie only in the exactness and adequacy of the analysis of the given situation *in concreto* and, under certain circumstances, in the unambiguous expression of the universal norms. However, if both these things are absolutely clear—this is the tacit view—then there can no longer be any doubt about the concrete imperative. Whoever knows the universal laws exactly and comprehends the given situation to the last detail, knows also clearly what he must or may do here. An ethics whose norms are theocentric, will naturally admit in this theory that the living God can, in the nature of things and basically, manifest his will in the concrete situation—a will which need not be derivable either from a universal norm or from the situation distinct from that manifestation, and which must then nevertheless be obeyed. Yet either such a case will always be regarded as an exception, or such a particular commandment of God will, in spite of everything, be subsumed under the general divine norms or be counted as a factor in the given situation. And so, nothing in the fundamentals of the general theory of a syllogistic, deductive ethics is altered by this case.

We want to approach our problem from a different angle. Let us presuppose (in an almost impossible oversimplification of the problem) that we have clarified and mentally penetrated a certain situation through and through, and that we have comprehended it by some sort of faculty of human knowledge in the moral field—let us say, by the virtue of prudence, etc. Let us suppose further, that all the universal material norms of ethical action, which can in any way apply to this case, are displayed before our eyes in all their clarity. Suppose that by reason of both these presuppositions, we have formulated a concrete moral demand of which we can say with certitude: by fulfilling this demand, we certainly do not offend against any of the universal norms applicable to this case—and also do not offend against any demand made on us by this situation, in so far as this situation has become a reflex datum for us through its analysis into propositions. The question then is this: is the fulfilment of the imperative identical in the concrete with what we are morally obliged to do here and now? Once more: the question is not whether even what we ought to do here and now might perhaps be permitted to offend against the imperative produced in the manner described. Any question of this being possible must be put out of our mind from the very start. Rather, the question is merely whether this imperative is simply identical with what we are obliged to do here and now. And this question has not yet been answered simply by what we have just described as unquestionable. It has not yet been answered for at least two reasons. Firstly: it is at least

conceivable that—even in a concrete situation—all the universal norms
that can be found still leave different ways of acting open to us as being
allowed and possible in their respective spheres. Indeed, this will happen
very often. In such a case, is all of what is allowed before the tribunal of
the universal norms actually possible morally, or can it also happen that,
from some other source altogether, only one of these 'permitted' possibilities of action is designated as the only morally right one in the concrete? Anyone who opts for the first alternative, presupposes what has
first to be proved, viz. the proposition that what ought morally to be done
in the concrete is nothing more than merely a case and specifying application of the universal norms. This, however, has to be proved and this is
precisely what we are questioning. And secondly: even if in the dimension of what is reflectively assignable, the dimension of the describable
difference of possible actions and behaviours, only one action is morally
permitted in a determined situation according to the universal norms
—when, therefore, the syllogistic deduction has seemingly succeeded
unequivocally—even then there still remains the question as to whether
just this apparently one and unambiguously determined action could not
take quite a different form in a dimension which can no longer be adequately regulated by the universal norms, and yet be here and now the
only right one and the one carrying the moral obligation. Taking both
reasons together, it is possible to ask: is what corresponds to the universal
norms simply identical with what ought to be done here and now, and is
what obeys these norms also simply without further qualification what is
morally permitted? More concisely still: Is the concrete moral action
merely a case of the universal moral good?

This however, seems completely open to question. The concrete moral
act is more than just the realization of a universal idea happening here and
now in the form of a case. The act is a reality which has a positive and
substantial property which is basically and absolutely unique. To prove
this in a precise and sufficient manner goes beyond the possibilities offered here. We can only give a few indications of what we mean. We can,
to start with, say from a more Christian and *theological* standpoint: Man
is destined to eternal life as an individual and someone in the concrete.
His acts are, therefore, not merely of a spatio-temporal kind as is the case
with material things; his acts have a meaning for eternity, not only morally but also *ontologically*. Now we must, however (even for ontological
reasons), hold fast absolutely to the fact—even if this is not obvious to
everyone at first sight—that something which is merely a case and a
circumscription of something universal, something which *as* an individual
and concrete something is just sheer negation, also cannot have—*as*
something individual—any real, eternally valid significance. Man with his
mental and moral acts, therefore, cannot be merely the appearance of the
universal and of what is—in this universality alone—'eternal' and ever-

valid in the negative expansion of space and time. In him, the individual, there must rather be a given a positive reality; expressed differently: his spiritual individuality cannot be (at least not in his acts) merely the circumscription of an in itself universal nature through the negativity of the *materia prima*, understood as the mere repetition of the same thing at different points in space-time. We must realize that a contrary view would be profoundly unchristian, and that anyone who does not see this, really has no right to protest against a medieval Averroism or against a modern Idealism. The assertion of something positively individual, at least in man's spiritual personal acts, does not moreover need to appear unscholastic, indeed not even really un-Thomistic. Of course, anyone who cannot rise to the metaphysical thought that (in good scholastic language) God cannot even *de potentia absoluta* create a second Gabriel—in other words, anyone who cannot rise *at all* to the notion of something individual which is not the instance of some universal idea, of something repeatable—cannot follow our thought here from the very start. Anyone, however, who can grasp this Thomistic thought of something real which cannot be subsumed unequivocally under a universal idea or under a law, cannot reject the idea from the very start that something like this is conceivable—indeed, must be postulated—also in man as a spiritual person, as that existent who does not resolve himself completely into *forma-materia-esse*. We may also say: if (and in so far as) man as a spiritual person participates by his acts in the permanency-in-itself of the pure form, which does not resolve itself in its ordination to matter as the principle of repeatability, then he must also participate in that spiritual individuality of the spiritual which has a positive individuality, an individuality which is not merely the sameness of the repeated universal and not merely a case of the law. Seen in this way, we therefore have to say: in so far as man belongs to the material world by his concrete activity, his activity is an instance and fulfilment of something universal which determines his actions as something different from the individual and opposed to it, i.e. as a *law* expressed in universal propositions. In so far as the same man subsists in his own spirituality, his actions are also always more than mere applications of the universal law to the *casus* in space and time; they have a substantial positive property and uniqueness which can no longer be translated into a universal idea and norm expressible in propositions constructed of universal notions. At least in his actions, man is really also (not only) *individuum ineffabile,* whom God has called by his name, a name which is and can only be unique, so that it really is worthwhile for this unique being as such to exist for all eternity.

It also cannot be said that such an individuality of a spiritual act has no place in the real world, or that one cannot conceive anything by it. For, first of all, there is the whole almost unascertainable field of different possibilities which remain open to the morally acting man within the scope of what is morally commanded and allowed. In every case in which a man decides, *within* the ethical sphere of the universal norms, on one of several possibilities—in which he 'chooses' *within* the sphere of the universally and positively moral good—this (non-derivable) concretion of his moral 'being-thus', brought about by a decision, is undoubtedly conceivable as the coming-to-light' of his ineffable moral individuality and not just as the merely arbitrary selection from among certain possibilities, as if these are equally-valid in the last resort and as if, in relation to them, the 'just-this' and 'not-that' has no further positive and ethical meaning. And furthermore: even in a case where the deductive, syllogistic formation of conscience from the universal norms and the concretely given situation seemingly leads to the unequivocal result of a concretely one imperative, the latter can still in actual fact be realized in the most diverse ways and with the most diverse inner attitudes. Even a case where these differences are no longer traceable, where one could conceive of exactly the same case as repeatedly realizable, *only* proves (this and nothing more) that something uniquely and positively individual cannot be expressed reflectively and after the manner of a proposition—that it cannot be the object of a reflective objective knowledge which can be articulated in propositions. It does not, however, prove that there cannot be a case of the positively ethico-individual element of a personal action.

The following must be added to what has been said: this positively individual element in the moral action (an action which is more than the fulfilment of the universal norm or of an abstract being: 'man') is even as such to be conceived absolutely as the object of a binding will of God. It would be absurd for a God-regulated, theological morality to think that God's binding will could only be directed to the human action in so far as the latter is simply a realization of the universal norm and of a universal nature. If the creative will of God is directly and unambiguously directed to the concrete and the individual, then surely this is not true merely in so far as this individual reality is the realization of a case of the universal——rather it is directed to the concrete as such, as it really is—to the concrete in its positive, and particularly its substantial, material uniqueness. God is interested in history not only in so far as it is the carrying out of norms, but in so far as it is a history which consists in the harmony of unique events and which precisely in this way has a meaning for eternity. The fact that this divine binding force, which regards the individual reality as such, cannot be expressed in a general proposition, is no proof of its non-existence, but arises out of the nature of things. The perception of this 'individual norm' (if we are going to use this term for the binding will of God in so far as it regards the uniquely individual which, precisely in its particular positivity, cannot be specified in the universal which can be contracted in 'cases') cannot come about in the same way as the perception of the universal law, viz. by an abstraction which forms notions of essences. Yet this fact is also no proof for the non-existence of such a perception and for the consequent impossibility of such an 'individual norm' or 'existential norm' as something actually binding.

No matter how inadequate the reasons offered in the present context, it can surely be said that there is an individual ethical reality of a positive kind which is untranslatable into a material universal ethics; there is a binding ethical uniqueness—by which we do not mean to say that *every* ethical individual reality must also necessarily and always be a binding moral reality, and that therefore there also cannot be anything individually or existentially ethical which remains free. In so far as there is a moral reality in an existential-ethic sense and of a binding kind which nevertheless cannot (in the very nature of things) be translated into universal propositions of material content—there must be an existential ethics of a formal kind, i.e. an ethics which treats of the basic elements, the formal structures and the basic manner of perceiving such an existential-ethic reality. Just as, on the one hand, there cannot be any science of the individual considered as a really individual singular as such and yet, on the other hand, there is a universal formal ontology of individual reality, so (and in this sense) there can and must be a formal doctrine of existential concretion, a formal existential-ethics.

A further question would be whether we could not understand the whole teaching on Choice in the Spiritual Exercises of St Ignatius much more profoundly and exactly if we were clearly conscious of such an existential-ethics and the way of finding an ethical existential-imperative. According to the usual theory about the finding of the correct imperative in the concrete (which we have outlined at the beginning of the chapter), the third time for making a choice named in the Exercises would have to be the real and decisive way of coming to a decision. But according to St Ignatius this time is only something secondary compared with the first and second times for choice. We may perhaps hazard the assertion that—as regards this point (as also many others)—our average theology and ethics has not yet caught up with the unconscious theology underlying the Exercises.

In the usual theory of sin we treat sin too exclusively as the mere offence against a universal divine norm. Could not an existential-ethics help us to see more clearly that sin, over and above its property of being an offence against the law of God, is also and just as much an offence against an utterly individual imperative of the individual will of God, which is the basis of uniqueness? Would we not perceive sin more clearly in this way as the failure of the personal-individual love of God? Even though all this has been developed in a formal ontology which in itself is of a philosophical kind, would it not offer a set of categories applicable and useful in a theology of the supernatural as an immediate personal encounter with the personal God as he is in himself?

In an essay about the 'Individual in the Church', the author of the present study has drawn attention to the significance of the question developed here for the position of the individual in the Church. We can merely make reference to this here. If there is an existential-ethics, then there is also a sphere of decision for the individual in and for the Church, which cannot be taken away from the individual by a material command of the ecclesiastical authority.

Has not our theory consequences also for a more profound theology of obedience in general, in the Church, and in the life of the religious? Is obedience to a person giving commands merely the respect for the objective rightness (to be presumed in the individual case) of the individual command, which is right as measured by the objective universal norms of a material kind on which it is based, or must obedience in some cases —and where and when—also be exercised as an act of homage to the individual will of the person commanding which can no longer be thought of as an interpretation and application of the universal and, in themselves, intelligible norms? When and towards whom is this second sort of obedience conceivable?

Would it be possible to find reasons, in the proposed theory, for a difference between the teaching and pastoral offices as two spheres which are not adequately reducible to each other? That such a question also has very practical consequences for the life of the Church in the concrete surely does not need a great deal of explanation here.

Does our theory not permit us to contribute something also to the question about the relation between the hierarchical and charismatic elements in the Church and in her history? Is not the Hierarchy as such the bearer and guarantor of the correct application of the permanent norms instituted together with the Church? However, if the Church acts in her history and if every action is always also more than just the application of the universal norms to the concrete case and given situation, then must there not be a function in the Church which takes in precisely this divinely inspired individual impulse given to the action of the Church and gives it its validity in the Church—a function which cannot be replaced by the administration and right application of the universal norms? Must this function always be originally found and united in the person of the bearers of the hierarchical powers? And if not (as is undoubtedly the case, after all, according to the evidence of Church history), does the Hierarchy not have the duty then to accept such impulses from those quarters in which they originally strike the Church in the providence of God: even from the charismatics, the prophets or whatever one may wish to call these antennae of the individual divine imperatives given to the Church? Can this provide us with a rational basis for 'public opinion' in the Church?

2. The Fundamental Option*

Man's basic freedom is not a mere choice between objects. It is the achievement of his choice of self. This self-choice, which cannot be avoided, is by its very nature either self-realization in the direction of God or a radical refusal of self to God. This basic freedom is achieved over the period of man's lifetime. As the total project of his human existence it is man's "fundamental option." A shift of emphasis from the individual act in which man chooses between objects to the perduring intentionality of man's fundamental option has profound consequences for moral theology. One of Rahner's major contributions to contemporary moral theology has been precisely his systematic justification for this change of emphasis.

It is decisive for the Christian doctrine of freedom that this freedom implies the possibility of a 'yes' or 'no' towards its own horizon and indeed it is only really constituted by this. This is true not merely and not even primarily when God is given and represented systematically in concepts and categories but also when he is given unsystematically but originally in our transcendental experience as the condition and moment of every activity directed towards the contemporary world in which we live. It is true in this sense that we meet God everywhere in a most radical way as the most basic question of our freedom, in all things of the world and (in the words of scripture) above all in our neighbour. Why then, more precisely, is the transcendental horizon of freedom not merely the condition of its possibility but also its proper 'object'? Why do we not act in freedom not merely towards ourselves, our surroundings and the people around us either in conformity to reality or in a destructive way within that infinitely wide horizon of transcendence from which we freely confront ourselves and the world in which we live, and why is this horizon itself also the 'object' of this freedom in our yes or no to it in itself? This horizon is once more *per definitionem* the condition of the possibliity of saying no to it. This means that in such a 'no' it is unavoidably negated as the condition of the possibility of freedom and is also at the same time negated as an unthematic 'object' or even (in explicit or practical 'atheism') as a conceptually mediated object. Thus, in the act of the negating freedom there is present a real, absolute contradiction in the fact that God is affirmed and denied at the same time; in it this ultimate monstrosity is both withdrawn from itself and, by the fact that it is necessarily made objective and mediated in the finite material of our life in its temporal extension, made relative by being introduced into temporality. The real possibility, however, of such an absolute contradiction in free-

*From *Theological Investigations*, vol. VI, pp. 181-88.
© 1969 and 1974 by Darton, Longman & Todd Ltd.

dom cannot be denied, though it is indeed disputed and doubted. This happens in ordinary everyday theology whenever it is said that the only thinkable mode of freedom is that the infinite God in his objectivity can only evaluate a little 'bending' of finite reality, the offence against a concrete and merely finite natural structure, for what it is, viz. something finite; he therefore cannot evaluate it by an absolute prohibition and an infinite sanction and cannot characterise it as something directed against his own will as such. The 'will', against which such a sin really offends (such a theology would say), is after all the finite reality really willed by God, and to suppose an offence against God's will over and above this is to falsely turn God's will into a particular category of reality alongside the finite thing which is willed. Yet there is the possibility of a free 'no' towards God. Otherwise freedom would basically have no real orientation to the subject (of which we will have still to speak explicitly), i.e. the fact that freedom is concerned with the subject itself and not just with this or that thing. Let us grant that the act of freedom is really concerned with the subject itself, since this subject is transcendence. Let us grant furthermore that the individual intramundane beings encountered by us within the horizon of transcendence are not events within a space which remains untouched by what is in that space, but are the historical concreteness of the encounter and projection of this source and goal that support our transcendence. In this light freedom towards the encountered individual beings is always also a freedom towards the horizon, the ground and abyss, which allows them to present themselves to us and lets them become the inner moment of our receiving freedom. In so far as and because the horizon cannot be indifferent to the subject understood as a *knowing* subject but is systematically or unsystematically that with which this knowing transcendence is concerned, particularly if this *'ad quem'* is not its explicit object, to that same extent and for the same reason *freedom*—even though it is always exercised on the concrete individual things of experience and through this becomes what it is—is primarily and unavoidably concerned with God himself. Freedom in its origin is freedom of saying yes or no to God and by this fact is freedom of the subject towards itself. Freedom is either indifferent to this or that, the infinite repetition of the same or of the contrary (which is merely a different kind of the same), a freedom of eternal recurrence, or the same 'wandering Jew', or it is necessarily the freedom of the subject towards itself in its finality and thus is freedom towards God, however unconscious this ground and most proper and original 'object' of freedom may be in the individual act of freedom.

We must add a second reflection to this, a reflection which alone brings to light the ultimate theological reason for freedom as freedom towards God, but one which can only be briefly indicated here. The supernatural and historical concreteness of our transcendence is never given as some-

thing merely natural but is always embraced and taken up by a supernatural dynamism of our spiritual being which tends towards the absolute
nearness of God. In other words, God in the concrete is not present
merely as the horizon of our transcendence, one which always withdraws
itself and refuses to give itself; rather, understood as this horizon, he
offers himself to be directly possessed in what we call divinising grace.
Given all this, the freedom in transcendence and in the yes and no towards the ground of this transcendence is given a directness towards God
by which it becomes most radically capable of saying yes and no to God
as such. This happens in a way which would, of course, in no way be
already given by the abstract formal concept of transcendence directed
towards God as the merely distant and repelling horizon of our exercise of
existence and it is such that it cannot be derived from this concept alone.

FREEDOM AS TOTAL AND FINALISING
SELF-MASTERY OF THE SUBJECT

Freedom, as we have said, cannot be viewed in a Christian sense as an
in-itself neutral capacity to do this or that in an arbitrary order and in a
temporal series which would be broken off from outside even though,
from the point of view of freedom, it could go on *ad infinitum*; freedom is
rather the capacity to make oneself once and for all, the capacity which of
its nature is directed towards the freely willed finality of the subject as
such. This is obviously what is meant by the Christian statement about
man and his salvation and damnation when he, the free person, must
answer for himself and the totality of his life before the judgement seat of
God, and when the eternally valid sentence about his salvation or damnation in accordance with his works is passed by a judge who does not
regard merely the appearance of his life, the 'face', but the freely governed core of the person, the 'heart'. It is true that man's formal freedom
of choice and decision is more presupposed in scripture than used as an
actual theme. It is true also that the explicit theme in scripture, especially
in the New Testament, is for the most part the paradox that man's freedom, while remaining responsible and without being destroyed, is en-
slaved by the slavery of the demonic powers of sin and death and to some
extent even of the law, and must first of all be liberated to make way for
an inner inclination towards the law (we will discuss this later). Yet it
cannot be doubted that for scripture both the sinful and the justified man
are responsible for the actions of their life and to this extent are also free
and that freedom, therefore, is a permanent constitutive of man's nature.
The proper nature of freedom, however, appears precisely in so far as
freedom is the basis of absolute salvation and damnation in Christian
revelation, and this finally and before God. For a merely profane every-

day experience, freedom of choice may appear merely as the characteristic of the individual act of man, which can be attributed to him in so far as it is actively posited by him, without this positing being already causally predetermined and in this sense forced by some inner condition of man or some external situation. Such a concept of freedom of choice atomises freedom in its exercise and thus distributes it exclusively to the individual acts of man, acts which are only held together by a neutral, substantial identity of the subject and of the capacities positing them all, as well as by life's external space of time. Freedom in this sense is merely freedom of acts, imputability of the individual act to a person who remains neutral in himself and hence (as long as the external conditions are given for this) can always determine himself anew. Once we see in a Christian sense, however, that by his freedom man can determine and dispose himself as a whole and finally, the idea of responsible freedom is changed and deepened immensely. This means that man does not merely perform actions which, though they must be qualified morally, also always pass away again (and which after that are imputed to him merely juridically or morally); man by his free decision really *is* so good or evil in the very ground of his being itself that his final salvation or damnation are really already given in this, even though perhaps in a still hidden manner. Freedom is first of all 'freedom of being'. It is not merely the quality of an act and capacity exercised at some time, but a transcendental mark of human existence itself. If man is to be really and finally able to be master over himself, if this 'eternity' is to be the act of his freedom itself, if this act is to be really able to make man good or bad in the very ground of his being, and if this goodness or badness is not to be merely an external, accidental event happening to man (so that this act would merely, contrary to its goodness, draw something which remains good into damnation), then freedom must first of all be thought of as freedom of being. This means that man is that being who is concerned in his very being about this being itself; he is always a being who already has a relationship towards himself, a subjectivity and never simply a nature; already a person . . . never just 'something there' but always already 'for himself', 'existing'. Nothing happens to this being which does not affect its relationship to itself in some way, or if it does, it becomes subjectively and salvifically significant only in so far as it is freely 'understood' and subjectively taken over by the free subject as such in a quite definite way; its 'ego' cannot possibly be passed over, it simply cannot be turned into an object and can never be replaced or explained by something else, not even by its own reflex representation of itself; it is genuinely original, never based on something else and hence cannot be derived from or proved by anything else. Its relationship to its divine origin must never be interpreted according to the notion of causal and formal relationships of dependence as operative in the categories of the realm of our experience in which the source keeps and binds and does not set free, and in which therefore independence and dependence grow in inverse and equal proportion. Man, by his freedom of being, is always the incomparable being who cannot be adequately classified into any system and cannot be adequately subsumed under any one concept. He is in an original sense the untouchable, but therefore also the lonely and insecure, a burden to himself, who cannot by any means 'absolve' himself from this once-and-for-all lonely self-being and who can never 'unload' himself on others. Hence, freedom is originally also not primarily concerned with this or that which one can do or not do; freedom is not originally the capacity of choosing any object whatsoever or the ability of adopting an individual attitude towards this or that; it is rather the freedom of self-understanding, the possibility of saying yes or no to oneself, the possibility of deciding for or against oneself, which corresponds to the knowing self-possession, the understanding subject-nature of man. Freedom never happens as a merely objective exercise, as a mere choice 'between' individual objects, but is the *self*-exercise of the man who chooses objectively; only within this freedom in which man is capable of achieving himself is man also free with regard to the material of his self-achievement. He can do or omit this or that in view of his own self-realisation that is inescapably imposed on him. This self-realisation is a task he cannot avoid and, in spite of all the differences within the concrete material of his self-achievement, it is always either a self-realisation in the direction of God or a radical self-refusal towards God.

It must of course be realised that this basic nature of freedom is achieved over a whole period of time and that the total project of human existence, one's own total self-understanding or *'option fondamentale'*, frequently remains empty and objectively unfulfilled. It must be borne in mind that not every individual act of freedom has the same actual depth and radical nature of self-disposal and that, although each individual act of freedom wants to venture total and final self-disposal, all such acts always enter into the totality of the one, total act of freedom of the one, whole temporally finite life, precisely because each one of these acts is exercised within, and receives its weight and proportion from, the horizon of the whole of human existence. Correspondingly, the biblical and Augustine concept of the heart, the concept of subjectivity in Kierkegaard, the notion of *'action'* in Blondel, etc., shows understanding for the fact that there is such a basic act of freedom which embraces and shapes the whole of human existence. This act is indeed realised and can be exercised only by means of those individual acts of man which can be localised in space and time and which can be objectified with regard to their motives. Yet this basic act cannot be simply identified by an objective reflection with such an individual act; it does not represent either the merely moral sum-total of these individual acts nor can it be simply identified with the moral quality of the last of the free individual acts exercised (before death). The concrete freedom of man by which he decides about himself as a whole by effecting his own finality before God, is the unity in difference of the formal *'option fondamentale'* and the free individual acts of man no longer attainable by reflection, a unity which is the concrete being of the subject of freedom having-achieved-itself. In all this, to emphasise this once more and explicitly, freedom—precisely speaking—is not the possibility of always being able to do something else, the possibility of infinite revision, but the capacity to do something uniquely final, something which is finally valid precisely because it is done in freedom. Freedom is the capacity for the eternal. Natural processes can always be revised again and directed along a different path and are therefore for this very reason indifferent. The result of freedom is the true necessity which remains.

FREEDOM REGARDED AS A DIALOGIC CAPACITY OF LOVE

This self-perfecting of freedom into the eternal 'moment' is, as we have said, its self-realisation before God. Freely posited salvation or damnation, consisting in the gaining or loss of God, must not be understood as a merely external reaction of a judging or rewarding God but is itself already performed in this freedom. Freedom, if it is to be able to effect salvation or damnation and hence the determination of the whole man, of itself brings into play the whole man with his mutually interactive relations to his origin and future. Freedom is always self-realisation of the objectively choosing man seen in view of his total realisation before God. In this way, considered as the capacity of the 'heart', it is the capacity of love. This answer is not so self-evident if we ask: what is the basic act of man into which quite absolutely he can synthesise his whole nature and life, the act which can embrace everything and incorporate everything within itself, everything which goes under the name of man and the life of man, happiness and despair, everyday life and starlight hours, sin and redemption, past and present. Yet this is really the case: the love of God, and this love alone, is capable of embracing everything. It alone places man completely before the one without whom man would be merely consciousness of radical emptiness and nothingness; it alone is able to unite all man's many-sided and mutually contradictory capabilities because they are all orientated towards that God whose unity and infinity can create the unity in man which, without destroying it, unites the diversity of the finite. Love alone allows man to forget himself (what a hell it would be if we were not able to do this in the end); it alone can still redeem even the darkest hours of the past since it alone finds the courage to believe in the mercy of the holy God. Love alone reserves nothing to itself and therefore can also decide about the future (which man, in the anxiety about his finiteness which must be used sparingly, is otherwise tempted to save up). Because it loves the one who has never regretted the venture of such a world of guilt, malediction, death and fruitlessness, love can also love this earth together with God. Love of God is the only total integration of human existence, and we have only grasped it in its dignity and all-embracing greatness if we have understood it to be this and once we suspect that it must be the content of the moment of eternity in time and hence the content of the eternity with God himself which is born out of it.

This love is not a determined, assignable performance which one could define exactly, but rather that which every man becomes in the irreplaceable characteristic of his always unique realisation of nature, something which is known only once it is accomplished. This is not to say that there is in no sense a universal concept of love, as seen in the statement that man is obliged to love God and to say that the whole divine law consists in this. Man is, in spite of all this, obliged to love God with his *whole* heart . . . and this one heart which man must stake, the innermost centre of his person, is something unique. What it bears within itself in its uniqueness, what is staked and given away in this love is known only once it has been done, at the stage when man has really caught up with himself and thus knows what is in him and *who* he is in the concrete. In this love, therefore, man enters into the adventure of his own reality, an adventure which to begin with is veiled from him. He cannot survey and evaluate from the very start what is really demanded of him. *He* is demanded, he himself is ventured, he in the concreteness of his heart and his life which, only when accomplished, reveals what this heart is that had to venture and squander itself in this life. In the case of all other efforts, we may know what is really demanded of us. It is possible to gauge, compare, ask oneself whether the stakes and the gain are worth it. One could justify such a demanded effort by something else, by a result which shows it to make sense, but in the case of love this is impossible. Love itself is what justifies love, but this only in any real sense when with the whole heart and with all one's might it has been carried to the very end.

The Christian ethos does not basically consist in the respecting of objective norms imposed by God on reality. All structures of things are *lower* than man. He can alter them, bend them as far as possible; he is their master and not their servant. The only ultimate structure of the person which manages to express it completely is the basic capacity of love, and this is without measure. Thus man too is boundless. Every sin is at root merely the refusal to entrust himself to this boundlessness; it is a lesser love which, because it refuses to become the greater, is no longer love at all. Of course, so as to know what this means, man requires objectifications which he encounters in the multiplicity of commandments. This is true but everything which thus appears in this multiplicity of commandments is the objectification or partial accomplishment or preliminary beginning of a love which itself has no norm by which it could be measured. One can speak of the 'commandment' of love as long as one does not forget that this 'law' does not command man to do *something* but imposes a person as a task on himself, that person who can love only by accepting that love belonging to God in which God does not give something but himself.

3. The Dignity and Freedom of Man*

Transcendental anthropology can determine the abiding characteristics in which the essential dignity of man consists. Man is a free, incarnate spirit. He is also a God-oriented, community-building person whose world of goals and values is structured by the multiplicity of societies to which he belongs. From these transcendentally grounded a priori characteristics of man a good many of the prescriptions of traditional natural-law morality, pertaining to individual and social ethics, can be derived. However, the other prescriptions of natural-law morality must be established by an empirical reflection on man's historical and social experience. The vast range of the contemporary empirical sciences makes this reflection both difficult and, at times, inconclusive. Furthermore, the results of the positive and social sciences have made it evident that a good many human characteristics which were once thought to be unchangeable structures of human nature must now be assigned an historical origin. Consequently, Catholic moralists must accept the fact that the empirical grounding of these principles will reveal that many of them rest on mutable and culturally determined characteristics of man rather than on his immutable nature. Moral theologians must take science, culture, and history much more seriously than they have in the past, and they must be much more open to mutability in the Church's moral teaching.

Furthermore, although the demands of the natural law and of man's membership in the Church and civil society give legitimate authority the right to restrict the scope of man's freedom, there must always remain a zone of personal freedom in the economic and social spheres and in the areas of religious and cultural values. Unjustified a priori restriction of human freedom constitutes a grave injury to the dignity of the person.

In view of the biological, cultural and cultural-historical mutability of man, it is no easy task to attain an exact metaphysical understanding of

*From *Theological Investigations*, vol. II, pp. 236-41, 248-52.
© 1963 by Darton, Longman & Todd Ltd.

the permanent, necessary nature of man underlying his historical mutability. Such a knowledge is not to be gained by a mere collection of factual evidence of what can be observed at a moment of time in the individual man—by using, as it were, the methods of the natural sciences. For this would imply that what can be thus observed is 'everything', or that everything observed is necessary for the nature or in accordance with it. A knowledge of essences (*Wesenserkenntnis*) which includes the concrete knowledge about the possibilities of nature (which in part are to be freely realized), must rely rather on a twofold method:

(i) On a transcendental method. Everything which already reaffirms itself with implicit necessity in the very *question about* the nature of man and in the very way man puts this question (i.e. more strictly speaking, in the metaphysical aspect of the knowledge man has of himself), belongs to the metaphysically necessary nature of man and to the moral perfection of that nature. Anything in this knowledge which is not transcendentally 'lasting' in this sense, need not on that account be accidental; but the question of its belonging to the necessary nature of man does in this case require to be proved separately and cannot be presupposed as self-evident.

(ii) The reflection on the historical experience man has of himself, without which the notion of man remains 'empty' and without which this notion has no clearness and consequently no power in history. Such reflection is indispensable because only in this way can we recognize the metaphysical possibilities of man as a free being which, because he is free, cannot be adequately deduced from something else clearly given. Since this reflection, being itself a 'historically becoming' process, is essentially unfinished, the understanding of the essence is permanently *in via* in spite of its *a-priori* and transcendental metaphysical element. To give an *adequate* design of man (what he is and ought to become) by an *a-priori*-rationalistic reason is impossible. Man must always refer *also* to his history and thus even to his future in order to know what he is. And conversely, the critique of the experience of self, which is necessary because not everything which is, is right and 'rational', refers the historical experience back to the transcendental, metaphysical method of self-knowledge and to God's judgement on man in revelation. Because man really knows 'concretely' about himself in this historical experience only—an experience which is still in a state of becoming—there is no manifest knowledge of essence without *Tradition* (of a natural kind and of the kind of saving history) and without a *venturing*, planning, devising anticipation of the future (which is itself grasped in an intramundane, 'utopian' manner and in a revealed 'eschatology'). All that follows, about the dignity (i.e. the nature) of man, must be understood with the reservation that the second element of this knowledge of essence is brought out merely formally and not in its reflex content. Finally, it must be noted that nothing can be explained here regarding these questions by something which is itself no more than an independent and lucid hypothesis, but that every notion refers to everyone for its explanation, and that such explanation must always merely elucidate the explaining and the explained and at the same time remove them into the obscurity of mystery.

The essential dignity of man consists in the fact that, within a sexually differentiated community in spatio-temporal history, man, by spiritually recognizing himself and freely identifying himself, can and ought to open himself (in the direction of immediate personal communion with the infinite God) to the love in Jesus Christ which communicates God himself. His dignity may be regarded as something pre-established (*vorgegebene*), i.e. as a capacity and a task, or as something fulfilled. Fulfilment, the gaining and preservation of the pre-established dignity constitutes itself the final and definite dignity of man (which, therefore, can be lost). The pre-established dignity cannot simply cease or become non-existent, but can exist as something denied, as foundation for damnation and judgement. In so far as this nature is from God and directed to God, receiving from him and opening itself in his direction, it is a nature in which the given dignity is always both the innermost being of man and what lies above man and hence partakes in the remoteness, the mysteriousness and namelessness of God. It only unveils itself completely in the knowing-believing-loving dialogue of man with God, and hence can never be given simply in the manner of object-like objectivity. We perceive God in a mirror and in images only; the same is equally true of man and of his destiny, for he is from God and directed towards God.

The dignity of nature is *pre*-appointed (vor-*gegeben*) to man for his free self-understanding—as the goal of his freedom, as its salvation or judgement.

The dignity of man's nature may be regarded formally, i.e. in advance of the question whether, by exercising his free choice, which is dependent of course on redemptive grace and the judgement of God, his dignity brings about his salvation or God's judgement upon him. Regarded in this way, the dignity of man's nature embraces the following moments which mutually determine each other:

a. Man's personal nature (in its specifically created and human characteristic), i.e. the 'natural' being of man. This means:

(i) *Man is Spirit*: in the perception of the spatio-temporal, he is always dependent on the total unity of reality, i.e. on God, who existed before the multiplicity of his immediately-given objects. This is true even in his own case, understood as a subject set off from the object and (implicitly) perceiving.

(ii) *He is freedom*: about this we will have to say more later.

(iii) *He is an individual*: he is not merely an instance of the universal;

each man is someone unique and ultimately never someone who can be totally deduced; his individuality in being-thus and in action is not merely the negatively spatio-temporal application of a universal or of a universal idea, which circumscribes him in the here and now. Because he is an individual, he has a valid existence which, as a real existence, does not coincide with his spatio-temporal existence; he is 'immortal' and the subject of an eternal destination and destiny. This is why the individual man, who is now, may never be forcibly sacrificed, in a manner which destroys him, for the future of 'humanity', of the others who come after him. The present is never just the material for a utopian intramundane future.

(iv) *He is a community-building person*: Person is not the opposite to community; rather, both are correlative realities, i.e. *qua* person, man is intended for community with other persons (God and men), and there is community only where there are *persons* and where persons are protected; he is a perfect person in the measure in which he opens himself in love and service for other persons. A genuine problem of opposing tensions exists only where (and in so far as) there is a question of striking a balance, in the plurality of human existence, between personality (or community) on *one* particular human level (as, for instance, on the level of economics, of the State, of the Church) and the same sort of community (or personality) on *another* level.

(v) *He is* (qua *human* person) *an incarnate, mundane person* who realizes himself in his ultimate core only in a spatio-temporal, pluralistic expansion, in concern for his bodily existence (economy) and within a community communicated in a tangible manner (marriage, parent-and-child relationship, the State, Incarnation, Church, sacraments, symbol, etc.). The personality of man, therefore, cannot be relegated to an absolutely internal realm. It requires of necessity a certain space for realizing itself. Such a space, although it is to a certain extent 'external' to it (body, earth, economy, sign, symbol, State), is nevertheless essentially necessary and hence must be so constructed that it permits personal self-realization. Seen even from this point of view, a retreat into the merely 'private', the inner 'conscience', the 'sacristy', etc. is contrary to nature.

b. The supernatural existential. This means: the person, as we have just outlined him, is called to direct personal communion with God in Christ perennially and inescapably, whether he accepts the call in redemption and grace or whether he closes himself to it in guilt (by the guilt of original sin and of personal sin). The person is addressed by the personal revelation of the Word of God in saving history which finds its climax in Jesus Christ, the Word of the Father become flesh; the person is unquestionably situated within the offer of his interior, saving and divinizing grace, he is called to the community-forming visible manifestation of this personal state of 'being directly called before God' which is the Church.

c. The supernatural existential is related to what we have called the personal nature of man, as a gratuitous gift of God, as grace. In this way man exists in nature and 'supernature'. This does not, however, mean that it is left to his free choice whether he intends to understand himself as a purely natural person or as a person called to direct communion with God by grace.

With this essence and this dignity of man there is given a plurality of human existential dimensions (Existentialien):

a. He is a *corporeal-material* living being, in a biological community of life with its material surroundings, and with a care for its will to live.

b. He is a *spiritual-personal,* cultural being with a diversity of personal communities (marriage union, family, kinsfolk, a people, the State, the community of nations), and with a history.

c. He is a *religious, God-centred* being (by nature and grace), with a 'Church', in a history which either damns or saves.

d. He is a *Christ-centred* being, i.e. his being possesses an ontic and spiritual-personal capacity for communicating with Jesus Christ in whom God has forever made the countenance of a man his own and has opened the reality of man, with an unsurpassable finality, in the direction of God; only thus was the real possibility of a direct communion of all men with God established with finality. Hence we can only speak ultimately of God by engaging even in the midst of all this (in the midst of theology) in anthropology; and ultimately any information about anthropology, about the nature and dignity of man, can be given only when we engage in theology about God and from God.

While the many existential dimensions must be distinguished, they and their achievement cannot be divorced from each other 'spatially' in the concrete. Each one of these existential dimensions is really dependent on the other. The lowest dimension is determined by the highest and vice versa; the whole being of man must work itself out in each one of them in particular. Every attempt by a dimension to make itself independent and self-sufficient, even merely in its own realm, contradicts the fact that man, without prejudice to any true and genuine plurality of his ontological moments, is first and last, originally and by destination, *one person*. Hence, for instance, economics or even economic legislation do not enjoy a 'pure' autonomy from the laws of the spiritual person, i.e. from ethics.

On the other hand, man in his self-knowledge, which must always proceed from a *multiplicity* of perceived objects and remains dependent on this multiplicity as such, can never perceive himself adequately from *one* principle, in such a way that he could adequately deduce from this his existential dimensions and their structural laws. There is, therefore, a permanent plurality of sciences of man and a relative individual structure of laws for each existential dimension and of the powers administering and forming it, which must be respected by every other.

Because this plurality possesses in its turn a structure and a superior and lower order, the claim of the higher dimension takes precedence over that of the lower one in any (apparent or, for the meantime, rightful) case of conflict.

If, on the one hand, freedom considered simply in itself, i.e. freedom of exercise and not merely freedom in what is done, belongs to the absolute dignity of the person and if, on the other hand, it is dependent for its exercise in the concrete on conditions of an external and internal kind, then the *concession* of these possibilities of the exercise of freedom to a sufficiently large extent is demanded by the dignity of the person. To deprive the person totally of this scope for freedom would, therefore, still be a degradation of the person even when the thing to be done would still be attainable without this concession of scope for freedom. *Simply* to deprive a person of the scope even for morally wrong decisions of freedom (even if or in so far as such a thing is or were possible) cannot, therefore, be the business of any man or of any human society in its dealings with other men. Even this would be an attempt on the dignity of the person and of his freedom which is not merely a means to an end (i.e. of the good realized without freedom) but is also itself a part of the goal (viz. of the person). The *unconditional* refusal of the possibility of an objectively and morally wrong decision would amount to a suppression of the very scope for freedom itself.

The scope for freedom thus demanded as the possibility of the exercise of freedom must—without prejudice to the plurality of moments of human existence—extend through all the dimensions of this existence on account of the mutual interconnection of the dimensions of human existence. To try to exclude some particular material of finite goods for freedom from this scope for freedom right from the start and absolutely, and to try to limit freedom *a priori* to certain other fields of personal freedom, would violate against the principle formulated above and would represent a grave injury to the dignity of the person. Hence there must be a zone of personal freedom in the sphere of economy, of the formation of communities, of the creation of objective cultural values, in the religious field, in the sphere of Christian values, whether or not these realms in particular and taken simply by themselves could 'function' sufficiently even without such a concession of freedom.

The moral law as such (in contrast to the forced compliance with it) is not a limitation of freedom, since it does after all presuppose freedom of its very nature and turns to it (since it is fulfilled only when it is obeyed freely), and since it orientates freedom to its own essential goal, viz. the true achievement of the person. The law (*qua* liberating law of freedom) can do this, to be sure, only if it is more than a merely destructive demand which provokes guilt, i.e. in so far as it is not a demand made on the powerless from without but the imperative expression of a power from within which is granted to the person in the concrete order of salvation only by the pneuma of God.

The freedom of the personal decision for which we are responsible ourselves and the consequences of which we must bear ourselves is a higher value (because more personal) than material security of physical existence as such. The flight from freedom into the enclosure of a merely secure life is, therefore, immoral. Wherever (and in so far as) a certain freedom and security of the material conditions of life belong to the necessary practical prerequisites of personal freedom, they are sanctioned by the dignity of human freedom and must be demanded in the name of this freedom—they must, therefore, be fashioned in such a way that the freedom of man itself is not sacrificed to the desire of possessing these material goods.

There can nevertheless be a justified limitation, not indeed of freedom as such, but of the scope for freedom. For the latter is (a) changeable and finite from the very start and independently of any human intervention and (b) is unavoidably changed in one person (even to the extent of a restriction) by the claim to freedom made by another person. Restriction of the scope for freedom of one person even when voluntarily posited by another cannot therefore be immoral, but flows precisely from the nature of the freedom of finite persons who exercise their freedom in a common space of human existence.

Such a limitation of the scope for freedom is thinkable as legitimate on various counts and in different ways:

a. As making it impossible to have a total or partial, but unlawful, restriction of some people's scope for freedom by others. For instance, the principle of the lawfulness of compulsion in a formal democracy: the freedom of political groupings is conceded only to those who also recognize this freedom in others; against enemies of democratic freedom we may proceed with compulsion. Or: anyone who steals is put in prison; society's reply to the unlawful limitation of freedom in the material realm of the free shaping of one's life is the enforced limitation of the freedom of movement. This principle of the enforced protection of the freedom of the many against someone who threatens freedom is not, however, the sole principle of the lawful restriction of freedom. There are others which are equally essential.

b. As an *educative* restriction of the scope for freedom with a view to the liberation of freedom. Man, on account of the uninvited influences exerted on him from without, is not simply and from the very start in lordly possession of complete control over his personal power of decision. He can be swept away involuntarily (before any action of his

freedom takes place) to do actions which either lack freedom and responsibility completely or possess them only to a diminished degree, and
which then become an obstacle to and restriction of the possibilities of his
freedom for good. He can be corrupted in advance of his decision. The
enforced restriction or elimination of such influences imposed by others
(viz. 'those charged with upbringing', such as the State, the Church, etc.)
is not an attempt on freedom, even when it is done in the face of objections from the one who is not really limited by this in any proper sense. In
this respect it would be a false, utopian outlook of an optimistic or pes-
simistic kind if we were to think that man can, from a certain age on-
wards, do without any such, to-a-certain-extent enforced education by
others (i.e. an education which does not merely appeal to the free good
sense of the other by exhortation and instruction, etc.) or if, on the other
hand, we tried to keep *every* possibility for evil always and everywhere
away from him.

c. Whenever the legitimate demand for an objective action (be it
legitimate by reason of the things itself or by reason of obligations freely
contracted towards it) is of its nature independent in its objective being of
whether its performance is constituted by freedom or without it—and to
the extent in which this applies—then the enforcing of some action is not
contrary to the nature of freedom.

d. Difficulties arise in the case of someone, on the grounds of conscience, refusing to do something which is objectively justified and hence
legitimately enforceable, by maintaining that conscience forbids him to
perform this task (refusal to do military service, etc.). In such a case the
following has to be said:

(i) The one who makes the demand must re-examine the justification
for his demand very closely, out of respect for the freedom and conscience of the person who refuses.

(ii) He must ask himself whether he has merely the right or is furthermore morally bound to make this demand.

(iii) If the former, then he can desist from enforcing his demand. In
many cases such a course will even be advisable or demanded by general
considerations.

(iv) If the latter, then he has the right and duty to enforce his demand
(in so far as this is possible) by using coercive measures proportioned to
the importance of his demand. For it is then not really a case of a conflict
between freedom-conscience, on the one hand, and coercion, on the other
hand, but between freedom and conscience *on both sides*. The tragic
conflict between the objectively justified and obligatory demand, on the
one hand, and the subjective conscience in good faith, on the other, is
insoluble in practice. Its tragedy must be accepted with patience and
mutual respect as a sign of the imperfection of the order here below.

e. The performance of actions and adoption of attitudes which essentially include the free 'yes' as one of their internal constitutive moments (and to the extent in which they do this), must not be coerced. The only law that remains valid in this case is the law of what ought to be done, and no longer the law of what must be done. The actual demarcation of the one case from the other is indeed difficult, because the concrete execution can include both moments. On account of the higher dignity of freedom as compared with the doing of something, we must decide against the use of coercion in a doubtful case.

4. The Faith Instinct*

Renewed emphasis on individual discernment does not mean that the teaching function of the Church's general directives can be safely under-played. Rahner insists on the Church's right and obligation to take an authoritative stand on the great moral issues which contemporary tech-nology and politics have raised in our generation. True, the range of unrevisable conceptual statements through which the Church can express her moral teaching has been diminished. Philosophical pluralism, the vast scope of scientific knowledge and technology, and the culturally conditioned character of much that was once considered "human na-ture" have made it increasingly difficult to reach morally certain conclu-sions through deductive arguments from theoretically unshakeable general principles. Nevertheless the Church remains the authoritative re-ligious and moral teacher of mankind. When she is challenged by the momentous moral issues, concerning which contemporary Christians must make decisions, the teaching Church may not simply fall silent and leave her children to their own resources. Yet, in order to make the moral pronouncements which she is called upon to make today, the Church will often be forced to resort to her "instinct of faith." Her magisterium will have to come to its conclusions through a non-formal mode of inference which is analogous to prudence, although not identical with it. Since the Church is illuminated by the light which comes to her through her loving faith commitment to the Word, who is Wisdom, she will be able to make the moral judgments which she must make today in order to fulfil her teaching mission. There is no necessity that the Church's moral conclu-sions be analytic or deductive. Neither need they be unrevisable. It is not necessary that the Church possess explicit awareness of how her conclu-sions have been reached. The Church need only know that these are the moral judgments which she must make now to meet the needs of the faithful in their present situation. Rahner's "faith instinct" is an exten-

*From *Theological Investigations*, vol. IX, 227-28, 230-31, 238-41.
© 1972 by Darton, Longman & Todd Ltd.

*sion to the sphere of the Church's moral teaching of the informal per-
sonal knowledge of the Revealing God which he used in his account of
the development of dogma. The Church's fidelity to the Revealing God
and the presence of the Holy Spirit within her ground the moral truth of
the word which must be spoken* now *in the name of Christ.*

*Rahner's critics, while conceding the brilliance of his theology of the
"faith instinct," complain of its incompleteness. Rahner admits that the
Church's sinfulness can affect the truth of her ordinary teaching. We
need a theology, similar to Rahner's formal existential ethics, which
would provide the thoughtful Christian with some* norms *which he could
use in evaluating the often conflicting moral statements of bishops and
theologians. When is the ordinary magisterium of the Church an expression of her "faith instinct" and when is it an expression of her sinful lack
of vision?*

*Rahner's demand for a formal existential ethics, his morality of the
fundamental option, and his theory of the Church's "instinct of faith"
have exercised considerable influence on Catholic moral theology. The
general principles of his moral theology have been taken over and developed systematically by a number of Catholic moralists, notably by
Josef Fuchs, S.J., of the Gregorian University at Rome.*

It is impossible simply to dismiss the thought of man's 'genetic manipulation' as an unethical project. As far as a Christian understanding of
mankind is concerned, man is not simply the product of 'nature', as if
nature *alone* were able and authorised to determine and model man's
being. Man is not only the being who is commissioned by God to further
God's work of creation, the being who both may and must 'subdue the
earth', i.e. his environment. Rather man is characteristically the being
who has been handed over to himself, consigned to his own free responsibility. In this sense he *must* 'manipulate' himself. Freedom is the inevitable *necessity* of self-determination, by which man (though starting out
from a 'beginning' which is a prior datum and within a perspective of
already pre-empted possibilities) *makes himself* what and who he wants to
be and ultimately will be in the abiding validity and eternity of his free
decisions. The fact that in earlier times this planned self-determination
('self-manipulation') took place almost exclusively on the individual,
moral-transcendent plane of convictions and of conscience may perhaps
initially obscure our view of the nature of man in this respect, but it does
nothing to change the *fact* of this transcendental necessity: to the extent
that man is 'handed over' to himself, he *is* 'self-manipulating' (within the
limits set by his 'nature' and 'history'). Today this fundamental essence
of his has now also broken through into history and society: today he is
able to manipulate himself in tangible, bodily and societal terms, and—a

radical difference here from earlier times—he can plan this manipulation rationally and steer it by means of technology.

Genetic manipulation is only one particular instance of this more general phenomenon. Consequently the formal, abstract concept of (genetic) self-manipulation does not automatically imply a morally repugnant act: man does not simply perform actions *external* to himself, merely suffering his own self passively: man is such that he actually 'performs' himself. Since the latter is in accordance with his nature, this kind of 'self-manipulation' is legitimate too, if it is true that a moral action is one which is in accordance with the subject's nature. The fact that today man is able to do this in ways which were previously not accessible to him does not change the abstract, formal concept of self-manipulation. This applies, for example, in the case of genetic self-manipulation if we take a preliminary 'abstract' look at it. For here, as in other methods of psychological, physiological and social self-manipulation, we must distinguish clearly between the process in its material content as such (i.e. the changing of hereditary material), and the conscious controlling of it, which does not automatically involve an artificial, arbitrary alteration which uses man himself as a means. For the moment we shall deal only with outlining the formal and abstract issues of the problem. The moral quality of control as such is determined by the moral quality of the process itself: if a thing is permissible, it may be expressly desired and consciously implemented.

Now a particular kind of 'change' of hereditary material is morally permissible. For it actually occurs legitimately, within certain limits, whenever a person chooses a marriage-partner, and whenever two human beings consummate their marital union sexually. Of course this kind of self-manipulation does not penetrate deeply into the human material as do psychological and pain-killing drugs and all cosmetic techniques in their different ways. But there are examples which show that, considered in the abstract, in this field of quite ordinary 'genetic manipulation' no moral objection can be raised on account of the conscious controlling of the process in itself. For example no-one would think of raising a moral protest if a married couple were to opt for a particular coitus which they knew beforehand (supposing that they could) would produce a boy, rather than for another one, equally possible, but which would lead to the birth of a girl. But such a case would constitute materially and formally a 'genetic manipulation' according to our terms so far (which cannot embrace the concrete phenomenon of modern genetic manipulation in all its aspects). Thus the abstract concept of genetic manipulation is not subject to any moral reservations.

Clearly this does not take us very far, for it is plain that not everything that *can* be done is morally justifiable. In our case the moral quality of a *concrete* genetic manipulation depends on several factors:

1. It depends on the concrete subject of the manipulation: a married

couple is something quite different from the state, for instance, or any other active subject taking such measures.

2. It depends on the concrete, premeditated result on the whole human being: to intend to produce a human being who would never be morally responsible for himself would be immoral, even if such a human being might be very 'useful' for the particular purposes of other men.

3. It depends on the concrete method employed in genetic manipulation: initially we cannot be certain that each *technologically successful* development can be fitted into the *whole* of human reality without being contrary to the latter's nature. But unless this is safeguarded, any such development is thoroughly immoral.

All three aspects of the moral evaluation of concrete genetic manipulation can be reduced to a common principle: its *concrete* reality must be adjudged according to whether it is appropriate to or contrary to the nature of man.

At this point we encounter the real difficulties of the question. Is there such a thing as an unchangeable 'nature' of man against which we can measure the appropriateness or inappropriateness of a particular genetic manipulation? With all our knowledge of man's immense malleability in the biological, psychological, cultural and social spheres, do we still have the courage to talk about the 'nature' of man? Do we know precisely where the limits of man's nature are to be found? We are even more at a loss if it is true that man is not only placed in a process of natural historical development, but also can and must change *himself* if he is to come to full stature and find true selfhood. Even if there is such a thing as this 'nature', can we recognise it, if by 'nature' we mean, not the tangible, concrete constitution of man as he is at any one time, but what is thought to be perennially valid and hence normative throughout all historical change? If there is such a 'nature' of man, if it is somehow present to man's understanding of himself, whether propositionally or not, do we come across it in any other way than in a particular historical form, where we are unable to distinguish clearly and unequivocally between the nature 'in itself' and its concrete, variable form? Is it not the case that saying 'No' in the name of morality and humanity has often been merely the mistaken and ultimately ineffectual refusal on the part of historical man to change himself and experience a new form of his reality, a new form of his 'nature'? May not the reverse be true, in a way: can there be a moral judgment based not simply on the 'eternal nature' of man as a *primary* 'law of nature', but one which draws its imperative from the particular form of man's nature which is committed to him at any one time as his historical destiny, such that he cannot act with impunity contrary to it, even if he has the power to do so? How can we recognise the boundary between the foolish 'No' of man when he will not let himself be changed, and *this* 'No', through which man holds fast to a particular form which,

though historically limited, is the currently imperative form of his historical nature? If man is essentially an inhabitant of 'civilisation' and never
merely a factor of nature, is it not possible to think that now this 'civilisation' is shaping his very self and no longer only his environment? This too
could be considered as 'genetic manipulation'.

At first sight it would appear that, in order to form an opinion of the
moral quality of a particular instance of genetic manipulation, one would
need to have a clear answer to all these questions, as well as the courage
to give a definitive answer. At this juncture it will be obvious, however,
that we can neither assume such an answer as given nor set out to provide
one.

Before trying to find a way of solving the problem under discussion without having to go into all the fundamental ethical questions which we have
just raised, we must clarify certain fundamental problematical issues as
they affect our particular question. Whatever the situation may be as
regards the current judgments of modern men and specialists, man *has* a
knowledge and understanding of his own nature, and this can exercise a
normative function in his moral evaluations. But the question remains as
to how far, if at all, this knowledge of the nature of man can take us in our
particular inquiry. This dual statement must be expanded somewhat.

Man is essentially the *subject*: he is a person, aware of himself as a free
being, and related, in this freedom, to the absolute mystery which we call
'God'. He experiences this *a posteriori* in his 'passive' subjectivity, in the
flesh of history, in language and in the objective account of himself which
he finds in 'civilisation'. Man's nature is constructed with a built-in transcendental necessity: man must inevitably affirm his own nature even in
an action which seeks freely to deny it. Here we need not go into the
question whether, further than trying to eliminate his nature as an
individual—suicide being the most radical case—mankind as a whole
could throw off its nature by implementing a process of 'civilisation in
reverse', cultivating a species of intelligent animals which would live only
unto themselves without being answerable for themselves. Such an action
would be the most radical conceivable genetic manipulation. But *qua*
action even this would be still the action of beings who would be denying
explicitly what *implicitly* they cannot but affirm. The action itself, like
individual suicide, would do nothing to deny the transcendental necessity
of man's nature. For because of his subjectivity, i.e. his *a priori* limitless
transcendentality, he cannot be mistaken for merely the highest 'stage' of
animal development. Hence it is clear that what we call 'immorality' is
when *this* transcendental nature is violated by man's self-determining
action. Yet this does not imply straightway that what is moral simply
coincides with what is appropriate to this *transcendental* nature.

In the case of those realities which have many layers and which cannot be
adequately reached by analysis, there exists a *moral* mode of knowing.

This moral knowledge itself has a structure which is both universal and not exhaustively analysable in conscious reflection. In a certain way it exercises a critical function in an area where 'is' and 'ought' *mutually* determine each other, but where what is 'objectively' right only becomes transparent to the person who has already embraced the correct attitude to it.

In other words, to adopt a term from the contemporary theology of faith, there is also a *moral* instinct of faith, i.e. a universal knowledge of right and wrong belief. This 'instinctive' judgment cannot and need not, however, be adequately subject to analytic reflection. In the more concrete questions of morality this faith-instinct is clearly indispensable because such complex realities are involved which cannot successfully be subjected to analytic reflection—and yet they must be evaluated morally all the same. Wherever the judgment of this moral faith-instinct attempts to express itself in words regarding a particular issue, it naturally and inevitably works with the categories of rational analysis, 'reasons', conceptual arguments etc., and thus conceals its own character. But at bottom it knows that its judgments are not the resultant and formal logical sum of the rational considerations which it is able to 'objectivise'. Traditional moral theology has no name for the activity of this moral faith-instinct, although the instinct plays its part in the former. For instance, a merely 'rational' scrutiny of moral theological 'proofs' will often reveal——initially to one's great surprise—that, looked at purely 'logically', they already presuppose what they claim to be 'proving', or else they have recourse to Holy Scripture or the Church's magisterium as a final court of appeal, in spite of the fact that they were supposed to be dealing with questions of natural law, requiring an *inner* justification. What is really behind these 'proofs'? Under certain circumstances they are not as bad as they seem. They are ultimately an expression of the universal faith-instinct, which is by no means identical with its objectivisation in analytic terms.

Of course there are dangers in citing this kind of knowledge *sui generis*: it can be used merely to avoid producing what is sometimes actually possible, namely, a more precise rational, analytic justification; it can be used as an argument where it does not, in fact, exist, where there is merely false 'evidence' rooted in historically conditioned prejudices, whether those of tradition, society or class ideology. Consequently it is fundamentally legitimate to be critical of this approach, especially when one thinks how much mischief and crime was perpetrated during the Nazi period in the name of 'the healthy instinct of the people'. But such criticism must neither dispute nor disregard the reality and rights of this universal instinct in reason and faith, irrespective of what it is to be called and how it is to be described and analysed from the point of view of formal epistemology.

Furthermore, this mode of knowing is active in human life wherever someone is 'committed' to a particular attitude: it is even active where the rationalistic sceptic gives expression to his scepticism *vis-à-vis* all so-called 'taboos', as he calls those things he wishes to reject. Denying the existence and legitimacy of such a mode of knowing cannot get rid of it: it can only obstruct the process of critical reflection upon opinions, opinions which are themselves—explicitly or implicitly—dependent on the results of this mode of knowing. One can only proceed with caution with regard to something if one has not, at the outset, denied its existence. Nor does this mode of knowing mean to curtail or even replace rationality, for it possesses this very rationality as one of its own elements. But it is necessary because what is moral, the concrete action to be performed, corresponds automatically to the unity of experienced and conceptual reality. It cannot wait while conceptual analysis—an essentially endless process—makes its conclusions; it demands that one should enter into the darkness of reality (which is never completely transparent) and have the courage to take the step from theory to practice. This action is never the mere application of concepts to an empty world of matter, enjoying no reality but what the abstract concepts give it. This kind of universal moral instinct of faith and reason can calmly take 'risks' provided that it is self-critically aware that its judgments contain unreflected elements which are, as such, contingent, subject to change; and that consequently a *different* judgment may be shown to be correct at a later time. All the same, a particular contingent judgment of this kind can still be the only correct one *in its situation.* The making of it requires a universal knowledge of the current situation; this knowledge is correctly grasped in the 'instinctive' judgment which recognises what is currently and properly called for, and this results in an 'appropriate' judgment.

Since it is made 'in general' and 'in principle', the judgment made by a universal moral faith-instinct is not simply identical with what traditional moral theology calls a 'prudential' judgment, nor with what I have described as an individual existential moral decision, which cannot be adequately reduced to general concepts and their application to particular 'cases' and thus requires a 'logic of existential decisions'. The fact that there are these other phenomena in the moral field shows too, however, that what we have called the 'universal moral faith-instinct' must be present in the sphere of theoretical moral reasoning as well. For this *fundamentally synthetic* knowledge, formed by the unity of a prudential judgment and a unique moral existential situation, must clearly also be the case where the situation is 'per se' morally 'general' in nature, since this too is inaccessible to *adequate,* exhaustive reflection and analysis. Taking due account of this connection between the modes of knowledge, it is also justifiable to refer to the following moral phenomena as a demonstration of the mode of knowledge we have been discussing: the choice of a career or a marriage-partner is (or ought to be) a decision of solemn moral

significance. Everyone admits—including the Church—that in considering the moral correctness of this kind of decision one may be aware of a
large number of points of view and reasons for and against a particular
decision; but in addition to all these factors the whole process of reflection includes a synthesising element, which cannot itself be reflected upon
in isolation and yet must be present, so that, from among all the conflicting reasons for and against, one may observe the plain inner security
which witnesses to a moral decision.

Here we cannot describe *how* this actually happens. It is certainly true
that, in the examples we have quoted, the decisions involved are essentially individual in character (not least with regard to their objects). But
we have already remarked that this same synthesising function of knowledge, by which we are able, so to speak, to see the wood in spite of all the
trees, is also necessary where what is involved is only a *general* moral
reality. And this latter is more complicated than the simple text-book
model employed in the usual kind of moral theology.

The terrible consequences of ignoring the universal moral instinct of
faith and reason, or of not having the courage to rely on it, can be seen
only too clearly, it seems to me, in a particular example of the most recent
past. I refer to the simulated crisis of conscience concerning the production of a cheap Napalm bomb for the war in Vietnam, which Günter
Wallraff fabricated and set before several prominent German moral
theologians for their decision. We shall not relate the whole story in detail
here. It is well known. In short it shows clearly that whenever a moral
theologian merely dissects such a particular 'case' into a thousand aspects
and individual problems and has the courage only to make abstract deductions from more general principles, merely engaging in 'casuistics';
whenever he fails to react simply and plainly from the instinct of faith to
the single totality of the 'case', he arrives at 'solutions' which are simply
blind to concrete reality; in plain language, they are *false*. Such 'solutions' do not exhibit the uncompromising simplicity of decisions which
are truly Christian and human, and only reveal their own impotence. In
order to see the helplessness of moral theology when it proceeds solely by
analysis and deduction, one need only refer to the whole complex of
problems involved in the moral evaluation, according to Catholic and
Protestant moral theology, of making and using biochemical weapons.
Even the Council was not able unequivocally to overcome this kind of
mentality, which paralyses any action which could be said to be clearly
Christian.

XII

The Church and the Sacraments

1. The Fundamental Sacrament
and the Sacraments*

Rahner's theology of the Church and the sacraments is an extension and development of his Christology. The Logos, the Father's real symbol, expresses himself in the Incarnation through the real symbol of his human nature. Thus Christ becomes the social and historical offer of God's grace to the human race. When, under the influence of the Indwelling Holy Spirit, this grace is accepted, the "economic Trinity" comes to dwell in the individual human soul.

Christ's Church, through which he continues to dwell in the human race, is the definitive people of God, established through his Incarnation. Consequently the Church, in her social and hierarchial form, is a visible sign in which Christ dwells and through which he continues to make a manifest offer of his grace to all men. The Church then is the real symbol through which the Incarnate Word expresses himself in human history.

Since the historical, socially organized Church is the symbol through which the grace of Christ is manifestly offered to each individual, the grace of Christ is also the grace of Christ's Church. Therefore, because of her connection with the Incarnation, the Church of Christ is necessary for salvation with a necessity, not just of precept, but of means. No man can hope to receive the grace of Christ, even as an anonymous Christian, without entering into a positive relation with the Church, although this relation may vary greatly in the degree of its intensity.

As the visible sign which manifests Christ's offer of grace to every individual, the Church is the fundamental sacrament of Christ's grace. Her nature exercises its proper activity when she stands before every man as a visible sign with which the promise of saving grace is infallibly connected.

*From "The Church and the Sacraments" (*Quaestiones Disputatae* 9) in *Inquiries*, pp. 202-11, 214-15. © 1963 by Herder KG.

For this reason the Church's nature as the real symbol of the Incarnate Christ provides the theological grounding for the seven visible signs which are called her sacraments in the strict sense of the term. For these sacramental signs are the manifold ways through which the visible, socially organized Church comes to meet the individual soul as a living, indefectibly operative offer of God's grace. In other words, the concrete, individual sacramental signs are the real symbols through which the Church expresses herself as the fundamental sacrament of Christ's grace.

Rahner's metaphysics of the sacramental sign enables him to explain how they give grace ex opere operato *in a systematically consistent way. For Rahner, the fact that the sacraments confer grace* ex opere operato *does not mean that their recipient should have greater assurance of receiving grace through them than he would by seeking grace through a non-sacramental sign, such as a prayer. Neither does it mean that he should be less concerned about his own subjective dispositions. Certainty of receiving grace is not the distinguishing mark of the sacrament. Subjective dispositions are so important that they can nullify a sacrament and prevent it from being a genuine sign of grace.*

The distinction between the ex opere operato *operation of the sacraments and the* ex opere operantis *operation of the non-sacramental sign therefore is not based on greater certainty of their giving grace. It is built rather on the diverse origin of these two types of sign. The sacramental sign is presented to the individual by the socially organized Church acting according to her nature as Christ's fundamental sacrament. Only the Church acting this way possesses infallible assurance that Christ's irrevocable promise of his grace is connected with a particular sign, even though the actual reception of grace may be prevented by the subjective dispositions of an individual recipient. Only those signs which the Church has infallibly recognized as connected with Christ's irrevocable offer of his grace are sacraments in this strict sense. The individual Christian who seeks grace through a non-sacramental sign does not possess the same assurance of the connection between his sign and the promise of Christ's grace. It is this infallible assurance of the connection between the sign and the promise of Christ's grace that is signified by the phrase that the sacraments confer grace* ex opere operato.

EXPLANATION OF THE SACRAMENTAL STRUCTURE OF THE CHURCH AND ITS ACTUALIZATION IN THE SEVEN SACRAMENTS GENERALLY

The Church is not a mythical entity to be hypostasized or personified in a false way. By the will of Christ her founder she is the organized community of the people of God, established through the incarnation in the unity of the one human race. Even if such a society is represented by individual human beings, it still remains a community. Such a collectivity may in a true sense continue in being even when all its members are asleep and the common business or activity for the moment has completely ceased. But in order to exist, nevertheless, a community has to fulfil its nature, must actually function. The enduring existence of such a society can to be sure find concrete expression in the most diverse ways, and manifest itself with greater or less intensity in visible historical form. And a community of spiritual persons depends much more than a real individual person on such *actus secundi* (operations flowing from a nature and expressing it), because it is only an association. One can confidently say that once a society renounced once and for all its own actualization and functioning, it would by that very fact cease to exist altogether. That holds true of the Church too. The Church exists in the full sense, in the highest degree of actual fulfilment of her nature, by teaching, bearing witness to Christ's truth, bearing the cross of Christ through the ages, loving God in her members, rendering present in rite in the sacrifice of the mass the saving grace that is hers.

If it is true to say that the Church as the continuance of Christ's presence in the world, is the fundamental sacrament of the eschatologically triumphant mercy of God, then salvation is offered and promised to the individual by his entering into positive relation to the Church. This positive relationship may possibly have very different degrees and grades of intensity, but if the individual is to attain salvation, can never entirely be lacking. God's life is offered to men plainly and once and for all in Christ, through whose incarnation the people of God exists. This has socially organized form in the Church, which is consequently the abiding and historically manifest presence of this saving grace in Christ, the fundamental sacred sign or sacrament of this grace. From this the necessity of the Church for salvation—at root it is the necessity of Christ himself —directly follows. Its necessity as a means is also clear, the kind of necessity which is presupposed by the question of a moral claim to men's obedience. We have also, of course, in the distinction between the aspect: people of God, and the aspect: juridical constitution of that people, within the one complete unity of the Church, an objective means of discerning degrees of intensity in membership of the Church, so that in fact there can be no instance of saving grace of which one would have to say, that it had no connection with the Church and with membership of the Church. So though the individual, in what concerns his own personal sanctification, works out his own unique, irreplaceable salvation in personal freedom, he always does so by finding his way to the Church. For the Church is the presence of saving grace in the world. To deny the ecclesiastical character of all grace and redemption would either imply that grace is not always related to the incarnation, to history and so to the Church, or else it would imply that one can attain salvation without the grace of Christ.

If, however, the means of grace, its presence, has a sacramental structure, that is, is based on the unity of grace and its historically manifest concrete embodiment, this must also be true of access to this means or fountain of grace, of entry into it, and of any further acceptance of grace by the individual from it. That does not imply that any and every conferring and acceptance of the grace present in the Church as the fundamental sacrament, has in every case the nature of a sacrament in the strictest and technical sense of the word. It has been sufficiently indicated already, and we cannot go into the matter further here, that any grace-giving event has a quasi-sacramental structure and shares in Christ's character as both divine and human. But when the Church in her official, organized, public capacity precisely as the source of redemptive grace meets the individual in the actual ultimate accomplishment of her nature, there we have sacraments in the proper sense, and they can then be seen to be the essential functions that bring into activity the very essence of the Church herself. For in them she herself attains the highest degree of actualization of what she always is: the presence of redemptive grace for men, historically visible and manifest as the sign of the eschatologically victorious grace of God in the world.

Now if the Church as the people of God in a socially organized form is the enduring historical presence of the eschatologically triumphant grace of God and of Christ in the world for the individual, the obtaining of grace by the individual cannot consist simply in his approval and consent to the mere presence of this redemptive grace. A community with an organized structure only acquires by its own act reality and validity for the individual who at first is outside it. A society must "enrol" him if he is to enter it. It is only in that way, then, that it is manifest that God's redemptive grace in Christ is a free grace, his own operation in us and not a factual reality always of necessity present, and in regard to which it is really only a question for us, of what attitude we choose to adopt towards it. The actualization or accomplishment of the eschatologically victorious redemptive grace established in the Church for the world and offered to all men, takes place, therefore, (in instances where this accomplishment is realized fully and perfectly), in an act of the Church in the individual's regard, whereby the gratuitous character of redemptive grace is proclaimed. This act of the Church in regard to man necessarily bears within it the structure of the Church's own nature. It is sacramental in accordance with the Church's character as the primal sacrament of grace. It is to be remembered here that we have called the Church the fundamental sacrament, not by a vague borrowing of the concept of sacrament known to us already from the current teaching about the sacraments, but by deriving our concept from Christology. Therefore fundamental sacrament means for us the one abiding symbolic presence, similar in structure to the incarnation, of the eschatological redemptive grace of Christ; a presence in which sign and what is signified are united inseparably but without confu-

sion, the grace of God in the "flesh" of an historical and tangible ecclesiastical embodiment, which therefore cannot be emptied of what it
signifies and renders present, because otherwise the grace of Christ (who
always remains man), would also be something merely transitory and
replaceable, and in the last resort we would still be under the old covenant. Consequently, because first of all and independently of the usual idea
of a sacrament, we envisage the Church as the fundamental or primal
sacrament, and form the root idea of a sacrament in the ordinary sense as
an instance of the fullest actualization of the Church's essence as the
saving presence of Christ's grace, for the individual, we can in fact obtain
from this an understanding of the sacraments in general.

THE NATURE OF A SACRAMENT IN GENERAL, VIEWED IN RELATION TO THE CHURCH AS FUNDAMENTAL SACRAMENT

We have, of course, no intention of attempting to deduce in precise
detail from this conception all the basic characteristics of the sacraments
as they are listed in the treatises on the sacraments in general. Nevertheless a few indications must be given.

Our viewpoint permits a deeper understanding of the meaning of *opus
operatum*. When applied to one of these acts of the Church in regard to an
individual in which her nature is accomplished, this expression simply
says what we said about the Church in general when we explained that
she is the definitive sign, impossible to deprive of meaning, of God's
grace in the world, which is rendered present by being manifested in this
way in the Church.

The concept of *opus operatum* is, of course, not as simple as might at
first appear. We are leaving out of account the fact that in standard
theology it is not identical with the concept of a sacrament, as there are
instances of it which are not sacraments (the mass as sacrifice; indulgences too, according to a commonly held view). The idea in itself too
presents considerable difficulties which can perhaps be solved more easily with the present approach than if one starts from the individual sacraments themselves and tries to build up the concept of *opus operatum* from
them. In the usual account, the concept means that grace is conferred on
the recipient through the positing of the sacramental sign itself, and
neither the merit (holiness) of the minister nor that of the recipient is
causally involved (Denzinger 849, 850f.).

It is explained that God has linked his grace once and for all to the
making of this sign and that through this connection established by God
himself between sign of grace and grace signified, any objection that the
sacramental *opus operatum* is being understood in a magical way *ipso*

facto vanishes, all the more so as the need for inner receptiveness and for appropriation in faith of the grace conferred is not only not excluded but is expressly taught by the Council of Trent (Denzinger 797f., 819, 849). All that is correct and at first sight quite clear. But we must note that in the first place the Council teaches the necessity, if the sacrament is to be received with fruit by an adult, of a right disposition: active co-operation in the reception of the sacrament with faith and love. Consequently the sacrament in its concrete reality involves, like the *opus operantis* (the dispositions of the recipient), an element of uncertainty about grace, of doubt about its factual efficacy. With the sacrament a person knows just as little as he does with his merely "subjective" actions performed in faith, whether it has really given him God's grace. Just as little and just as much. That is after all an undeniable fact which is hidden in the popular view of the sacraments by what the average person thinks *opus operatum* implies. Everyone has heard Catholics say, or has himself thought, that when someone prays or repents of his sins, he is not as sure that God has heard him or forgiven him as he is if he goes to the sacraments. Since Scotus more or less, this idea has been one of the standard arguments in apologetics to show the necessity or utility of the sacrament of penance, confession, even when this is not strictly obligatory because no grave sins are in question. The idea of *opus operatum* in fact current, contains an element of what one might almost call physical certainty of functioning, which does not belong to it in more accurate theology. Conversely one can certainly affirm that God has attached the unconditional promise of grace and help to other realities as well as to the sacramental signs. If someone prays in the name of Jesus for saving grace and for nothing else (and in a particular case he knows as much or as little whether he is doing so as he does about his dispositions when he receives the sacraments), he knows with infallible certainty that God hears him, even if perhaps the precise mode of the answer remains hidden and must be left in God's hands. It is not a cogent objection to this example to say that here the prayer as *opus operantis* represents a "merit" and consequently the obtaining of grace and its measure depend on the measure of this subjective merit, whereas fortunately this is excluded in the case of the sacraments, where God acts towards men according to his own generosity and good pleasure. This does not meet the difficulty. For the measure of grace in the sacraments is dependent on the quality of the recipient's dispositions (Denzinger 799).

Furthermore, even if the prayer is meritorious, God's hearing the prayer is not based on the merit that accrues through the prayer, but as all theologians agree, on the fact that in prayer as such, appeal is made for Christ's sake to the infinite generosity of God. It is to this prayer that God has promised an absolutely certain hearing. Consequently one can say in a general way with regard to the two instances that in both of them, the sacrament and the prayer, and not only in the one where we employ the term *opus operatum,* we have occurrences to which, if they are true and genuine, God has absolutely promised his grace. Other acts could be quoted as well as prayer, that have a similar character, and we only omit them because in this connection they occupy a less prominent place in the average Catholic's awareness of his faith: reading of Scripture, listening to the word of God, and others. But in both the instances we are dealing with, grace is also conferred according to the measure of the recipient's dispositions which, of course, in the last resort are themselves a gift of grace. In both cases, too, the operative cause is not really the (supernatural) merit of man (which exists) but God's promise. So where is the real difference between the *opus operatum* of the sacraments and these other instances of grace being conferred, which we do not call sacraments?

In order to be in a position later to give as concrete an answer as possible to this question, let us illustrate once more with an example. Someone repents of his sins with genuine contrition and conversion, in his own conscience. If he does this, he knows with absolute certainty, by reason of the faithful and irrevocable words of the divine promise, that God truly forgives him his guilt. What happens then is an actual instance of grace being conferred, not a merely "subjective" desire for it to happen. Another man confesses his sins contritely in the sacrament of penance. He knows that God forgives him his guilt by the Church's power of the keys, if he is truly and genuinely repentant. In neither case is there absolute certainty about the fulfilment of the condition. In both cases, over and above what the man does and experiences, he must also trust in God and his inscrutable judgment, seeing that in both cases he is obliged to trust firmly and unshakenly (not to know), with simple and childlike hope, (for God is greater than our heart), that God will truly have produced by his grace the necessary condition, our "good will". In the first case we speak of *opus operantis,* in the second of *opus operatum.* What is the difference between the two?

First of all it must be calmly and candidly recognized that the difference is not at all as radical as a rather mediocre theology would have it. Supernatural activity where grace is conferred and promised to us by God, infallibly on his part, and sacramental activity, are not identical. The second is only one of the possible kinds of the first. And as regards our question itself, the answer can only be that in the first case the sign (the prayer, repentance, in other words what the individual as such privately does), to which God has attached his grace, is itself intrinsically fragile, vulnerable, capable that is of becoming invalid of itself, and of being for its own part deprived of the character of visible expression of God's promise of grace. In the second case the sign has an irrevocable eschatological validity; in itself it is the sign of the eternal irrevocable covenant of God with men, a sign which so shares in the eternity and irrevocability of God's salvific will, that the sign itself can never lose the quality of being the visible expression of God's consenting answer to man. It can meet with refusal from man, who can reject the word of God and let it stand against him. But since Christ, and only since him, man can no longer prevent this word's being permanently addressed to him, calling him and not being withdrawn; or that this word summoning him to grace is irrevocably present in the sacramental sign, inseparable from it.

An historically tangible concrete act of a human being, a prayer for instance, does not in itself possess this, because of itself it can be empty of the content that of itself it expresses, and because it is not an act that is accomplished by the Church as such. In such instances one can always say no more than: If this concrete phenomenon really contains what it purports to contain, then the grace of God is bestowed. With the sacraments of the new law, however, one can say unconditionally: Here in all truth a manifestation of God and his salvific will is taking place. It may remain questionable whether here and now grace is received. But it is not questionable that in general grace is in fact received under these signs, for the Church as a whole has also the promise of her own subjective holiness produced and preserved by efficacious grace. Above all, it is not questionable that God here and now in the sacrament offers his grace. Consequently *opus operatum* means the unambiguous, abiding promise irrevocably made by God, and as such recognizable and historically manifest, of grace for the individual human being, a promise made by the God of the new and eternal covenant. The statement that it is a conferring of God's grace without the subjective merit of the minister or the recipient of the sign, is only the negative and therefore secondary formulation of this positive content of the concept.

2. The Causality of the Sacraments*

The fact that the sacraments are real symbols through which the Church expresses herself explains the nature of their causality. The Church is an intrinsic symbol of the eschatologically triumphant grace of God. Christ acts through the Church in regard to an individual human being by giving his action spatio-temporal embodiment by having the gift of his grace manifested in the sacrament. The sign is constituted as sign by the giving of God's grace which becomes present in it. Thus the visible form of the sacrament is an effect of the coming of grace. Since in the

*From "The Church and the Sacraments" (*Quaestiones Disputatae* 9) in *Inquiries*, pp. 219-22. © 1963 by Herder KG.

*self-embodiment of grace in the sacraments grace occurs, the sacraments
can cause grace in the human soul. Furthermore, since the metaphysics
of the symbol demands that grace become ontologically present in the
sacramental sign, the sacraments can cause what they signify without
violating the fundamental law of Thomistic metaphysics*–agere sequitur
esse.

The sacraments precisely as signs are causes of grace. [It] is a case here
of causation by symbols, of the kind that belongs to what by its very
nature is a symbol. By such "natural symbols" or intrinsically real symbols, we mean for our purpose here, the spatio-temporal, historical
phenomenon, the visible and tangible form in which something that
appears, notifies its presence, and by so doing, makes itself present, body-
ing forth this manifestation really distinct from itself. With natural symbols, the sign or symbol as a phenomenon is intrinsically linked to what it
is a phenomenon of, and which is present and operative, even though
really distinct. In fact we must distinguish between two aspects: the dependence of the actual manifestation on what is manifesting itself, and the
difference between the two. To cite a comparable relationship, a spiritual
being is an intellectual substance, yet only constitutes itself as such, as
mind, by there emanating from it what is not identical with itself, its really
distinct power of knowing. A proportionately similar relation holds between phenomenon and underlying reality. Hence it is possible to perceive
why the symbol can be really distinct from what is symbolized and yet an
intrinsic factor of what is symbolized, essentially related to it. In the same
way there holds between what we have called an intrinsic or natural
symbol and what it signifies neither a nexus of transitive efficient causality, nor the relation of subsequent notification of something that has already taken place and is in being, by an extrinsic announcement of the
state of affairs which is quite unaffected by it. It is a case of an intrinsic
and mutual causal relationship. What is manifesting itself posits its own
identity and existence by manifesting itself in this manifestation which is
distinct from itself. An example of this relationship is available for the
scholastic philosopher in the relation between soul and body. The body is
the manifestation of the soul, through which and in which the soul realizes
its own essence. The sign is therefore a cause of what it signifies by being
the way in which what is signified effects itself. The kind of causality
expressed in such a conception of symbolism occurs on various levels of
human reality. In substantial being (body as the sign or symbol of the
soul); in the sphere of activity (bodily gesture through which the inner
attitude itself which is expressed by it first attains its own full depth). On
this level of activity the informative expression, without prejudice to its
essential connection with what is expressed, may be posited quite freely
and take the form of a legal reality. When, for example, what is signified is

itself freely posited, the sign can share this characteristic. In other words, even a sign freely posited and belonging to a juridical order can be what we have called an intrinsic or essential symbol.

This concept of the intrinsic symbol, though developed so briefly here, must now be employed if we are to grasp what characterizes sacramental causation, and if we are to do this on the basis of the ecclesiological origin of the sacraments. The Church in her visible historical form is herself an intrinsic symbol of the eschatologically triumphant grace of God; in that spatio-temporal visible form, this grace is made present. And because the sacraments are the actual fulfilment, the actualization of the Church's very nature, in regard to individual men, precisely in as much as the Church's whole reality is to be the real presence of God's grace, as the new covenant, these sacramental signs are efficacious. Their efficacy is that of the intrinsic symbol. Christ acts through the Church in regard to an individual human being, by giving his action spatio-temporal embodiment by having the gift of his grace manifested in the sacrament. This visible form is itself an effect of the coming of grace; it is there because God is gracious to men; and in this self-embodiment of grace, grace itself occurs. The sacramental sign is cause of grace in as much as grace is conferred by being signified. And this presence (by signifying) of grace in the sacraments is simply the actuality of the Church herself as the visible manifestation of grace. Consequently the converse holds. The relation between the Church as the historical visible manifestation of grace and grace itself, one of reciprocal conditioning, extends into the relation between sacramental sign and grace conferred. The sign effects grace, by grace producing the sacrament as sign of the sanctification effected. This, of course, can only be said if the Church as an entity is truly and inseparably connected with grace. Only then is her act, when it is an unconditional realization of her essence, (that is of the Church as the presence of grace), essentially and irrevocably a manifestation of grace, so that the manifestation necessarily renders present what is manifested.

This accounts for the connection between *opus operatum* and the causality of the sacraments in relation to grace. Both are rooted in the same nature of the Church as the essentially primal symbol of grace inseparable from what is symbolized (grace).

This kind of causation is sufficient in this matter. All theologians agree that one satisfies the Church's doctrine that the sacraments are a "cause" of grace, provided one holds firmly that grace is conferred "on account of" the sacramental sign. No more is defined, and even the theory that the sacraments are only *condiciones* of the conferring of grace has never been officially rejected. Our interpretation fits all this. Provided the sign is an effect of God the dispenser of grace, it is true to say: This grace is conferred here and now because embodied, and by taking concrete form, in the sacramental manifestation. This statement is not falsified by there being other instances of the conferring of grace in which such sacramental embodiment does not occur. Even in regard to the grace conferred the two kinds, sacramental and non-sacramental, are not identical.

3. Christ's Institution of the Sacraments*

Once the Christian understands the relation of the Church as the fundamental sacrament of Christ's grace to the individual sacramental signs, he will not need "proof texts" from Scripture and tradition to support his faith in Christ's institution of the individual sacraments. The Church's infallible knowledge of her own nature as the manifest offer of Christ's grace to individual men will give the Christian unshakeable assurance of the connection between the irrevocable promise of Christ's grace and the sacramental signs through which she expresses herself as the fundamental sacrament of his grace.

Rahner's theology of the sacraments is highly systematic. It follows from his ecclesiology, which in turn depends on his Christology, both of which are structured by his metaphysics of the symbol.

Of course, the connection between the Church as fundamental sacrament and the individual sacraments is not unique to Rahner. It is rather commonplace in contemporary theology. Rahner's uniqueness lies in his systematic justification of the connection between the two and in his metaphysical account of the causality of the sacraments. The sacramental sign operates ex opere operato *because it is infallibly connected with the irrevocable promise of God's grace. When the individual soul does not frustrate that promise by his evil subjective dispositions, the sacramental sign becomes a real cause of grace. The offered grace, whose presence in the sacramental sign as its symbol constitutes the sign a sign, is now received by the human soul. Through that participation by the soul of the grace present within the sign, the sacramental sign causes what it signifies. Thus the causality of the symbol, which cannot be reduced to moral causality or mere instrumental causality, both accounts for the unique causality of the sacraments and links their operation systematically to the primordial sacramental activity of the Church as the fundamental sacrament, the indefectible manifest offer of Christ's grace to men.*

From the principle that the Church is the primal sacrament it would be possible to see that the existence of true sacraments in the strictest traditional sense is not necessarily and always based on a definite statement, which has been preserved or is presumed to have existed, in which the

*From "The Church and the Sacraments" (*Quaestiones Disputatae* 9) in *Inquiries*, p. 223. © 1963 by Herder KG.

historical Jesus Christ explicitly spoke about a certain definite sacrament. This would have its importance for apologetics of a less anxious and worried kind in the history of dogma, in the matter of the institution of all the sacraments by Christ. A fundamental act of the Church in an individual's regard, in situations that are decisive for him, an act which truly involves the nature of the Church as the historical, eschatological presence of redemptive grace, is *ipso facto* a sacrament, even if it were only later that reflection was directed to its sacramental character that follows from its connection with the nature of the Church. The institution of a sacrament can (it is not necessarily implied that it must always) follow simply from the fact that Christ founded the Church with its sacramental nature. It is clear too that, properly understood, the treatise *De sacramentis in genere* is not an abstract formulation of the nature of the individual sacraments, but a part of the treatise *De ecclesia*. It rightly precedes doctrine about the individual sacraments, it does not follow as a subsequent secondary generalization; for only on the basis of the doctrine about the Church, the fundamental sacrament, can the sacramentality of several sacraments be recognized at all.

4. Episcopate and Primacy*

The Church which is the fundamental sacrament of Christ's grace is the visible, socially organized Church. This means that it is the hierarchical Church. The pope has, by divine right, full, immediate, and ordinary episcopal primacy of jurisdiction over the whole Church, including her bishops.

Nevertheless, the bishops are not just functionaries of the pope. The episcopal college exists in the Church by divine right and the pope cannot usurp its rightful jurisdiction.

The contemporary Church has need of deeper theological reflection on the relationship between the Roman Pontiff and the episcopal college. Pastoral theologians should also concern themselves with the role of the individual bishop within his own diocese. The necessary unity of the Church under the Roman Pontiff should not be so rigid that it impedes healthy pastoral initiative by local bishops or discourages the pastoral diversity which is required in a world whose nations have become aware of their legitimate cultural diversity.

According to defined Catholic doctrine, the pope personally possesses a full, immediate, ordinary and general episcopal primacy of jurisdiction

*From "The Episcopate and the Primacy" (*Quaestiones Disputatae* 4) in *Inquiries*, pp. 330-31, 336-39, 378-79. © 1962 by Herder KG.

over the whole Church and over her every part and member, including the bishops. On the other hand it is definitive Catholic teaching (though not as yet defined in terms of such conscious clarity) that the episcopate exists of divine right in such a way that the pope, for all his jurisdictional primacy, cannot abolish it, that the bishops are not to be considered mere functionaries or representatives of the Roman Pontiff, that they have, rather, their own proper power to tend their flocks, not in the name of the pope, but in Christ's name and their own, and are therefore successors of the apostles by divine disposition. "The episcopate exists in virtue of the same divine institution on which the papacy rests; it too has its rights and duties, which the pope has neither the right nor the power to change. It is therefore a complete misunderstanding . . . to suppose . . . that the bishops are only instruments of the pope, officials of his without personal responsibility." "According to the constant teaching of the Catholic Church, as expressly declared also by the Vatican Council, the bishops are not mere instruments of the pope, not papal officials without responsibility of their own, but established by the Holy Spirit and taking the place of the apostles, as true shepherds they tend and rule the flocks entrusted to them . . ." Thus the statement of the German episcopate of 1875, which enjoyed the express and solemn approbation of Pius IX.

But this only raises in more urgent fashion the problem of the content of this episcopal power of jurisdiction which belongs to the whole episcopate by divine right and which the pope cannot retain for himself. No doubt it must be possible to say more about this content than theological textbooks and canon law expressly state. Much (not all!) that bishops do as a matter of course and that is also permitted by the Holy See as a matter of course is not mere *de facto* custom, something the pope could as well withdraw from the bishops, or has to give them merely because an official must have certain permanent powers if he is not to be useless, but is *iuris divini,* even when not explicitly so conceived. This is not to say (as has already been emphasized above) that concrete, definitely fixed individual rights of an *individual* bishop as an individual must be *iuris divini* in such a way that the pope could not deprive the bishop of one of these particular rights. Such a claim would be of no practical use and would really be senseless, because it could only fortify, and provide some content for, the episcopal jurisdiction if the bishop were declared legally irremovable. But since this is impossible, any attempt to define the content of the *ius divinum* in the bishops' jurisdiction by listing inalienable particular rights is futile from the start.

Nevertheless this is not to say that, apart from its general origin, the *ius divinum* of the bishop is impossible to define. Though the attempt to fix the material limits of the rights of the papacy and the episcopate is not feasible for the reasons indicated above, and though we cannot ascertain a residue of particular episcopal jurisdictional rights which escape papal supremacy, nevertheless the inalienable episcopal *ius divinum* need not be thought void of any real content.

THE IUS DIVINUM *OF THE WHOLE EPISCOPATE IS THE MATERIAL AND COGNITIVE GROUND OF THE* IUS DIVINUM *OF INDIVIDUAL BISHOPS*

Its exact definition must proceed on the one hand from the nature of the universal Church, and on the other from the nature of the episcopate as a college (the successor of the apostolic college, which as a college takes precedence over the individual apostles and their powers, and is not merely the sum of the individual apostles and their powers).

The first point of departure is obvious: the nature of the Church is always the permanent foundation of the nature of her governmental powers, even though we cannot deduce, from any abstract concept of the nature of the Church alone, her exact juridical structure, which is at least in part an additional positive institution of Christ, so that an exact concept of the Church entails some knowledge of her juridical constitution, of the authorities that govern her, and of their rights and duties. Yet recourse to the theological nature of the Church which underlies her juridical structure is always advisable, even necessary, if one is seeking an accurate notion of her organs of government.

But the second approach mentioned above is the decisive one in our case. The answer to the problem of the *ius divinum* of the individual bishop lies in the *ius divinum* of the universal episcopate. To understand our point, we must remember that the papal power over the individual bishop, even to the point of deposing him, cannot and may not, by a simple extension, be exercised over the universal episcopate; that, therefore, the pope's rights over the universal episcopate are not the mere sum of his rights over the individual bishops. Therefore the papal rights over the individual bishop must be exercised in such a way that the divine right of the universal episcopate as a college is not, in effect, abolished or its nature threatened. The fact that a particular limitation of a bishop's episcopal rights by the pope happens to be canonically and dogmatically legitimate in a particular case, does not at all imply that the same limitation can by divine right be imposed on the rights of the universal episcopate. Because the universal episcopate, as the apostolic college living on in history, has *qua* college inalienable rights and duties *iuris divini,* the pope is obliged to take care, lest some of his measures, legitimate when imposed on an individual bishop, infringe the original right of the universal episcopate—for example, if the sum total of such measures taken against many bishops should make the rights (and duties) of the universal episcopate illusory in practice, or reduce them to a dimension where they might survive in practice, but without any clear juridical status.

Even if it cannot be said that the pope has only those rights over individual bishops which he has over the universal episcopate as such, neither can one conversely conclude from the papal right over the individual bishop to the existence of that same right over the bishops as a whole. A simple example, obvious and familiar: the pope could remove a particular bishop and install an apostolic vicar or administrator, that is, a papal official, in his place. Nobody can conclude from this that he could do this with all the bishops at one time. This would amount to abolishing the episcopate itself, which the pope cannot do. One can even go so far as to say that the full participation of a bishop in the rights and duties of the universal episcopate is *de iure* to be presumed, so that the contrary, in the case of a particular bishop or a particular measure, must be proved, even though the burden of proof and the actual proof is left to the conscience of the pope, against whom the individual bishop has no legal recourse. Therefore, *iuris divini,* the rights of the universal episcopate can be taken from an individual bishop only to the extent which the concrete circumstances show to be lawful and equitable.

But with this the problem is not solved, only transferred. The problem of the content of any single bishop's divinely given jurisdictional power becomes the problem of the jurisdiction of the episcopate as a whole. And, according to the history of the Church, which, on the whole, may be taken as a guide to what is legitimate, the divine right of the episcopate is not (materially, at least) bound to any absolutely fixed form as its realization in the concrete. Then again, the episcopate is obviously the subject of these divine rights only insofar as it is unified in the bishop of Rome, that is, it is not really a subject of rights as a college *vis-à-vis* the pope, but in unity with him.

But subject to these presuppositions and qualifications, the question can and must be put whether and how the content of the episcopate's rights *iuris divini* can be more precisely defined. The problem is a difficult one, one that theology to date can hardly claim to have properly posed, much less adequately answered.

The Church today contains peoples, territories, civilizations, the differences of which are much greater, even within the life of the Church, than has ever been the case before in the Church. That these differences have so far remained para-canonical and para-liturgical, and can therefore escape the notice of the naïve and superficial observer, does not change the fact. The only difference in earlier times was between a Christianity in a single highly civilized area, and a Christianity among nations with less developed civilizations. Today for the first time a Christianity is needed for areas historically different but culturally equal. We can today no longer afford to identify Christianity with European and North American

Christianity. This same pluralism is growing relentlessly even within the old Western world, for despite our unified civilization the underlying differences are awakening to clearer consciousness and more deliberate self-assertion.

The stagnation of the Asian missions among the Far Eastern civilizations, and in awakening Africa, shows (if differently in each case) that a non-Western Christianity must be developed there, or the Gospel will not advance, because its success until now (whether it wished or no) has been in large part due to the preponderance of Western civilization. In the past, this may indeed have been an instrument of supernatural providence through which the force of the Gospel could be proclaimed, but today it is a means of declining efficacy. In this situation very much will depend on whether the Church unhesitatingly and confidently opens herself to such a pluralism, or whether, out of a cautious conservatism, she decides that unity must be maintained through the maximum possible uniformity. She can accept such a pluralism with perfect equanimity. She has systematically developed the principle of unity in her law and dogma for one hundred years past, she possesses in the Holy Ghost the most potent principle of unity, and she has in the history of the early Church and in the Uniate Churches of the Middle East a ready example in her own history to show that the unity of the Church is compatible with the pluralism of the churches. An episcopate of divine right should be the embodiment and guarantor of such a pluralism, which will be the more necessary in the future.

5. The Charismatic Element in the Church*

The hierarchy has an indispensable role to play in the Church. Her founder has given legitimate authority to the pastors of his community. Nevertheless the Church's teaching and sanctifying mission has not been entrusted exclusively to her officeholders and the Church must be extremely sensitive to the personal intimations of God's will and to the pastoral inspirations which have been given to charismatic individual Christians. The Church's leaders must not endeavor to manage everything in the Church bureaucratically "from the top down." They must rather encourage apostolic initiative "from the bottom up" on the part of charismatic individuals and charismatic pastors. The Church's ideal is the harmonious cooperation of her hierarchical and her charismatic element. It should never be the absorption or the elimination of one element by the other.

*From *The Dynamic Element in the Church*, pp. 50-53.
© 1964 by Herder and Herder, Inc.

Pius XII wrote in the encyclical *Mystici corporis:* "But it must not be supposed that this co-ordinated, or organic, structure of the Body of the Church is confined exclusively to the grades of the hierarchy, or—as a contrary opinion holds—that it consists only of 'charismatics', or persons endowed with miraculous powers; though these, be it said, will never be lacking in the Church. . . . But when the Fathers of the Church mention the ministries of this Body, its grades, professions, states, orders and offices, they rightly have in mind not only persons in sacred orders, but also all those who have embraced the evangelic counsels and lead either an active life among men, or a hidden life in the cloister, or else contrive to combine the two, according to the institution to which they belong; also those who, though living in the world, actively devote themselves to spiritual or corporal works of mercy; and also those who are joined in chaste wedlock. Indeed, it is to be observed, especially in present circumstances, that fathers and mothers and godparents, and particularly those among the laity who co-operate with the ecclesiastical hierarchy in spreading the kingdom of the divine Redeemer, hold an honoured place in the Christian society, and that they too are able, with the inspiration and help of God, to attain the highest degree of sanctity, which, as Jesus Christ has promised, will never be wanting in the Church. . . ." Christ "established that authority, determined by appropriate precepts, rights and duties, as the primary law of the whole Church. But our divine Saviour himself also governs directly the society which He founded; for He reigns in the minds and hearts of men, bending and constraining even rebellious wills to His decree. . . . And by this interior government He, 'the shepherd and bishop of our souls', not only cares for each individual but also watches over the whole Church: enlightening and fortifying her rulers so that they may faithfully and fruitfully discharge their functions; and (especially in circumstances of greater difficulty) raising up in the bosom of Mother Church men and women of outstanding sanctity to give example to other Christians and so promote the increase of His mystical Body." (*A.A.S.* XXXV [1943], 200ff.; *C.T.S.* translation, *The Mystical Body of Jesus Christ* [London, 1948], pp. 13-14; 23-24).

If we reflect attentively on this teaching, it is possible for us to say that there are persons in the Church endowed with the charismatic gifts of the Spirit outside the sacred ministry. They are not merely recipients of orders from the hierarchy; they may be the persons through whom Christ "directly" guides his Church. Obviously office is not thereby abolished. The Lord, of course, guides and rules his Church, the same encyclical tells us, through the medium of the sacred ministry. Holders of office themselves can receive, in addition to the authority of their charge and its proper administration under the protection of the Spirit, direct impulsions of that kind from the Church's Lord. But if Christ directly operates in his Church apart from the hierarchy, if he rules and guides the Church through charismata that are not linked to office and in this sense are extraordinary, and if, nevertheless, there is a valid and irrevocable official ministry in the Church, then harmony between the two "structures" of the Church, the institutional and the charismatic, can only be guaranteed by the one Lord of both, and by him alone, that is to say, charismatically.

Now it is no doubt a rule, a normative principle and a law for the spiritual gifts themselves, that they should operate in an "orderly" way, that they are not permitted to depart from the order prescribed by authority. As a consequence it is possible to use as a criterion of their authentic spiritual origin the fact whether or not they do this. Yet this formal rule alone would not of itself guarantee the actual existence of harmony. For though official authority might be sufficiently protected by the rule from merely apparent spiritual gifts, the charismata also need to be protected from the authorities. Provision has to be made that bureaucratic routine, turning means into ends in themselves, rule for the sake of rule and not for the sake of service, the dead wood of tradition, proud and anxious barricades thrown up against new tasks and requirements, and other such dangers, do not extinguish the Spirit.

No really effective remedy against them is ensured by the formal principle that official authority must not extinguish the Spirit, any more than it is merely by the punishment that in the long run always falls on authority if it trusts more to the letter than to the Spirit. The effective guarantee is not given by official authority and its principles alone. Even though the authorities can only sin against the spiritual gifts by transgressing the very principles of their own authority, it is not thereby excluded that those in office might not discern their own principles clearly enough in the matter, that they might do prejudice to them and be in danger of excluding the charismatic element from the Church as a nuisance. Safeguard that is effective and certain to be effective is only to be looked for from the Lord of both. He is the transcendent source of both, and he himself is the support that he promised to his Church always and victoriously, consequently he can ensure the unity of the two elements. Their unity cannot itself be institutionally organized, it is itself charismatic, though this charisma is promised to the Church as one that will endure till the end. It will have to be considered presently what practical conclusions follow from this fundamental idea, which is based on the papal teaching about spiritual gifts and immediate relationship to Christ on one hand, and the institutional component of the Church on the other.

We must add another remark here concerning the texts quoted above. Spiritual gifts need not necessarily and in every case occur in a miraculously extraordinary form. Every genuinely Christian life serves the Body of Christ, even if it is lived in an "inconspicuous" (rather than "unimportant") place in the Church. It is the charismatic features of the Church as a whole which must in addition be of a striking character. For the Church, of course, is to be by her inexhaustible plenitude of holiness a sign set on high among the nations, and herself the proof of her divine origin and mission, as the First Vatican Council taught (Denzinger, *Enchiridion Symbolorum,* No. 1794). St. Paul too assumes the same (for example in Galatians 3:2), for by the charismata the pagan is to recognize and acknowledge in adoration that "God is among you indeed". But that does not mean that because the Church's charismatic character functions as a mark of credibility, the spiritual gifts in her individual members must necessarily be something extraordinary.

6. The Parochial Principle*

The Church of Christ has been a "local Church" from its beginnings. It has been a community of local dioceses under their local ordinaries who are not just functionaries of the pope. For centuries the real local Church for the ordinary Christian has been his parish. It is here that the Eucharist is celebrated and the gospel preached by his local pastor and the parochial clergy. Therefore one of the basic principles of a solid pastoral theology. has been and remains the parochial principle. The people of God should be divided into local units so that their spiritual needs can be taken care of by their local pastor and his assistants.

The parochial principle is a valid one. It should be honored and never downgraded. Nevertheless, it is not and never has been the exclusive principle of the Church's pastoral theology. More than ever today the social, economic, and cultural differences between men and the need for a more individual type of pastoral care require that in a sound pastoral theology the parochial principle be balanced by several other pastoral principles.

The parish (which in the early Church coincided practically with the diocese) is in a sense the diocese in miniature. The parish in itself exists indeed only in virtue of human law and hence has not basically the same irrevocable necessity as the diocese. Thus the bishop can to a great extent (and within the framework of canon law) make use also of other instruments besides the parish (and parish priest) in the fulfilment of his pastoral duty. Nevertheless, the parochial structure is a consistent development and practical application of the principle of the territorial diocese ruled by the bishop as pastor of the whole flock. The parish, too, can in this sense claim to be a realization of the divinely-wise and ever-valid principle which the Founder of the Church has established within her for

*From *Theological Investigations,* vol. II, pp. 290-91, 306-07.

© 1963 by Darton, Longman & Todd Ltd.

all time, viz. that she should convert men into Christians, men who have a home and are a people. When principles of pastoral organization begin to vie with one another, it remains an indisputable fact that the parochial principle can claim to be the oldest and most venerable principle applied by the Church on the authority of Christ; one man is in charge of the whole pastoral work done among a group of people who are collected together under him because they have their home on the same soil. If this principle has eternal validity for the over-all structure of the Church (and hence also permanent meaning and utility), it cannot be absolutely false for the smaller structures of the Church.

Let us pass on now to the pastoral argument for the parochial principle. The pastoral effort requires a living centre on account of the unavoidable and immense variety of its activities, means and forms and of individuals with whom it is concerned. From this centre everything derives its proper place, right measure and correspondingly greater or lesser importance, and this centre is a safeguard both against a kind of planless hypertrophy and against an atrophy of particular pastoral activities. This living centre can only be the Altar, even though genuine Christian life and ecclesiastico-sacramental life do not by any means coincide, i.e. even though Christian Priesthood and Liturgy are not the same thing and genuine Christianity itself must come to grips with the whole of reality (and hence also with 'profane' reality), making it subject to its law. Yet it remains true that wherever pastoral care exercised in federations, associations, organizations, etc., more or less cuts itself loose from the central concern of all Christianity which man, as a member of the holy people of God, adores through the Sacrifice of our Lord and—truly and historically—encounters in the Sacrament of the God of grace and eternal life, this 'care of souls' becomes a mere empty business, an exclusive interest in local club life, a rationalistic urge to reform the world and an officious organization-fever, by which the members seek their own advantage and not God. The Altar, however, stands first and foremost in the parish church. For the parish church is the representative of the diocese and the primary place for the care of souls according to canon law (if only for the reason that the parish priest has the right and duty of the care of souls of *all* Christians living in his territory). Hence, if every pastoral work finds its central point in the Altar of Christ, then the life of the parish, issuing from the altar of the parish church, is and remains *the* basic form of the care of souls. In this way we also have a guarantee that individual pastoral endeavours preserve their mutual relations and proper proportion, by the very fact that in the parish they reach man under the very respect which even by nature is one of the most many-sided and yet most uniform, viz. man as member of a natural, spatial community. Such an organization has also fundamentally the greatest stability in times of crisis. The most primitive structure is also the most indestructible. The bond uniting kith and kin, as realized in the natural community, belongs to the most primitive forms of human society. And the parish builds on the foundations of the natural community. Consequently, taking things as a whole, the parish, and hence also its pastoral function, has (after the family) the greatest social, spiritual and thus also pastoral resistance of all human associations, both against internal tendencies to dissolution and against external influences.

Looking back over the reasons against the exclusive validity of the parochial principle, the *conclusions* so far reached may be easily formulated. The parochial principle, in its fundamental reasoning, is the 'territorial principle', since the objectively decisive reason for it lies in the fact that man becomes the object of the care of souls in a suitable, and indeed unavoidable, manner precisely in so far as he has a 'home' (*Heimat*), a *'place-where-he-is-quartered'* (*Stand-ort*). The reasons which militate against the exclusive validity of the parochial principle, both on the part of the object and on the part of the minister of the care of souls, are all based on the fact that man has his 'station' (*Stand*) in life (taking the word here in its widest sense as referring to the differences in occupation, intellectual differences, differences in sex, age, culture), which owing to present-day sociological conditions no longer corresponds completely in practice with the narrow confines of the immediate locality where he lives. Now, in so far as man's social differences in this widest sense furnish a basis for the possibility and duty of an extra-parochial care of souls exercised in view of these differences, we may speak of the application of a 'social-differential principle' (*Standesprinzip*) to the care of souls. Our third reason against the exclusive validity of the parochial principle for the pastoral ministry was based on the fundamental right of the individual in the Church to form 'free-groups'. In so far as such extra-parochial 'free-groups' give grounds for the possibility and (in certain circumstances) duty of an extra-parochial pastoral care, we may speak of a 'free-group principle'. And so we may formulate the results of our inquiry so far by stating that the parochial principle is not the only legitimate principle for present-day pastoral practice. Side by side with it, and possessing their own validity, there are the *'social-differential principle'* and the *'free-group principle'*—even if social differences (in the meaning used here) and free-groups do not take the form of mere expressions of the individual parish. The 'federation principle' implied several times during our discussion of the parochial principle is, in the terminology adopted here, a combination of the social-differential and free-group principles. For a 'federation' (*Bund*) (prescinding from its *supra*-diocesan organization) is a 'free-group' whose organizational principle is to be found in the 'social-differential' (i.e. occupational and similar differences). To this extent the 'federation principle' is also justified by our reflections.

7. Freedom in the Church*

If public opinion and a healthy diversity of viewpoints are to be allowed the freedom of expression which they must have in order to allow God's will to manifest itself in the Christian community, clerical totalitarianism must disappear. Freedom of speech and action must be assured by a wider application of the principle of subsidiarity. Only in this way will her wide variety of apostles and scholars be able to make their proper contribution to the life and teaching of the Church.

Even within her life of religion, the Church must combat the tendency among her own members of taking refuge in the mass and taking flight into a merely collective religious life, as is manifested by too great a dependence on others, by the fact of shying away from personal responsibility or waiting for ecclesiastical directives from above in the wrong circumstances, or by the opinion that everything is morally as it should be merely by the fact that the Church has not issued an explicit and detailed verdict, and by the dwindling of a *personal* private life of piety both of the individual and in families, in spite of their participation in the official liturgy, etc.

If, in conclusion, we are to give some indication of certain concrete instances where room should be left for freedom *inside* the Church particularly at the present time, then the following must be said:

(a) Even within the Church there should be room and toleration for the expression of opinion, i.e. Public Opinion. Pius XII himself pointed this out and stated that the absence of such public opinion in the Church would be a fault for which both the pastors and the flock would have to take the blame. The following are the Holy Father's actual words (*Osservatore Romano*, 18th February 1950):

> Public opinion is the natural portion of every normal society composed of human beings. . . . Whenever there is no manifest expression of public opinion at all, and above all whenever one must admit that public opinion does not at all exist, this lack must be regarded as a fault, a weakness and a disease in the life of that society. . . . In conclusion, We wish to add a few words about public opinion within the pale of the Church (in respect of those matters, of course, which are left to free discussion). Only those will be surprised at this who do not know the Catholic Church, or at least know her only badly. For, after all, she too is a living body, and there would be something lacking in her life if there were no public opinion in the Church—a lack for which the pastors as well as the faithful would be to blame. . . .

*From *Theological Investigations*, vol. II, pp. 106-07.
© 1963 by Darton, Longman & Todd Ltd.

(b) There must be room in theology for research, for different schools and directions of thought, for experiments and progress, within the framework of actual dogmas and any other really obligatory doctrines.

(c) There is, if we may express our meaning in so profane a manner, a lawful 'freedom of association' for Christians within the ecclesiastical sphere. Even in this sphere is it a valid rule that higher forms of organization must not be allowed to suppress, in favour of a kind of 'State Socialism' which organizes things in a bureaucratic manner from above, the spontaneous individual life of fellowships which grow up within the Church from below. Such methods would be more convenient and would make it easier to survey everything, but they would not be more successful in the long run and would, in fact, mean the death of any true Church life. An exaggerated principle of parochial and natural social groupings offends against the rightful freedom of the Christian in his religious life.

(d) Side by side with the official function which is transmitted in a juridical manner, there is and must also be the charismatic and the prophetic in the Church which cannot be officially organized right from the start but must, in all patience and humility, be given sufficient room for growth, even though its bearers are sometimes rather 'inconvenient'. It is written: 'Do not extinguish the Spirit.'

8. The Church of Sinners*

Since the Church is Christ's community of redemption, Christians have been ready enough to acknowledge the sinfulness of the imperfect men who are her members. They have been less ready to accept the equally important truth that the Church herself is sinful. Sin and sanctity coexist dialectically in the Church herself, not just in her individual members. The Church's sinfulness manifests itself, for example, in the untimely and inappropriate enactments of her leaders and in the shortsighted and defective teaching of her theologians. For both have their root in the bias, impatience, or lethargy of sinful human nature. Still the Church remains always the holy Church. She is both the home of saints and the source of their supernatural sanctity. Sound spirituality is always mindful of the coexistence of sinfulness and sanctity within the Church.

The Church of God and of his Christ is a Church of sinners. What is meant by this will be explained in two groups of ideas: sinners in the Church, and the sinful Church.

*From *Theological Investigations*, vol. VI, pp. 256, 258-63, 267.
© 1969 and 1974 by Darton, Longman & Todd Ltd.

1. It is an article of faith that *sinners are members of the Church*. Even sinners who are destined to be lost can truly and really belong to the Church. This is a truth of our faith which the Church has constantly taught, in patristic times against Montanism, Novatianism and Donatism, in the Middle Ages against the Albigenses, against the Fraticelli, against Wyclif and Hus, and in modern times against the Reformers, against Jansenism and the Synod of Pistoia. The proposition that sinners, those deprived of grace or those foreknown by God as destined to be lost, are not members of the Church is a formal heresy which has been definitively condemned by the Church.

It is true that this 'belonging of the sinner to the Church' must be viewed from another side as well, that is, it must be negatively delimited, for the sinner does not belong to the Church in the same full sense as the justified person.

The Church has, to a certain extent, a sacramental structure. But in a sacrament we must distinguish between the sacramental sign as such (and the conditions for its 'validity') on the one hand, and the sacramental sign in so far as it is really the cause of sacramental grace and filled with it, on the other. The two concepts must be kept carefully distinct; for it is possible to have in certain circumstances a 'valid sacrament' which in point of fact does not cause any grace in the recipient of the sacrament. Now in a certain sense the Church is the basic sacrament (*Ursakrament*); hence in her case we must make a distinction between her visible appearance as a body in so far as this is a sign of grace, and this visible appearance in so far as it is a reality filled with grace, and accordingly also between a (merely) 'valid' and a 'fruitful' membership of the Church. The sinner has the first kind of membership of the Church, but not the second. But by making this distinction the continuing membership of the sinner in the Church is not being reduced to a harmless formality of an external, juridical kind. It is true that the sinner still belongs to the visible appearance of the Church, but his visible membership of the Church has ceased to be the efficacious sign of his invisible membership of the Church as a living, holy community. In a certain sense the sinner has turned this sign into a lie (rather like someone who receives a sacrament validly but unworthily); for he has robbed his continuing membership in the Church of all the meaning and effect to which it is by its entire nature ordered: the inner, living union of men with God and with each other in the Holy Spirit.

2. With this we come to establishing the express point which this doctrine primarily enunciates in all its clearness: *the Church is sinful*. After what we have just said it is already impossible to maintain any longer as consistent with the faith that there are admittedly sinners 'in' the Church as an external confessional organisation but that this fact tells us nothing about the Church herself. For we have already seen that these sinners,

according to the teaching of the Church, are real members, parts, and therefore integral pieces of the visible character of the Church herself. We must now elucidate this a little further.

In order to see our way more clearly, we must keep in mind two things. If we were merely to say, 'Certainly there are sinners in the Church, but this fact has nothing to do with the real Church', we would be assuming an idealistic concept of the Church which from a theological point of view is very questionable. 'Church' is then an idea, an ideal, an ought-to-be, something to which appeal can be made from the concrete reality, something which is meant to be reached only asymptotically, as it were, by slow approximation. That is something which we can of course always love, to which we can fearlessly commit ourselves; it is something untouchable, beyond the reach of the wretchedness of daily life. But this is not really the meaning of the theological concept of 'Church'. In this latter concept the Church is something real: it is the one and only Church which exists and in which we believe, in all cases always including the visible and juridically organised assembly of the baptised, united together in the external confession of their faith and in their obedience to the Roman pope. And it is precisely of this Church that it is impossible to say that she has nothing to do with the sins of her members. Obviously she does not approve of sin; obviously there will always be within her ranks men (and perhaps many men) whom we must call, in some real sense of the word which we need not discuss further here, holy men. But if she is something real, and if her members are sinners and as sinners remain members, then she herself is sinful. Then the sins of her children are a blot and a blemish on the holy mystical Body of Christ itself. The Church is a sinful Church: this is a truth of faith, not an elementary fact of experience. And it is a shattering truth.

Furthermore, we must consider a second fact. If what we said is true, then it is also self-evident that the official representatives of the Church, those men whom a superficial theological consciousness especially among the Catholic laity likes to regard exclusively as 'the' Church (as though the laity, too, were not the 'Church', as though they represented merely the object of the Church's ministration, an error emphatically opposed in Pius XII's encyclical on the Church), that those men too can be sinners, and in fact have been and are in a very noticeable way. But then it is again even clearer that the concrete Church is sinful (and once again, only in the concrete is she the 'Church'). For it is surely beyond dispute that the sins in question do not occur merely in a realm of the 'private life' of these ecclesiastics, but may also influence very substantially their concrete mode of action as official representatives of the Church. When the Church acts, gives a lead, makes decisions (or fails to make decisions when they ought to be made), when she proclaims her message, and when she is obliged to proclaim it in accordance with the times and historical situations, then this activity of the Church is not carried out by some abstract principle and not by the Holy Spirit alone, but rather this whole activity of the Church is at the same time the activity of concrete men. And since they can in fact commit sin, since they can be culpably narrow, culpably egoistic, self-satisfied, obstinate, sensual or indolent, this sinful attitude of theirs will naturally affect also those actions which they initiate precisely *as* ecclesiastics and in the name of the Church as acts of the concrete Church. There exists no dogma according to which the assistance of the Holy Spirit which always remains with the Church would limit the effect of the sinfulness of the men who administer the Church to their purely private lives and not permit it to have any influence on those events which must be characterised as unmistakably acts of the Church, if the concept of the Church is not to evaporate into the abstract ideal of an invisible Church. It is true that the Christian's conscience can, if he thinks himself capable of attempting it, discover such motivations; he can also, indeed he *must,* refuse obedience in a case where he is commanded what is sinful, but he cannot withdraw himself from obedience to the Church as long as he himself is not commanded to do anything sinful (even though he may think that the command springs at least partially from sinful narrowness, obstinacy and love of power), and above all—and this is here the only point—he cannot dispute the fact that such actions of ecclesiastics are actions of the Church. This means it must be conceded that the Church can be sinful in her actions. It goes without saying that this happens in opposition to the impulse of the Spirit and the norms and laws always proclaimed by the Church. But this is surely what is so great about this *faith* in the sinful Church, that she can really do all these things and yet (unlike all human organisations falling away from their original ideals) remain the bride of Christ and the vessel of the Holy Spirit, the only means of grace, from which no one can separate himself by appealing to her own ideal, accusing her of no longer being what she 'once' was (she never was it), or what she ought and claims to be.

Of course we hasten to add that it is not as though the Church were the pure paradox of a union of visible sin and invisible grace. She is holy because she is constantly in a vital contact with Christ the source of all holiness; she is holy, because her whole history with all its ups and downs is constantly pressing forward in the power of her living source, the Holy Spirit, towards that ultimate day to which all her truth, her law and her sacraments are ordered, towards that day when God himself will appear unveiled in his world. She is and remains infallible whenever she makes a solemn dogmatic decision under precise conditions which we need not here further determine. Her sacraments are independent of the worthiness of their ministers, they have an objective validity and efficacy, they are holy and make holy. She never falls victim to the temptation of accommodating to the weakness and mediocrity of men the truth and the norms which her very human preachers proclaim. (How far from self-evident is this miracle of the power and the grace of her holy Spirit; yet it is ever renewed through the centuries!) At all times in a sinful world she has championed the holiness of God and of his Christ, and if we had really grasped how easily man tends to regulate his principles according to his deeds, we would recognise in the eternal 'contradiction' between the holy preaching and the all-too-human life of the preacher of the Church's gospel not so much a stumbling-block as a demonstration of the effectiveness of God's Spirit in a holy Church. The Church is also really so holy in so many of her members, and this holiness can be ascertained even empirically, that for the man of good will, enlightened by the grace of faith, even her outward appearance bears all the marks of a constant motive for faith and an irrefutable witness to her divine commission. In a way which is not at all self-evident but extraordinary, she has really been in all ages the eternally fruitful mother of saints, the holy Church, the bride of Christ, whose appearance even now holds out for the man of faith the promise that she will one day be the bride able to enter without spot or wrinkle the wedding feast of the lamb—on that day when the light of eternal life will reveal what in reality she *is* even now under the appearance of the woman of sin.

But all this does not give the Church or us her children the right to put a gulf of arrogance and superiority between her and the sin which is not only in the world but also in the Church and through which she herself is really sinful, and this in a way in which she alone can be sinful (even where she is much better than those who are outside); for she alone can distort by her sin the eternal visible presence of Christ in the world which she is and so wrap a shroud about him—and do this in the face of men who must seek him as a matter of life and death!

If then holiness *and* sin co-exist in the 'image' presented by the Church (and the Church is essentially 'image', a sign making historically accessible the grace of God in the world), this is of course not to say that sin and holiness in the Church have the same relationship to the hidden essential purpose of the Church and therefore belong to her in the same way. The holiness made tangible in her history is an expression of what she is and will remain infallibly and indestructibly until the end of time: the presence in the world of God and of his grace. The Church is always something more than an association, more than a 'juridical Church' and confessional organisation, because the Holy Spirit has indissolubly united himself to her. And this Holy Spirit of God, in himself hidden, recreates over and over again in the palpable holiness of the Church a visible manifestation of his continuing presence capable of convincing the world. In this holiness—not in sin—are we given 'phenotypically' the inner glory which constitutes the permanent heritage out of which her whole character is fashioned. By contrast with all other historical structures, including the 'Church' of the Old Testament, this bodily manifestation of the Church cannot be so distorted by sin that the life-giving Spirit would abandon her or be unable any longer to be historically manifested in her. For the power of death will not overcome her (cf. Mt 16:18).

But what is to be our attitude if we clearly catch sight of sin in the face of our holy Mother the Church, if in the sacred precincts of the House of God we encounter failure, corruption, the feathering of nests, the lust for power, gossiping, under-the-counter dealing or narrow-mindedness? We should see these things as men fully conscious from our own experience of being ourselves sinners. When we see the sins of others it is so easy for us to forget that we are all-too-prone to pray, 'Lord, I thank you that I am not as one of these sinners here, like these self-righteous Pharisees in the Lord's House', in other words, that even in the pose of the humble Publican we can be . . . Pharisees. If sin in the Church serves first of all to call to mind our own sinfulness, if it shocks us into remembering that *our* sins are the sins of the *Church*—whether we are priests or laymen, powerful or lowly people in the kingdom of God—that we all contribute our share to the Church's penury and want, and that this is the case even though our sins may not figure in any chronicle of the Church's scandals, then we have taken up the proper, that is the Christian, position to see the sins of the Church in their true light. Perhaps we will even then remonstrate, complain, struggle and attempt to better things, in so far as it lies within our power or falls to our duty; but first we will weep over our own sins by means of which we ourselves are crucifying the Son of God in his Church and obscuring the light of the gospel for the world.

9. The Diaspora Church*

The Church of the future will be a diaspora community. Christians will be scattered in small groups through a vast secular society which will afford them no sociological support for their belief. Unless their diaspora community is to fall back upon itself and become a ghetto, the Christians of the future will have to cultivate a deep personal commitment to their faith and an outgoing attitude toward their world. Thus personal initiative will be supremely important in the diaspora Church. Individual responsibility will be cultivated in vital parish communities and in the small informal groups which God inspires to give witness to their faith of their own accord. The Church of the future must point its pastoral practice toward the development of personal conviction in her members and the exercise of individual apostolic action by the Christians who are surrounded by a secular culture.

*From *Theological Investigations*, vol. VII, pp. 89-90, 92-95, 97-98.
© 1971 by Darton, Longman & Todd Ltd.

The Christian recognises the diaspora in which he has to live today, wherever he may be, as the setting of his Christian life as something in which an ultimately positive significance is to be found. When I use the term 'diaspora' I am using it in the biblical sense in which it is currently employed, not in the sense ascribed to it until recently, in which it designated the situation of a Catholic minority in the midst of a majority of Protestants. This nineteenth-century idea may still have a certain validity in the field of pastoral care, and still point to certain needs which have to be fulfilled. But this meaning is more and more receding into the background, and the term is being applied more and more to a fresh phenomenon, which we now have to examine. This is the society which is based on a multiplicity of ideologies: the society which, taken as a whole, and from the point of view of its constitution, its special patterns and its culture, bears the stamp of other influences besides the purely Christian one. In this society Christians, whether Catholic or Protestant, live, provided they are true Christians, in common as brothers in the diaspora. It is the diaspora in this sense, in which non-Christian liberal humanism, militant atheism and the atrophy of religion are everywhere apparent, that is referred to when we use the term 'diaspora' here; the diaspora which all Christians have in common, in comparison with which the differences between the various Christian confessions seem not indeed unimportant, but historically speaking secondary. This diaspora must be seen by the Christian of today as the divinely ordained 'situation' of his own Christianity. It is the setting in which his free and personal act of faith is posited, a faith which cannot be overthrown in favour of any social ethic, the situation of free decision, of personal responsibility, of personal avowal of one's faith. And all this gives a fresh application to the old adage that Christians are not born but made. This is the situation which had to arise as a necessity of saving history. Christians know that on the one hand, if their own theological expectations of the future are to be fulfilled, they will always exist as the creed that is under attack, and on the other that when all kinds of far from homogeneous cultures are permitted to exist each in its own sphere as parts of one and the same world history, an attack on any one of them will only come from without, from those who do not belong to that particular culture. We Christians accept this situation. Certainly, in common with all other citizens we want to have the right to co-operate in the sphere of public life. Certainly we also demand that in cases in which, in spite of all variations within the community, the unified political system makes it quite unavoidable for all to have one and the same form, the Christian history of our people and the fact that the great majority of the people want to be Christians even now shall be respected. We demand in the name of freedom and tolerance that he who, in effect, gives the casting vote shall not be the one who is most radical in denying Christianity. But we Christians have no interest in maintaining

Christian façades behind which no true Christianity is alive, and which serve only to compromise and to discredit such true Christianity.

In the situation of a complex society made up of heterogeneous elements and of a diaspora extending through the whole of that society, the Church necessarily changes from a Church of regional and national communities to a Church of believers. What we mean by this is that the members of a Christian community constitute this community not solely in virtue of the continuity of office and the stability of the institutions governing the relationships between those members, though these factors can have a decisive influence upon the lives of the individuals even prior to the personal decision of faith which each one takes for himself. A further factor is precisely this free personal decision of faith which each individual member has won his way to in striving to come to terms with the pluralistic environment. Without impugning the sacramental significance of baptism (including infant baptism) it can be said that for the purpose of the concrete social realities of this environment the Christian community no longer depends (or at least depends less and less) upon baptism and the ecclesiastical institutions as such, but rather on the free exercise of faith. We are, of course, living through a period of transition from the regional or national Church to the Church of believers, and the Church cannot, in her solicitude for the salvation of all, use her official institutions arbitrarily to accelerate this process of transition. At the same time she must recognise that in this situation one new member who decides to join her from his own genuine decision of faith carries more weight than three who, while belonging or seeming to belong to her, really do so only because of the weight of social tradition.

In this situation two points of importance emerge with regard to the community, and therefore with regard to the task of the individual Christian in the Church as well. On the one hand there must be a continual emergence of genuine new communities. The Church must be manifestly seen to be sustained by the faith of all not merely in her institutions and her official organisation, for this depends upon itself and regards the Christians merely as the subject of its own salvific activities. Church means people of God. Church is identical with ourselves—all of us who believe and bear witness to the world as a community of faith, of eternal hope and love, to the grace and pardon of God in Christ. If such a community is to exist and to constitute a living representative of the Church at one particular place, then the bond of brotherhood between all the members of the community must transcend all differences of individual functions in the community and all distinctions between those who hold official positions in it and those who do not, necessary though such distinctions may be. This bond of brotherhood must overcome and endure through all such distinctions. It must be possible for the established authorities and the ordinary Christians to communicate with one another.

All must feel personally responsible and be ready to give their active participation, their hearts and, where necessary, their material resources too in order to ensure the vitality of the community. We must come to know each other and cohere, must play our part in maintaining the liturgy and the attitude of neighbourliness. We must not be willing merely to receive the Church, but must be ready to give; we must positively want to make contact, to get to know people, to help and to serve. The community must recognise that it, and in it the Church, is not merely an organisation based on religious techniques with the function of satisfying individual religious needs, but the community of those who, because they are united in Christ, are also united among themselves. They must be united in such a way that their communal life signifies not merely philanthropy or benevolence towards their fellow men, not merely orthodoxy or reception of the sacraments, not merely a willingness to pay the Church's dues, but truly that love which, confronted in the concrete with a 'neighbour', a 'fellow worker in the household of the faith', does not fail, but rather proves itself.

The other point which is relevant to the contemporary 'diaspora' situation, and which concerns every Christian in his task as a Christian and as a member of the community of the Church, is this: The community for which each one is responsible must not on any account become a ghetto. This is easy to say, and sounds obvious, yet it is difficult to put into practice. There is no need here to enter into a discussion as to whether the Church of believers, the future community of the believers which has already begun to exist, should be regarded as already and inevitably having the sociological status of a 'sect', (taking this term in a completely neutral sense, and as it is used in the sociology of religion), or whether it is too misleading to formulate it in this way, since it suggests one specific state of affairs. At any rate the community, both in the present and in the future, must be a community of brothers who know one another and love one another, a community that coheres, that creates the kind of environment which is so necessary of common convictions, common aims, mutual help and mutual love, an environment in which Christian faith can develop without restriction, and can exploit all the possibilities so as to become a vital force. But then the danger inevitably arises of a community of this kind becoming a sect in the bad sense, of it forming a ghetto, living as a sort of religious 'back to the land' community. This makes it all too possible to arrive at the unfortunate situation of withdrawing, from an intellectual, cultural and social point of view, into a sort of 'hole-and-corner' existence, having too little to do with normal life, feeling that one belongs to an esoteric and exclusive club, in which the members mutually confirm one another's positions. All this on the grounds that the estimate which the world, the public at large, makes of the Christians is that they represent a *quantité négligable* of harmless religious ideologists or fanatics whom one does not have to take seriously because they are incapable of coping with the realities of life. This is not how it must be. The Christian community must not be a fire that warms only itself.

For the community of the present day to reconcile both of the tasks confronting it, to be truly a family united by one faith, and at the same time an open missionary community, venturing boldly on intercourse with the world, is not easy. It is not easy to ensure that the nucleus of the community shall not be made up of individuals who have nothing else to do than to be pious. This is not to say anything against those individuals who, in the wisdom of old age and under the shadow of approaching death, are pious in a very true sense, and are so precisely because to be anything else in this situation would simply be cowardice and a flight from reality. But in its more active sections the community must be made up of those who recognise that in the celebration of the mystery of the Lord's death it is the focal point of their own lives that is made sacramentally present. They must be coming fresh from their work in the world precisely to the recognition of this fact: to find in the dead and risen Lord the ultimate outpouring of grace upon human existence in this present world, and so to go out once more from the experience of, and the act of receiving, this grace to joy and confidence in the fact that their worldly life has been redeemed in its worldliness, and while remaining worldly. But it will be necessary to construct far clearer and more convincing concrete prototype examples than hitherto of what the way of life and social patterns of such communities must be in order for the men of today to feel immediately at home in them. These examples must include preaching, confession, liturgy, work for neighbours in the parish, the charity of the community as a whole. When all this still leaves so much to be desired it becomes absolutely the first duty and task for the Christian of today to collaborate patiently and unselfishly in the construction of such communities, and not to take the lack of them as an excuse for holding himself dispensed from selfless service of this kind.

XIII

Spirituality

1. Justified and Sinner at the Same Time*

Rahner has been a prolific spiritual writer. His published works include two retreats for priests and a large number of conferences given to diverse groups of priests, religious, lay men, and lay women. The selections printed in this chapter are only a sample drawn from the vast number of his spiritual writings. Although they touch on central themes of his spirituality, they give no idea of the range, variety, and pastoral concern which has made him one of the most appreciated spiritual writers in Central Europe.

Reflecting his own Ignatian formation and drawing on his own theology of the Church, Rahner makes one of the foundations of a sound spirituality the Christian's realization that he is at once justified and a sinner —simul justus et peccator. The Christian is a sinner because of the ingrained self-love which inclines him to sin, at least venial sin, and to habitual imperfection. Yet the Christian is also justified because Christ's grace within him contends against his human sinfulness. This dynamic opposition between grace and sin in the Christian soul is very familiar to the countless Christians who have made the first and second weeks of Ignatius' Spiritual Exercises. Familiar too is Rahner's firm affirmation of man's total dependence on the grace of Christ for any progress in the spiritual life.

Thus the teaching of the permanent sinfulness of man by venial sins represents a continuous question for us as to what we really are deep down. We must always answer this question in a positive sense, placing our hope in the grace of God but we can never do this proudly and self-assuredly with a theoretical certitude of salvation.

Hence we must somehow pass beyond the distinction between mortal and venial sin, however much it is materially and objectively correct,

*From *Theological Investigations*, vol. VI, pp. 227–30.
© 1969 and 1974 by Darton, Longman & Todd Ltd.

since it cannot be carried through completely in concrete reflection on our own existence. On the one hand, we are in fact sinners who hope always to be allowed to escape again out of their sinfulness into the mercy of God. On the other hand, there is justice, and if it is really in us through God's grace, it is always also threatened and tempted and hidden from us.

The doctrine of permanent, habitual justice through infused sanctifying grace must not be understood as if this justice were a purely static possession or static quality in man. Rather, this justice is always tempted and threatened by the flesh, the world and the devil. It is always dependent again on the free decision of man. In spite of its character of a state it is suspended, as it were, on the point of the free grace of God and on the point of man's freedom. The grace of justification must always be accepted and exercised anew again, since basically it is always given anew again by God. This permanent condition of grace is always exposed to the freedom of man. The freedom of man in its turn can accept and preserve God's grace only in and through the free grace of God which God has granted and must grant to us ultimately without any merit whatsoever on our part. Since our justice is always under attack, it must always be given to us anew by God's favour and grace. It is therefore also the ultimately indisposable justice. Certainly we believe in God's salvific will . . . but this salvific will, when referred to and having become effective in each of us, is the immense and incomprehensible miracle of God's absolute favour. Man's free 'yes' to God's liberating grace is itself once more a gift of God's grace. Thus we must declare our own freedom to be once more a grace of God, a freedom which is not only a capacity for acting in a salvific way but also an act which really opens itself towards God. Of ourselves *alone* we cannot do anything at all which could make God direct his grace towards us, for our prayer for grace is based on unasked for grace which must give us both the power to pray and the act of praying itself. God must always anticipate us with his grace. Even when we think we are doing, and actually do, the most personal and original things, we experience precisely in this the earlier and more powerful deed of God in us. Of ourselves we are always sinners. Of ourselves we would always turn away from God if God's grace did not anticipate us. In view of the completely uncontrollable grace of God, of tempted justice, uncontrollable justice, we are always sinners. In this sense, it is possible to find an always true and decisively important Catholic sense in the formula 'Just and sinner at the same time'.

Even when justified, man remains a pilgrim. As such he has not only an external space of time to live through, but he is 'on the road'. In his personal history of salvation he is in search of something permanent, indestructible and final. We are on pilgrimage in the faith. We possess God only on the ground of hope. We reach out in hope for what is to come, that which is not yet given to us. Thus possession is given by hope, and by this same hope possession is also withdrawn from the free direct grasp of man. By our free personal history we must first catch up with what by God's deed which justifies us we already are. We are pilgrims in faith and hope, in ever new temptations and trials, by always accepting God's grace anew in freedom. We come from Adam and the land of darkness and look for the eternal light and bright perfection. Since the one great movement of our existence out of our lost condition towards God always still carries within itself the source from which this movement originates, we are 'just and sinners at the same time' by being sinners in the state of becoming who are still in search of perfection. This does not mean, as has already been said, that these two things, remaining always the same, confront one another in a simple static dialectic. Yet the concrete salvific activity of man is always simultaneously characterised by the starting-point from which we came, by our own lost condition which we have left behind, and also by the goal which we already possess in hope but towards which we also still reach. Here is realised the being-by-becoming of the creature. One can only recognise created man in his historical being-by-becoming, in his tension between beginning and end, by pointing to the beginning and the end. Every moment of this becoming is characterised by both, since this movement has an *a quo* and an *ad quem*. Seen as a future citizen of eternal glory, man always moves between the beginning and the end. This 'at the same time' is not a simultaneity of beginning and end, but an 'at the same time' in the tension between both.

Thus the Reformation formula of the *simul justus et peccator*— if only the factors of a Catholic 'no' to this formula remain clear—has a perfectly positive meaning for Christian existence. The Catholic Christian especially should not interpret himself as the 'good man' who basically and really, unless he steals silver spoons or poisons his neighbour, lives from the very start as a good man in grace, so that, as modern sentiment often maintains, it is really God who must justify himself before man and explain why there is too much suffering, darkness and confusion in the history of the world. The Christian must have understood that of himself he is nothing but nothingness and that left to himself he is nothing but sin. Wherever he discovers something good in himself, he must acknowledge it as a causeless free grace of God. Hence even the Catholic Christian should not spread out his justice before God. He should rather from day to day accept his justice, which in fact divinises him, as an unmerited gift of God's incalculable favour. If he wants to express this by saying that he is always and of himself a poor sinner and always someone justified by God's grace as long as he does not close himself to this grace of God by disbelief and lack of love, then he is quite at liberty to do so.

Even Catholics like St Theresa of the Child Jesus have done this. When they dared to stand before the countenance of God, they came of and for themselves with empty hands and confessed themselves like St. Augustine to be sinners. In this consciousness of their own sinfulness they discovered in themselves that miracle which means that God fills our hands with his glory and makes our heart overflow with love and faith. Anyone who confesses that of himself he is a sinner, experiences precisely in this that grace of God which really and truly makes him a saint and a just man. Then God absolves him from all sin so that he is really and in truth, to the last root of his being, a holy, just and blessed child of God.

2. Ignatian Mysticism of Joy in the World*

In the selection printed below Rahner gives an eloquent expression of his own thoroughly Ignatian spirituality. He shows how Ignatius' Trinitarian mysticism, which like all genuinely Catholic piety is a piety of the Cross, is nevertheless a mysticism of joy in the world. The celebrated Ignatian indifference is the Christian's calm surrender to the God who is in the world precisely because he transcends it. Thus Ignatian indifference becomes "seeking God in all things." True presence to the world requires as its condition of possibility the ascetic fuga saeculi *on which monastic piety placed such great importance.*

The harmonious unity between Rahner's Ignatian piety and his systematic theology is evident in this short article. It is this deep-seated unity between Rahner's spirituality and his theology which has made his two priests' retreats such profound, nuanced and theologically convincing presentations of The Spiritual Exercises.

We may now state that Ignatius was really a mystic. There can be no doubt about that. With this bare statement we must here be satisfied. Not as though we had no historical information about his mysticism: we cannot of course use as a term of comparison our knowledge of the interior lives of the great Spanish mystics Theresa and John of the Cross, nevertheless we are very well informed about the mystical grace-life of St Ignatius as well. A careful analysis of his Book of Exercises, of his autobiographical notes, of the fragments of his diary, of the information given by his trusted companions—by a Laynez, Nadal and Polanco—give us indeed a quite clear picture of his mysticism. But we do not want to tell here the story of his *pati divina*, as he himself called it. Neither its characteristics: his mysticism of Jesus and the Cross, his priestly liturgical mysticism, his mysticism of the Trinity; nor the history of his mys-

*From *Theological Investigations*, vol. III, pp. 280–81, 290–93.
© 1967 and 1974 by Darton, Longman & Todd Ltd.

tical progress: from the first visionary experiences in Manresa, his primitive Church, as he called this period, through the time in upper Italy whose climax was the vision of La Storta, to the Roman period, the time of his mystical completion, where he lives always in the presence of his God in a manner beyond the visionary, so that Laynez, the great theologian and trusted friend, can say of him: '*visiones omnes tum reales . . . tum per species et repraesentationes iam transgressus versatur nunc in pure intellectualibus, in unitate Dei*'. Whoever knows but a little of the theory of Catholic mysticism will be able to gauge at least from a distance what these simple words of Laynez permit us to surmise of the long ascent of this mystic, until he entered into the simple, illuminated darkness of God: *in unitatem Dei*.

But we are not concerned to speak of these things here. For we have to treat of his mysticism here only in so far as it renders comprehensible the fact and the nature of that which we commonly call Ignatian joy in the world. When we seek to comprehend his mysticism under this aspect, then it is obviously no longer of importance to isolate that characteristic of mystic piety by which it is distinguished from a 'normal' piety and way of prayer, one which does not possess the characteristic of immediate contact with God in the same way and to the same degree as is met with in the experience of the mystic. Therefore as long as we keep in mind that the characteristic piety of a mystic is given a special depth and power by the specifically mystic element of his piety, we may simply proceed to discuss the character of Ignatian *piety,* from which the fact and the meaning of its acceptance of the world will become understandable.

When we try to explain Ignatian piety under this aspect, then—so it appears to us—we have to lay down two propositions about it:

1. Ignatian piety is a piety of the Cross, and therein is revealed its inner continuity with the universal stream of Christian piety before it and so its Christian character.

2. Ignatian piety, because it is Christian, is directed to the God *beyond* the whole world, and it is precisely in the emphasis of this attitude that its peculiar character is to be found, as well as the foundation for the fact and the meaning of its joy in the world. We shall proceed in what follows to discuss these two propositions.

Ignatian piety is a piety of the Cross, like all Christian mystic piety before it. One would lay oneself open to the danger of completely misconstruing Ignatian piety, were one to overlook this first fundamental characteristic. We must take note of the fact that Ignatian piety is and intends to be primarily 'monastic' piety; 'monastic' not in a juridical sense, nor monastic in the external arrangement of the community life of his disciples, but 'monastic' in the theologico-metaphysical sense which constitutes the first and last meaning of this word. What we mean to say by that is that Ignatius in his life, in his piety, and in the spirit which he impresses upon his foundation is consciously and clearly taking over and continuing that ultimate direction of life by which the life of the Catholic Orders, the *'monazein'*, was created and kept alive. Proof of this is the simple fact that he and his disciples take the vows of poverty, chastity, and obedience. And with them they necessarily take over the attitude of the *monachos,* of one alone in God far from the world. Ignatius stands in the line of those men who existentially flee into the desert in a violent *fuga saeculi,* even though it may be the God-forsaken stony desert of a city, in order to seek God far from the world. It is nothing but superficiality if one allows the difference in external mode of life between Jesuit and monk to mask the deep and ultimate common character which dominates the ideal of every Catholic Order.

Ignatius approaches the world from God. Not the other way about. Because he has delivered himself in the lowliness of an adoring self-surrender to the God beyond the whole world and to his will, for this reason and for this reason alone he is prepared to obey his word even when, out of the silent desert of his daring flight into God, he is, as it were, sent back into the world, which he had found the courage to abandon in the foolishness of the Cross.

From this results the double characteristic which is proper to Ignatian joy in the world: the maxims of *'Indiferença'* and of 'finding God in all things'. The first is the presupposition of the second.

Indiferença: the calm readiness for every command of God, the equanimity which, out of the realization that God is always greater than anything we can experience of him or wherein we can find him, continually detaches itself from every determinate thing which man is tempted to regard as *the* point in which alone God meets him. Hence the characteristic of Ignatian piety is not so much situated in a material element, in the promotion of a particular thought or a particular practice, is not one of the special ways to God, but it is something formal, an ultimate attitude towards all thoughts, practices, and ways: an ultimate reserve and coolness towards all particular ways, because all possession of God must leave God as greater beyond all possession of him. Out of such an attitude of *indiferença* there springs of itself the perpetual readiness to hear a new call from God to tasks other than those previously engaged in, continually to decamp from those fields where one wanted to find God and to serve him; there springs the will to be at hand like a servant always ready for new assignments; the courage to accept the duty of changing oneself and of having nowhere a permanent resting-place as in a restless wandering towards the restful God; the courage to regard no way to him as being *the* way, but rather to seek him on all ways. Moved by such a spirit, even the passionate love of the Cross and of sharing in the ignominy of the death of Christ is still ruled by *indiferença*: the Cross, yes, *if* it should please his divine Majesty to call to such a death in life. *Indiferença* is possible only where the will to a *fuga saeculi* is alive, and yet this *indiferençia* in its turn disguises that love for the foolishness of the Cross into the daily *moderation* of a *normal style of life* marked by *good sense*. Filled with such *indiferençia*, Ignatius can even forgo manifestations of mystical graces —after all God is beyond even the world of experience of the mystic—he can forgo the mystical gift of tears because the physician wanted it—Saint Francis had angrily rejected precisely the same remonstrances of the physician.

In brief: such *indiferençia* becomes a seeking of God in *all* things. Because God is greater than everything, he can be found if one flees away from the world, but he can come to meet one on the streets in the midst of the world. For this reason Ignatius acknowledges only one law in his restless search for God: to seek him in all things; and this means: to seek him in that spot where at any particular time he wants to be found, and it means, too, to seek him in the world if he wants to show himself in it. In this seeking-God-in-all-things we have the Ignatian formula for a higher synthesis of that division of piety into a mystical one off flight from the world and a prophetic one of divinely commissioned work in the world, which is customary in the history of religion. In that formula these contradictions are in the Hegelian sense 'resolved' ('*aufgehoben*'). Ignatius is concerned only with the God above the whole world, but he knows that this God, precisely because he is really above the whole world and not merely the dialectical antithesis to the whole world, is also to be found *in the world*, when his sovereign will bids us enter upon the way of the world.

If we leave aside the somewhat excessively Greek colouring of the concepts, we can find the problem of the dialectic between flight from the world and acceptance of the world repeated in the dialectic between the two medieval Christian concepts of *contemplatio* and *actio*, of *vita contemplativa* and *vita activa*. *Contemplatio* is adherence to the God who is the goal of Christian existence, therefore to the God of a supramundane life. *Actio* is the fulfilment of one's duty within the world, including that of natural morality. This indication of the designation of these concepts allows us to understand the formula of Ignatian acceptance of the world which originated in the first circle of his followers: '*in actione contemplativus*'. Ignatius seeks only the God of Jesus Christ, the free, personal Absolute: *contemplativus*. He knows that he can seek and find him also in the world, if this should please him: *in actione*. And so he is prepared in *indiferençia* to seek him and him alone, always him alone but also him everywhere, also in the world: *in actione contemplativus*.

Here we must break off. We were unable even to touch on many questions which would have to be inserted in any closer investigation into what has been said, or which could follow as new questions as a consequence of what we have said. Thus we have not touched, for example, upon the question of the specific formation which the Ignatian basic attitude receives by its dedication to the apostolate in the service of the Church and her mission. We were likewise unable to discuss how this Ignatian outlook, which is after all primarily that of the monk, of the member of a religious Order, would present itself, if it were transferred to the level of a properly lay piety.

The Cross of Christ belongs to our Christian existence, and when we actually meet it in our personal life, in the fate of our people, when the hour of darkness appears to have descended, then this is not for us Christians a failure of our true life, but the distress which is necessarily felt by him who does not have and does not want to have a permanent abode here, because he is on the way to the God beyond all the fulfilment of this world, because he is a ὑπερκόσμιος. And yet according to Clement we should be κόσμιοι: enter into the world and its work with the strength born of our superiority to the world, sent by him with whom we are united in the one mystical life. Κόσμιος χαὶ ὑπερκόσμιος.

To such an attitude Ignatian piety and mysticism can lead us. Ignatian affirmation of the world is not a naïve optimism, not an installing ourselves in the world as though we had in it the centre of our lives. Ignatian joy in the world springs from the mysticism of conformity with him whom we have joined in the flight from the world contained in the foolishness of the Cross. But once we have found the God of the life beyond, then such an attitude will break out of deep seclusion in God into the world, and work as long as day lasts, immerse itself in the work of the time in the world and yet await with deep longing the Coming of the Lord.

3. The Nature and Necessity of Asceticism*

Ignatian joy in the world can be purchased only at the price of asceticism. In this selection, taken from his first priests' retreat, Rahner explains why Christian asceticism cannot be deduced from the demands of the natural order alone. It is not philosophical self-discipline. Christian asceticism is conscious surrender to the grace of Christ. It is a planned and deliberate development of the believing, hoping, and loving life in us according to the laws of nature and grace. The surrender of legitimate worldy goods in a life of ascetic devotion is both an exercise of the life of faith, hope, and charity and a public witness to it. The source and motivation of a life of Christian asceticism is the love of God. Its faithful practice is a testimony to the Church's eschatological hope. Since the

*From *Spiritual Exercises*, pp. 69–75.
© 1956 by Herder and Herder, Inc.

*Christian life is a life of surrender to grace, some form of self-denying
asceticism must be a part of every Christian's life.*

1. *Asceticism in the Broad Sense.* The "spiritual life" is life with God
and toward God. We are leading this life when we forget outselves for
God, when we love him, praise him, thank him. "Spiritual life" in grace
means that we realize the inner divine life in ourselves; it means waiting
for eternity in faith, hope, and love, bearing the darkness of human existence; it means not identifying oneself with this world, living according to
the prayer contained in the Didache: "Let this world pass away and let
the grace of God come."

All that is certainly an unforced gift of the free grace of God: especially
with regard to the presuppositions and situations in which God has placed
us, and which open up for us the area of our freedom even though our
freedom cannot control them; we mean, for example, our time and incli-
nations, our character, what we have inherited, our fellow men, the social
and religious milieau in which we were born, the "other things" given us
by God in order that we might find him; and this free gift is also our own
performance or realization, that is, the "spiritual life" that we put on and
actualize in ourselves is at the same time the freely given grace of God.

But while praising grace we should not forget that it does not always
rush over us in a wave of victory, sweeping aside all obstacles; nor is it a
simple and unhindered growth; neither does it develop our "spiritual life"
only to the extent that we suffer all in silence, leaving everything else in
the hands of God. Generally speaking, the "spiritual life" is grace precisely because it must be painstakingly cultivated day by day; it requires
constant training and drilling. In short, the "spiritual life" is also (even
though not exclusively or even predominantly) *work, planned exercise,*
and *conscious development* of the believing, hoping, and loving life in us
according to the laws of nature and grace, and according to the motives of
a total dedication to God. This aspect of the "spiritual life" is what we
mean by "asceticism" in the broad sense.

In these exercises, each one of us should ask himself whether or not he
is an ascetic in this sense, or whether, until now, he has remained an
amateur Chistian, perhaps protected by grace, perhaps kept more or less
on the right path by reason of his surroundings and moral code. Perhaps
the greatest gifts of grace come to us where we have not sought them;
perhaps God gives grace to us even though we do not bother much about
it; perhaps he runs after us, pursues us through the events of our life in
such a way that much later we can say to God's mercy: God has been
able to bring good out of all the stupidities of my life; my laziness and
indolence, my reluctance and tepidity, my stubborn attitude have not kept
him from remaining by my side and putting up with me day after day. That
may very well be! But it does not free us from the obligation of doing

something ourselves in an orderly fashion. This "something" may be different in youth and old age, but it must have its place in a man's religious life. (An older person who has reached a certain maturity through his experiences of the grace of God, can allow himself a certain freedom in the systematic development of his "spiritual life," that we cannot allow ourselves and which would be very dangerous for us.)

2. *Asceticism in the Strict Sense*. Asceticism in the strict sense is a part of the asceticism spoken of above, but only that part which is specifically Christian. This asceticism is Christian self-abnegation in the true sense —an abnegation which gives up positive values in this life, and not just useful things that are a mere means to the end (*bona utilia*, for example); it also gives up (preserving, of course, the proper relationship and subordination to higher values) personal values (*bona honesta*), such as marriage and the freedom to develop one's personality by disposing of material possessions that make for independence.

a) *The Meaningfulness of This Asceticism*. Asceticism in this sense, at least basically and in its actual practice, cannot be deduced from the mere natural order. Nor does the natural law even suggest it. Values of intrinsic worth should not be given up in the natural order except under the pressure of circumstances. To give them up in this order would be impossible ontologically and perverse ethically. All resentful disdaining of earthly goods from the point of view of the world—because a natural ethic considers them to be cheap or dangerous or common—is by that very fact objectively false and suspect, from a psychopathological point of view, in its basic motivation. Moreover, it would undermine the true meaning and the genuine realization of Christian self-denial.

From a purely natural standpoint, it could happen that a person, by reason of special circumstances (which themselves contain the necessity of attaining a certain good, and this necessity at the same time excludes the attainment of another good), would actually be hindered from attaining an incompatible good. An example would be to give up different aspects of the present standard of living in order to train one's nature to act in harmony and in order to take the offensive against concupiscence. But this is not the meaning of the asceticism that is specifically Christian. In this regard, a person might pose the question whether or not the choice of the evangelical counsels for most men is really the "better way" to bring order into the drives in the personal whole. It is a simple fact that the evangelical counsels create new dangers. (One would be forced to draw some painful false conclusions if one wished to interpret the "heroic deeds" and the "excesses" that have occurred in the history of Christianity in this way. We cannot explain the radicalism and immensity of the penance found in the lives of the saints by appealing to a motive of self-discipline; nor can it be explained by "pious folly" or "influences of a general, historical, spiritual nature" which really have nothing to do with Christianity.) But if penance is not discipline, then we are forced to object, against every such attempt to establish asceticism, that specifically Christian asceticism (for example, the evangelical counsels) can never be established with this type of an argument. For such discipline, asceticism belongs strictly to this world. And this explanation forgets that Christian asceticism, as an essential part of Christianity itself, must necessarily partake of the scandal of Christianity and its separation from the world. Therefore, it can only be truly understood from an understanding of Christianity itself.

Since asceticism is a virtuous striving for Christian perfection, and since this perfection must be formed by charity, asceticism itself can only adequately be grasped from the standpoint of charity. For this, however, neither the difficulty of the renunciation nor the example of Christ would suffice; it would just avoid the question. For example, a suicidal offering of one's own life would certainly be "hard," but, as a fundamentally immoral act, it could never be a true realization of the love of God. And why did Christ choose poverty, chastity, and obedience as the concrete ways of realizing this love? Did he choose them?

There must be an objective inner connection between self-denial and love. This connection consists in the fact that the renunciation of values that, from an earthly point of view, are unrenounceable is the *only possible* representation of love for the eschatological-transcendent God; for the God who is not only the ultimate meaning and guarantee of the world, but also who wished to meet us directly in love as himself. The revelation of such a love, which must always also be a quest for a return of love, is necessarily an intrusion into the isolation that the world would like to preserve; it is a rupture in which the world, even insofar as it is willed and governed by God, is reduced to a thing of only secondary importance—to something provisional, and our existential focal point is placed outside of it as the area of the tangible and the accessible.

Every naturally good act can be elevated by grace and informed by charity so that it is a co-realization of the redeeming divine love. But this does not mean that the transcendence of this love "appears" in the naturally good act. Precisely because it is naturally and morally good does it have a meaning in this world—a justification and an intelligibility in itself. God's transcendent otherness cannot be made manifest in itself in such acts. Therefore, he remains silent above the order of grace and its meaningful direction that surpasses the dimensions of this earth. Our confession of the transcendent God and of the relativity of this world, wrought by his direct gift of self to us, can only "appear" through the sacrifice of this world; this is a manifestation of faith and love that surpasses the world and its goods, even when these are of a personal nature. At the same time, it is nothing but an anticipation of Christian death—practice for it and its affirmation. For in death the totality of man's reality is absolutely put in question by God. There, in the most radical way, man is asked whether he allows himself to be disposed of in the obscure, incalculable beyond add by this "allowing" deny himself; whether he wants to understand the radical sacrifice of all "other things" from the cross of Christ as a true falling into the love of God.

If Christian asceticism in the strict sense is thus a mere anticipation of Christian death, nevertheless the throwing of oneself into the merciful hands of the transcendent God only becomes *visible* in the *freely chosen* anticipation. For death and only death is the complete sacrifice of this world, and thus the most radical possibility of faith, hope, and love. But it is also a "must" that is imposed on us by God. Our freedom can accept it in sin or redemption without affecting its outward appearance, that is, without removing its "obscurity." Asceticism, therefore, as the free sacrifice of values that should not be given up from an earthly point of view, is the only way in which our confession of the eschatological-transcendent God can "appear" in a palpable way.

b) *The Necessity of This Asceticism.* That we actually make the renunciation of values that should not be given up from an earthly point of view an expression of our love for God, and in this way may and indeed must anticipate our death, can only be explained ultimately by a positive call of God (either of a general or a private nature). Supernatural love could also be realized in naturally hidden and so unapparent morally good acts (as redeeming love); and it could also be realized in the silent, patient bearing of suffering and death (as transcendent love). (Certainly, asceticism would be at least meaningful, if not absolutely necessary, as a "preparation" for such suffering, so that then death—as in the case of Christ—can become the absolute culmination of our freedom precisely in absolute weakness.)

But the clear, positive will of God in this matter is manifested in the structure of the Church. She is the primordial-sacramental tangibility of the eschatological presence of the salvation of God in the world. Accordingly, God wills that she make the eschatological transcendence of the love that constitutes her inner nature palpably apparent. This occurs sacramentally especially in baptism and the Eucharist, where a man partakes of the death of Christ and actually announces it until His reappearance; it occurs existentially in specifically Christian renunciation. Christian asceticism, therefore, is an unsurrenderable part of the Church's essence. As a life lived according to the evangelical counsels, it is not only the normal, persisting, and existence-determining norm for individuals, but it is required at all times in one form or another from all members of the Church.

Because the Church is not an ultimate guarantee that the world will

make magnificent progress, because she is rather one that puts her hope
in that which is yet to come, because she is the community of those men
who have the courage based on faith, hope, and love to look for that
which really counts in that which is yet to come, who do not try to
construct the kingdom of God in this world, but wait for it as a gift of God,
sent into this world (a gift that will signify the eschatological elevation and
transformation of this aeon), who, moreover, must visibly live their faith,
hope, and love before the whole world and so become witnesses—for
these reasons, there must be a self-denying, specifically Christian asceticism in the life of each and every one of us. Each one of us has many
things to give up that would not be sinful to keep, that could be meaningful, beautiful, and a positive enriching of his human existence, because
—especially if he is a priest—he must represent the Church, because he
must live as an example for the world in a way that shows that he truly
believes in eternal life, and that he does not belong to the children of this
world who just happen 'also" to believe in some kind of a future life.

4. The Evangelical Counsels*

*Rahner's reflections on explicit faith as a loving commitment to the
Incarnate Word support his extremely coherent theology of the evangelical counsels. The counsels are the lived expression of the Church's
supernatural faith, hope, and charity. The communal life of the counsels,
led under vows, is a corporate expression of the Church's teaching. It is a
living symbol of Christ's saving grace and a visible sign of the Church's
eschatological hope in Christ.*

*Although by no means universally accepted, Rahner's theology of the
evangelical counsels is one of the most consistent theological justifica-
tions of religious life to win serious attention in the post-counciliar
Church. Its justification of the corporate visible testimony given by each
religious institute to the Church's eschatological hope gives a precise
reason for the unique place occupied by religious congregations in the
visible teaching Church. Its equal demand for worldly work and eschatological renunciation of worldly goods is a strong defense against an
immanentist conception of religious life which, carried to its logical conclusion, could reduce religious life to a form of secular humanism.
Rahner's conception of the religious life has been strongly influenced by
his membership in the Society of Jesus. Nevertheless, the systematic
theology which supports it extends its applicability to all religious congregations.*

*From *Theological Investigations*, vol. VIII, pp. 159–67.
© 1971 by Darton, Longman & Todd Ltd.

THE STATUS OF CHRISTIANS UNDER THE
EVANGELICAL COUNSELS AND IN THE WORLD

The evangelical counsels are the expression and the manifestation of a faith that is reinforced by hope and love as well. In this they are distinguished from 'this worldly' goods (those of riches, power and development of the personality), though these two are capable of being integrated into, and subsumed under grace (though they do not make grace manifest in any direct sense). The evangelical counsels also represent an attitude of withdrawal as opposed to an unreserved striving for position in the world, for the world lies prostrate 'in the evil' of infralapsarian sinfulness. Now since the evangelical counsels do constitute an expression and a manifestation of a faith that hopes and loves in this way, the epithets 'better' and 'more blessed' as applied to them in that *objective* sense which accords them a pre-eminence over the opposite way of life, are altogether appropriate. The truth of this has always been acknowledged by scripture and tradition prior to any application of them to the merely individual case. In this sense, therefore, they have a relatively greater suitability as a means of exercising love for one who has been called to follow them. Objectively speaking, therefore, the evangelical counsels do have a certain general pre-eminence over other ways of life. But this pre-eminence, taken precisely in the sense intended here, does *not* mean that the actual fact of fulfilling them in practice *ipso facto* and necessarily means or guarantees that a greater love of God is achieved than is, or can be, achieved even apart from these counsels. It does not mean that for every individual (or even for normal cases) the 'means' which is better for that individual constitutes the most perfect realisation of the love of God that is possible. It does not mean that one who practises the evangelical counsels is *ipso facto* 'more perfect' than the Christian 'in the world'. But it does mean that the evangelical counsels (considered as a renunciation, though admittedly such renunciation can also be present in other ways of life) constitutes an objectivation and a manifestation of faith in that grace of God which belongs to the realm beyond this present world. And this objectivation and manifestation *precisely as such* are not achieved in any other way of life. Objectivation means—from the ontological point of view—that in the case of a being subject to physical and historical modalities certain ultimate and basic orientations have to be achieved, and these can be achieved only in an 'other being', though they are not identical with it. (For this reason this 'other being' can never show quite unambiguously what these basic orientations of the first being are.) This 'other being', therefore, has the value of an 'ontic symbol' and is the expression of these freely adopted orientations. Again from the ethical point of view it is the 'means' by which these orientations are in fact achieved. 'Everything' (sin excepted) can be the 'material' which is integrated into a 'faith' orientation, and is constituted as such by it. But not everything is on that account *ipso facto* an objectivation and manifestation of faith itself in the sense intended precisely *here,* though, of course, it is also true that positively to opt for certain 'this worldly' goods as 'material for integration' in this sense can in itself be a 'means' of causing faith to grow.

We have not yet arrived at any clear and universally accepted terminology to give a satisfactory expression to this state of affairs with regard to the 'objective' pre-eminence of the evangelical counsels. If we merely say that the counsels are the 'better *means*' for achieving a believing love, then this use of the term 'better' immediately raises the question of what this is intended to signify, if the counsels are, nevertheless, *not* the better means for the majority of men. It also gives rise to the further question of whether a satisfactory answer is arrived at merely by adding that these 'means' are better 'in themselves'. For when we use the term 'means' we imply a relationship not merely to the end in view for which the means are employed, but also to the subject whom these means are intended to help in the attainment of that end. If, therefore, we say that these means are not the 'better way' for the majority of men, what, in that case, can it still mean to say that they are the better means 'in themselves', seeing that we are nevertheless concerned to point out that this 'in themselves' does not apply to the majority of cases even when there is no question of acting contrary to their nature and so sinfully? The term 'means' is valid as an expression of the relationship between counsel and perfection only to the extent that this expression makes it clear that perfection is never formally constituted as such by the counsels, and that the counsels do not constitute a higher form of perfection (one which is inaccessible to the 'ordinary' Christian). Rather it must be taken as signifying that the counsels are ordered to *that* perfecion to which all are called; that the counsels precisely do *not* of themselves constitute a closer form of following Christ, a more intimate unity with God, but rather are there *for* these ends. But the term 'means' is inadequate because of its nature it tends to suggest that there is an objective relationship between perfection and counsel (the case is rather as if one were to call the body and its actions the 'means' of the personal fulfilment of the spirit). If we really say that the counsels arë the 'objectivation' of faith and love then this easily gives rise to the misunderstanding that they alone, and not every rational activity of the Christian in this world, can be the concrete realisation of faith, that only the renunciation and sacrifice entailed in the counsels are able to constitute faith as lived in the concrete, of being faith 'spiritually', instead of realising that 'everything—including our worldly activities—which we do' is able to become this if only we do it in the name of Chirst. We must therefore simply shift by saying that the counsels are the sole mode in which faith achieves its objectivation *and manifestation,* though when we say this what we mean is that in the counsels *alone* (in contrast to other

forms of renunciation, and especially to that which consists in consciously and explicitly embracing 'passion') faith arrives at a state of
objectivation in which it becomes manifest precisely because all forms of
objectivation which entail a positive assent to the world also conceal faith
(where this is not thought of and practised as a mere ideological superstructure imposed upon one's ordinary life), since even without faith they
continue to be meaningful. Since they do constitute an objectivation of
the faith in this way, making it manifest (and thereby bearing witness to
it as well), the counsels are, of course, precisely *not* mere empty manifestations of faith which have nothing to contribute to the actual exercise of
it because their nature is such as can only be realised in the act of objectivation and manifestation. On the theory put forward here, therefore, the
evangelical counsels are of their nature the historical and sociological
manifestation of the faith of the Church for the Church and for the world.
But to proceed from this (this point must straightway be added here) to a
denial of the fact that the counsels also have an 'ascetical' significance for
the individual would be an utter misconception. Admittedly it remains
true that this faith also achieves manifestation and objectivation in the
freely accepted inescapable 'passion' in the life of every true Christian
(not in 'passion' as such, but in the 'death' which we accept in 'obedience' in that 'passion' as in the case of Christ himself). But it is precisely
in order to inculcate this attitude of obedience that the counsels are given,
to exercise man, by anticipation, and to prepare him for death. They are
not intended to be anything more than this. And in freely accepting the
element of 'passion' we are, materially speaking, achieving precisely the
same effect as appears in the counsels: the free acceptance of a renunciation which, from the point of view of this world, is irrational.

The statement 'the evangelical counsels are the "better way" ', therefore, is not an assertion that those who practise them have reached a
higher stage of perfection. For the sole measure of the degree of perfection which the individual achieves is in all cases the depths of his love for
God and his neighbour. This statement refers rather to the fact that the
counsels are 'means' (an objectivation and a making manifest) of faith and
love (a) *relatively speaking* in their reference to the individual called to
follow them. Here a contrast is established between his situation under
the counsels and the situation which would be his if *he as an individual*
were to refuse them; (b) *absolutely speaking* to the extent that they alone,
considered as a renunciation and a practising of the passion of Christ
himself, can be said to have the character of an objectivation and manifestation of faith and love (not only as preached but as assumed and lived).
Here there is a contrast between the way of life prescribed by the counsels and the other 'material' for a Christianity that is lived to the full,
which is capable of being integrated into this fulness of Christian life
because, as having positive existence in this world, it is the material in

which the Christian can express his affirmation to the world. But even when it does this it cannot make manifest the 'transcendence' of grace and of faith.

THE ECCLESIOLOGICAL (SYMBOLIC) SIGNIFICANCE OF THE EVANGELICAL COUNSELS

The evangelical counsels are distinguished from other forms of renunciation and of accepting in faith the 'passion' of personal existence in that they have a *status* (in virtue of their unambiguously clear sociological orientation, their permanence, their clearly defined meaning and also the vows which are taken to follow them in the presence of the Church herself). This status which the evangelical counsels impart makes them (and those who practise them) an element in the 'visible' Church. In virtue of this fact they have an essential function to perform in the Church prior to any question of the 'useful works' which the orders perform on the Church's behalf (by giving an example of moral living, by their apostolate, prayers, etc.). The Church is not only the fruit of salvation which springs from a reality hidden within her (the grace of the Spirit which quickens and sanctifies the Church herself). She is also a permanent and quasi-sacramental sign of salvation in her visible manifestations in history. But it is not only in virtue of her preaching of the word and conferring the sacraments that she has this significance of a historical presence. If this were the case she would only be the sign of the grace which is *offered* by God. But she must be something more than this. She must be the sign of the actual fact that grace has been accepted, that it is already at work eschatologically, and is already in fact triumphant. Now she is a sign in this sense not in her institutional, but rather in her charismatic aspects if, and to the extent that, this fact is objectified and made manifest for all to see on the sociological and historical plane. And this is precisely what is achieved in the life governed by the evangelical counsels insofar as these are visible in the Church's communal life. The evangelical counsels constitute that element in the Church which makes her a sign, a sign of the fact that in her eschatological faith she is reaching out for a goal that lies beyond this present world. They also constitute that element in the Church which makes her a visible sign of the fact (which is the real reason for the foregoing) that she is the community triumphantly possessed by the grace of God. Of course, the mere fact of observing these counsels being practised in the life of the *individual* for various reasons is not of itself, unequivocally, and in a way that objectifies it beyond all doubt, an existential symbol of the faith that really is present in the Church (which must be so present because the eschatological Church, in contrast to the synagogue, must be, as a whole, she who really is indefectible in her belief). But the reality of the evangelical counsels as lived in the Church taken as a whole does nevertheless constitute a sign in this sense. In terms both of material fact and of epistemological theory the situation here is the same (and in fact ultimately for the same reason) as with martyrdom considered as an objectivation of, and a witness to faith on the part of the Church, whose faith is, in a true sense, indefectible. Like martyrdom the evangelical counsels too are, in their fulness and totality signs in the Church of the fact that God's grace is effectively triumphant in the faith of the Church. Now the Church must be a witness precisely in this sense. But she is a witness in this sense only through the evangelical counsels (we are abstracting here from martyrdom considered as the active acceptance of 'passion' in the absolute, the state in which 'passion' and ascesis are brought together, for it is precisely *not* simply in 'normal' times alone that martyrdom can represent a rival to the Church's constitution in this function of being the sign of the real and effective faith that is within her). Thus it can be seen that these evangelical counsels belong (even if not in a form which is institutionally defined in any precise sense as a matter of the Church's law) to the essence of the Church because it is not only the official dispensers of the Church's truth and grace who constitute an essential part of her, but the grace that brings about her triumphant acceptance of truth and grace as well—this latter grace as received and as manifesting itself for what it is.

As witness of the fact that it is precisely the grace of *Christ* that is accepted in faith by the Church this witness has a *soteriological* character. It attests the fact that the Church (as a whole) freely submits herself to the Passion of Christ to the extent that this constitutes a free acceptance of death in a spirit of obedience, and thereby brings about salvation. It also has an *eschatological* character, not strictly speaking to the extent that the evangelical counsels already contain the future life of heaven by anticipation already in the here and now. Rightly understood this can be said of grace itself and the fulness of it as attained on this earth. This is in accordance with the fact that in empirical terms it must be said that justification is already achieved 'in the here and now' (notwithstanding the fact that this concept applies primarily to the definitive consummation of salvation). But if this were all we were saying then it would be true of *every* kind of Christian perfection and every act of striving for such perfection. The counsels themselves as such, to the extent that they are distinct from that which constitutes their basis, the grace of justification and love, do not 'anticipate' eternal life as such. For they are, of their very nature, a renunciation, and this is no true characteristic of final perfection. In particular when, according to many Fathers of the Church, virginity in the earthly sphere is conceived of as an anticipation of life in heaven, as *vita angelica,* a life similar to that of angels, this is the outcome of a pietistic Neoplatonism, in support of which Mt 22:30 cannot be invoked. Marriage does not make a man 'earthly'. But the counsels can and must be understood as an eschatological witness to the extent that they objectify and make manifest that faith which reaches out in hope towards that future state which is the consummation of the grace which is received in this faith. To the extent that this objectivation and manifestation of the triumph of grace and of faith is the objectivation of that grace which embraces the world (even though this is achieved precisely through the Cross) and glorifies it, this 'sign' character of the counsels is essentially focused upon the Church, in which the consecration of the world takes place and the worldly becomes identified with the Christian. It is not only for practical reasons that there must be something more in the Church than the *mere* practice of the evangelical counsels. Such a thing would actually be *unfitting.* The fact that some of the members of the Church live a 'worldly' life, that Christianity has also its 'everyday', and therefore almost anonymous aspects in the way in which it is lived, so that Christians act as the 'pagans' also act—this is something that belongs of necessity to the mode in which the Church manifests herself, and is inherent in her nature. The life of Christians in the world has a message for those who live under the evangelical counsels. It tells them that their actions too, do not compel grace, but rather that grace is bestowed upon those actions. The life of the evangelical counsels has a message for Christians 'in the world'. It tells them that they too are pilgrims, to whom grace comes from above and not *as a result of* their worldly activities (even though it does come *in* those activities). Both 'states' in the Church mutually contribute to one another according to the gifts which are given to each in particular precisely as proper to itself.

Of course, a further consequence of all that has been said is that the counsels must be lived in a manner (and that too precisely with regard to their sociological and 'institutional' aspects) which makes it clear that they have the force not only of objectivation but of a manifestation too of the faith of the Church. But at this point fresh questions are raised for today. The poverty of the orders seems often to have very little 'poor' about it. The evangelical state of virginity all too often vanishes into the vague indefinability and ambiguity of the attitude of contemporary society towards sexual love. Obedience appears as a way of organising the communities on the grand scale such as also occurs in other contexts and with greater severity. All this constitutes a threat today to the ecclesiological function of the evangelical counsels, and raises fresh questions concerning the contemporary forms of religious life.

5. Religious Obedience*

Rahner's writings on obedience, which now strike us as being mild and extremely reasonable, aroused considerable controversy in the early days of aggiornamento *and provoked a great deal of popular interest. The following selection, taken from his second priests' retreat, gives a succinct, non-technical expression of Rahner's understanding of religious obedience.*

Religous obedience cannot be justified theologically simply on the basis of the renunciation of the religious' own will. The religious' submission to authority is a selfless exercise of faith. But, since it is religious obedience, it does not absolve either subjects or superiors from their personal responsibility to discern and to carry out the concrete intimations of God's will which come to individual religious. The value of a personal surrender to God in faith can never consist in a flight from mature individual responsibility. At times the will of God and the good of souls may require that a religious represent vigorously against a misguided or ill-informed order of his superior. On such occasions a religious must not shirk his duty to represent for fear of displeasing a superior.

There is an evangelical counsel, which is folly to the world, which would be meaningless apart from a radically realised faith. There is a religious obedience which requires us to sacrifice and renounce very positive values. The recompense of this renunciation is one that cannot be known or enjoyed in this world. Humanly speaking at least, it is possible from time to time to find obedience working out in the religious life as something like stupidity, when someone has slipped into it and cannot prove the appropriateness of such obedience in this world. We must appreciate and stick to this sense of obedience as the Christian's renunciation and as practice for a radical renunciation which is always imposed in the long run and which the Christian will never be spared.

Even if it seems externally that the obedience involving a commitment of faith is not being asked of us, the fact remains that religious life as a whole, in its diffuse, general routine, without the will to this evangelical renunciation, would scarcely present a summons to a life's dedication. The whole of our life stands or falls only by the rules, by the constitutions, by the stereotyping of our life under a common denominator of renunciation, which at most overlooks the boredom, the lack of human feeling, the parsimony. But this is not an advantage and does not indicate any religious achievement: it is merely symptomatic of a deficiency in authentic, human vitality.

If however this vitality is present, then the religious life, particularly in

*From *The Priesthood*, pp. 110–113.
© 1973 by Sheed and Ward Ltd.

its prosaic routine and normality, provides a challenge to obedience for someone who can bear this—especially if he is alive, humanly authentic and rich—only in a spirit of faith. If, instead of undertaking this task, he were to sink into mediocrity, to cut himself off from real life, to capitulate and compromise, and in this humanly defective state to take on the religious life, he would be like a person who had only managed a lesser calling although he had been meant for a greater; if we endure the religious life only in this way, reducing our claims and sinking into mediocrity then we have misunderstood the meaning and purpose of obedience.

The fact that obedience is hard for us makes no difference. It would even be a bad sign either for our spirit of asceticism or for our human authenticity, vitality, and strength, if there seemed to be nothing more to obedience than regulated mediocrity, a life without sensations or excitement, a smooth, comfortable, bureaucratic existence. We would be doing our duty and receiving our food in return, we would be contented and therefore would not make any great claims on life. This is not what religious obedience really means. It is really the sacrifice of a value of central importance as an act of faith.

OBEDIENCE IN THE SERVICE OF THE CHURCH

Our religious obedience has of course another aspect: the ecclesial and apostolic aspect. This obedience, of a world-denying, ascetic character, as a mysterious, almost incomprehensible sacrifice of faith, is also placed at the service of ecclesial objectives. Firstly, at the service of the community life; secondly, at the service of the Church's apostolate. It is as a result of these things that religious obedience and ecclesial obedience to superiors in the Church acquire a new, additional meaning which has a positive value and is important for its own sake, which can sustain and justify religious obedience, not indeed as a whole, but still to a large extent.

A religious order placed at the service of the apostolate has a common task. A common work, a common external aim, needs a structuring, a unification, a general orientation of effort, and from this aspect too needs obedience. Thus ascetic obedience acquires a very practical purpose and meaning. This involves the danger of mistaking and overlooking the ultimate, religious, ascetic, even mystical aspect of faith. Obedience can retain the most essential supernaturally ascetic meaning, even when religious superiors or other authorities in the Church issue orders which seem very problematic, perhaps very stupid, very wrong, very old-fashioned in relation to the apostolic purpose of obedience. It is obvious however that obedience does not cease to have meaning or justification when this apostolic objective is not attained. This of course does not meant that every order of a superior is as such always legitimate.

AUTHORITY AND OBEDIENCE

A third point that we must consider is authority and obedience in the pluralism of reality and of the Christian virtues. What does this mean? We have already observed that even the radical renunciation involved in the evangelical counsels is not intended as an absolute, physical sacrifice of the values represented there (leaving aside for the time being the question of marriage and celibacy). In any case, it is possible to want to be absolutely poor in a material sense without actually being poor. Nevertheless, in this respect too, by comparison with the attitude of the lay Christian, it can be a question only of a different emphasis, important quantitatively, but not of an ultimately essential difference. The layman too must renounce things which represent positive values for him, at least when God does actually take them away.

On the other hand, the religious cannot possibly live only on asceticism. A life wholly dominated by this asceticism as renunciation and sacrifice of human values would not be Christian, but perhaps Buddhist. If the Christian wanted to turn renunciation into a single-minded attitude, monopolising all his life, he would be denying in practice, if not in theory, the reality of the human values which are not pure grace; these values would not be brought into the consummation of the kingdom of God. Both attitudes would be heretical, for ultimately the perfection of man and of the Christian consists in the absolute and final salvation of Christian and human realities by the supreme values of divine grace, of uncreated grace, down to the transfiguration of the body.

The attitude of the Christian, also of the Christian who is a religious, must imply always and everywhere the ultimate affirmation of God as God of nature and supernature in regard to all created things. That is why *a priori*, renunciation as such can never be absolute. This holds too for obedience.

Obedience cannot exist without an autonomous disposal by the individual of his freedom. Obedience and authority are very important factors in the life of the religious, which he must respect; but they could never completely guide his life. Even the religious who would leave it to his superior to approve, confirm, direct and guide the smallest details of his life, still cannot avoid putting some suggestions before the superior. Even if he declares that he will leave everything to the absolute discretion of the superior and thus allow himself to be treated "like a stick in the hand of an old man" or "like a corpse," he is by that very fact making an autonomous gesture which he could not have left to the superior to initiate.

Simply because I am free—and obedience itself is dependent on this—I must necessarily have autonomous impulses which cannot be ruled by the superior. Heaven does not first ask the superior what inspirations and impulses to bestow on the individual. The situation has changed then, even for the superior, before questions are asked. He can then always still give directions, he can choose; but he directs what has already begun, his choice has already been made by someone else. It is only as one factor in a plurality of impulses, dynamisms, that he tries to see something of what he can do about projects put before him and submitted to his authority. This does not mean merely that obedience is kept within proper and reasonable limits, which all ascetic tirades cannot set aside, but that a very considerable responsibility is imposed on us.

In other words, I can never say that everything is in the best of order because the superior has given his blessing. I have to recognise that, in spite of my obedience, I have an absolute responsibility before God which neither superiors nor obedience can take away from me. This is a truism, but you would not think so when you read the normal ascetic effusions on obedience. They overlook this fact, but they do not thereby encourage obedience: they make asceticism too cheap. For this renunciation of my freedom, of my autonomous responsibility, even with the best will in the world on the part of the most punctilious superiors and on the part of the most obliging subjects, can in fact only go part of the way. It cannot go further, since the superior cannot have merely *materia prima* to deal with in the subject, but is facing another person, someone with charisms, with the autonomous impulses of his freedom.

If authority and obedience constitute one element in a greater reality and in a pluralism of the Christian virtues, obedience cannot be made to bear the whole burden of a man's spiritual life and way of life, of decisions and guidance. Superiors cannot want this, even if they sometimes behave as if they preferred subjects so completely obedient.

Here again it is clear that this pluralism is in a sense incalculable. How far I may permit myself to be influenced by the superior, how far I am active myself, when I make my own plans and when I take over what others have planned: all these things must remain within the framework of obedience. When the superior says, "Thus far and no farther", he is right and his "No" will be respected. But the possibility remains of adding larger or smaller doses of obedience and no one can deprive me of the right to make my own estimate of the dosage.

St Ignatius does in fact say here and there that we must fulfil every wish of the superior. But he is not all that serious about it: in practice, he shows that he has no great opinion of subjects who do this. Within the framework of obedience, I must do things which are not at all to the liking of the superior. If he simply will not have this, he should have the guts and the manliness to accept his responsibility and say: "That must stop!"

But in pastoral practice, in education, in scholarship, you cannot adapt yourself one hundred per cent to just any arbitrary wishes, opinions, attitudes or tastes of the superior. This would be impossible if only because you cannot in the last resort jump out of your skin, and because a superior may not always be particularly sympathetic to you.

Obviously we can assume that our superiors never order anything which they consider subjectively to be a sin. But we must certainly allow for the possibility of superiors ordering something that is objectively against the commandment of Christ and the Church and of moral theology: something that is objectively impossible for the subject, but is not perceived to be such by the superior. In such a case, a person must really have the courage to appeal to his conscience and refuse to obey the commandment. This does not often occur, but its rarity may perhaps be due to the fact that we are too lax. But if anyone were to think that these simple and obvious facts justified him in grumbling, protesting, muttering about his conscience whenever something was not to his taste, he would be wrong. We cannot hope to avoid such wrong conclusions if we simply pigeon-hole the correct principles, suppressing them without openly denying them.

PRACTICAL CONCLUSIONS

There must be a real will to obedience as an act of selflessness in faith: the will and desire to experience in this life an absolute test of faith. Why should we not want at some time to face a situation in which we are really obeying without being praised by superiors, without being recognised by men, because we seek nothing but God and because by the very fact of exercising our freedom we are surrendering ourselves to God?

Moreover, it is a part of true obedience to take the initiative and make our own decisions in the line of duty. We have not only the right, but today more than ever the duty, to take the initiative. Our apostolic situation particularly presents so many facets today, is so complicated, so far beyond the supervision of the individual superior, that a religious order would be a boring, dismal set of people unless its subjects also developed a large measure of initiative. However intelligent the superior may be, he cannot really understand something about all the modern opportunities for the apostolate. If he is intelligent and does not think he knows something about everything, he can lead his subjects only in a very formal sense; he can often in a way say no more than: "Think this over sensibly and, if you decide you must act differently, then do so. You also have my blessing for it." Thus each takes on and has to bear a large measure of responsibility.

There is also a responsibility of our own, of which no one can deprive us, even if something is quite clearly ordered; for then too we can at least be asked if we have seriously and honestly tried to discover whether sin is involved or not. This much is not only our right, but our duty. We can certainly assume that what is ordered is morally unobjectionable. But we can have no more than a presumption. We are never dispensed from the responsibility of forming our conscience in regard to what is ordered.

Real obedience includes the courage to be a troublesome subject. Not a grumbler, not one who is always complaining, who always knows better, who cannot fit in anywhere, who presumes *a priori* that whatever the superiors order is absurd and unreasonable until the contrary is proved. There are subjects like this and to some extent we have all been among them. If an unsympathetic superior orders us to do something, we are very easily inclined—and this is understandable—to look first for reasons for saying that it is absurd, instead of trying at once to understand its meaning. But all this does not alter the fact that we must have the courage to be troublesome subjects.

And, independently of the question whether a definite obligation is imposed, we should also have the will and strive constantly to be amiable, friendly, agreeable subjects, meeting our superiors too in a proper, manly and refined manner. This too belongs to the marginal, human phenomena of a religious obedience.

6. Lay Spirituality.*

Christian spirituality should not be considered the special province of priests and religious. The laity have a specific spirituality of their own, based on their sacramental incorporation into the Church.

Rahner has written a great deal on the role of lay men and of lay women in the contemporary Church. In the future diaspora condition of the Church, when the Church becomes a small minority of believers scattered among a largely unbelieving population, the role of the laity in the Church's life, worship and apostolic activity will be much greater than it has been in the past.

Like most contemporary theologians, Rahner believes that there is urgent need to develop a specific spirituality properly adapted to the needs of the lay men and lay women of the contemporary world.

At the beginning of this chapter we formulated this proposition: by sacramental consecration and empowerment every Christian in the Church is constituted, qualified, and in duty bound to a position of active

*From *Nature and Grace*, pp. 110–113.
© 1963 by Sheed and Ward Ltd.

co-responsibility inside and outside the Church. The narrow framework of this short essay did not permit us to give anything more than the most general substantiation and interpretation of this proposition. But at least this one point should have become evident: "laity" means in the Church the opposite of what it means in secular usage, for instance, in the sentence, "He is an utter layman in the field of criminal law." In the secular sphere "laity" means those who cannot have a voice, who have nothing to say, who are excluded from a certain area of life and responsibility. "Laity" means just the opposite in the area of theology.

Of course, it may be true, in accordance with the latest studies, that the application of this word to the baptized, believing Christian, in order to connote his difference from the clergy, is not immediately derived from the biblical concept of "the people of God" (from the *laos theou*, with which it is *linguistically* connected) but rather that from the very beginning it carried with it a suggestion of "layhood." However it would be and actually is catastrophic if the Christian has merely one realization concerning his own Christian position, i.e., that he is not a cleric and therefore must play a totally subordinate and more or less passive role in the Church. Every Christian is indelibly sealed by his Baptism; every Christian through Baptism is an anointed and consecrated person, a temple of God, a chosen, elect soul, one who is called to the community of those who know and confess that God has had mercy on the world and has called it into His life. Every Christian is the sharer in an active function inside and outside the Church. The word of God is also placed on his lips, even if he has no mission or power to preach in the official assemblies of the community. For he ought to carry the message of the Gospel from the community assembly to the very place where it should proceed if it has any meaning and power, namely, where life is being lived, a life which yearns to be illumined and redeemed by God's Word. The baptized Christian may articulate this word primarily—though he should not confine himself to this—by the sincere activity of his own life and not through his own words. He can apply to himself, as a divinely sealed member of the Church of the Word, the saying: "Woe to me if I did not preach and did not bear witness."

Every Christian is through Baptism and all the other sacraments co-responsible for the task of the Church: that through the Church the grace of God becomes tangible and convincing in the world which has been redeemed by God's love and still has to be redeemed by continuing to experience and perceive the fact of her redemption. This is always an activity within and without. Within because we who are Christians must always become Christians anew; without because by far the greater part of the world has not yet *com*prehended what it has already *ap*prehended in the depths of its consciousness and what can be understood as the grace and promise of being definitively taken over by God's grace.

It remains true and ought not be hushed up, since there is no need to do so, that the unordained Christian who is not charged with a mission of Orders and leadership in the Church clearly differs from a cleric. In this respect a subordination and difference of rank in the Church exists according to Christ's will. But this gradation and distinction of dignity is totally directed to certain definite ecclesiastical-social functions in the structure of the Church's life and has no relevance with reference to holiness, the embrace of God's love, or even necessarily the objective salutary value of the function itself. For a free charism received by a layman in the Church with respect to the salvation of men and the world can be effectively of greater significance than the exercise of an institutional, official, or even a sacramental power. Nor does this difference of rank result in a division of classes as regards the radical demands of God or the inescapable duty to keep and preserve the world in all its dimensions as the reality of God's creation and to bring it to the reality of the Redemption.

If we mull over all these points and look for a very simple formula which would summarize everything, then we might say: through the sacraments the layman in the Church is not, of course, a cleric (since both have different tasks within the Church which mutually condition one another). But having seen and said this we might well say: the layman in the Church is not a layman—but a Christian. And each layman is asked whether he wishes to be what he already is.

XIV

Ideology, Eschatology, and the Theology of Death

1. Ideology and Christianity*

*Christ is the Absolute Future of human society. The union of humanity
with the Triune God at Christ's second coming will be the culmination of
the work of creation and redemption. Christianity therefore is essentially
a history and, as such, is a religion of the future. The Church's eschatological hope in her Absolute Future protects her against the aber-
rant ideologies which mistake some finite reality, within the world or
beyond it, for the Infinite God. Since Christianity is not and cannot be an
ideology, Christians must be tolerant toward the variety of religious and
political view points which exist in the modern world. The Church must
avoid identifying herself with the fanaticism of particular ideologies. She
must not transform the Christian Revelation into an ideology by en-
deavoring to confine the transcendent mysterious God within the intramundane categories of particular political or social systems. Neither
may she imply that the uncontrollable God of Christian hope can be won
by any definite techniques of social planning or of political activity.*

Ideology, it must be emphasised right away, is understood here in a
negative sense. In other words, it is understood as an erroneous or false
system which must be rejected in view of a right interpretation of reality.
We can prescind in this from the question as to whether the false 'system'
is clearly constituted by theoretical reflection or whether it represents
more an unreflected attitude, in the sense of a mentality and arbitrarily
and freely created mood. It remains a completely open question here, of
course, as to where this sort of ideology is to be found in the concrete; in
other words, whether, for example, every metaphysics is to be understood as an ideology in this sense. What, however, distinguishes such an
ideology in its essence from simple, basically open error, is the voluntary
element of closure by which the ideology understands itself as a total

*From *Theological Investigations*, vol. VI, pp. 43-45, 52-57.
© 1969 and 1974 by Darton, Longman & Todd Ltd.

system. To this extent, ideology is then a fundamental closure in face of the 'wholeness' of reality, one which turns a partial aspect into an absolute. Bearing in mind common usage, one would have to complete this abstract description of the nature of ideology by pointing out that—in so far as reality as a whole can demand recognition from man—the conversion of a partial aspect of reality into an absolute takes place with a view to practical action, and thus usually takes the form of a basic determination of political activity; indeed, in its ultimate intention, it will try to determine the norm for the whole life of a society. From this point of view, ideology could also be defined with R. Lauth as a pseudo-scientific interpretation of reality in the service of a practico-social orientation which it is meant to legitimate retrospectively. This formal definition of the nature of an ideology, regarded as a definitive erection into an absolute of a partial aspect of the whole of reality, makes it *a priori* possible to recognise a threefold form of ideology. This is not meant to imply that these three forms are ever realised in a pure state and completely separated from each other but that there is in a real sense an ideology of immanence, an ideology of 'transmanence' and an ideology of transcendence. We will now give a short explanation of this division.

Ideologies of immanence convert certain finite areas of our experiential world into absolutes and regard their structures as the law of reality as such. This group embraces the greater part of what is normally referred to as ideology: nationalism, the ideology of 'blood and soil', racialism, Americanism, technicism, sociologism and of course that materialism for which God, spirit, freedom and person signify just empty talk in the real sense of the term. The opposite of the ideology of immanence—an opposite we often fail to recognise immediately—is the ideology of 'transmanence', i.e. supernaturalism, quietism, and certain forms of utopianism, chiliasm, indiscreet 'brotherhood', etc. In this kind of ideology, the ultimate and infinite—that which permeates and governs all areas of reality—is turned into an absolute (or better, perhaps, is totalised) in the sense of cheating the relatively ultimate finite reality—that which is already always given and accepted—out of its relative rights; the relatively ultimate is passed over and one tries to project and manipulate it purely from the standpoint of that absolutely ultimate reality: this is the typical danger for the philosopher and the religious person. The third form of ideology is called the ideology of transcendence. This tries to overcome the first-mentioned forms of ideology but in its turn hypostatises in itself, as the only valid thing, the actual empty formal process of surmounting what is meant by the first two forms of ideology. In this case, what is immediately given in experience is devalued negatively into historism, relativism, etc., and what is properly transcendent is experienced merely as something which refuses to communicate itself, as something unspeakable. From this stems the ideological programme of unrestrained and so-called 'openness' for everything and anything, an attitude which timidly avoids any clear engagement in anything definite, with the result that such a professedly typical Western attitude is then brought face to face with the demands of a Western ideology; in this lies the ever new attraction for Western intellectuals of that communism which demands 'engagement'.

The reproach is made against Christianity that it too is such a negative ideology. Before we can reflect on this claim and on the reason why this reproach is quite unjustified, it will be necessary to reflect at least briefly on the reasons which can provide apparent justification for the interpreting of Christianity as an ideology.

Christianity is essentially a history, since it directs man's attention towards spatio-temporally fixed events of human history understanding them as saving events which find their unsurpassable summit, centre and historical measure in the absolute saving event of Jesus Christ. If this history itself is part of the nature of Christianity, and not just an accidental interchangeable stimulus of that transcendental, supernatural experience of the absolute and forgiving nearness of the holy mystery which overcomes all intramundane forces and powers, then Christianity appears clearly as the negation of every ideology of transmanence and transcendence. (This must not be understood as the annihilation of transcendence, but must be seen as the negation of the ideologisation of transcendence into a bare and empty formalisation of genuine transcendence.) Two things will have to be understood if we are to be able to think of this concept. Firstly, it will be necessary to make clear the inner connection between the genuine and unsurpassable historicity of Christianity in its turning to history regarded as a real event of salvation and the transcendental nature of Christianity understood as the openness by grace to the absolute God; in other words, it will have to be shown that genuine transcendentality and genuine historicity determine one another and that man by his very transcendentality is referred to real history, a real history he cannot 'annul' by *a priori* reflection. Secondly, it will have to be understood that by the genuine imposed nature of real history, man is empowered and indeed bound to take things really seriously even in his profane existence and to be really involved in the external historical reality, even where he recognises and experiences by suffering the contingency and thus the relativity of this historical reality. As regards the first question, it must be said straight away that the correctly understood history of man is not an element of mere chance imposed on man in addition to his existence as a being of transcendence but that it is precisely the history of his transcendental being as such. He does not live out his existence orientated to God in a pure or even mystical interiority, in some sort of submersion running away from history but lives it out precisely in the individual and collective history of his very being. Hence Christianity can still be seen to consist absolutely in the grace-constituted transcendental being of man and yet still in very truth be the actual history in which this being is achieved and which confronts man himself in spatio-temporal facticity. Truly there is then a history-of-salvation of the human word in which the divine word gives itself; the Church furthermore is truly the assembly of salvation and the sacrament, even though all these historical objectifications of man's absolute depth-of-being open to God's grace only have and retain their own nature when all these historical manifestations appear as what they are, namely as instruments of mediation and signs pointing to the incomprehensibility of a God who communicates himself in all truth and reality to man through these signs so as to become directly present in an absolute and forgiving manner. If and as long as these historical mediations are really mediations to the presence and acceptance of the mystery of God, and while retaining their relative nature yet prove themselves even in this way as unavoidable for the historical being of man in this aeon before the direct vision of God is reached, history and transcendence will never be subject in Christianity to an ideology of immanence, i.e. to the idolisation of intramundane powers, or to an ideology of transmanence and transcendence, i.e. to the idolisation in empty, formal abstractions of man's transcendentality by grace. Two further points must be noted in this connection. Firstly, the historicity of man, understood as mediation of his transcendental being elevated by grace reaches it unsurpassable climax in Jesus Christ, the God-man; in him God's promise of himself to the world, its historical mediation and its acceptance by man have become absolutely one in a union which is not fusion and yet eliminates separation; thus this represents the historically unsurpassable eschatological communication of God to man himself through the history of grace in the world (without it being thereby possible simply to identify in some monophysite sense the historical mediation of God and God himself); man can and must accept this mediation-by-immediacy to God as something quite irreplaceable, by humbly accepting it in his own transcendentality by grace as something which is historically ordained and freely contingent. Man's reference to this historical mediation of his own grace inserted in the ground of his being does not take place merely or in the first place by a theoretical, historical knowledge about these historical events of salvation, a sort of knowledge which could be suspected as an ideology; it is given in an immediate, realistic manner which, through the living unity of the history of salvation, through the Church (which is more than just the subsequent totality of the theoretical opinions of those who agree), through sacraments and worship, through what we call anamnesis, tradition, etc., bursts open any merely theoretical information. Because man is mediated to the historical event of salvation and this mediation does not take place merely by way of theoretical information—since he experiences this mediation as the event of his own transcendental and supernaturally elevated being—he has always gone beyond the three above-mentioned basic forms of ideology. Secondly, it must be stated here that the necessary historical mediation of transcendentally established grace also draws the Christian's attention to the fact that he can and must also take his 'profane' history absolutely seriously. He does this not by turning it into an ideology and by thus erecting it into an absolute, but by the fact of experiencing it as the concrete expression of the will of God who posits it in freedom: thereby he both removes it from himself as the conditioned and historically contingent and lends it the seriousness proper to the situation in which an eternal destiny is decided before God.

We wish now to add some of the consequences of our basic thesis to the aforegoing fundamental reflections on why Christianity is not an ideology.

(a) Christianity is not an ideology. From its nature and reflex doctrine about this its own reality, we could certainly derive general norms about God-conformed human activity, even in the sphere of the profane world, norms whose ultimate import is to preserve the openness of man to the God of absolute and forgiving nearness, and this in all dimensions of human existence, i.e. not limiting faith to a particular human existential dimension but making it the inner, formal law of man's whole life. But these general norms, in so far as they are contained in the message of Christianity and are proclaimed in the Church by her magisterium, leave room for imperatives and programmes which are determined by situations and history. Two conclusions follow from this. On the one hand, the Church as such cannot become the direct and, as it were, official bearer of such concrete imperatives or of such concrete, history-forming guiding ideas; she cannot tell the Christian concretely in his individual and collective history what he must do exactly here and now; she cannot relieve him of the burden of the daring historical decision and its possible failure, and she cannot preserve him from the fact that history frequently gets into impossible situations. In other words, the Church must defend herself against becoming an ideology, if this is understood in the sense of a historical guiding idea which believes that if it is to have any real historical impact it must assert itself absolutely. On the other hand, the refusal by the Church to becoming an ideology in this sense does not mean that the Christian as such has no obligation in his individual and collective decision, and by reason of his Christian responsibility, to decide on some definite concrete imperative for the here and now and to bear the burden and risk for actions subsequent on such a concrete imperative. If his transcendentally Christian being realises itself in its history, and this in all its dimensions, then, even though the Church as such cannot furnish him with them, this quite simply entails the necessity and duty of finding concrete imperatives of his historical action in the midst of Christian existence. The Christian accepts this Christian responsibility for concrete decision in his historical situation; he takes this responsibility seriously as being obedience to the absolutely binding will of the living God; yet he does not turn this decision into an ideology since, without holding everything to be relative in a quietistic or sceptical way, he always lodges his decision again within the providence of the incontrollable Lord of history, in whose grace the success and failure of this decision can be saved and become availing unto salvation, and who can expect other decisions in conformity to his will from other ages and indeed enable men to take them.

(b) If Christianity is not an ideology—if, in other words, the imperatives and concrete decisions about intramundane actions and positions which Christians may and must have, must not be turned into an ideology—then there must be tolerance among Christians as an expression of the necessary avoidance of particular ideologies in the Church. Such tolerance is necessary because it is not to be expected that this choice of concrete imperatives, this interpretation of the historical moment and the decision for a particular path of history, will always be seen to be the same for all Christians. The struggle between such different decisions will be utterly unavoidable even among Christians; it cannot be avoided by any purely theoretical debates since this would presuppose that, at least in principle, the concrete imperatives for the here and now can be derived from universal principles and from a purely statistical, neutral analysis of the particular situation; such a possibility is a rationalistic error, since every decision for a concrete action adds a non-derivative factor to the *a priori* intuition of essences, viz. the choice of concrete existence from among many possibilities. Precisely because we cannot avoid a struggle, i.e. a real competition between opposite tendencies of realisation beyond the plane of the purely theoretical, there must necessarily be among Christians and in the Church what is meant by tolerance: understanding for the other's position, fairness in battle even when it is conducted seriously, that rare unity in determination with which one fights for one's own position, and the readiness to allow oneself to be defeated and to remain in the totality of the Church which decides differently.

From what has been said above about anonymous Christianity, as being the very opposite to an understanding of Christianity as an ideology, it follows then that there must be a similar attitude of positive tolerance towards non-Christians; this tolerance distinguishes the firmness and missionary zeal of the Faith from the fanaticism which is and must be characteristic of an ideology because only by such fanaticism can an ideology safeguard its strict boundaries against the greater reality surrounding it; Christianity in contrast is of its very nature commanded to look for itself in the other and to trust that it will once more meet itself and its greater fullness in the other.

2. The Christian Future of Man*

As an abiding witness to the world's Absolute Future, the Church is an eschatological community of supernatural faith and hope. The Church's consciousness that she is the definitive community of the Incarnate Word is her assurance that she will continue to exist as an institutional community until the history of God's identification with the world through the Incarnation of the Word reaches its culmination at the Parousia.

The Christian does not believe, however, that only members of the institutional Church can work effectively for the Absolute Future. In his Providence God can use anonymous Christians to achieve his purpose, and the Church's assurance that she will perdure as an institutional community does not mean that she will not be a diaspora Church, a small minority of explicit believers scattered among a secularized population which has little explicit knowledge of Christ or conscious identification with his eschatological community.

Christianity is a religion of the future. It can indeed be understood only in the light of the future which it conceives as an absolute future gradually approaching the individual and humanity as a whole. Its interpretation of the past takes place in and through the progressive unveiling of an approaching future, and the meaning and significance of the present is based on the hopeful openness to the approach of the absolute future. After all, Christianity understands the world within the framework of salvation *history*; this means, however, that properly speaking and in the last analysis it is not a doctrine of a static existence of the world and of man which, remaining always the same, repeats itself in an of-itself-empty period of time, without actually progressing; rather, it is the proclamation of an absolute becoming which does not continue into emptiness but really attains the absolute future, which is indeed already moving *within* it; for, this becoming is so truly distinguished from its yet-to-come future and fulfilment (without implying pantheism, therefore) that the infinite reality of this future is nevertheless already active within it and supports it as an inner constitutive element of this becoming, even though it is independent of this becoming itself (and in this way every form of primitive deism and any merely external relationship of God and the world are

*From *Theological Investigations*, vol. VI, pp. 60-63, 65-68.
© 1969 and 1974 by Darton, Longman & Todd Ltd.

eliminated from the very start, and the truth *in* pantheism is preserved). The real nature of man can therefore be defined precisely as the possibility of attaining the absolute future, i.e. not this or that state which is always embraced and thus made relative again by some other and greater future still to come and yet imposed as a task, which would then also be recognised as such a relative future. Christianity, therefore, is the religion of becoming, of history, self-transcendence, and of the future. For Christianity, everything given is something imposed as a task, and everything is understandable only by what is yet to come. The tending towards a still outstanding future has indeed its own measure and a nature behind it which projects a horizon of the possible in front of it, and also a law in accordance with which it takes up position. But since the absolute fullness of the divine reality is the ultimate reason, and since this very God who starts everything by giving himself as the end is the ultimate goal, any understanding of being and nature conforms to reality only if it seeks to understand in the light of that future which unveils the beginning for the first time.

Christianity is the religion of the *absolute* future. We have really already indicated the meaning of this in the previous paragraph. Man (and humanity) is the reality which knowingly and willingly is always ahead of itself, the reality which constitutes itself by projecting its future, or better, by projecting itself (i.e. its nature) towards *it* (or, since it is a question of the projecting of the *absolute* future which *per definitionem* cannot really be planned and formed: lets this future approach him). If this is so, then the decisive question for a metaphysical anthropology will be whether the future, towards which man projects himself, is merely a categorial future, i.e. one whose single and distinct, and therefore spatio-temporally bound elements form this future in combination (possibly planned and manipulated, possibly also always more complex), so that being something finite, it is always still basically encompassed by a further empty future possibility, *or* whether the unsurpassable, infinite future as such comes towards man and hence the possible space of the future and the future in the present become identical.

With regard to this question, Christianity opts for the second possibility: the absolute future is the true and real future of man; *it* is a real possibility for him, it is offered to him, it is something coming towards him, it is the future state and its acceptance is the ultimate task of his existence. Since the only way in which man can be concerned about a feasible future which has a spatio-temporal point and which is constructed out of the partial elements of his world, is by passing beyond it into the basic totality of unbounded possibility, man's intramundane care always contains (at least implicitly, and often perhaps also deliberately pushed aside) the question about the possible encounter with this infinite totality as such; in short, with the absolute future. Christianity answers this question in the sense that this absolute future is not only the always still absent condition of the possibility of a categorised intramundane planning of, hoping for and attaining of the future, but also becomes as such the communicated, attained future of man itself.

Christianity therefore poses man the *one* question as to how he wants basically to understand himself: as a being only acting *in* the whole but having nothing to do with the whole as such, even through projection towards the whole as an asymptotic horizon is always the condition of the possibility of his knowledge and action; or as a receptively acting being *of* the whole, a being which has something to do even with this condition for his knowledge, action and hope as *such* and which allows this totality, the absolute future itself, to approach it and to become an event for it in the action by which it creates the future within the bounds of this totality. This ultimately is the only question posed by Christianity. It follows from the very nature of the totality of the absolute future that this totality cannot really become the object of a proper classification or of a technical manipulation, but remains the unspeakable mystery which precedes and surpasses all individual cognition and each individual action *on* the world.

A mere glance at the current concepts of Christian dogmatic theology in which this thesis of Christianity as the religion of the absolute future is expressed, will show us that Christianity really understands itself in this way. Absolute future is just another name for what is really meant by 'God'. For the absolute future by its very concept cannot exist as a future which is manufactured out of finite, individual material and by classifiable combination; but it cannot be a merely empty possibility in the sense of being the not-yet-real, even when seen as the end and warrant of the dynamism of the world's and man's movement into the future, or as the sustaining hope; if it is the sustaining ground of the dynamism towards the future, then it must be the absolute fullness of reality. In point of fact the absolute future understood *in this way* is precisely what we call God. Conversely, from what has been said, there follows a twofold conclusion concerning God. Firstly, it follows that he is known precisely *as* the absolute future; in other words, he is not one object among many others with which one is concerned as individual objects within the unbounded system of co-ordinates of knowledge and planning action for the future, but rather is the ground of this whole projection towards the future. Knowledge of God is therefore always included when man projects himself towards the future, especially when man gives no name to this whole but tries to leave it unspecified. Secondly, God—understood as the absolute future—is basically and necessarily the unspeakable mystery, since the original totality of the absolute future, towards which man projects himself, can never really be expressed in the precise characteristics proper to it by determinations taken from intramundane, classifiable experience; thus he is and remains essentially a mystery, i.e. he is known *as* the essentially transcendent, of whom it is of course said that, understood precisely as this mystery of infinite fullness, he is the self-communicating absolute future of man.

Even though it is the religion of the absolute future, a religion which remains neutral in the face of the individual and collective aims of man and leaves them free, Christianity has an inestimable significance for this movement towards genuine and meaningful earthly goals. Christianity, it is true, does not maintain that only *its* followers can serve this earthly future objectively and with the involvement of the whole man. This would be no more true than to say that it regards itself as the sole genuine bearer of such intramundane aims for the future or that it disputes the fact of having been in quite a few cases an actual obstacle to such efforts on account of the historico-ecclesiastical forms in which it has manifested itself. There are obviously men who—without being manifestly Christians—spend themselves in selfless service for the welfare and social development of man. Christianity, it is true, maintains by its very teaching about the oneness of the love of God and of neighbour that whenever someone serves man and his dignity lovingly and in *absolute* selflessness, he affirms God at least implicitly and also works out his salvation before God by his affirmation of absolute moral values and imperatives . . . but it does not maintain in any sense that this is possible only in someone who is explicitly a Christian.

Nevertheless, Christianity even taken as the thematically explicit religion which sees God as the absolute future, has great significance for intramundane society and its goals. By its hope for an absolute future, Christianity defends man against the temptation of engaging in the justified intramundane efforts for the future with *such* energy that every generation is always sacrificed in favour of the next, so that the future becomes a Moloch before whom the man existing at present is butchered for the sake of some man who is never real and always still to come. Christianity makes it comprehensible why even *that* man preserves his dignity and intangible significance who can no longer make any tangible contribution to the approach to the intramundane future. Christianity lends ultimate radical significance to the work for this intramundane future: it declares in its teaching on the unity of the love of God and of neighbour that the positive relationship to man is an indispensable, essential element and the irreplaceable means for the relationship to God, the absolute future (and 'salvation'). If, however, this man who is to be loved cannot exist except as someone who makes projects with a view to his future, then this means that the love of God understood as the love of neighbour cannot exist without the will to *this* man and hence also to his intramundane future. This does not ideologise this will or estrange it from itself, but merely makes it explicit in its absolute dignity and in its radical nature as an obligation.

[Christians] believe, however, that God sends himself precisely in this way to men as the absolute future for man, and that he can and must therefore be named and expected by man. This is what they understand by religion. Religion for them is not the solution of those questions arising in this world, as it were functionally, *between* individual realities in their mutual relationships; it is the solution of the question which refers to the *whole* of these many different realities. Since this question will always remain, religion too—Christianity—will always remain, since its nature consists precisely in not confusing the question of the world with the question *in* the world.

This permanent religion will always remain as an institutional religion. Since man must *also* accomplish, in a reflex way, even his transcendental relation to the one totality of his existence, his world and his future, he has to accomplish it also in conceptual categories, in concrete actions, in the social order, briefly: in a Church. He cannot do it in any other way. If, therefore, the religion of the future is to be present always, then it will always be there as a social quantity. This quantity in its historical concreteness will always depend *also* on the profane order of secular society. Since Christianity has no concretely binding view of this profane society and is also incapable of prophesying about it, it cannot make any prediction about the *concrete form* of its own socio-ecclesiological structure of the future.

Since Christianity—however much it knows itself to be the religion which in itself is meant for all men—knows in the *very* nature of things and in its *eschatology* that it will be a controversial and even rejected institution until the dawn of the absolute future itself, this reason alone suffices to prevent it from counting on ecclesiastical and secular society ever becoming even merely materially identified. It itself is after all the socially organised community of free belief in the absolute future, of a belief therefore which is necessarily based on the individual decision of each person. Hence it cannot expect in any way that all men will ever *in actual fact* belong to it. Since the earthly future of mankind, however, tends more and more towards a social organisation of mankind as one and as a whole, and not to historically and geographically limited cultures particular to each individual people, a situation is rapidly approaching when everyone will be the neighbour of everyone else. This means that in future there also will be no more *homogeneous* regional strata and societies in the Christian sense. In the historical and social unity of the one humanity, Christianity will therefore be everywhere as well as being everywhere merely a part of humanity, since presumably embracing only a minority.

3. The Church and the Parousia of Christ*

The Church as the eschatological community of faith and hope does not simply abide through human history. Through her work in the world she actively contributes to its progressive development. This means that Christians cannot be indifferent to the legitimate worldly hopes of modern man which are nourished by his growing confidence in his ability to bend the course of nature to his will. Nature can no longer be simply accepted as a given. The manipulation of nature is a task for which man as homo faber *must assume responsibility. Since the order of creation is included within the order of redemption, the Church is obliged to guide her children in the active planning through which they will shape the future of the world.*

Faith and hope are not merely human attitudes towards something to come, and therefore only promised, but they are man's personal self-realisation, the ultimate and most necessary principle for whose being and actualisation is the grace of God itself. But this is not any kind of aid given to an act which would still be merely human and creaturely and rob the aid and the divine word of revelation of its power by making it subject to the *a priori* of human nature. The grace of faith and hope in the last analysis (leaving out of account creaturely and necessary effects of grace which can rightly in their turn be called grace) is God himself making it possible by his communication of himself to man for his act to remain truly human and yet to be the hearing and the uttering of the Word of God as such and not merely of the response to it within the horizon of mere finitude and merely human-spiritual transcendence; this self-communication of God as the reason for hope results in man's hope grasping not merely the *concept* of a future hoped-for object within the horizon of human desire but the hoped-for object itself.

In so far as faith and hope have what is believed and hoped for, namely the God of eternal life, as the inner principle of faith and hope and to that extent experience in the act of believing and hoping this *a priori* principle of faith and hope itself notwithstanding its necessary categorial mediation through the human word, and although it is not represented objectively in its own self, we must without hesitation speak of an experience of grace, of revelation, and of faith. In it the Church is not only in fact given the eschatological gift by which she is herself constituted but this is experienced. The Church is the community of those who already possess the eschatological gift which is God himself, who in full liberty really accept

*From *Theological Investigations,* vol. VI, pp. 304-05, 310-12.
© 1969 and 1974 by Darton, Longman & Todd Ltd.

this possession, who confess in faith that this possession and its acceptance has been caused by the free action of God's love, and who hope for the unveiling of this possession by the power contained within it. She belongs therefore to the present time in so far as she is still moving towards the goal by faith and hope, that is in so far as she must still let the Parousia of Christ come upon her, and at the same time she belongs to eternity, as she moves towards her end in virtue of the future which has already arrived.

The Church's experience of herself as the community which possesses the eschatological good of salvation 'only' in faith and hope is naturally not only an experience of faith and hope to the extent that what is really believed and hoped is experienced through the mediation of human categorial objectivity in a way which is itself again merely abstract. This mediation is a concrete historical one and signifies for faith and hope real darkness, trouble, constancy in the face of always new and unforeseen situations, of contradiction on the part of unbelief, of despair, of a future Utopia conceived within the limits of this world. In brief, the concrete history of the Church is the means by which the transcendental experience in faith and hope of grace as the divine life itself is objectified and so becomes in the concrete the object of man's saving decision. And this history of the Church's experience is therefore at once a means and a temptation for faith and hope. If one were to deny to history a positive function as a means one would fundamentally be disputing that in her explicit confession of faith, which is after all part of the dimension of history, the Church is herself again a work of grace and not only a merely human reaction to a grace which remains meta-historical. If one were to deny in this history the character of temptation for faith (in theory or in practice), then the Church would be regarded fundamentally as the manifest presence of God in the world and faith and hope would become an evident possession of eternal life, which could at the most be hidden in some way by that human history which remains extrinsic to salvation and its possession and does not play any part in the history of salvation as such.

In this section we would like at least briefly to touch upon a question which was left open in the previous section, namely the question what exactly is the relationship of the Church as institution and official ministry to the Church as eschatological entity. The eschatological character of the Church was after all developed from the concept of the Church as the fruit of salvation, not so much from the Church as means of salvation. Now these two aspects are essentially interdependent, even though they cannot be simply identified with one another. For the Church is at least in part the means of salvation precisely in so far as she is the believing and confessing community, constituted by the predetermining power of God's grace, of those who glory in the triumphant grace of God's divinising and forgiving self-communication to mankind and who with missionary zeal as 'God's co-workers' in the service of grace move men precisely through this confession of faith to accept divine grace.

Our treatment of the subject of the Church and eschatology would be left incomplete if we did not also cast a glance at those this-worldly future hopes and Utopias which exist today in a way and with an urgency which was impossible in earlier ages. Obviously even in earlier times man was a being who could and had to fashion his life actively in freedom. But in earlier times, and particularly at the time of the origin of Christianity, the area of man's capacity springing from his inner nature of freely and actively fashioning his own being was so narrowly limited and so well within his range of vision, that its possibility for the future had in practice to be experienced as the more or less near present. Man could at that time have only an inner attitude of surrender or protest against a fate laid upon him in point of fact simply by nature: he could not really be the active, creative designer and planner of himself, the world he lived in, and so also of a more remote future. But this is something which he can do today. He does not just more or less accept Nature as his world, but he changes it and fashions it into that world which he has of his own accord determined to live in. Nature is no longer merely the given unalterable stage upon which he acts out his being, including the history of his salvation and damnation, but the mere material, the quarry, out of which he first constructs the scenery in the midst of which as expressing his own self-understanding he wants to live out his historical existence. The practical possibilities of such an active self-realisation in the active transformation of the human sphere of existence are today perhaps still very limited: but this future has begun, and there is an enormously increased area of the future which man anticipates in his planning.

Christianity must come to meet this really new experience of man's existence; it cannot be mastered immediately and adequately from the New Testament alone, for such an existential experience did not exist at that time to any notable extent. The Church as the eschatological community of salvation living in the faith and the hope of a future which is the gift of God himself and which is not designed and created by man, must come to terms with this new existential experience of modern man to whom is opened both for himself as an individual and for mankind as a whole a real and extensive future which can be foreseen, planned and realised. This will mean in the first place, that Christianity should recognise the fundamentally Christian roots of this situation of modern man and so accept it as being itself genuinely Christian. In point of fact this situation has a Christian origin, firstly because Christianity of its very essence conceives the totality of reality primarily as history and Nature as one element of this, and not *vice versa*; secondly, because Nature as truly created and thereby as *not* divine and the role of God as the personal partner of man signify that it is not a numinous Nature but the Word of God and man himself who are the real representatives of God in the world and that Nature is in reality that which man is to make subject to himself, because it is nothing else than the continuation of his bodiliness and therefore reaches its fulfilment in him and his history: it is not the other way about, man ultimately sharing the extra-human and infra-human destiny of nature.

Once the Christian antecedents of man's new situation as *homo faber sui ipsius et mundi* are seen in spite of all the *hybris* and corruption which surrounded this new understanding of existence at its birth and still surrounds it today as it continues upon its both beneficial and harmful way, then Christianity must unhesitatingly recognise that future plans and future utopias within this world are not only from the Christian standpoint legitimate, but are the destiny which God's providence has assigned to man, in the carrying out and suffering of which alone can he live his Christian calling genuinely and completely today. Only on this condition can Christianity say to the man of today that his future, too, stands under the sign of creatureliness, of sin, of law, of death, of pointlessness and of redemption by Christ and that this future, too, is redeemed and sanctified and given its own proper meaning by the fact that it is already overtaken by the future of Christ come upon us and by the divine self-communication, and that therefore this future too, if it is to bring man his salvation, must happen in the *kairos* of Christ. But the Church must see (and live out) the fact that she is not the true and credible eschatological community of salvation by being the resentful, ineffectual and fearful host of those who deny themselves the greatness, the duty and the danger of this world of the future or who have taken up towards it an attitude which regards it exclusively as material, indifferent in itself, for the practice of Christian virtue, material without any of that original, worldly value which precisely as secular and worldly must be accepted by the Christian as a Christian without again sublimating its worldliness in a religious sense. What all this signifies more precisely in the concrete, how in this situation the different Christian professions each have their own specific tasks, opportunities and dangers of failure, cannot be considered any further here. But this will have to happen, if the Church's understanding of herself as the eschatological salvation-community to which God has given himself and which still waits for his kingdom, is today not to be misinterpreted by the Church herself and misunderstood by non-Christians.

4. On Christian Dying*

The individual Christian will not have to wait until the Parousia to meet his Absolute Future. Each human subject will encounter God at the moment of his death. Death is the moment of final and irrevocable decision. At the instant of its death each human soul, freed from the resistance of its "nature," will either ratify or reverse the fundamental option of its life in a single act of total and irreversible self-commitment. The outcome of that total and definitive act of self-commitment is either salvation or damnation. Sinful souls may still require the purification of Purgatory, but each soul's ultimate destiny is settled by the choice of its fundamental option at the instant of its death.

Rahner's theology of death is an extension of the theology of the fundamental option and of the theology of concupiscence which we have seen in previous chapters. These theologies in their turn were developments of the metaphysics of the incarnate human spirit which Rahner established in Hearers of the Word. *Rahner's theology of death, like his theology of the departed soul's continued relation to historical society on earth, depends on that metaphysics for their grounding. They are strictly systematic positions.*

The deepest and most ultimate reason for the connection with and orientation to death which is most intimately inherent in man, which makes him mortal and in virtue of this fact renders all men now and for ever subject to death in the truest sense, is the freedom of the spirit. It is this, ultimately speaking, that makes man mortal, and mortality in the biological sense is only the manifestation and the realisation in the concrete of this mortality, which has its origin and basis in the freedom with which man is endowed as spiritual. How then can this be the case? Freedom is not the power constantly to change one's course of action, but rather the power to decide that which is to be final and definitive in one's life, that which cannot be superseded or replaced, the power to bring into being from one's own resources that which must be, and must not pass away, the summons to a decision that is irrevocable. If freedom were capable of achieving only that which could subsequently be abolished by a further free decision, then freedom would be nothing more than power over that which is purely neutral and indecisive, that which is always open to subsequent revision, a miserable sort of freedom, condemned, as it were, to proceed in futile circles without any final resting place, ultimately meaningless. If, therefore, man *is* personal freedom, then it follows that he is one who uses the resources of his own innermost nature to

*From *Theological Investigations*, vol. VII, pp. 287-91.
© 1971 by Darton, Longman & Todd Ltd.

form himself by his own free act, for by the exercise of this freedom of his he can definitively determine the shape of his life as a whole, and decide what his ultimate end is to be, the ultimate realisation of his own nature, beyond all possibility of revision.

Now the physical side of man's nature, in which he actively works out the shape of his life as person and brings it to its consummation, is so constituted that it sets him in the dimension of that which is constantly open to further development. It follows from this that while it can be the dimension in which freedom is exercised *in fieri,* it cannot be that in which the fulness of freedom is achieved, the dimension of that consummation to which freedom finally and definitively attains. Freedom enters into the dimension of becoming and of openness to further development only in order to achieve its own consummation. To this extent it is exercised at this physical level of man's being only in order to pass beyond it and transcend it, and so to attain to its definitive goal. The free man is willing to accept the limitations of mortality only in order that the exercise of his freedom on this plane may enable him to attain to that true immortality which lies beyond, and which consists not in an unending evolution in time but in the achieved finality of eternity itself—in that, therefore, which is beyond time.

At its deepest level the exercise of free decision bears upon death itself. It must do so because, in order to arrive at its own final perfection it must will death as that which puts an end to the mere prolongation of temporal existence. It is only on the surface of our awareness that we shrink from death. At its deepest level this awareness of ours craves for that which is imperfect and incomplete in use to be brought to an end in order that it may be finally perfected. Indeed if anyone told us that our present state would last for ever we would regard this in itself as tantamount to being damned, for it would mean that every fleeting and transitory moment of our existence was *ipso facto* deprived of its true value, a value which consists in the fact that each of these moments provides us with the possibility of making a decision of final and permanent validity. For the outcome of the free act is always something which endures.

Of course Christianity recognises a special kind of perfection to be attained through the exercise of freedom, one that goes beyond that which death brings, namely that state of perfection in grace which the first man was offered the possibility of attaining to in Paradise. In this situation of primæval blessedness to man would not simply have enjoyed an indefinite prolongation of his earthly life; here too his freedom would have defined some state of final perfection which would have been achieved by some radical transformation of the physical side of his human nature as realised in the concrete. But in Paradise the physical side of the man who had attained to the state of Paradisal perfection would have undergone an extremely radical change. It would have been raised to a state of glorifica-

tion in which it was no longer subject to constant change and flux, unfolding itself in an unending series of transformations. At the same time,
however, primordial man would not have relinquished the physical side of
his nature as we have to relinquish it now in order to achieve our own
perfection. To that extent this necessity of death to which we are subject
is a sign of the guilt in Adam of the whole race, a manifestation of the
sinfulness of all. But even this does not derogate from the fact that death
precisely *as* that which perfects us and raises us above the continuous
flow of time, as the incursion of that finality which is posited once and for
all in freedom, is on a higher level than the mere process of becoming
which we now call life. The one death which comes to all is natural and in
harmony with our natures inasmuch as it is the birth of that finality aimed
at in freedom which is the ultimate object of man's will at its most basic
and fundamental. Death is 'unnatural' in its immediate effect upon the
physical side, which is an essential part of man's nature, inasmuch as in
death this cannot at once be transformed and raised in glory to that state
of final perfection for which man's life, taken as a single and continuous
whole, is designed. Instead at first this physical side of our nature simply
falls away from us as something which we have to transcend and get
beyond, and is relinquished as though it were of no permanent significance.

Thus from our consideration of the universality of death, inasmuch as
this is an article of faith, we have been brought spontaneously and inevitably face to face with quite different and far deeper factors which are
essentially inherent in death. Death is the breaking in of finality upon
mere transience—that finality which is the concretisation of freedom
come to its maturity. But when we make this assertion we intend it as the
Christian answer both to the materialist teaching that at death man ceases
totally to exist, and to the teaching of the transmigration of souls, which
implicitly denies the unique and final value of this earthly life and its
importance as providing the opportunity for absolute decision (in reality
this latter doctrine recognises only the miserable fate of being condemned
to the eternal cycle of birth and death). But while all this is true as far as it
goes, a further point must straight away be added to it: this act of freedom
which ultimately determines what man's final state is to be comes to its
fulness, as we have seen, in death. For that very reason it constitutes the
absolute climax of the process of enfeeblement and deprivation of power
in man.

The freedom which is exercised on the physical plane is, in fact, that
freedom by which man lays himself open to intervention from without,
submits to control by another power or powers. The physical side of
man's nature constitutes the sphere in which the interplay takes place of
action from within himself and passion as imposed from without. As a
physical being endowed with freedom man has to take cognisance of the

fact that he occupies an intermediary position. He is neither wholly self-directing nor wholly subject to control by another, but half-way between these two. The mysterious interplay between action and passion in the exercise of human freedom appears above all in the fact that it is precisely at the very point at which man freely achieves his own perfection that he is, at the same time, most wholly subject to control by another. The ultimate act of freedom, in which he decides his own fate totally and irrevocably, is the act in which he either *willingly accepts or definitively rebels against* his own utter impotence, in which he is utterly subject to the control of a mystery which cannot be expressed—that mystery which we call God. In death man is totally withdrawn from himself. Every power, down to the last vestige of a possibility, of autonomously controlling his own destiny is taken away from him. Thus the exercise of his freedom taken as a whole is summed up at this point in one single decision: whether he yields everything up or whether everything is taken from him by force, whether he responds to this radical deprivation of all power by uttering his assent in faith and hope to the nameless mystery which we call God, or whether even at this point he seeks to cling on to his own autonomy, protests against this fall into helplessness, and, because of his disbelief, supposes that he is falling into the abyss of nothingness when in reality he is falling into the unfathomable depths of God.

On the basis of this it is possible for us to realise that death can be either an act of faith or a mortal sin. In order rightly to understand this we must consider (and perhaps it would have been clearer to make this point right from the first) that the actual act of dying does not necessarily occur at that point in time in the physical order at which doctors suppose it to take place, and at which it is considered to take place in the popular estimation when men speak of the final departure and of death as coming at the end of life. In reality we *are* dying all our lives through right up to this, the final point in the process of dying. Every moment of life is a stage on the way to this final goal, a stage which already carries this end within itself and derives its significance from it, just as when one sees a shot fired one can already estimate, even as it is travelling, where the impact will fall. Life, therefore, is in a true sense a process of dying, and what we are accustomeed to call death is the final point in this life-long process. Dying takes place throughout life itself, and death when it comes is only the ultimate and definitive completion of the process. Now this death in life or living death, as it may be called, can become one of two things: it can be made into an enduring act of faith in the fact that our lives and destinies are being directed and controlled by another and that this direction is right; the willing acceptance of our destiny, the ultimate act of self-commitment to that destiny, a renunciation which we make in anticipation of our final end because in the end we must renounce all things; also because we believe that it is only by this poverty entailed in freely accepting our own destiny that we can free ourselves for the hand of God in his unfathomable power and grace to dispose of us as he wills. *Alternatively* this death in the midst of life can become an act of desperately clinging on by main force to that which is destined to fall away from us, a protest, whether silent or expressed, against this death in life, the despair of one who is avid for life and who imagines that he has to sin and so to obtain his happiness by force. The death that is accomplished in life, therefore, must be really the act of that loving and therefore trustful faith which gives man courage to allow himself to be taken up by another. Otherwise it will become the mortal sin which consists in the pride of seeking one's own absolute autonomy, anxiety (*Angst*) and despair all in one.

5. The Life of the Dead*

Since man is an incarnate spirit, the human soul, even after death, retains its relation to the material world. Thus the dead are still concerned with the evolution of the world's history. Man's ultimate future, his union with the Trinity at the Parousia, is a human *future. Therefore it requires the resurrection of the body and a glorified life in a new heavens and a new earth. So Christ's Second Coming will be truly the glorification of his material creation.*

But if immortal man thus claims against time's mere dissolution that which is valid in his personal existence, it is only God's word of revelation which tells him clearly what is the actual concrete meaning of his being. It makes him experience his possible eternity for the first time, by revealing to him the *actuality* of eternity. The fulfilment revealed in the gospel message is manifold in content: eternity as the fruit of time means to come before *God* either to reach pure immediacy and closeness to him face to face in the absolute decision of love for him, or to be enveloped in the burning darkness of eternal god-lessness in the definitive closing of one's heart against him. Revelation, building on the grade of God and its power, presupposes that *every* man, no matter how his ordinary life appeared on earth, achieves so much spiritual and personal eternity in his life, that the possibility inherent in his spiritual substance is realized in fact as eternal life. Scripture knows of no life which is not worthy to be definitive, it does not recognize any life as superfluous. Since God knows each man by name, since *everyone* exists in time before the God who is judgment and salvation, *everyone* is a man of eternity, not just the enlightened spirits of human history. Further, the theology of St John makes it

*From *Theological Investigations*, vol. VII, pp. 287-91.
© 1971 by Darton, Longman & Todd Ltd.

clear that the existence of eternity is seen as inserted in time, and that hence eternity grows out of time and is not just the after-thought of a reward appended to time. The *reality* of the blissful life of the dead is described in Scripture by innumerable images: as rest and peace, as a banquet and a state of glory, as being at home in the Father's house, as the kingdom of the eternal lordship of God, as the fellowship of all who have been perfected in bliss, as the inheriting of the glory of God, as day without night, as satisfaction without satiety. Throughout all these words of Scripture we sense the same thing: God is the absolute mystery. And hence the consummation, the absolute nearness to God, is itself an ineffable mystery to which we go and which the dead who have died in the Lord have found. There is not much we can say. But it is the mystery of unspeakable *bliss*. No wonder then that the sheer silence of bliss cannot be heard by our ears. And finally: revelation tells us that the *whole* of the unity of temporal man is given its definitiveness, so that it may also be called the resurrection of the flesh. And this doctrine of Scripture is not merely enunciated in words: it is experimentally seized in faith as a dawning reality in the resurrection of the Crucified.

In the Christian doctrine proposed by the Church of the 'immortality of the soul' and of the 'resurrection of the flesh' the whole man in his unity is always envisaged. This affirmation does not deny or call in doubt that there is a differentiation intrinsic to the definitive state of man which corresponds to the justifiable distinction of 'body' and 'soul' in his makeup. But if, as cannot be doubted, the 'resurrection of the flesh' in the creed of the Church means the definitive salvation of man as a whole, then the doctrine of the immortality of the soul, being a truth of faith and not just a philosophical tenet, is also concerned in fact with such a life, such a 'soul' as for instance Jesus placed in the hands of his Father as he died. Hence this assertion is also directed to the *whole* reality and meaning of man as he depends on the creative and life-giving power of God, *whereby* of course it refers also to what the philosopher as such may call soul in contrast to body, with a destiny which he may try to trace after death. It would indeed be the moment to ask the philosopher what right he has to follow the fate of an isolated element of the whole, and not rather investigate the destiny that would transfigure the one, whole man; though perhaps indeed the philosopher, for his own part, would not dare to call this unimaginable but hoped-for transformation of the whole, valid and permanent, the 'resurrection of the flesh', and would still be inclined to give the name of 'soul' to what has become definitively and permanently sensible in the whole, regarding it to some extent as an extract of corporeal being which has become definitive in death.

There is this further difference between what the *Catholic* faith has to say of the dead and the belief of most Protestant Christians. It maintains firmly in the doctrine of purgatory that death does indeed make definitive the freely matured basic attitude of man, which again is purely by the grace of God, since this finality is good. But it also maintains that the many dimensions of man do not all attain their perfection simultaneously and hence that there is a full ripening of the whole man 'after' death, as this basic decision penetrates the whole extent of his reality. Such a difference of phasing, which results from the plurality of man's structure, is in fact also to be seen in the contrast between the fulfilment of the individual in death and the universal consummation of the world, between the finality achieved by man in death and the clarification and perfection of this fulfilment which is still to come in the transfiguration of his bodily existence. Since it cannot be denied that there is an 'intermediate state' in the destiny of man between death and bodily fulfilment, unless one holds that what is saved is not what was to be saved, there can be no decisive objection to the notion that man reaches personal maturity in this 'intermediate state'.

6. The Resurrection of the Body*

As we have seen, man is an incarnate historical spirit. Therefore a purely spiritual union with God, a Visio Beatifica *in which man's glorified body would have no part, cannot be the final perfection of man. Christ's victory, the triumphant result of his work in creation history, cannot have as its goal the disappearance of his material creation. Thus those blessed men and women who share in Christ's triumph at the Second Coming will be fully human members of the perfect society which will live with the Incarnate Christ on His glorified earth.*

When we Christians profess our belief in the 'resurrection of the body', what then do we really mean by it? What is the least we mean by it?

'Body' (*Fleisch*) means the whole man in his proper embodied reality. 'Resurrection' means, therefore, the termination and perfection of the *whole* man before God, which gives him 'eternal life'. Man is a many-sided being which in (and despite) its unity stretches, as it were, through several very different dimensions—through matter and spirit, nature and person, action and passion, etc. And so it is not surprising that the process of man's perfecting and the entrance into this perfection is not in itself a simple and identical quantity in every respect. And it is not surprising that the 'moment' of completion of such a stratified being is not simply the same for every one of these dimensions. Hence, as the

*From *Theological Investigations,* vol. IV, pp. 351-53.
© 1966 and 1974 by Darton, Longman & Todd Ltd.

Church's consciousness in faith has come to comprehend ever more clearly—instructed as it has been by the beginnings of such a comprehension in the Scriptures—the continuing reality of the personal spirit can already reach the direct communion with God by the event and moment which, looked at from its intramundane side, we experience as death. In so far as this union with God constitutes the innermost being of blessed completion, 'heaven' and 'eternal happiness' can already be given with death (Denz 530). Nevertheless, the deceased remains 'united' with the reality, fate and hence the temporal events of the world, however little we are able to 'picture' to ourselves such a continuing belonging-to-the-world and however few immediately comprehensible statements on this matter are contained in the Scriptures. We must simply try to realize clearly and soberly that a spiritual union with God cannot be regarded as something which grows in inverse proportion to the belonging to the *material* world, but that these are two quite disparate matters in themselves. Thus basically, for instance, there can be vision of God before death, and 'separation from the body' for the soul in death does not by a long way need to mean *ipso facto* a greater nearness to God. Remoteness-from-the-world and nearness-to-God are not interchangeable notions, however much we are accustomed to think in such a framework.

The deceased remain therefore (despite the *visio beatifica*) united with the fate of the world.

This world in its totality has a beginning and a history; it goes on towards a point which is not the end of its existence but the end of its unfinished and continually self-propagating history. It is true, we may not succeed in representing to ourselves concretely *how* it will be possible at some time to separate its continued existence in itself, on the one hand, and its transition into the unknown (to our prevision), on the other hand; it may be impossible to imagine how the former continues while the latter ceases. We may not be able to say what the then remaining world will be like (all attempts to picture this to oneself never get beyond the image). And yet, for all that, this final state of the world as a whole, which will come at a certain point but has not come as yet, is more *conceivable* for us today than it was perhaps for earlier generations and especially for the ancients. For to them this world of their experience gave the impression of being something eternal; change and transitoriness was only a happening in the lowest stratum of all in this 'eternal' world of 'eternal' laws, which was enveloped by the quietly reposing serenity of celestial spheres; for them (even for the Christians), beatitude could, therefore, only mean leaving the sphere of the transitory for the blessed heavenly spheres intended for this 'migration' in the framework of saving history; the history of salvation took place in the 'heaven'-enveloped world, but was not the development itself of heaven. We today are becoming more clearly aware of the developmental character of our world as a whole, in spite of

the ultimate uncertainty of the natural sciences and the extremely profound problems of a 'harmonization' of theological data and our natural
knowledge of the world. We have come to realize the senselessness of
trying to retrace the existence of the world into the infinite; the world
itself, practically down to the last detail—and not merely the revolutions
of its stars—is temporal.

If we allow the 'becoming', time and history to be really temporal and
do not in the end turn them again into a false eternity, then we may say
(very carefully): it does not contradict the nature of the world that this
open, self-propagating history has a beginning and an end. Who can say
how far this end is the very 'running-itself-to-death' of the course of the
world itself (which is happening in accordance with its eternal laws), how
far a halt is called by the creative and restraining Word of God, how far
both of these things ultimately come to the same thing! We know at any
rate from the testimony of God that this history of the world will come to
an end, and that this end will not be a sheer cessation, a 'being-no-longer'
of the world itself, but the participation in the perfection of the spirit. For
this spirit is assigned a beginning, but in relation to God. And hence its
beginning is not the beginning of the end, but the beginning of a development in freedom towards freely achieved completion, which does not
let the becoming end up in nothingness, but transforms it into the state
of finality. Furthermore, the deepest conviction of Christianity and of
idealism is true: the personal spirit is the meaning of the whole reality of
the world and, in spite of all its biologico-physical insignificance, it is *not
merely* a strange guest in a world which, standing ultimately untouched
and indifferent opposite this spirit, carries on its own history; the personal
spirit, precisely as human spirit, is a material, mundane, incarnate—
indeed *intra*-mundane spirit. And so the end of the world is participation in the perfection of the spirit: the world remains, beyond its previous
history, as the connatural surrounding of the achieved spirit which has
found its finality in the fellowship with God and achieves its own history
and that of the world at the same point. If this is so, however, it is
necessary to consider what exact form this history of spiritual persons has
taken and is taking: it is a history which, as the history of mankind, has
taken place (consciously or veiled to itself) with, for and against the
Person of the One who—right through death and resurrection—possessed
the life of God and the history of a human reality at one and the same
time—Jesus Christ, our Lord. The end of the world is, therefore, the
perfection and total achievement of saving history which had already
come into full operation and gained its decisive victory in Jesus Christ and
in his resurrection. In this sense his coming takes place at this consummation in power and glory: his victory made manifest, the breaking through
into experience, and the becoming manifest for experience too, of the fact
that the world as a whole flows into his Resurrection and into the trans-

figuration of his body. His Second Coming is not an event which is enacted in a localized manner on the stage of an *un*changed world which occupies a determined point in space in this world of our experience (how could everyone see it otherwise, for instance?); his Second Coming takes place at the moment of the perfecting of the world into the reality which he already possesses now, in such a way that he, the Godman, will be revealed to all reality and, within it, to every one of its parts in its own way, as the innermost secret and centre of all the world and of all history.

BIBLIOGRAPHY

KARL RAHNER'S COLLECTED WORKS

Theological Investigations Vol. I: God, Christ, Mary and Grace. London: Darton, Longman and Todd, 1961; New York: Seabury Press, 1974.

Theological Investigations Vol. II: Man in the Church. London: Darton, Longman and Todd, 1963; New York: Seabury Press, to appear in 1975.

Theological Investigations Vol. III: Theology of the Spiritual Life. London: Darton, Longman and Todd, 1967; New York: Seabury Press, 1974.

Theological Investigations Vol. IV: More Recent Writings. London: Darton, Longman and Todd, 1966; New York: Seabury Press, 1974.

Theological Investigations Vol. V: Later Writings. London: Darton, Longman and Todd, 1966; New York: Seabury Press, to appear in 1975.

Theological Investigations Vol. VI: Concerning Vatican Council II. London: Darton, Longman and Todd, 1969; New York: Seabury Press, 1974.

Theological Investigations Vol. VII: Further Theology of the Spiritual Life 1. London: Darton, Longman and Todd, 1971; New York: Seabury Press, 1972.

Theological Investigations Vol. VIII: Further Theology of the Spiritual Life 2. London: Darton, Longman and Todd, 1971; New York: Seabury Press, 1972.

Theological Investigations Vol. IX: Writings of 1965-1967 1. London: Darton Longman and Todd, 1972; New York: Seabury Press, 1973.

Theological Investigations Vol X: Writings of 1965-1967 2. London: Darton, Longman and Todd, 1973; New York: Seabury Press, 1973.

Theological Investigations Vol. XI: Confrontations 1. London: Darton, Longman and Todd, 1974; New York: Seabury Press, 1974.

Theological Investigations Vol. XII: Confrontations 2. London: Darton, Longman and Todd, 1975; New York: Seabury Press, to appear in 1975

Sacramentum Mundi: An Encyclopedia of Theology. 6 vols. Ed. by Karl Rahner et al. London: Burns and Oates; New York: Seabury Press, 1968-1970.

Secondary Sources: General

Gelpi, Donald L., S. J. *Light and Life: A Guide to the Theology of Karl Rahner*. New York: Sheed and Ward, 1966.

Roberts, Louis. *The Achievement of Karl Rahner*. New York: Herder and Herder, 1967.
Vorgrimmler, Herbert. *Karl Rahner: His Life, Thought, and Works*. Glen Rock, N.J.: Paulist Press, 1966.

Bibliography to Individual Chapters

I-III PHILOSOPHICAL ANTHROPOLOGY

Rahner, Karl. *Spirit in the World*. New York: Seabury Press, 1968.
———— *Hearers of the Word*. New York: Seabury Press, 1969.
———— "The Concept of Existential Philosophy in Heidegger," *Philosophy Today* 13 (1969), 126-137.

Secondary Sources

Baker, Kenneth, S.J. *A Synopsis of the Transcendental Philosophy of Emerich Coreth and Karl Rahner*. Spokane: Gonzaga University, 1965.
Branick, Vincent P. *An Ontology of Understanding: Karl Rahner's Metaphysics of Knowledge in the Context of Modern German Hermeneutics*. St. Louis: Marianist Communications Center, 1974.
Donceel, Joseph, S.J. *The Philosophy of Karl Rahner*. Albany: Magi Books, 1969.
———— "Rahner's Argument for God," *America* 123 (1970), 340-342.
McCool, Gerald A., S.J. "The Philosophical Theology of Rahner and Lonergan" in Robert J. Roth, S.J. (ed.), *God Knowable and Unknowable* (New York: Fordham University Press, 1973), pp. 123-157.
MacKinnon, Edward, "The Transcendental Turn: Necessary But Not Sufficient," *Continuum* 6 (1968), 225-231.
Tyrrell, Bernard, S.J. "The New Context of the Philosophy of God in Lonergan and Rahner" in Philip McShane (ed.), *Language, Truth, and Meaning*. Notre Dame, Ind.: University of Notre Dame Press, 1972.

IV PHILOSOPHY AND THEOLOGY

Rahner, Karl. "Theology and Anthropology" in Patrick T. Burke, (ed.) *The Word in History*. New York: Sheed and Ward, 1968.

From *Theological Investigations*

———— "Philosophy and Theology," VI, 71-81.
———— "Theology and Anthropology," IX, 28-45.
———— "Philosophy and Philosophising in Theology," IX, 46-63.
———— "The Historicity of Theology," IX, 64-82.
———— "Theology and the Church's Teaching after the Council," IX, 83-100.
———— "Christian Humanism," IX, 187-204.

From *Sacramentum Mundi*

—— "Man (Theological Anthropology)," IV, 365-370.
—— "Person (Theological)," IV, 415-419.
—— "Philosophy and Theology," V, 20-24.

Secondary Sources

Imbelli, Robert P. "Karl Rahner's *Itinerarium Mentis in Deum*" *Dunwoodre Review* 12 (1972), 76-91.
McCool, Gerald A., S.J. "The Concept of the Human Person in Karl Rahner's Theology," *Theological Studies* 22 (1961), 537-562.
—— *The Theology of Karl Rahner*, Albany, N.Y.: Magi Books, 1969.

V. SCRIPTURE, TRADITION, AND THE DEVELOPMENT OF DOGMA

Rahner, Karl. *Inspiration in the Bible*. New York: Herder and Herder, 1966. Also printed in *Inquiries*. New York: Herder and Herder, 1964.
—— and Joseph Ratzinger. *Revelation and Tradition*. New York: Herder and Herder, 1966.
—— *Kerygma and Dogma*. New York: Herder and Herder, 1969.

From *Theological Investigations*

—— "The Development of Dogma," I, 39-77.
—— "Considerations on the Development of Dogma," V, 3-35.
—— "Theology in the New Testament," V, 23-41.
—— "What Is a Dogmatic Statement?" V, 42-66.
—— "Exegesis and Dogmatic Theology," V, 67-93.
—— "Reflections on the Notion of 'Jus Divinum' in Catholic Thought," V, 219-243.
—— "Scripture and Theology," IV, 89-97.
—— "Scripture and Tradition," VI, 98-112.

From *Sacramentum Mundi*

—— "Bible (Theology)," I, 171-178.
—— "Dogma," II, 95-98.
—— "Development of Dogma," II, 98-108.
—— "Dogmatics," II, 108-111.
—— "Revelation," V, 342-355, 358-359.

Secondary Sources

Bent, Charles N., S.J. *Interpreting the Doctrine of God* (Glen Rock, N.J.: Paulist Press, 1968), pp. 140-224.

VI THE THEOLOGY OF MYSTERY AND SYMBOL

From Theological Investigations

Rahner, Karl. "The Concept of Mystery in Catholic Theology," IV, 36-73.
——— "The Theology of the Symbol," IV, 221-252.

From Sacramentum Mundi

——— "Mystery," I, 133-136.

Secondary Sources

McCool, Gerald A., S.J., "Rahner's Anthropology," *America* 123 (1970), 342-344.

VII THE TRIUNE GOD

Rahner, Karl. *The Trinity,* New York: Seabury Press, 1970.

From Theological Investigations

——— "Theos in the New Testament," I, 79-148.
——— "Remarks on the Dogmatic Treatise 'De Trinitate,' " IV, 77-102.
——— "Observations on the Doctrine of God in Catholic Dogmatics," IX, 127-144.

rom Sacramentum Mundi

——— "Trinity," VI, 295- 08.

Secondary Sources

Clarke, W. Norris, S.J., "A New Look at the Immutability of God" in Robert J. Roth, S.J. (ed.), *God Knowable and Unknowable* (New York: Fordham University Press, 1973), pp. 43-72.
Donceel, Joseph, S.J. "Second Thoughts on the Nature of God," *Thought* 46 (1971), 346-370.
Kelly, Anthony J., C.SS.R. "Trinity and Process: Relevance of the Basic Christian Confession of God," *Theological Studies* 31 (1970), 393-414.
Robertson, John C., Jr. "Rahner and Ogden: Man's Knowledge of God," *Harvard Theological Review* 63 (1970), 377-407.
Trethowan, Dom Illtyd. "A Changing God," *Downside Review* 84 (1966), 247-261.

VIII THE INCARNATION

From Theological Investigations

Rahner, Karl. "Current Problems in Christology," I, 149-200.

———— "On the Theology of the Incarnation," IV, 105-120.
———— "Dogmatic Questions on Easter," IV, 121-133.
———— "History of the World and Salvation History," V, 97-114.
———— "Christology Within an Evolutionary View of the World," V, 157-192.
———— "Dogmatic Questions on the Knowledge and Self-Consciousness of
Christ," V, 193-215.

From *Sacramentum Mundi*

———— "Resurrection of Christ," V, 323-324.

Secondary Sources
*See articles by Joseph Donceel and Illtyd Trethowan listed under "The Triune
God."*

IX GRACE

Rahner, Karl. "The Order of Redemption within the Order of Creation," *The
Christian Commitment* (New York: Sheed and Ward, 1963), pp. 38-74.
———— "Nature and Grace," *Nature and Grace* (New York: Sheed and Ward,
1964), pp. 114-149.

From *Theological Investigations*

———— "Concerning the Relationship Between Nature and Grace," I, 297-317.
———— "Some Implications of the Scholastic Concept of Uncreated Grace", I,
319-346.
———— "The Theological Concept of Concupiscentia," I, 347-382.
———— "Reflections on the Experience of Grace," III, pp. 86-90.
———— "Nature and Grace," IV, pp. 165-188.

From *Sacramentum Mundi*

———— "The 'Existential,' " II, 304-307.
———— "Grace," II, 412-427.
———— "Potentia Oboedientialis," V, 65-67.
———— "Salvation (Universal Salvific Will)," V, 405-409.

Secondary Sources

Meyer, Charles R., *A Contemporary Theology of Grace*. New York: Alba
House, 1971.
Shepherd, William C. *Man's Condition: God and the World Process*. New York:
Herder and Herder, 1969 (a study of Rahner's theology of grace and the
Supernatural Existential).
Bechtle, Regina. "Rahner's Supernatural Existential," *Thought* 48 (1973), 61-77.

Eberhard, Kenneth D. "Karl Rahner and the Supernatural Existential," *Thought*
    46 (1971), 537-561.
Kenny, J.P. "Reflections on Human Nature and the Supernatural," *Theological
    Studies* 14 (1953), 280-287.
—— "The Problem of Concupiscence: A Recent Theory of Professor Karl
    Rahner," *The Australasian Catholic Record*, 29 (1952), 290-304; 30
    (1953), 23-32.
Motherway, Thomas. "Supernatural Existential," *Chicago Studies* 4 (1965),
    79-103.
Peter, Carl J. "The Position of Karl Rahner Regarding the Supernatural: A
    Comparative Study of Nature and Grace," *Proceedings of the Catholic
    Theological Society of America* 20 (1965), 81-94.

X. FAITH, HOPE AND, CHARITY

Rahner, Karl. *Belief Today*. New York: Sheed and Ward, 1967.
—— "The Faith of the Priest Today," *Woodstock Letters* 93 (1964), 3-10.

From *Theological Investigations*

—— "Intellectual Honesty and Christian Faith," VII, 47-71.
—— "The Need for a Short Formula of Christian Faith," IX, 117-126.
—— "Christianity and the Non-Christian Religions," V, 115-134.
—— "What Is Heresy?" V, 468-512.
—— "Anonymous Christians," VI, 390-398.
—— "Atheism and Implicit Christianity," IX, 145-164.
—— "On the Theology of Hope," X, 242-259.
—— "The Commandment of Love in Relation to the Other Commandments,"
    V, 439-467.
—— "Reflections on the Unity of the Love of Neighbor and the Love of God,"
    VI, 231-249.

Secondary Sources

Röper, Anita. *The Anonymous Christian* (with an afterword "The Anonymous
    Christian According to Karl Rahner" by Klaus Riesenhuber, S.J.). New
    York: Sheed and Ward, 1966.
Hillman, Eugene, C.S.P. "Anonymous Christianity and the Missions," *Down-
    side Review* 85 (1966), 361-380.
Maloney, Donald. "Rahner and the Anonymous Christian," *America 123 (1970),
    348-350*.

XI MORAL THEOLOGY

Rahner, Karl. "The Appeal to Conscience," *Nature and Grace* (New York:
    Sheed and Ward, 1964), pp. 39-63.

From *Theological Investigations*

———— "On the Question of a Formal Existential Ethics," II, 217-234.
———— "On the Dignity and Freedom of Man," II, 235-263.
———— "The Theology of Freedom," VI, 178-196.
———— "Practical Theology Within the Totality of Theological Disciplines," IX, 101-114.
———— "The Experiment with Man," IX, 205-224.
———— "The Problem of Genetic Manipulation," IX, 225-252.
———— "Practical Theology and Social Work in the Church," X, 349-370.

Secondary Sources

Bresnahan, James F. "Rahner's Christian Ethics," *America* 123 (1970), 351-354.
Dorr, Donal J. "Karl Rahner's Formal Existential Ethics," *Irish Theological Quarterly* 36 (1969), 211-229.
Moga, Michael, S.J. "The Existential Ethics of Karl Rahner," *Focus* (Spring, 1965).
Wallace, William, O.P. "The Existential Ethics of Karl Rahner: A Thomistic Appraisal," *Thomist*, 27 (1963), 493-515.
Fuchs, Josef, S.J. *Human Values and Christian Morality*. Dublin: Gill and MacMillan, 1970.

XII THE CHURCH AND THE SACRAMENTS

Rahner, Karl. *Free Speech in the Church*. New York: Sheed and Ward, 1960.
———— *The Episcopate and the Primacy*. New York: Herder and Herder, 1962. Also printed in *Inquiries*. New York: Herder and Herder, 1964.
———— "The Significance of the Order of Redemption within the Order of Creation," *The Christian Commitment* (New York: Sheed and Ward, 1963), pp. 75-113.
———— "The Individual in the Church," *Nature and Grace* (New York: Sheed and Ward, 1964), pp. 9-38.
———— *Theology for Renewal: Bishops, Priests and Laity*. New York: Sheed and Ward, 1964.
———— *The Dynamic Element in the Church*. New York: Herder and Herder, 1964.
———— *The Christian of the Future*. New York: Herder and Herder, 1967.
———— *The Church and the Sacraments*. New York: Herder and Herder, 1963. Also printed in *Inquiries*. New York: Herder and Herder, 1964.
———— and Angelos Haüssling, O.S.B. *The Celebration of the Eucharist*. New York: Herder and Herder, 1968.

From *Theological Investigations*

———— "Freedom in the Church," II, 89-107.

——— "The Church of Sinners," VI, 253-269.
——— "The Church and the Parousia of Christ," VI, 295-312.
——— "The New Image of the Church," X, 3-29.
——— "The Presence of the Lord in the Christian Community at Worship," X, 71-83.
——— "On the Presence of Christ in the Diaspora Community According to the Teaching of the Second Vatican Council," X, 84-102.
——— "Dialogue in the Church," X, 103-121.
——— "The Bishop in the Church," VI, 313-389.
——— "On the Relationship Between the Pope and the College of Bishops," X, 50-70.
——— "The Teaching of the Second Vatican Council on the Diaconate," X, 222-232.
——— "Peaceful Reflections on the Parochial Principle," II, 283-318.
——— "The Sacramental Basis for the Role of the Layman in the Church," VIII, 51-74.
——— "The Position of Woman in the New Situation in Which the Church Finds Herself," VIII, 75-93.
——— "The Eucharist and Suffering," III, 161-170.
——— "On the Duration of Christ in the Sacrament of the Lord's Supper," IV, 287-311.
——— "On the Duration of the Presence of Christ after Communion," IV, 312-320.
——— "Forgotten Truths Concerning the Sacrament of Penance," II, 135-174.
——— "The Meaning of Frequent Confession of Devotion," III, 177-189.
——— "Problems Concerning Confession," III, 190-206.
——— "Penance as an Additional Act of Reconciliation Within the Church," X, 125-149.
——— "The Renewal of Priestly Ordination," III, 171-176.
——— "Marriage as a Sacrament," X, 199-221.
——— "Personal and Sacramental Piety," II, 109-133.

From *Sacramentum Mundi*

——— "Church and World," I, 346-347.
——— "Magisterium," III, 351-359.
——— "Penance," IV, 385-389.

Secondary Sources

Carmody, John. "Karl Rahner's Brave New Church," *America* 130 (1974), 109-111.
Levi, Anthony. "The Religious Thinking of Karl Rahner," *The Catholic Mind* 64 (April 1966), 4-13.

XIII SPIRITUALITY

Rahner, Karl. *Encounter with Silence*. Westminister, Md: Newman Press, 1960.

—— *Spiritual Exercises*. New York: Herder and Herder, 1965.

—— *Servants of the Lord*. New York: Herder and Herder, 1968.

—— *On Prayer*. New York: Paulist Press, 1968.

—— *Watch and Pray With Me*. New York: Herder and Herder, 1969.

—— *The Identity of the Priest*. New York: Paulist Press, 1969.

—— *Leading a Christian Life*. Denville, N.J.: Dimension Books, 1970.

—— *The Priesthood* (An Ignatian Retreat for Priests). New York: Seabury Press, 1973.

From *Theological Investigations*

—— "Reflections on the Problem of the Gradual Ascent to Christian Perfection," II, 319-352.

—— "Justified and Sinner at the Same Time," VI, 218-230.

—— "The Ignatian Mysticism of Joy in the World," III, 277-293.

—— "Behold This Heart!: Preliminaries to a Theology of Devotion to the Sacred Heart," III, 321-330.

—— "The Passion and Asceticism," III, 58-85.

—— "Reflections on the Theology of Renunciation," III, 47-57.

—— "Self-Realization and Taking Up One's Cross," IX, 253-257.

—— "On the Evangelical Counsels," VIII, 133-167.

—— "On the Theology of Poverty," VIII, 168-214.

—— "Priestly Existence," III, 239-262.

—— "The Consecration of the Layman to the Care of Souls," III, 263-276.

NOTE: Volumes III and VIII of *Theological Investigations* are devoted to Rahner's Spiritual Theology.

Secondary Sources

Carmody, John T. "Rahner's Spiritual Theology," *America* 133 (1970), 345-347.

XIV IDEOLOGY, ESCHATOLOGY, AND THE THEOLOGY OF DEATH

Rahner, Karl. *On the Theology of Death*. New York: Seabury Press, 1961.

From *Theological Investigations*

—— "The Resurrection of the Body," II, 203-216.

—— "The Hermeneutics of Eschatological Assertions," IV, 323-346.

—— "The Life of the Dead," IV, 347-354.

—— "Ideology and Christianity," VI, 43-58.

—— "Marxist Utopia and the Christian Future of Man," VI, 59-68.

—— "The Church and the Parousia of Christ," VI, 295-312.

—— "A Fragmentary Aspect of a Theological Evaluation of the Concept of the Future," X, 235-241.

———— "The Theological Problems Entailed in the Idea of the 'New Earth,' " X, 260-272.

———— "Immanent and Transcendent Consummation of the World," X, 260-272.

———— "The Peace of Christ and the Peace of the World," X, 371-388.

From *Sacramentum Mundi*

———— "Beatific Vision," I, 151-153.

———— "Death," II, 58-62.

———— "Eschatology," II, 242-246.

———— "Hell," III, 7-9.

———— "Last Things," III, 274-276.

———— "Parousia," IV, 345-346.

———— "Resurrection," IV, 329-333.

Secondary Sources

Baltasar, Hans Urs von, *Word and Revelation* (New York: Herder and Herder, 1965), pp. 147-176.

Boros, Ladislas, *The Mystery of Death*. New York: Seabury Press, 1965.

Gleason, Robert W., S.J., "Toward a Theology of Death," *Thought* 32 (1957), 36-68.

Metz, Johannes B. *Theology of the World*. New York: Seabury Press, 1969.

———— "Political Theology," *Sacramentum Mundi*, V, 34-38.

Index of Persons

Anselm 19
Aquinas, Thomas xiv, xv, xvi, xviii, 1, 3, 4, 8, 9, 10, 12, 13, 20, 22, 30, 56, 66, 72, 79, 110, 114, 120, 132, 144
Aristotle 1, 72
Augustine 19, 129, 137, 140, 179, 214, 240, 259, 313

Baker, K. 363
von Baltasar, H. 371
Barth, K. 143
Baruzi, J. 28
Bechtle, R. 366
Bent, C. 364
Bergson, H. xiv
Bloch, E. 226
Blondel, M. xiv, 73, 259
Bonaventure xx, xxi, xxii, xxv, 136, 138, 240
Boros, L. 371
Branick, V. P. 363
Bresnahan, J. F. 368
Brisbois, E. 175
Burke, P. T. 363

Carmody, J. 369, 370
Clarke, N. 365
Clement of Alexandria 317
Constantine 206
Coreth, E. xvi

Dalai Lama 73
de Bérulle, Cardinal P. 136
Descartes, R. 73
Dessauer, P. 189
Dorr, D. J. 368
Donceel, J. 363, 365, 366

Eberhard, K. D. 367
Elizabeth of the Trinity 136

Faulhaber, Cardinal xiii
Fichte, J. G. xiv, xv
Francis of Assisi 316
Froschammer, J. 25
Fuchs, J. 271, 368

Galtier, Paul
Gelpi, D. L. 362
Gilson, E. xviii, xxvi
Gleason, R. W. 371
Grabmann, M. 133
Gregory of Nyssa 28
Günther, A. 25, 155

Haussling, A. 368
Hegel, G. xvi, xviii, xx, xxi, xxii, 11, 14, 146, 150
Heidegger, M. xvi, xvii, xix, xx, xxii, 17, 18, 31, 185, 240
Hermes, G. 25, 143
Hillmann, E. 367
Honecker, M. xviii
Hus, J. 301

Ignatius of Loyola 136, 253, 310, 313, 314, 315, 316, 317, 332
Imbelli, R. P. 364

Jans, A. 136
John of the Cross 28, 136, 313

Kant, I. xiii, xiv, xv, xvi, xviii, 17, 18, 73
Kelly, A. J. 365
Kenny, J. P. 367
Kierkegaard, S. 259

Lauth, R. 338
Laynez, D. 313, 314
Leibnitz, G. W. 19

373

Index of Subjects

Sabellian modalism 143
Sacrament:
 Christ as fundamental 278ff., 288f., 301
Sacramental theology 129
Sacraments 121, 129f., 138, 281, 288, 301,
 326, 340:
 Causality of 285ff.; Christ's institution of
 288f., 292; confer grace *ex opere operato*
 279, 282ff., 287f.
Salvation:
 and the Incarnation 193; and
 non-Christian religions 212ff.; and the
 Trinity 132, 134; apart from Christ 216f.;
 certitude of 310; community of 91;
 economy of 140, 144; God's universal of
 233ff.; natural and supernatural 194, 222;
 order of 182; revelation of 69, 71; see
 History of Salvation
Satisfaction 137
Saviour 168f., 294
Scotism 232
Scripture 91ff., 141f., 144, 180, 220, 222,
 247, 257, 275, 288, 356f., 359:
 and Tradition 97f., 176, 222, 288, 340;
 development of dogma in 83, 95f.
Secretariat for Unbelievers 306
Secular life 236ff.
Sein and *Seindes* 5, 58
Self-subsistence of man 14, 16, 18ff., 29,
 32, 39, 42, 54, 57ff.
Sense knowledge, sensibility xvi, 49f.,
 55ff., 62, 202
Sentences 132
Silence of God 45f., 207
Sin 210, 220, 253, 256f., 261, 265, 300ff.,
 310ff., 323, 354ff.; original 215f., 220, 265
Sinner:
 Church of sinners 300ff.; justified and
 sinner at same time 310ff.
Situation ethics 245ff.
Society of Jesus xiii, 322
Son (Second Person of Trinity) 128, 131f.,
 134ff., 139, 141f., 144, 214, 224, 304; of
 Man 152, 209
Soul, intellectual xiv, 51f., 120f., 192;
 relation of soul to material world after
 death 357ff.
Space xiv, 54, 56, 64f., 250 264
Spatiality 52ff., 129
Spirit 1, 20, 113, 115, 117, 161
Spirit in the World xvi, xvii, xviii, xxvii, 7,
 12, 19, 56
Spiritual Exercises 253, 310, 313
Spirituality, quality of man 51, 55, 200, 251
Spirituality 300, 310, 313, 334:
 lay xix, 337; Rahner's Ignatian 310,
 313ff.
Sufferings of Christ 160

Summa Alexandri 133
Summa Contra Gentiles 8, 9, 10, 201
Summa Theologiae xvi, 110, 132
Supernatural 75, 177, 183, 195, 198f.:
 effects a change in human consciousness
 173ff., 184; existential xxvi, 184f., 188ff.,
 196, 211ff., 220, 265; extrinsicist theology
 of 173, 175f., 185
Surnaturel 185
Symbol:
 analogy of the real symbol 121, 126; and
 causality of the sacraments 121, 129f.,
 279, 285ff.; and Logos 126; Being as
 symbolic 121, 123ff.; Church as symbol
 of Christ 128ff., 278f., 287; Logos as
 Father's real symbol 126ff., 131, 278;
 metaphysics of 120f., 154, 288; ontology
 of 121, 125f.; order of creation as symbol
 of order of redemption 190; 'overplus of
 meaning' 122; real xxvii, 120f., 131, 145,
 166, 190, 278f.; theology of 120ff.
Synderesis 43

Temporality 52ff., 129
Theological Investigations xxiii:
 I 96, 134, 153, 185, 199; II 245, 262, 296,
 299, 334; III 196; IV 95, 120, 136, 145,
 173; V 159, 166; VI 75, 211, 234, 255,
 300, 337, 343, 348; VII 305, 352, 356; IX
 66, 80, 89, 132, 205, 220, 270; X 220
Theology 95ff., 103, 108ff., 122, 132, 136,
 140, 187:
 and the sciences 81, 85, 87, 262;
 development of 97; historicity of 89;
 philosophizing in 66, 69, 75, 78, 81ff., 85;
 philosophy and 66, 69, 72, 75, 77, 79,
 81ff., 87ff.; unbridgeable pluralism of 81,
 83ff., 300
Theos:
 as the Father 135; in the New Testament
 134f.
Thomism; see Transcendental Thomism
*Le Thomisme devant la philosophie
 critiique* xiii
'Thrownness' 31f., 34
Time xiv, 54ff., 64f., 89, 159, 250, 264,
 353f., 356, 360
Tradition 97f., 176, 222, 288, 340
Transcendence 17, 21, 23ff., 37, 40ff., 47f.,
 54ff., 62f., 71, 112f., 147, 161, 180ff., 197,
 21 f., 255ff., 338ff.
Transcendental:
 approach 72; condition 15, 57, 67, 243;
 consciousness 13; deduction 25f., 55, 58,
 186, 247; experience 71; investigation 71;
 method xvf., xxviii, 72, 74, 189, 263;
 reduction 70; reflection xiii, xv;
 structures 69; Thomism xiii, xviff., xxvif.